THE
ATLANTIC
CROSSING GUIDE

THE
ATLANTIC
CROSSING GUIDE

Fifth Edition

Royal Cruising Club Pilotage Foundation
in association with the
Ocean Cruising Club

By Anne Hammick and Gavin McLaren
Revised by John Lawson

ADLARD COLES NAUTICAL
London

Published by Adlard Coles Nautical
an imprint of A & C Black (Publishers) Ltd
37 Soho Square, London W1D 3QZ
www.adlardcoles.com

Copyright © RCC Pilotage Foundation 1983, 1988,
1992, 1998, 2003

First edition published in Great Britain by
Adlard Coles 1983
Reprinted with amendments 1984, 1985
Second edition 1988
Revised reprint 1989
Third edition published by Adlard Coles Nautical, 1992
Reprinted with amendments 1994
Reprinted 1996
Fourth edition 1998
Fifth edition 2003

ISBN 0-7136-6075-9

The author, John Lawson, has asserted his right under the
Copyright, Designs and Patents Act, 1988, to be identified as the
author of this work.

A CIP catalogue record for this book is available from the British
Library.

A & C Black uses paper produced with elemental chlorine-free
pulp, harvested from managed sustainable forests.

Typeset in Sabon 9½/12 pt
Printed and bound in Singapore by
Tien Wah Press Limited

Some of the plans included have been based, with permission,
on British Admiralty Charts and Publications (Licence No HO
363/960/624/01).

CAUTION

Whilst every care has been taken to ensure that the information contained in this book is accurate, the RCC Pilotage Foundation, the authors and the publishers hereby formally disclaim any and all liability for any personal injury, loss and/or damage howsoever caused, whether by reason of any error, inaccuracy, omission or ambiguity in relation to the contents and/or information contained within this book. The book contains selected information and thus is not definitive. It does not contain all known information on the subject in hand and should not be relied on alone for navigation use: it should be used in conjunction with official hydrographic data. This is particularly relevant to the plans which should not be used for navigation.

The RCC Pilotage Foundation, the authors and publishers believe that their selection is a useful aid to prudent navigation, but the safety of a vessel depends ultimately on the judgement of the navigator, who should assess all information, published or unpublished.

CONTENTS

Foreword to the Fifth Edition   vii
The RCC Pilotage Foundation   vii
Preface to the Fifth Edition   viii

PART I – PREPARATIONS

1 The Philosophy of Ocean Cruising   1

2 The Boat and her Permanent Fittings   3
The hull – The rig – Below decks – The engine
and electrical system – Routine maintenance

**3 Equipment for Ocean and Warm Climate
Cruising**   15
Ground tackle – Anchors – Automatic steering –
Sails – Power generation – Awnings and forced
ventilation – Dinghies and outboards – Spares
and replacements – The toolbox

4 Ocean Navigation   26
The chart table – The log book – The compass –
Barometers and thermometers – GPS receivers –
Charts, pilots and other publications – Ocean
navigation in practice – Equipment failure

5 Electronics and Communications   32
Instruments – Navigation aids – PCs –
Communications – Receivers – Transmitters –
VHF – MF/HF and amateur radio – Satellite
communications – EPIRBs – GMDSS

6 The Crew   38
Recruitment – Replacements en route –
Training – Friction aboard – The skipper

7 Provisioning   41
Storing before departure – Storing for a single
passage – Provisioning in different areas –
Non-perishables – Fresh stores and storage –
Fishing – Liquid refreshment

8 The Mechanics of Ocean Cruising   45
Watchkeeping systems – Ship's time – Paperwork
– Money – Insurance – The law – Clothing –
Firearms – Pests – Communications with home

9 Safety   53
The deck: design features – Heavy weather – Gear
failure – Collision – Fire – Firefighting equipment –
Lifesaving equipment – Personal safety gear – Man
overboard – Illness and injury – Security

PART II – PASSAGES AND LANDFALLS

10 The North Atlantic – Background   61
Routes, seasons and timing – Winds and
weather – Ocean currents – Sources of
information – Charts – Pilots, guides and
sailing directions – Weather forecast
transmissions – Amateur forecasts – Traffic
Separation Schemes (TSS)

11 The British and European Coasts   69
Regional weather – Currents – Tides and
tidal streams – Approach and landfall –
Formalities – Facilities – Sailing directions
and yachtsmen's guides – Relevant ports
covered in Part III

12 Southwards in the Eastern Atlantic   74
Passage planning charts – Falmouth to
Madeira via the coasts of Spain and
Portugal – Falmouth to Madeira direct –
Falmouth to the Azores – Azores to Madeira –
Madeira to the Canaries – Canaries to the
Cape Verde Islands

**13 The Madeiran, Canary and Cape Verdean
Archipelagos**   77
Regional weather – Currents – Tides and
tidal streams – Approach and landfall –
formalities – Sailing directions and
yachtsmen's guides – Relevant ports
covered in Part III

14 The Trade Wind Crossing   82
Passage planning charts – Timing – The
trade wind belt – Ocean currents and swell –
Caribbean approach and landfall

**15 The Caribbean Island Chain (Windward and
Leeward Islands)**   85
History – Trade winds – Current and swell –
Navigation and pilotage – Anchorages –
Formalities – Currency – Facilities – Medium-
and large-scale charts – Sailing directions and
yachtsmen's guides – Chart packs – Relevant
ports covered in Part III

16 The Bahamas   92
Caution – Weather and currents – Navigation
and pilotage – Formalities – Facilities – Sailing
directions and yachtsmen's guides – Chart packs

17 North from the Caribbean Islands   94
Passage planning charts – Virgin Islands to
Florida via the Bahamas – Virgin Islands to
Beaufort, North Carolina – Virgin Islands to
Bermuda – Antigua to Bermuda – Bermuda to
Newport, Rhode Island – Virgin Islands to the
Azores

18 The North American Coastline   98
Weather and currents – Ice – Tides and tidal
streams – Approach and landfall – Formalities:
Canada – Formalities: the United States – The US
Coast Guard – Facilities – Sailing directions and
yachtsmen's guides – Chart packs – Relevant ports
covered in Part III

19 Bermuda   104
Weather and currents – Approach and landfall –
Formalities – Facilities – Sailing directions and
yachtsmen's guides – Relevant port covered
in Part III

20 The Azores Group   107
Weather and currents – Tides and tidal streams –
Approach and landfall – Formalities – Facilities –
Sailing directions and yachtsmen's guides –
Relevant ports covered in Part IIII

**21 Transatlantic in the Middle and Northern
Latitudes**   110
Passage planning charts – Weather patterns –
Ocean currents – United States to Bermuda –
Bermuda to the Azores – United States or
Canada to the Azores – Azores to northern
Europe – Azores to Iberia or Gibraltar – United
States or Canada to Europe via the mid-latitudes –
United States or Canada to Europe via the great
circle – Passages westward – Azores to Bermuda –
Azores to the United States or Canada – Europe to
the United States or Canada via the mid-latitudes –
Europe to the United States or Canada via the
great circle – Europe to the United States or
Canada via the northern route

PART III – PORT INFORMATION

Harbours selected as being suitable for landfall or departure and, where possible, having above-average facilities
by the standards of the area.

1 Crosshaven, Ireland   120
2 Falmouth, England   124
3 Plymouth, England   127
4 Brest, France   131
5 La Coruña, Spain   133
6 Bayona, Spain   136
7 Leixões, Portugal   139
8 Lisbon, Portugal   142
9 Lagos, Portugal   146
10 Gibraltar   148
11 Funchal, Madeira   151
12 Harbours in the Canaries   154
13 Porto Grande (Mindelo), São Vicente,
     Cape Verdes   161
14 Chaguaramas Bay, Trinidad   164
15 Prickly Bay, Granada   168
16 Bridgetown/Port St Charles, Barbados   170
17 Rodney Bay, St Lucia   174
18 Fort de France, Martinique   177
19 English Harbour/Falmouth Bay, Antigua   180
20 Road Town, Tortola/**Virgin Gorda Yacht
     Harbour**, British Virgin Islands   184
21 Fort Lauderdale, Florida, USA   187
22 Beaufort/Morehead City, North Carolina,
     USA   190
23 Norfolk, Virginia, USA   193
24 Annapolis, Maryland, USA   196
25 Newport, Rhode Island, USA   200
26 Rockland, Maine, USA   204
27 Halifax, Nova Scotia, Canada   208
28 St John's, Newfoundland, Canada   212
29 St George's, Bermuda   215
30 Horta, Faial, Azores   219
31 Ponta Delgada, São Miguel, Azores   223

Appendix A Suggestions for Further Reading   227
Appendix B Cruising Guides, Almanacs
     and Regional Weather   229
Appendix C Publishers   231
Appendix D Suppliers of Books and Charts   232
Appendix E Glossary of British and
     American Terms, Weights and Measures,
     and Conversion Chart   233
Appendix F The Beaufort Wind Scale   237
Appendix G Weather Forecasts   238

Index   243

FOREWORD TO THE FIFTH EDITION

Although this book is aimed primarily at helping those who are contemplating their first crossing of the North Atlantic ocean I would also commend it to experienced sailors to remind them of some of the fundamental issues involved in ocean cruising. The depth of experience that has been accumulated over 20 years and four previous editions is all captured here and set out in a very readable way. The book also provides port information for many harbours around the Atlantic and even if they are not on your planned itinerary the information may well be useful in an emergency.

The RCC Pilotage Foundation is most grateful to John Lawson who took on the task of editing this fifth edition at short notice. John has brought his customary energy and enthusiasm to the job in addition to his extensive knowledge of the subjects covered. A great deal of work has gone into upgrading the plans to full colour – a task much more complicated than it sounds. It is hoped that these will now give a clearer picture of each port.

The Pilotage Foundation is always pleased to have feedback on our publications and any comments or corrections should be sent either via the publishers or by e-mail to director@rrcpf.org.uk

Francis Walker
Director, RCC Pilotage Foundation
April 2003

THE RCC PILOTAGE FOUNDATION

In 1976 an American member of the Royal Cruising Club, Dr Fred Ellis, indicated that he wished to make a gift to the Club in memory of his father, the late Robert E. Ellis, of his friends Peter Pye and John Ives and as a mark of esteem for Roger Pinckney. An independent charity known as the RCC Pilotage Foundation was formed and Dr Ellis added his house to his already generous gift of money to form the Foundation's permanent endowment. The Foundation's charitable objective is 'to advance the education of the public in the science and practice of navigation' which is at present achieved through the writing and updating of pilot books covering many different parts of the world.

The Foundation is extremely grateful and privileged to have been given the copyrights to books written by a number of distinguished authors and yachtsmen including the late Adlard Coles, Robin Brandon and Malcolm Robson. In return the Foundation has willingly accepted the task of keeping the original books up to date and many yachtsmen and women have helped (and are helping) the Foundation fulfill this commitment. In addition to the titles donated to the Foundation, several new books have been created and developed under the auspices of the Foundation. The Foundation works in close collaboration with three publishers – Imray Laurie Norie and Wilson, Adlard Coles Nautical and On Board Publications – and in addition publishes in its own name short run guides and pilot books for areas where limited demand does not justify large print runs. Several of the Foundation's books have been translated into French, German and Italian.

The Foundation runs its own website at www.rccpf. org.uk which not only lists all the publications but also contains free downloadable pilotage information.

The overall management of the Foundation is entrusted to Trustees appointed by the Royal Cruising Club, with day to day operations being controlled by the Director. All these appointments are unpaid. In line with its charitable status, the Foundation distributes no profits, which are used to finance new books and developments and to subsidise those covering areas of low demand.

PREFACE TO THE FIFTH EDITION

The Atlantic Crossing Guide was first written in the early 1980s by Philip Allen, who used his and Colin McMullen's extensive experiences of ocean cruising to produce the first definitive guide on the subject. It has expanded considerably since then, principally in the Fourth Edition where Anne Hammick and Gavin McLaren brought it up-to-date with the many technical advances that had occurred, not least the advent of GPS.

Much of the original writing from the last edition, which would be hard to better, has been retained. The philosophy of ocean cruising changes little whatever material advances are made: the trade winds still – mercifully – blow, and the ocean currents pursue their inexorable paths; the hurricane season inevitably occurs within the same annual limits; rocks and shoals alter only marginally over the years and coral grows but slowly; manmade modifications to ports and harbours often only add icing to the cake. It is, however, in the design of yachts, their fittings and equipment that most changes occur, and advances in the electronic and electrical aids to the safety and comfort on board small yachts is now so rapid that many details of equipment will become out-of-date in the interval between writing the book and publication. This is particularly true in the fields of electronic charting and navigation, worldwide communications, and continuous and accurate weather forecasting. Only a decade ago these aids were confined to commercial vessels or the largest yachts, but now the reduction of power consumption, weight, size and price makes them available to the smallest boat. But let us not forget that any such aid is vulnerable to the ways of the sea – the old mantra of log, lead and lookout (distance, depth and knowing what is going on around you) is as important today as it has ever been – even in the wide open spaces of the Atlantic.

The section on the south Atlantic has been omitted in this edition following the publication of *South Atlantic Circuit* by Tom Morgan and the RCC Pilotage Foundation, but many photographs, particularly of the ports, have been added. The plans have all been redrawn and the whole book is now in colour. The selection of ports is largely a matter of personal choice, and only one has been changed. The information now given in each port section is presented so that a stranger arriving for the first time in reasonable weather and with the relevant charts, can enter without further or more detailed information.

A number of people have helped in this production, not least Anne Hammick and Gavin McLaren, whose advice has always been welcome, as has Gavin's invaluable initial work on the revision; and Ros Hogbin of the Pilotage Foundation has kept a critical and friendly eye on the book's progress at the same time as producing *The Pacific Crossing Guide*, the sister publication for the world sailor. *The Atlantic Crossing Guide* would not be the same without the immaculate plans produced by the cartographer Alan Whitaker, and the efforts of the many who produced photographs, which are acknowledged individually. I am particularly grateful to Ted Laurentius for information about St John's, Newfoundland; to Kit McCurdy for details about Halifax, Nova Scotia; to Trudi and son Martin Smyth and Thomas Herbert of Barbados for much information about that island and amateur radio nets; and finally, to the editorial staff of Adlard Coles Nautical, who have been unfailingly helpful, and are also responsible for the final design of the book – which I hope gives pleasure to many at the threshold of ocean voyaging.

John Lawson
Newton Ferrers
April 2003

PART I

PREPARATIONS

1 The Philosophy of Ocean Cruising

The most important quality in the ocean cruising skipper and his or her vessel is self-sufficiency. To some extent this may be said of anyone who ventures beyond the harbour mouth, but the coastal cruise will normally be planned around convenient harbours where water, fuel, provisions and, if necessary, repairs are available. Regular and accurate weather forecasts are also available when cruising within the home waters of most countries. Awareness of the need to become self-sufficient begins when, with growing experience, you venture further afield only to run short of some necessity in a place where it is simply not available.

Self-sufficiency implies many things. First, that the yacht herself is sound and seaworthy; second, that she has a crew capable of sailing and maintaining her and who can make all normal repairs, both in port and at sea; and third, that she is equipped and provisioned sufficiently to avoid running short of any essential item before a replacement can be found.

The sound and seaworthy ocean cruiser must be more than just a strongly built hull that does not leak, with an efficient rig and good gear. Of course, these things are essential, not only to avoid catastrophe, but also to inspire those aboard with a reasonable degree of confidence in the yacht's abilities. But she must also be seakindly and must have an interior in which it is possible for her crew to live in reasonable comfort for extended periods. While the average yacht spends most of her time at a mooring or in a marina, the ocean cruiser will spend weeks on end at sea, and those aboard cannot exist for that length of time on snacks and the odd hot drink. Neither can they be expected to catnap in insecure seaberths. The most limited resource aboard the ocean cruising yacht is the energy of her crew, and without regular food and sufficient sleep this cannot be maintained.

Self-sufficiency is of course a relative term, and a small community, such as the crew of a yacht, cannot survive for ever without calling on outside help. The newcomer to ocean cruising tends to overstock in the anxiety not to run short in far-off places. With growing experience it becomes apparent that some things can be replaced easily, others with difficulty, and a few only at home. One learns, too, that a place that is good for one thing may be unexpectedly bad for others, that water does not always come conveniently piped, and that when something which is bound to be needed later is available it had better be bought while the going's good.

The ocean skipper must also have a certain determination, a resolve that once a task has been started it will be carried through to its conclusion despite the difficulties that will arise. While most long distance cruising is pleasant and enjoyable, this will not always be the case. Some destinations may not be the paradise envisaged before departure – obstructive officialdom may cause frustrating delays, or the anchorage may turn out to be overcrowded or untenable due to wind or swell. On passage, there will sometimes be bad weather to endure and inevitably there will be the occasional gear failure and breakdown to be dealt with. Such problems may seem overwhelming at the time, but they are seldom insurmountable, and determination on the part of the skipper will overcome them. In retrospect, they will usually seem insignificant in the context of the cruise as a whole.

A yacht capable of crossing oceans is a complicated and diverse piece of equipment, and those aboard must possess the skills to keep at least the more important aspects functioning. The idea that 'I'm just the skipper, he's the engineer, she's the cook' is long dead aboard cruising yachts, and every ocean skipper must be resourceful enough to look after all the vital equipment on board, aided when appropriate by a manufacturer's handbook or well-illustrated manual. On a coastal cruise repairs to a torn sail, a slipping winch or a flooded engine can be left until the next harbour is reached, where expert help will probably be available. On an ocean passage these things will have to be dealt with by those on board – often by the skipper – usually in less than ideal circumstances and sometimes using improvised equipment and parts. He or she will have to be sufficiently resourceful to make at least temporary repairs.

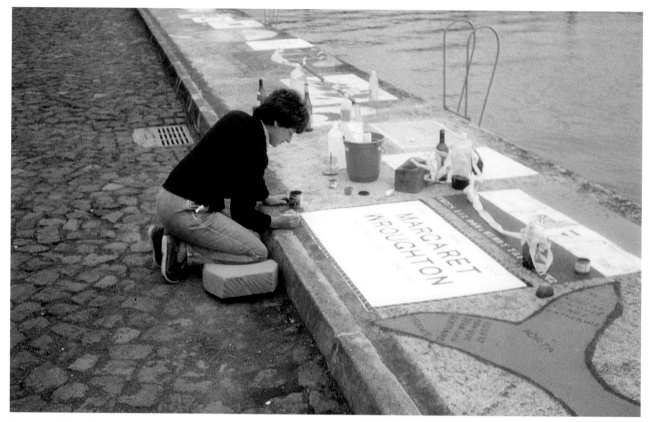

In many of the Atlantic's cruising ports it is traditional for a yacht to leave a record of her visit. Photo Gavin McLaren.

A self-sufficient, determined and resourceful skipper will certainly be able to make successful Atlantic crossings, but they must also decide what type of ocean cruising suits them. The boat can be very large or very small, or of any size in between. She may be fitted with a vast array of the latest high-tech mechanical, electrical and communications gear to make sailing effortless and to give all the comforts of home; at the other extreme she may have nothing more complex than a Primus stove aboard. For some owners it will be essential that she is fast and can make swift passages, but for others this is quite unimportant. In some boats, the sailing is all important, with time spent in harbour tolerated only to prepare for the next trip. For other yachts the passages are chiefly a means to reach a new cruising ground. Some cruisers never spend more than a couple of nights in one harbour and visit as many parts of a particular area as possible, while others prefer to linger and get to know fewer spots more thoroughly. Some are sociable and seek out the popular places, some are happy with their own company.

Most prospective ocean cruisers will have little choice in some of these matters. The size of boat and budget and the time available may be constrained. On other issues, you may already have strong views. But where you are uncertain – and have the choice – you should adopt a middle course. Choose a boat that is not too big, but not too small either. One that is not uncomfortably fast, but not unbearably slow; that is not brand new, but not excessively old. Have some mechanical

and electrical gear for comfort and convenience – but not too much, lest it take over. Plan to visit a selection of harbours in a cruising ground, not just one, but not all of them either. Experiment with traditional techniques, such as astro-navigation, but don't reject the modern alternatives.

This middle course will not be entirely perfect and, after experiencing a spell of ocean cruising, individuals will be able to improve upon it. By then, though, they will have a clear idea of their likes, dislikes and priorities, of what they feel is essential, and what can be dispensed with. But until that experience has been gained, the middle course is likely to be the best. At the least, it will not be disastrously unsatisfactory.

To live aboard a well-found boat and cruise in her over long distances is to experience a sense of independence and freedom that is almost beyond description. The petty annoyances of the land fall away, you live by the look of the sky, the feel of the wind, and the run of the sea. As time goes on and experience is gained, both you and your craft become increasingly efficient, able to deal with any eventuality, and that sense of affection and empathy felt by nearly all long distance sailors towards their vessels begins to make itself felt. Putting to sea, while still a busy time full of anticipation, loses some of its overtones of anxiety, and the prospect of an ocean passage is no longer quite as daunting as it once was. However, to reach this happy state you must observe the rules, which are simple but exacting: careful planning, good seamanship and vigilance.

2 The Boat and Her Permanent Fittings

There is no ideal type of ocean cruiser. Comparatively few yachts are designed specifically for ocean passage-making, despite the claims made by some manufacturers. The majority of people who make long voyages do so in the boats that they happen to own at the time, although they may have originally been bought with long distance cruising in mind. Successful Atlantic passages have been made in yachts of almost every type, and it is likely that a boat that has been cruised successfully in home waters for several seasons will be quite suitable. She will have the advantage that her owner will be familiar with her, and will trust her. The modifications she will need before an ocean voyage will vary according to her design; a yacht built purely with cruising in mind will need fewer changes than a cruiser racer.

Similarly, a yacht's age is unlikely to affect her suitability. The majority of ocean-going yachts are well past the first flush of youth and, providing they are structurally sound, yachts of almost any age should be quite capable of crossing the Atlantic. It is likely, however, that the older the yacht, the more work she will require before an ocean passage.

The hull

Although the vast majority of yachts are built of glassfibre, other materials are equally satisfactory for long distance cruising. Steel is often quoted as the ideal hull construction material, and it is certainly strong. But steel boats under 12m (40 ft) are likely to be heavy and the maintenance of a steel hull will be more time-consuming than that of a glassfibre one. It is worth remembering that corrosion occurs more rapidly in warm water, and a steel (or aluminium) boat will need considerably more looking after in the tropics than she will in northern climes. Similarly, the owner of a wooden boat must be prepared to spend a good deal of time on basic hull maintenance.

Of whatever material it is constructed, it is vital that the hull is sound. This implies that a steel or aluminium boat has not become dangerously corroded, that glassfibre has not succumbed to serious osmosis, and that wood has no worm, rot or sick fastenings. If a boat has not had a survey for several years, get one done at the start of the preparation process. Tell the surveyor your plans and ask him to look at the boat as a potential ocean, as opposed to coastal, cruiser. Even if his inspection reveals no significant problems, the reassurance will more than justify the cost. It is more likely, however, that the unbiased eye of the surveyor will find

some defects that have escaped the owner's attention. It will be far easier to rectify these before departure than to deal with them along the way.

Protection against worm is particularly important for wooden boats. Although attack by marine borers is possible in temperate waters, it is much more likely in the tropics and damage can be rapid and severe. Antifouling paint must be in perfect condition and will need to be renewed regularly. There are preparations of powdered copper in epoxy that may be more effective against borers and will last longer than conventional antifouling paint. The underside of the keel is particularly difficult to paint, and it will be rubbed off by even the most minor grounding. Consider having this vulnerable area sheathed with copper or glassfibre.

Skin fittings

Every hole in the hull should be protected by a seacock; below the waterline this is essential. Seacocks should

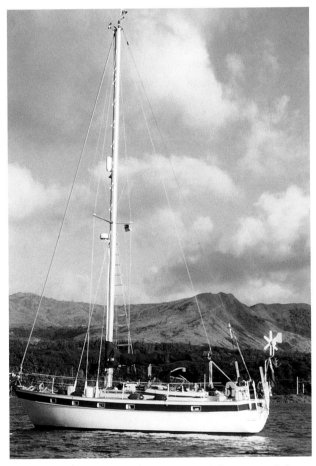

Haalberg-Rassys make ideal ocean cruisers, large enough for comfort, but easily managed by two people. Here Sadko lies in Guam. Photo Noël Marshall.

preferably be of the bronze cone type, although ball valves are adequate if they are made of suitable materials. In the interests of reducing costs, some builders fit ball valves more suitable to domestic water systems than the marine environment. Although these may outwardly appear the same as the proper fitting, and may last a good while in northern waters, they corrode rapidly in the tropics. Gate valves, which are operated by turning a handwheel, are sometimes seen. Although cheap, they are unreliable, and if they must be used at all it should only be above the waterline. Unlike a proper seacock, it is impossible to tell by looking at them whether they are open or shut; they are particularly vulnerable to corrosion; and they almost invariably leak a little.

Whatever type of skin fitting is used it must be in good condition. Each one should be stripped, examined and renewed if suspect. All seacocks should be dismantled, cleaned and greased regularly – a good rule of thumb is to do this every time the boat is antifouled.

Hoses connected to seacocks need periodic replacement, and if reinforced plastic hose has hardened it should be changed. Double hose or jubilee clips of good-quality stainless steel should be used to secure hoses to skin fittings, and softwood bungs in a range of sizes to fit every through-hull aperture kept handy. Ideally, each fitting should have its own plug attached on a lanyard, ready for immediate use in an emergency.

The stern gland

The stern gland is one of the most frequent sources of leakage, partly because access is often poor and adjustment difficult. If it is of the traditional type, the packing should be replaced before departure to ensure plenty of scope for further adjustment, but if on inspection the propeller shaft is significantly worn, no adjustment of the gland will prevent leakage and the shaft will have to be repaired or renewed. Spare packing of the appropriate size should be carried. The stern greaser needs to be turned regularly while the boat is motoring, so it must be installed in an accessible position; it should be large enough to limit refilling to an occasional chore.

The more modern design of stern gland relies on two perfectly smooth discs – usually of ceramic or carbon materials – pressing against each other to maintain a seal. One disc revolves with the shaft, while the other, connected to the hull, remains stationary. These seals are maintenance free and, if correctly installed, are completely drip free. Eventually the discs become worn and the complete unit must be replaced, an operation that requires partial withdrawal of the propeller shaft. There is little warning before failure occurs. The manufacturer should be able to give an approximate life of the seal (in terms of engine hours), and if it seems likely that this will be approached during an extended cruise, the seal should be replaced before departure. A spare seal should be carried.

Most engines are flexibly mounted and the stern gland must accommodate the movement of the shaft

that results. Normally this is achieved by connecting the gland to the hull using a short length of heavy rubber hose, secured with double hose clips. Failure of this hose will cause severe leakage, and it cannot be replaced without withdrawing the shaft. Unless its condition is beyond doubt, it should be replaced before departure.

Decks and hatches

Once certain that water cannot enter the hull from below, the possibility of it doing so from above must be considered. A watertight deck, cockpit, coachroof and hatches are essential for safety – and for comfort too. Few things can spoil the enjoyment of an extended cruise so fast as continuous wetness below decks.

The deck must be leak free. This may seem obvious, but there are a huge number of potential places where water can enter. Fastenings through the deck and topsides for headsail tracks, stanchions, winches, hatches, chainplates and a host of other fittings, and their watertightness is dependent on the sealing method and material used. Sealants have a finite life and will eventually need replacement.

Wooden decks need more looking after than do other types, particularly in the tropics. They should be protected from the sun as much as possible and never allowed to become really dry – a sluice-down with salt water morning and evening should be the rule. The seams will need attention from time to time; however, a complete recaulk is a major job, and if it is likely to be necessary it should be done before leaving. Teak laid over glassfibre, metal or plywood makes an attractive deck, comfortable to walk on and initially watertight. But when leaks do occur in such decks, it may be hard to identify their source. Water can travel between the teak and the base material for some distance, emerging into the accommodation far away from the fitting whose faulty seal admitted it.

Although it is rare for the cockpit to be completely filled during heavy weather it is a possibility that must be considered. In such conditions it is likely that the motion will rapidly throw a good deal of the water back out, but much will remain and the cockpit drains must be adequate. Look at the size of the cockpit in relation to that of the boat as a whole – a larger boat is better able to cope with the weight of water in a big cockpit than is her smaller sister. Cockpit lockers are notorious as a source of leakage in heavy weather, and a lot of water can get below through them. They must have stout lids, good seals and strong hinges and clasps to secure them in bad weather.

A bridgedeck between cockpit and companionway is a great source of structural strength, but even if there is no bridgedeck the companionway opening should not extend right down to the cockpit sole. If possible, there should be a permanent barrier up to cockpit seat level. If this is not the case, then consider temporarily sealing in the lower washboards when on passage. Washboards must be strong, and those that drop into slots should be capable of being secured or released from both the cockpit and below, with lanyards so that they cannot be lost. There should be at least one strong exterior attachment point for harness lines within reach of the companionway.

Hatches must be so well secured that there is no possibility of a hatchcover being ripped off by a powerful sea, and they must not leak. Frequently it is not the hatch itself that leaks so much as its fitting on the deck, in which case removal and rebedding may do the trick. Opening hatches and portlights depend on rubber seals, which also need periodic renewal.

Bilge pumps

Inevitably, a little water will occasionally find its way below, and at least two manual, high-capacity bilge pumps are essential. One should be operable from the cockpit (without the need to keep a locker open), preferably within reach of the helmsman, and the other from below. If an electric pump is fitted, it should be additional to, not instead of, these two pumps. Spare parts for all pumps should be carried.

No manual or electric bilge pump will be able to cope with the flow from even a minor below-water leak for very long – a fit man can pump about 90 litres (20 gallons) of water a minute, but he will soon tire. A large yacht, or one with a weak crew, should consider fitting a large-capacity pump driven directly from the engine via a clutch; this is the only type of pump that has the slightest chance of coping with the water from significant underwater damage for any length of time.

The rig

Just as there is no perfect hull material for a transatlantic cruiser, neither is there an ideal rig. Although the majority of today's boats are bermudan sloops or cutters, many schooners, ketches and yawls have made highly successful crossings. Gaff rig has its proponents, and it may be better downwind. Modern materials have produced the unstayed mast and wishbone rig adopted by the Freedom class, while junk rig enthusiasts point out its simple, low-technology advantages; both these types regularly cross the Atlantic. One thing, however, is certain. Whatever its type, the ocean cruiser's rig must be well-designed, regularly inspected and conscientiously maintained.

Masts and spars

Both keel- and deck-stepped masts have their own advantages and drawbacks, and both have been well proven at sea. A keel-stepped mast has at least some inbuilt support, and should it break it will probably do so high enough to furnish at least the beginnings of a jury-rig. However, it is difficult to prevent leaks where

A simple bar to protect the propeller will come into its own in New England waters where lobster traps abound. Photo Gavin McLaren.

it passes through deck or coachroof, and an older aluminium mast may suffer from corrosion at its heel. A mast stepped on deck is utterly dependent on the rigging for its support, and any failure there is likely to be catastrophic. While both types require considerable reinforcement below to prevent the hull distorting, usually a main bulkhead, a deck-stepped mast should also have a kingpost to transfer its loading to the hull.

Aluminium spars should be checked for corrosion around every fitting, particularly those of stainless steel. It is quite possible for the aluminium to degrade unnoticed, until either the fitting pulls out under strain or the spar simply tears and folds. Mast steps are a great convenience, but do add to the weight and windage aloft and may snag halyards, although some designs are less prone to this than others. As a preventative, a lanyard is often run from each step out to the nearest shroud; an alternative is to run a vertical light line down each side joining the outermost extremities of the steps.

Standing rigging

It is imperative to ensure that all standing rigging is above reproach as failure on an ocean passage may lead to disaster. The life of stainless steel wire is generally considered to be about ten years, although regular surveys may enable replacement to be delayed for a year or two. Failures most commonly occur where the wire enters a terminal, and these points should be examined frequently. The fracture of a single strand indicates that something is seriously wrong, and the shroud or stay should be replaced as soon as possible.

Either swaged or swageless terminals are fitted to the ends of the standing rigging. Swaging involves applying great pressure to the terminal in a special machine so that the metal is forced into the construction of the wire. Providing a conscientious operator using the proper machine has made them, swaged terminals are strong, but it is hard to tell a good swage from a bad one, as the defects are likely to be inside the fitting. Warning signs are ridging on the outside of the swage

Gaffers still regularly cross the Atlantic, and may be better in downwind sailing. Marguerite is nearly 100 years old and has at least two crossings to her credit. Photo Anna Brunyee.

itself, or a swage that appears bent. Both are symptoms of a poor joint. Although the legendary 'banana swage' is seldom seen, any fitting showing even the slightest trace of a bend should be replaced.

Because the condition of swaged joints is so hard to assess, swageless terminals (Norseman or Sta-lock) are preferable. Although initially considerably more expensive, these terminals can usually be reused when the wire has reached the end of its life. Other advantages of this type of terminal are that it may be fitted in a few minutes with no special tools, and that it can be dismantled periodically to inspect the condition of the wire inside. Even if swaged terminals are used, it is wise to carry a selection of swageless terminals and some spare wire for use in an emergency.

Stainless steel is vulnerable to repeated bending stresses and it is essential that the load is straight along the axis of the wire and fitting. All masts move a little in relation to the hull, and toggles accommodate this movement. These should be fitted between the bottle-screw and chainplate of all shrouds and stays and must allow complete freedom of movement. Stays upon which sails are set are subject to extra bending forces, as a glance up the luff of a headsail will show. It is essential that these wires be fitted with toggles at the mast end as well.

The fittings to which the rigging is fastened are as important as the rigging itself. The points of attachment of all standing and running rigging should be examined – chainplates (including those for forestay and back-stays), sheet tracks and eyebolts. Satisfy yourself that they are strong enough in themselves, and that their anchorage to the hull or deck, and the way in which the loads are spread, is adequate. The fittings aloft are equally important and should be periodically dismantled and carefully examined. The modern 'ball and socket' mast fitting, in which a hook-shaped terminal with a ball at its end is slotted into the spar, has failed so often that it is surprising to see it still used. It might be adequate for round-the-buoys racing, where the reduced windage it involves is advantageous, but has no place on an ocean passage-maker.

Any terminal, mast tang, chainplate or other rigging component that has ever sustained damage must be immediately suspect – even if returned into apparently perfect shape, it may have invisible faults that will weaken it seriously. Short of testing to destruction, it is difficult to check the state of older stainless steel fittings, although some new electronic techniques appear promising, and a surveyor specialising in the subject should be fully up-to-date. At the moment, however, the advice must be to inspect rigging regularly and to replace it periodically.

Do not necessarily heed the old advice that the rigging of a yacht bound across the ocean must be increased in size. This may have been true with galvanised wire, where increase in diameter gives a greater margin against corrosion. But the designer of a modern yacht will have specified the stainless rigging as part of a complete system. Increasing the wire size will disrupt that system; for example, the compression on the mast may be increased beyond the safe limits for the particular aluminium section used. Moreover, it is point-less to increase the strength of a single component of the rigging chain without considering the rig as a whole. To be worthwhile, heavier wires and bottlescrews prob-ably need heavier chainplates and mast tangs, and larger bolts to fasten them with – perhaps even rein-forcement to the hull. If the rig for your chosen ocean passage-maker seems inadequate, get an expert to advise you on the changes needed.

Running rigging

The strength and durability of modern synthetic ropes has made wire halyards unnecessary on all but the largest cruising yachts. Troublesome wire-to-fibre splices are eliminated and so are the jagged 'fish hooks', which are liable to injure fingers and clothes. To avoid chafe it is essential that the sheaves over which the halyards pass are large enough for the rope used, and that they are in good condition. Going aloft at sea is unpleasant, and in rough conditions may be impossible, so it is important to ensure that there are sufficient spare halyards to make a trip up the mast unnecessary should a halyard be lost aloft or damaged. An oversize topping lift will suffice for the main or mizzen and a spinnaker halyard for a genoa. The fittings at the masthead must be sufficiently strong for these secondary purposes, and the ropes must lead fairly without chafe. This is much more important on an ocean passage, where a spare halyard may be in use for days on end, than it is for coastal cruising where the

Chafe is one of the ocean cruiser's worst enemies. Here a temporary 'scotchman' has been made to protect a boomed-out jib sheet. Photo Gavin McLaren.

original halyard can be retrieved or replaced at the next port within a short time.

The modern tendency is for running rigging to be led aft from the mast to the cockpit. This has the advantage of reducing the number of times that it is necessary to go forward and, by using a set of jammers, a winch each side of the companionway under the sprayhood can serve almost all sail control purposes. To work efficiently it is essential that the turning blocks used be of the best quality, that lines run fairly through them, and that these are regularly inspected for chafe. Such convenience has a price, however, and the drawbacks should be considered. Even with the best hardware, friction will be increased and ropes will be subject to additional wear. The forward end of the cockpit is liable to become cluttered with lines, and winches and jammers fill the useful space under the sprayhood. With half-a-dozen jammers lying side by side, it is easy for the wrong one to be cast off inadvertently, particularly at night. Probably the most significant disadvantage of the 'lead everything aft' approach is that the deck outside the cockpit becomes unfamiliar territory and, when it is necessary to go forward, probably in response to some emergency, the positions of handholds, obstacles, clipping-on points and so forth will have to be thought about. For a crew who routinely go forward, such things are second nature – and so they are better placed to concentrate on the job in hand.

Below decks

Arrangements below decks will of necessity be a compromise between the requirements of extended periods at sea on passage and those of life aboard in harbour. A centre cockpit is probably only worthwhile if the aft cabin can be reached without a trip through the cockpit, and this generally limits this arrangement to yachts over about 11m (36ft). Above that size, the

advantages of a completely separate sleeping cabin, away from the saloon, become increasingly feasible.

Ventilation

If a yacht from cooler climes is to be taken to the tropics, the problems of ventilation should be studied with great care. The ideal is to have at least one good-sized hatch in each cabin, preferably of the type with reversible hinges, allowing it to be opened either forward or aft. A smaller hatch or opening port in the heads will also be appreciated. Opening ports in the living quarters are a great advantage in warm weather, but they must be of good quality otherwise they will leak. Lightweight aluminium frames have a tendency to corrode over time, and are vulnerable to distortion by misuse, and then they will never seal properly.

Dorade-type ventilators should have two holes in the top of the box, one over the watertrap and the other immediately over the deck inlet. In port, the vent can be put directly over the inlet with a cover on the other opening. The reverse position is used at sea. There should also be an emergency cover for the deck inlet in case the box is smashed.

Comfort below is greatly improved by proper insulation, which may also prove beneficial on the return to colder areas. In a steel or glassfibre boat the whole of the area under the deck and coachroof should, if accessible, be covered with one of the proprietary forms of expanded polyurethane, the thicker the better. This should not be done in a wooden boat where it might promote rot, but timber provides relatively good insulation anyway.

The galley

No crew will be at their best unless properly fed, making the galley one of the most important areas below. The general layout will probably not lend itself to major alterations, but even so certain improvements can be made. Whereas the average boat's galley is mostly used in port, the ocean cruiser's must continue to work efficiently at sea. The stove must be able to swing freely on its gimbals to at least 35° in either direction, while a high surrounding rail and efficient pot-clamps are essential; so is a protective 'crash bar' in front, both to protect the cook from possible injury and to decrease the likelihood of gas taps being turned on or off by accident. A stout strap should be provided to hold the cook in place or to lean against.

Even if bulk food stores are stowed elsewhere, the many items used regularly must be handy to the galley. This means safe stowage for a variety of containers – often bins or shelves with high fronts are more secure than lockers, which may dump their entire contents when the door is opened – and somewhere to put implements or open containers while in use. Work surfaces should have high fiddles, and should not be too large. Most galleys work well when the yacht is on one tack or the other, when everything naturally gravitates to, and remains, in the 'downhill' areas. It is much more difficult to arrange things to cope with constant rolling, but it is important to do so, as this is the motion most likely to be experienced during the crossing. Non-slip maps or cloths to stop things sliding around are remarkably effective in all but the most extreme conditions.

A deep sink is essential and it should drain on either tack. As well as its normal use for washing up, the sink will often be the best place to stow things temporarily during cooking operations. There should be a salt-water supply at the sink so that, even in harbour, the initial washing up can be done in salt water.

An important feature of the galley layout, and one that can sometimes be improved with a little thought, is that of ensuring that the cook can work without interfering with (or being hampered by) those who need to get past. If the cabin sole is varnished, some form of non-slip surfacing should be employed in the galley area. Provision must be made for rubbish – preferably two containers: one for biodegradable rubbish that can be disposed of at sea, and one for plastic and items to be taken ashore. On passage, where they will need to be retained on board for a lengthy period, these items should be thoroughly rinsed in seawater.

Cooking fuel

For most cruisers, the cooking fuel of choice is LPG (liquefied petroleum gas). Paraffin (kerosene) is still used by some who consider it safer, but supplies are increasingly difficult to obtain, as LPG is now widely used in even the remotest places. The quality of any paraffin available is often poor. If a paraffin cooker is fitted, then provision should be made to store fuel for about three months and it should be filtered. A good supply of

spares for a paraffin stove must be carried as their availability has declined along with the use of the fuel.

LPG is relatively cheap, but is unfortunately produced in different forms and pressures (propane and butane) and is supplied in a variety of different non-interchangeable bottles. There is a danger of explosion through carelessness or faulty installation; to some extent this can be guarded against by fitting a gas detector, but such a device is no substitute for regular inspection of the gas system and safe procedures when using the stove.

As mentioned, LPG comes in more than one variety. Broadly speaking, propane is supplied for boats in North America, Bermuda, the Caribbean and Scandinavia, while butane is more usual throughout the rest of Europe. The primary difference is one of pressure, propane being stored at considerably higher pressure than butane and needing a different regulator. Propane cylinders incorporate a pressure release valve, whereas some butane cylinders do not. Although in many places butane cylinders will be filled with propane without comment or objection, this is a highly dangerous practice – do not assume that just because the supplier agrees to do so it is safe. Most gas appliances will run off either fuel, provided that it is supplied through the correct regulator.

Throughout Europe the normal practice is for LPG bottles – be they propane or butane – to be leased. For practical purposes this amounts to much the same as purchase, but the bottles remain the property of the supplying company, who are responsible for their testing and maintenance. Subsequently, empty bottles are exchanged for full ones, with only the gas being charged for. Most yacht chandlers and many hardware shops carry a stock of full bottles in the popular sizes. The supplying company refills empty bottles at a regional depot. Outside Europe, it is normal for individuals to purchase their own bottles outright and have them refilled when necessary. In the United States, refilling facilities are available at many petrol stations and some marinas; most Atlantic and Caribbean islands have a single central refilling plant that will deal with bottles of almost all types.

Each European country has its own LPG supplying companies and bottles are not exchangeable between them. Companies *may* refill bottles from another supplier or country, but normally only if they are satisfied that the bottles are suitable and are in date for test. A visit to the nearest refilling plant will be necessary and there is no guarantee that it will have the necessary thread

A well-thought-out U-shaped galley, with everything to hand. Although there is a belt to secure the person doing the cooking, a 'crash bar' is needed to stop the cook being thrown against the stove. Photo Georgie McLaren.

adaptors to fill bottles other than its own. The only pan-European bottles are those from Camping Gaz, which may be exchanged in nearly all European ports and in most of the Atlantic and Caribbean islands. Unfortunately the bottles are small, the gas expensive, and only butane is available. Camping Gaz bottles are not fitted with safety valves and should *never* be filled with propane.

The best gas system to fit for an Atlantic cruise will depend upon the route to be taken; however, the following guidance is given:

1 A British yacht should be fitted with a Calor Gas system. If it is certain that the United States will not be visited, then an existing Calor butane system will suffice, but it would be preferable to fit a propane regulator and exchange butane for propane bottles before departure, as propane will be available throughout the voyage. Only in France, Spain and Portugal will it be difficult to get propane bottles refilled, but it will be possible. If retaining a butane system, then one or more Camping Gaz bottles (with the necessary adaptors) may be useful in areas where they are readily exchangeable. If planning to visit the United States, then the change to propane should be made before departure. Calor propane bottles can be refilled using the standard US fittings (but see note below).

2 An American yacht will find her propane system quite adequate until she reaches Europe. There it may be possible to get her cylinders refilled, provided that there is the documentation to prove that they are suitable for the purpose and in test date, but it may be a time-consuming process. If planning to remain in a single European country for a length of time, it will be preferable to lease local propane cylinders, and to fit the necessary adaptors to connect them to the yacht's propane regulator. If the intention is to visit several European countries over an extended period, then it will be more convenient for the yacht to be converted to a butane system using Camping Gaz cylinders. The exception to this is in the Scandinavian countries where only propane may be available.

All yachts should ensure that their bottles are in good condition before departure, and that they will remain in test date throughout the cruise. Bottles that are dented or have become rusty are unlikely to be acceptable for refill, so it is worth looking after them. Bottles should be marked with their tare weight and never overfilled. Cylinders could become hydraulically full (and burst) through expansion of the LPG with increase in temperature, so never overfill cylinders. In hotter – tropical or semi-tropical – regions, cylinders must only be filled to 70 per cent of their capacity to allow for this expansion.

Note: Although American and Calor propane connectors appear identical, they are not absolutely so. An American propane connector can be attached to the female fitting on a Calor bottle and a gastight seal can be made. However, it is physically impossible to get a UK Calor connector into an American female bottle fitting.

A great deal of useful information on gas systems is contained in the leaflet *LPG (Bottled Gas) for Marine Use*, published by Calor Gas Ltd and available free from showrooms or direct from the Boating Industry Liaison Officer at the company, telephone (UK) 0845 766111, or www.enquiry@calorgas.co.uk.

Gas is potentially dangerous, and basic safety procedures must be laid down and then stringently observed. The ideal is to turn the gas off at the bottle as soon as it is no longer required. If, as is usually the case, this means going out into the cockpit and opening a locker, a shut-off valve for routine use should be fitted where the piping enters the cabin. Alternatively, a shut-off valve at the bottle can be electrically operated from a switch near the galley. But either device must be far enough from the stove to be accessible in the event of fire. Newer gas stoves and other gas appliances are likely to be fitted with some form of flame failure device. However, this will not prevent leaks from defective piping.

Stove and gas system spares should be carried. If burners rust out or a regulator fails, replacements will be almost impossible to find. It is worth carrying a simple alternative method of heating food, either a single-burner Primus with some paraffin and priming alcohol, or a miniature camping stove with a supply of solid fuel tablets. On an ocean passage a diet of uncooked food palls quickly.

Refrigeration

Although not absolutely essential, some method of keeping food and drink cool in the tropics should be high on the agenda, the choice being between an insulated icebox and a refrigeration system. An icebox has the advantage of simplicity and reliability, but is dependent on ice from ashore; with the increased use of refrigerators, block ice is becoming harder to find. An icebox is of limited use on longer passages, although with really good insulation a block of ice will last a surprisingly long time.

Refrigeration systems fall broadly into two categories, those that are directly driven from the yacht's engine (or auxiliary generator), and those that run from the ship's electrical system. The former are usually considerably more powerful, enabling a larger volume to be cooled and ice to be made, but will require the engine to be run at least once, and often twice, every single day. Running a diesel on such a comparatively light load in harbour will do it no good and, in crowded anchorages or when alongside, may be antisocial.

In the tropics, a electrical refrigeration system will be the largest consumer of electricity on board. Indeed, its requirements will probably exceed those of all the other electrical equipment combined. Whatever type is fitted, in tropical waters it will use at least twice the number of amp-hours that it would in temperate conditions and this energy will have to be put back into the battery. An electrical fridge should therefore be considered in the context of the boat's overall electrical and charging systems. All fridges should use water to cool the refrigerant; air-cooled systems are hopelessly inefficient in hot climates. Fridge systems contain an unhealthy mix of metals, so ensure that sacrificial zincs are fitted in the cooling circuit.

The amount of energy a fridge consumes, or the amount of ice an icebox requires, is directly proportional to the efficiency of the insulation of the box, and a system designed for northern waters will almost certainly need extra insulation. A minimum of 10cm (4in) of modern insulation, preferably closed cell polyurethane foam, is needed, although 15cm (6in) is preferable, and is the minimum for any part of the fridge/icebox that is against an engine compartment bulkhead. The insulation should incorporate a vapour barrier, and a reflective layer to reduce radiated heat transmission. A tightly fitting lid, with efficient neoprene seals, is essential, and a drain (with a swan-neck to prevent cold air escaping) should also be provided.

Water tankage

In many boats, it will be necessary to increase fresh water capacity before undertaking an ocean voyage. About 2.5 litres (just over ½ Imperial gallon/nearly ¾ US gallon) per person per day should be sufficient in cooler areas, but is barely enough in the tropics and allows nothing for personal washing or laundry. Allowance must also be made for a longer than anticipated passage time. The calculation for the Canaries/ Barbados voyage with a crew of three might be:

> 2.5 litres x 3 people x 24 days = 180 litres
> 50% reserve = 90 litres
> Total required = 270 litres (about 62 Imperial
>   gallons/75 US gallons)

It should be stressed that this is the absolute minimum consistent with safety, and 400 litres (88 Imperial gallons/106 US gallons) or more would be preferable. At least 45 litres (10 gallons) of this should be carried in plastic containers, reasonably accessible in case of emergency; as fresh water is lighter than salt water, these containers will float.

The water supply should be split between at least two tanks, and for preference these should not interconnect. The best arrangement is to have three tanks; the suction from each should be from the top via a stand-pipe so that a fracture in the pipework will not allow the tank to drain away. The suctions should be connected to the water distribution system via a set of valves so that an individual tank can be selected for use.

On passage, water consumption must be monitored and the skipper must always have a good idea of the amount remaining in each tank. It is prudent to check the actual capacity of each tank by filling it from a container of known volume rather than relying on the figure provided by the manufacturer. Most tank gauges are notoriously unreliable, and a better method of keeping track of consumption at sea is to use a 5- or 10-litre (1- or 2-Imperial gallon) plastic can as a service tank, with all water used coming from this can. Each time it is refilled, the fact is recorded, and so the amount of water used is always known. It is often said that the contents of one water tank should be left unused until near the end of the passage to allow for an unexpected emergency, but this is not good advice. Each tank should be used for a day or two in turn throughout the passage, so that the quantities in each remain roughly the same. In that way, the consequences of the loss of one tank's contents will be minimised.

While at sea a pressure water pump should invariably be switched off when not actually in use, and it may be better to disconnect the pump when on an ocean passage and to rely on the hand pump – which will in any case be needed as a back-up. Having to work hard for fresh water deters most people from being careless with it!

The plastic containers mentioned above, in which reserve water should be carried, will also be invaluable in those places where it is not possible to fill the tanks by hose. It may sometimes be necessary to carry water several hundred metres before transporting it out in the dinghy, and for this reason 5- or 10-litre (1- or 2-Imperial gallon) cans will be preferable to the unwieldy 22-litre (5-Imperial gallon) variety. They are also easier to stow, and should one can split at sea only a small part of the reserve will be lost.

Reverse osmosis watermakers, which produce fresh water from seawater, are increasingly popular, and though still costly, their price has fallen considerably in recent years. They may be driven by the ship's electrical system, or directly from the engine or generator – the latter arrangement is preferable if useful quantities of water are to be produced. Manually operated models are also available, but these are only suitable for use in survival situations. As long as it continues to work, a watermaker will allow more water to be used at sea, but such a complicated device cannot be completely relied on, and there must always be sufficient water remaining in the tanks to enable a port to be reached, even if only under strict water rationing. The watermaker should therefore be run frequently in the early part of an ocean passage to keep the tanks fully topped up.

In harbour, a watermaker will eliminate the need to go alongside for fresh water, or to carry it in cans, and will allow the more generous use of water for laundry and cleaning. Some may consider that these advantages hardly warrant the complication or expense, but it is significant that those long distance cruisers who have fitted a watermaker usually maintain that it is the last mechanical device that they would forgo.

Most voyaging yachts need extra storage space. Here a bunk has been converted into a shelf with cupboards. Photo Gavin McLaren.

Berths

Along with regular food, adequate and relaxing sleep will do much to keep those aboard not only functioning through the worst conditions, but also reasonably cheerful. It is desirable for there to be as many good seaberths as there will be people aboard for the passages; it is *just* acceptable for there to be one fewer, but this will mean hot bunking and should be avoided if at all possible. In harbour, berths that would be untenable at sea, perhaps those in a forward cabin, can be used. A good seaberth is one in which it is possible to sleep in any weather and on any point of sailing. Ideally it should be as close to the centre of the boat as possible, to reduce the motion, should be parallel to the fore-and-aft line, should be located so that normal watchkeeping and ship's activities do not disturb the sleeper and should not need to be unrigged when not in use. Few seaberths achieve these ideals, but they are worth striving for.

In practice, quarter berths, the saloon settees, and possibly pilot berths rigged above them, will probably have to suffice. In a centre-cockpit yacht the aft cabin may be used. Wherever the berths, it is absolutely essential that the sleeper cannot be thrown out however extreme the conditions. High leecloths or bunkboards will be needed, and they must be strong – as must their attachment points. In many pilot berths, the canvas base is supported by a full-length bar that ships into bulkhead sockets at the head and foot of the berth. This bar must be positively fastened into the sockets and not rely merely on the weight of the sleeper to keep it in place.

Berths must not be so wide as to allow the occupant to slide from side to side as the yacht rolls, which they are likely to do for most of a trade wind crossing. Nor must they be so narrow that they stop the occupant turning over. Leecloths of smooth plastic fabrics should be avoided; in the tropics the minimum of bedding, if any, will be needed, and such materials adhere to the skin. Acrylic canvas is very much more comfortable.

Every effort should be made to avoid the crew having to sleep in the saloon when the yacht is in harbour, although it may be necessary for occasional guests to do so. A permanent harbour-sleeping cabin

A high leecloth and a narrow bunk provides the occupant with secure sleep, whatever the yacht's antics. Photo Ashley Crawford.

will make life in port very much more civilised. Having to make up bunks each evening and stow them each morning may be acceptable for a few weeks' holiday, but is tedious for long-term living aboard.

Stowage

The ocean cruising boat will need more space devoted to stowage than will her coastal counterpart. Much of this will be devoted to food stores, but extra sails, clothes, spares, tools and all kinds of other paraphernalia must also be accommodated. The modern-production boat tends to be lacking in storage space. Fortunately, she is also likely to have more berths than are good for her, and one or more of these will probably have to be converted into storage space by building in lockers, partitioning into bins, or whatever method seems most suitable. If extra crew are taken on for the ocean passages it is important that they are allocated a dedicated locker for their clothes and possessions.

Lockers – whatever they are to hold – should be lined so that water cannot spoil their contents. This is easy to do in a wooden hull where battens or hardboard can be fixed over the timbers, but may be less easy with steel or glassfibre. Never allow a locker shelf, or the cabin sole, to be fitted right up flush with the hull. If this is done, any water trickling down will collect on the shelf, soaking the contents, and probably causing rot in the longer term.

It is better to have many small lockers than a few large ones – the larger a stowage, the more likely it is to have everything on top and nothing to hand. In a modern glassfibre yacht with modular joinery there are often many inaccessible spaces behind the joinery work or under the sole. These can often be opened up, lined, and fitted with a door or hatch to provide extra stowage. Space under the sole is particularly suitable for heavy items, provided that they are protected against the water that will inevitably find its way there from time to time.

The engine and electrical system

The engine and electrical system should be in first-class condition before departure. More extended cruises are delayed, curtailed or abandoned as a result of mechanical or electrical failure than for any other reason. Engine problems are usually caused by lack of maintenance or poor installation. The electrical system usually fails because it is inadequate to meet the extra requirements placed upon it.

The engine

The engineless cruising yacht is now so rare as to be almost extinct. As anchorages become more crowded,

so manoeuvring under sail alone has become increasingly nerve-wracking. A few harbours, and most marinas, are impossible to enter except under power. The increased electrical demands of modern yachts mean that an efficient and powerful battery charging system is needed, which the engine can provide. Finally, engines themselves have become lighter, more reliable and relatively cheaper over the years.

On most Atlantic cruises an engine is needed less for propulsion at sea than for battery charging and harbour work. Only if the range under power is several hundred miles will an engine be much use for propulsion on passage, although sometimes it may be profitable to motor a shorter distance to find the wind, or to speed the last lap to the destination.

The engine should be thoroughly checked before leaving home waters. It will be far easier to have major work done at this stage, even if it is not yet absolutely necessary, than along the way. Engine mounts should be examined, as should all flexible hoses – those whose condition is not first class must be renewed. If the engine is past the first flush of youth it may be wise to have the alternator and starter motor overhauled and to renew the thermostat. If it seems likely that they may be dirty, fuel tanks should be opened up and cleaned; injectors and fuel pumps will benefit from being serviced before departure. The exhaust system should be thoroughly checked and any suspect components renewed – corrosion in this system is particularly common. There must be some method of closing the exhaust overboard discharge – water flooding back through the exhaust system in heavy weather has destroyed countless engines. Fresh- and saltwater cooling systems need descaling periodically. A fresh-water cooling system should contain the correct proportion of antifreeze; icing is unlikely to be a problem, but antifreeze is also an effective anti-corrosive. The engine compartment should be thoroughly clean.

Comprehensive engine spares should be carried. Most engine manufacturers can supply a kit of long-range spares, or at least a list of recommendations. Also, plenty of fuel filters are essential. If routine – or not so routine – maintenance requires any specialised tools, these should be carried. Diesel mechanics are to be found almost everywhere and, even if more used to fishing boats or tractor engines, they will be able to carry out work on a yacht's diesel provided the correct spares and tools are available.

Having set off with an engine in good condition it is relatively easy to ensure that it remains so. The manufacturer's service schedule should be meticulously followed. Modern, lightweight diesel engines are particularly hard on their lubricating oil. This must be changed and a replacement filter element fitted at the correct intervals. If the engine is regularly run on light load – to power a fridge or to charge the battery for example – then the oil and filter should be changed more frequently. Fuel filters should also be changed regularly, and it is good practice to install double fuel filters in parallel so that a clean one is always available for use.

Working on the engine is much easier if it, and its compartment, are kept clean, which will also enable minor leaks to be identified and rectified early.

The electrical system

The demands placed on yachts' electrical systems have increased dramatically in recent years. Unfortunately the systems themselves have often not developed at the same pace. This may not be significant for the average cruiser, which is limited to weekend sailing and the occasional two- or three-week cruise. That pattern of use is likely to involve a proportionally much greater use of the engine, and therefore the alternator, than an extended voyage. During a home-waters cruise it is likely that at least the occasional night will be spent connected to shore power, when the battery can get a good charge. But the ocean voyager must be completely independent of the shore during the passages, and even when in harbour they are much more likely to be at anchor than alongside. The ocean voyager's electrical demands must therefore be met entirely from onboard resources.

The design of the electrical system is a complex matter, and if in doubt expert advice should be sought. There are also some excellent books on the subject. It is not possible in this book to duplicate these sources of information, but the following points are worth considering.

It may seem obvious, but is an often overlooked fact, that every amp-hour taken out of the battery must be replaced by an amp-hour put back in. (In reality, because of the characteristics of batteries, every amp-hour taken out must be replaced by more than that – usually about one and a quarter amp-hours.) However big the battery, however powerful the alternator or efficient the auxiliary charging devices, however smart the regulator or accurate the battery metering instruments, there is no avoiding this principle. Generally speaking, the bigger the battery bank, the longer can be the interval before the amp-hours used have to be replaced; the bigger the alternator, the more rapidly can the recharging be done. Smart (modern electronic) regulators enable the full potential of a powerful alternator to be used without damaging the battery.

The rate at which the amp-hours used can be put back in varies not only with the power of the alternator, but also with the capacity of the battery – the bigger it is, the more rapidly can it accept a given number of amp-hours. Some 50 amp-hours can be returned to a 300 amp-hour battery much more quickly than they can be to a 100 amp-hour one. It is generally damaging to a battery for it to be regularly discharged below about 45 per cent of its capacity; it is time-consuming to recharge it above about 85 per cent, although for long battery life this should be done periodically.

Given these simplified facts, some general guidance for an ocean cruising yacht's electrical systems can be given. The amp-hours used each day in harbour and at sea must be estimated. When doing so, allowance should be made for the longer nights of the tropics and for the very much greater load that any electrically powered fridge will take in a warm climate – the daily consumption of such a fridge is likely to be at least twice that in temperate conditions. It is wise to overestimate the total daily amp-hourage rather than to underestimate it. Domestic battery capacity in amp-hours should not be less than three times the maximum of the sea and harbour estimate. If space and weight considerations allow, a greater capacity should be fitted. Rated continuous alternator output in amps should be around a third of the battery capacity in amp-hours. Again, a larger alternator will do no harm, though to gain full benefit a smart electronic regulator should be fitted. These are general guidelines for a system that can be maintained with less than two hours of engine running each day. A system that falls significantly outside these parameters will need longer and/or more frequent periods of charging. Alternative means of charging are considered in Chapter 3, but (apart from a large yacht's dedicated diesel generator) they should in general be considered as additions to, rather than substitutes for, the engine charging system.

Unless it can be started by hand, the engine should have its own dedicated battery, kept fully charged. The electrical system should be designed so that this battery cannot inadvertently be used to power the domestic system, while at the same time provision should be made for the domestic batteries to be used to start the engine should its own battery fail. This is usually achieved either by manual switches or blocking diodes. A battery state indicator is also useful, and should be installed in such a way that it can indicate the state of each battery individually.

Corrosion

Any water-cooled engine is liable to be affected by galvanic or electrolytic action. A salt-water cooled installation should have sacrificial zincs somewhere in the water jacket, and these will need regular inspection and replacement. Even when fresh-water cooling is used, the heat exchanger is exposed to the corrosive action of hot salt water and an anode may be needed for its protection. Galvanic corrosion is rapid in tropical waters and must be guarded against. Most boats will need at least one external hull anode correctly bonded to the metal fittings. This is a complex subject and, unless you are an expert, get a surveyor who specialises in this field to check your system during your preparations. Anodes should be in good condition before departure, and at least one spare carried.

Routine maintenance

Keeping up with routine maintenance is essential to the smooth running of the long distance cruising yacht. Part of it will be cosmetic – brightwork in particular deteriorates rapidly in the tropical sun – but more is related to

Routine maintenance of all equipment subject to salt spray is essential. The important thing here is to remember which bit goes where. Photo Georgie McLaren.

safety at sea. Regular inspection on the 'stitch in time' basis will often avoid more serious damage. Checking sails for worn stitching, running rigging for chafe, shackles and other metal fittings for rust, corrosion or abrasion – all may avert failure at a critical moment. Mechanical equipment (including the winches) will need periodic servicing, halyards should occasionally be end for ended to even out the wear, the outboard motor will

benefit from a fresh-water flush from time to time, and once in a while the sprayhood and dodgers will need cleaning. These tasks, and a myriad of other similar ones, are part of the normal routine aboard a long distance cruiser, and most owners find it satisfying to keep their yachts in good shape.

One advantage of the ever-increasing number of yachts based in the Caribbean is the dramatic improvement in facilities, including those for hauling out, over the past two decades. However, most slipways and travel lifts are in regular use and it may be necessary to book well in advance. If you have a full set of plans for the boat it can do no harm to carry them with you, though photographs to show sling positions, hull shape and length of keel may be of more practical use. In tropical waters much routine work on the hull can, if necessary, be done with the boat afloat. With snorkel and facemask it is easy to keep the hull clean and regularly inspect the rudder fittings, propeller and anode.

Before going to sea, make a comprehensive list of items to be checked and mark each item off as you complete it. Examine the rigging meticulously – an inspection aloft should be made regularly and certainly before each ocean passage. Ensure that rigging screws are properly secured, that every shackle is moused (small plastic cable ties are good for this), and that all masthead sheaves are running freely. Check the engine is in good shape, that the batteries are topped up if necessary, and that they are well charged. Navigation lights should be checked individually, a task often best done several nights before departure.

The spares and tools most likely to be required will naturally vary from boat to boat, but some suggestions will be found in Chapter 3.

3 Equipment for Ocean and Warm Climate Cruising

Much of the equipment discussed in this chapter may already be on board, particularly if the yacht has already cruised extensively in home waters, but its importance is such that it deserves further mention.

Ground tackle

For most people, one of the greatest differences between cruising in home waters and cruising long distance will be anchoring. Away from northern Europe and the major American yachting centres it is normal to spend time in port at anchor. Often this is because alongside berths are simply not available, but even when there is a marina, considerations of privacy and security often make the anchorage preferable. Other advantages in the tropics are that there will be less trouble from insects, the breeze will keep the yacht cooler, and her crew will be able to swim from her.

The ground tackle must be able to cope with bad weather too. On hearing a gale warning at home, most people think in terms of finding a secure mooring or sheltered marina berth (not least because these now occupy so many of the former best anchorages). On an ocean cruise there will be many occasions when there is no alternative to riding out bad weather at anchor, sometimes in indifferent holding or poor shelter, and possibly with rocks or coral heads astern. At these times the safety of the yacht, and her crew, will depend entirely on her ground tackle and the skill with which this is deployed.

Anchors

Most cruising yachts use a CQR, Danforth or Bruce as their main anchor. All three have imitators, which are unlikely to be manufactured to the same exacting standards. The CQR is probably the favourite general-use anchor and can often be stowed permanently on the bow roller; the Danforth may be superior in very soft ground, but is difficult to handle. So too is the traditional Fisherman anchor, but it is the only one that will hold in thick weed. The Bruce claims to overcome both these problems, but may have difficulty in digging into very hard bottoms. A relative newcomer to the anchoring scene is the Delta anchor. This appears superficially

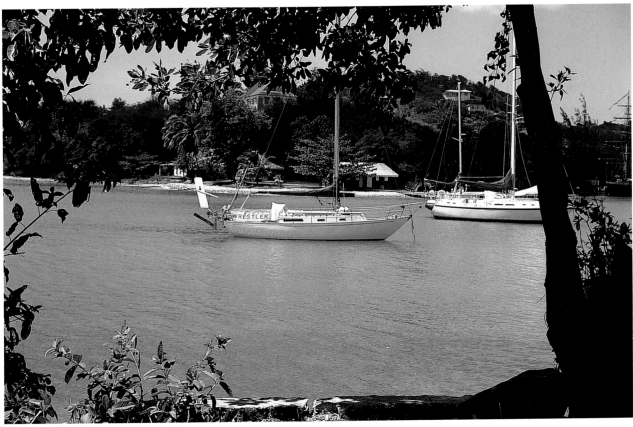

The Rustler 31, though designed as a cruiser racer over 30 years ago, remains a good example of the smaller cruising yacht. Here Wrestler of Leigh, *veteran of four transatlantic passages, lies at anchor in Vigie Cove, St Lucia. Photo Anne Hammick.*

similar to the CQR, and is made by the same company, but it is a one-piece anchor. Among the claims made for it are ease of stowage, strength, and very high holding power in a variety of bottoms. Those who have used it are impressed.

Every cruising yacht should carry at least three anchors, preferably not all of the same type. Anchor manufacturers and cruising reference books provide tables giving recommended weights for various types of anchor, and the skipper should study these. For peace of mind, skippers would be wise to choose anchors somewhat heavier than those recommended, and one (not necessarily the one in daily use) should be considerably heavier for use in extreme conditions. A windlass becomes worth its weight aboard a yacht of over about 9m (30ft). Above 11m (36ft), a power-operated windlass becomes increasingly attractive, particularly for a shorthanded crew. Although the current it draws will be high, it will only be used for brief periods – and so overall power consumption will not be particularly great. On many of the occasions that it is used the engine will be running. Among the advantages of a power windlass are readiness to anchor in deeper – and therefore probably less crowded – water, a willingness to move and re-anchor if the first attempt is not in exactly the right place, and readiness to lay out plenty of cable without concern for the effort involved in recovering it. This last factor is a considerable safety advance, as chain still in the chain locker does not increase holding power.

Anchor cable or rode

The main anchor cable or rode may be of chain or of rope. Rope has few advantages except in a very small yacht, where it may be impossible to stow a sufficient weight of chain. Rope is particularly liable to chafe on unseen rock or coral and provides no natural catenary to ensure a horizontal pull at the anchor. To help overcome this, if rope must be used, then a length of chain should be inserted between the rope and the anchor; this may also help to overcome some of the chafe. Rope cable will not self-stow, and compared to chain has a relatively short life. A yacht lying to rope will also require considerably more room in the anchorage – typically a seven to one scope is needed. Finally, rope is much more liable to be snagged by passing yachts or dinghies.

Chain increases holding power to such an extent, both through its own weight and by forcing the anchor to lie flat and dig in, that a scope of three to one is sufficient in normal conditions. Increasing the scope is a powerful weapon if the wind increases. This, together with its long life and invulnerability to chafe, make it the unhesitating choice of at least 90 per cent of experienced cruising yachtsmen. Additionally, except in really windy conditions in shallow water, chain will drop almost sheer from the bow, and thus be next to impossible for others to snag. Chain is far easier to handle and stow, particularly if a windlass is fitted. Self-stowing

will be improved if the chain falls straight down from the chain gypsy (wildcat) into a deep locker; the windlass, navel pipe and locker may have to be moved aft to get the necessary fall for reliable self-stowing.

There are few anchorages along the normal Atlantic route with depths much in excess of 15m (50ft), and provided chain is to be used, then 60m (200ft) should be sufficient. In a larger yacht, 90m (300ft) would be preferable; a third of this might be a separate length stowed in the bilge to be used with a second anchor in extreme conditions. Even if chain is routinely used, a mixed cable – 15m (50ft) of chain plus 75m (250ft) of three-strand or multiplait nylon – will be needed for those occasions when a second or third anchor must be taken out by dinghy, a task that is difficult with chain. This line will also be invaluable in those steeply shelving Caribbean anchorages where one drops a bower anchor and takes a stern line ashore, and should therefore not be permanently attached to the chain.

It is seldom a steady pull that breaks out an anchor. Far more often it is snatching and jerking that are to blame. An anchor weight is one way of preventing this, but the weight needs to be at least 20kg (44lb) to do much good. An alternative is to use a nylon spring. Here, after the anchor has been set, one end of a length of nylon rope is attached to the chain and the other secured to a cleat in the bow. Chain is then veered until the nylon takes the weight, and the chain hangs in a bight beneath it. (The chain should always be made fast in case the nylon parts.) Some 3–4m (10–13ft) of nylon is adequate, and it should not be too heavy or otherwise it will not be sufficiently elastic. Routine use of a spring has the additional advantages of reducing the noise transmitted up the chain as it moves around on the bottom and of taking the strain off the windlass.

Automatic steering

Unless there will always be a crew of at least three aboard, some form of automatic steering device will be more than a luxury. Even with a larger crew it will make life considerably easier. Autopilots use electronic systems to steer the yacht, and vane gears use the wind to do the same. Both devices have their advantages – and disadvantages – and many ocean cruising boats are fitted with both.

Vane gears

The principal advantage of a vane gear is that it requires no electrical power, and being a purely mechanical device should be reliable. This alone is enough to outweigh any disadvantages and to make it the choice of many skippers. Vane gears are easily understood, and the crew can generally carry out maintenance and minor repairs. A good gear will steer a yacht however heavy the weather. The disadvantages are cost, weight (this is particularly important in a very small yacht as the weight of the gear is in just the wrong place), and vulnerability to damage in harbour. (The better gears can often be easily removed to circumvent this.) Major repairs, particularly to the aluminium models, may be beyond local resources in all but the major yachting centres. Vane gears will not normally steer the yacht under power, and many are not particularly efficient in very light downwind conditions. They can be time-consuming to rig and set up after leaving port.

There are three types of system. They steer relative to the apparent wind, and when that changes the yacht's course will change too. All have a vertical wind vane, normally made of plywood, arranged so that when the yacht is on course the vane faces into the apparent wind. When the yacht veers off course the vane turns or tilts on its axis, and this motion causes the gear to bring the yacht back onto the correct heading.

In the oldest type, a linkage connects the wind vane directly to the yacht's rudder (or to a trim tab on its trailing edge). It is the simplest gear, and the only one that the average owner is likely to be able to build himself, but as it generally lacks power is suitable only for smaller yachts. It is now seldom seen.

The second type of gear is completely self-contained and uses an auxiliary rudder. The wind vane turns this rudder, or a trim tab attached to it, when the yacht is off course. The boat's main rudder is either left free to trail or, more commonly, set in the position that makes the vane gear work easiest. This type of gear avoids complicated connections to the wheel or tiller, and has the considerable advantage of providing the yacht with an auxiliary rudder, should the main one be lost or damaged. However, the steering forces are directly transmitted from the auxiliary rudder to the hull – normally to the transom. This may not have been designed or built with these sideways forces in mind, and so before fitting this type of vane gear, the designer or builder may need to be consulted. The Hydrovane is the most common example of this system.

The third type of vane gear is the servo pendulum. The Monitor and Aries gears are the most prolific makes, but there are many other manufacturers. In these gears, movement of the wind vane rotates a blade in the water. This blade, or servo-oar, is free to swing from side to side (hence the name servo pendulum) and, once it has been rotated out of the fore-and-aft line, the water flowing past it causes it to do so. This swinging movement is used to turn the yacht's rudder via a system of steering lines connected to the wheel or tiller. Servo pendulum gears are powerful and, as the power comes from the flow of water past the servo blade, the faster the yacht is travelling the more powerful they become. The steering forces act on the yacht's rudder and its fittings; the forces on the gear itself are only those required to move the helm. Although this is the most complex, and therefore the most expensive, type of vane gear it is the choice of most experienced voyagers – and thus the variety most commonly seen.

A typical servo pendulum self-steering gear. This Aries has steered for about 40,000 miles and is still going strong. Photo Gavin McLaren.

Whatever type is fitted, for a vane gear to work well the sails need to be trimmed to balance the yacht. The system must be arranged so that it can be disconnected instantly in an emergency, as it will be impossible for a helmsman to overcome the movement of the gear by brute force. It takes time to learn how to get the best out of a vane gear and to discover the most efficient way to arrange tiller or wheel lines. It is advisable therefore, if at all possible, to fit the chosen gear and experiment with it for at least one season of local cruising before using it to cross the Atlantic.

Autopilots

An autopilot uses a compass sensor, an electronic control system and an electric power unit to steer the yacht. In smaller sizes these three components may be combined into a single unit and models are available for either wheel or tiller steering. Larger units for wheel-steered yachts may either be mounted in the cockpit and turn the wheel via a belt and wheel drum, or may be mounted below decks and connected into the steering system there. This is the better arrangement as the power unit will be out of the weather and less vulnerable to accidental damage, or to theft. The electronic control systems vary in sophistication, with the most advanced models incorporating circuits that automatically adjust the autopilot for weather helm, sea state and steering load; these are said to reduce the power the autopilot will use. Most models can be fitted with a small wind direction sensor, so that the course may be set relative to the apparent wind. It is sometimes possible to use the masthead wind direction sensor for this purpose. Some autopilots can be connected to GPS receivers so that the yacht is automatically kept on track and steered to the chosen waypoint. This is a dangerous practice – particularly in a sailing vessel – and should be avoided.

The principal advantage of an autopilot is that it is cheap and easy to fit, at least in the smaller and medium sizes, and is light and simple to use. It will steer in the lightest winds and when under power. It avoids clutter on the stern and, if lost or damaged, is relatively easy to replace. Its main disadvantage is lack of reliability. Electronics and salt water are uneasy companions. (For this reason, the built-in units are considerably more dependable than the cockpit-mounted ones.) It is rare to meet a voyaging yacht that has been cruising for any length of time without having an autopilot problem. Experienced cruisers who rely on them for ocean passages carry at least one complete spare system.

The other significant drawback is that autopilots are completely dependent upon electric power and, in most cases, plenty of it. Running an engine or generator regularly will almost certainly be necessary to meet the demand. Should the engine fail, then the autopilot will fail shortly afterwards. Of the alternative charging devices mentioned later in this chapter, only the towing generator is likely to provide enough power, and then only when the yacht is moving fast. Finally, it is impossible for the majority of owners to make any sort of repair to an autopilot and problems will have to be dealt with by a specialist, who may well have to order components for a particular model.

Without doubt, the ideal is for the ocean cruising yacht to fit both a vane gear and an autopilot. The drawbacks of the one are largely compensated for by the advantages of the other. The vane gear will be the main helmsman on ocean passage. The autopilot will come into its own in very light weather, when under power and for short coastal sails. The reassurance of having two independent systems, each able to do the bulk of the steering during the crossing, is overwhelming – particularly for the shorthanded crew.

Sails

If ordering new sails give careful thought to their weight and design. Cruising sails need not be heavier than racing sails, and unless those already on board are showing signs of wear and tear there may be no need for new sails in any case. However, if ordering new for cruising, cloth that is 1oz heavier than before will be

money in the bank. If the boat has done much racing she may well have more sails than will be needed on an ocean cruise, when she might carry the following:

- Mainsail
- Two or three headsails (whether or not roller furling is fitted)
- Storm jib
- Trysail
- Mizzen and mizzen staysail if a ketch or yawl
- Asymmetric spinnaker or cruising chute if already on board

A major enemy of sails is sunlight, and their casualty rate will be high unless care is taken to protect them. Covers for main or mizzen are essential, roller-furling headsails must either have a cover or protective strips on the leech and foot. Sails that have to stay on deck when in harbour must be bagged. For preference, these bags should be of a heavy acrylic material as light nylon gives little protection from UV rays. Triple stitching is essential on sails, and it is helpful if the thread can be of a contrasting colour so that damage can more easily be spotted, and it must be UV resistant. Careful attention should be paid at all times to ways of avoiding chafe – the most likely place for this to occur is where a mainsail touches the lower shrouds when running downwind. It is worthwhile reinforcing the mainsail on either side in the way of the spreaders and lower shrouds to absorb the chafe.

Mainsails

Few yachts today carry mainsails cut specifically for ocean cruising, and a well-made sail suitable for coastal sailing will be quite satisfactory. It should have a minimum of two – and if a trysail is not to be carried, three – reefs, and there is some advantage in having these arranged so that the boom end will be raised a little as each reef is pulled down. This will reduce the risk of dipping the boom into the water when rolling. There should be a jam cleat on the leech for the leech line at each reef position, but these will usually not be accessible without sheeting in the sail. Consider running the leech line over a sheave on the headboard and down, within the tabling, to corresponding jam cleats on the luff of the sail. The method used to secure slides to the sail should be beyond reproach, and some spare slides should be carried. The clew of the sail carries a very considerable vertical strain; if the foot is fitted directly into a groove in the boom (without slides), a lashing through the clew cringle around the boom will help to prevent the sail gradually pulling out. Fully battened mainsails are now common. Such sails set well, and are easy to hoist and lower, but some have batten cars that are less than satisfactory. A fully battened main is very vulnerable to chafe where the battens press against the shrouds and at the luff, and some extra protection will be needed here.

In-mast reefing mainsails are increasingly popular, and those who have used them speak highly of them. A well-made gear is quite up to the demands of ocean passage-making, but it must be absolutely impossible for the system to jam. Should it do so in a rising wind there may be no alternative to going aloft and cutting the sail away. The clew is normally outside the mast when the sail is furled, and so is particularly vulnerable to sunlight – therefore sacrificial tabling or some form of small cover may need to be devised for it. With this gear a separate trysail should certainly be carried.

Trysails

Opinion about the need for a trysail is divided, and some long distance cruising skippers do not carry one, preferring to rely instead on a very deep third reef on the mainsail. This may be adequate on a small yacht, but a trysail is preferable and should certainly be carried aboard a vessel over about 11m (36ft). Ideally it should have its own separate track, which will make it very much easier to rig and hoist in storm conditions. A major advantage of the trysail is that it is set loose-footed, and so can be used if the main boom is damaged – a bermudan mainsail set without a boom is seldom much use, even if deeply reefed. The trysail will also come into its own on an ocean passage if the main is damaged beyond repair. These two uses alone justify carrying one, quite apart from heavy weather considerations. The trysail may also be useful as a roll damper when running downwind under double headsails.

Headsails

Roller-furling and reefing headsails are now the norm rather than the exception, although many cutters retain a hanked-on staysail. There appears to be little doubt that if a reputable gear is chosen and correctly fitted, the likelihood of problems is low. It will need to be well maintained; in particular, the system should be dismantled periodically so that the condition of the forestay can be checked. The sail must be protected from sunlight and, although strips on the leech and foot are effective to some extent, it may be better to remove the sail and stow it below during a long stay in port. This should certainly be done if strong winds are expected.

If using a roller headsail it may become necessary to deal with a jammed gear at sea. If the jam occurs with the sail reefed it will not be possible to lower it. The best way to furl the sail in this situation will be to motor in circles, passing the sheets around the sail, something best practised for the first time on a windless evening in harbour, preferably without an audience! At least one reserve headsail of no 2 genoa or working jib size should also be carried, and the means of setting this – a spare stay, halyard and sheet leads – should be provided. Regardless of what other headsails are aboard, it is essential to carry a small, heavy storm jib, set on a wire luff, and fitted with shackles to pass around the stay at head and foot for extra security. If using roller furling, either a permanent or temporary inner forestay will be needed on which to hoist the storm jib. This forestay may need extra support, either from running backstays or additional lower shrouds swept well aft, and the deck fittings must be substantial.

Downwind rig

The principal transatlantic yacht routes are downwind, particularly the trade wind east-to-west crossing. Unfortunately the bermudan rig is not particularly efficient on this point of sailing – this is an area where gaff rig has a distinct advantage. Ocean cruisers need to organise their yachts so that they can be sailed downwind safely, efficiently and comfortably for prolonged periods. There are three methods for achieving this.

One way is to rely on an asymmetric spinnaker. A symmetric spinnaker set flying has no place in a serious cruising yacht unless the crew is of racing proportions. Little needs to be said about it here as the arrangements for coastal cruising under this sail will be quite satisfactory. A snuffer or other furling device will increase confidence in its use. Chafe can be a problem where sheets and guys cross the guard rails and at the pole end. Unless the halyard block is perfectly fair, chafe at the masthead can occur unnoticed and the nip should be freshened regularly. If complete reliance is to be placed on this rig, sails of various sizes will be needed for differing wind strengths. Few skippers are happy to leave a vane gear or autopilot in charge when under spinnaker, although in strong winds a servo pendulum gear should be adequate. For the majority of ocean

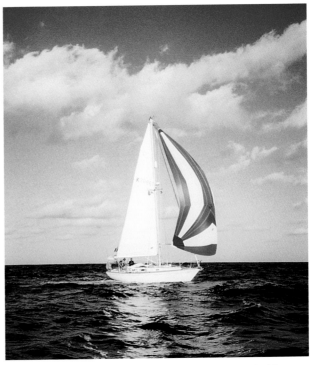

Light trade winds encourage spinnakers, especially if taking part in the ARC rally. Here Jessamy has a snuffer at the head for ease of handling. Photo Myles Higgin.

cruisers, a spinnaker – if used at all – will only be set under settled conditions and probably only during the day. At other times she will revert to one of the other two common downwind rigs, twin headsails, or main and poled-out genoa.

A true twin headsail rig, high cut and with twin poles stowed up and down the mast, was for many years the hallmark of the ocean cruiser. The rig evolved not so much for its efficiency as for its self-steering attributes. Before the advent of reliable vane gears, twin headsail rig was the only way that most yachts could be persuaded to steer themselves before the wind. For this reason it remains the easiest rig on the helmsman, whether human or mechanical. Other advantages are that it is remarkably free from chafe, wear and tear on the mainsail is avoided, and there is no danger of an accidental gybe. Drawbacks are that with no fore-and-aft canvas to steady her the yacht is likely to roll heavily, and that once the gear is rigged, manoeuvrability is considerably reduced. Setting the trysail and sheeting it hard amidships may ease the rolling. It will gybe repeatedly, but will come to no harm. Double headsails need at least one pole, and preferably two. If only one is available, the main boom will serve as the other, supported by the topping lift and with a foreguy holding it as far forward as the shrouds will allow. The headsail sheet is run through a block at the boom end. Poles attached to a track forward of the mast also need to be controlled by a topping lift, together with a guy led to the quarter, and a foreguy led to the foredeck. This will ensure that should the sail have to be got in in a hurry, the pole will remain safely stationary, to be dealt with later. The foreguy will also prevent the pole

being driven aft into the shrouds should the end dip into a sea.

Nowadays the headsails themselves are unlikely to be special sails, kept for this purpose alone, and they do not need to be of equal size. The usual arrangement is for one sail to be the normal roller-furling genoa, and for the other to be a spare headsail hanked to a temporary stay. An alternative is to have two identical or similar sails, each set in one of the twin grooves of the roller gear. These sails can be furled and unfurled together as the wind strength varies. Those who have used this arrangement are enthusiastic about it, often describing the headsail furling line as the throttle. But the loads on the furling gear will be larger than normal and it must be man enough for the job.

The simplest downwind rig is mainsail and boomed-out genoa. The main – reefed as necessary – will be set to leeward, and the roller genoa poled out to windward, the pole being secured as described previously with topping lift, guy and foreguy. The roller genoa is reefed and unreefed as the wind strength varies. Advantages of this rig are that no special gear or sails are needed, and that the yacht is likely to roll less than under the twin headsail rig. More significantly, she is much more manoeuvrable; the headsail can be sheeted to leeward and the yacht brought onto the wind quickly without touching the pole at all. The drawbacks are that there will be more wear and tear on the mainsail and it is vulnerable to chafe. This can be minimised by using a tightly set-up foreguy and, if necessary, a block and tackle between the centre of the boom and the lee rail to prevent the boom, and therefore the sail, moving up and down against the lee rigging.

Note the main boom is well strapped down to prevent mainsail chafe against the shrouds. Photo Gavin McLaren.

Power generation

Many cruising yachts rely solely on their main engine for the generation of electricity, particularly those whose power requirements are low. However, the amount of electrical equipment aboard cruising boats has increased steadily over recent years, and its importance to the voyager seems to have increased too. Additional methods of power generation are regularly fitted to ensure that this electrical equipment remains available. It should be appreciated, though, that 'alternative' energy sources – solar or wind power – are unlikely to completely meet the needs of an electric fridge or autopilot. Such devices will, however, reduce the frequency and length of time that the main engine will need to be run.

Wind generators

There are a number of wind generators on the market specifically designed for the yachtsman. They vary greatly from small trickle chargers to large machines capable of producing up to 250 watts in a reasonable breeze. In most types an alternator is driven by a propeller with three to six blades, and the unit is mounted aft on a pillar or the mizzen mast above head height and clear of all rigging. Some have the blade tips protected by a guard, but even with this they can inflict lethal injuries. There is at least one type that can also be used with a water impeller which revolves on a bracket under the transom, and this is not so vulnerable to inquisitive or hungry fish as an impeller towed astern. The noise in harbour from a wind generator will be considerably less intrusive than running the main engine or an auxiliary generator, which can be regarded as antisocial in marinas or crowded anchorages.

To a greater or lesser extent, all wind generators make a noise, and should be tested before purchase to find out whether this is acceptable. The type and output of the machine must also be considered, whether as a trickle charger or a serious alternative supply of power. None of them produces a significant output without at least 10 knots of relative wind.

Water-powered generators

Towed water-powered generators are capable of producing more power than wind generators, but they have some disadvantages. They will only produce a charge when underway, and usually at some speed, and will do nothing in harbour when the need to top up the batteries may be more pressing. A towed impeller, though, is an attraction to predatory fish, and while spares can be carried, it can become an expensive business. Lastly, the presence of a line astern is likely to be forgotten if the engine has to be used in an emergency, such as man overboard, or even when started to enter harbour.

Solar panels

Solar panel technology has improved markedly in recent years and modern panels are considerably more efficient than older ones. Their power output is still severely limited, though, and even a large array will only produce worthwhile amounts in the tropics. The manufacturer's figures should be treated with considerable scepticism and are unlikely ever to be achieved in other than perfect conditions, ie with the panel completely free from even the slightest shadow, connected to the battery through perfect wiring and held at right angles to the sun. Such a

Solar panels well sited on a much-travelled Victoria 40, Tacit. *Photo Roberta Bromley Etter.*

situation is unlikely to be achieved in practice. It should not be forgotten that, for 12 hours of the day, solar panels will produce no power at all, and for at least a couple of hours either side of sunrise and sunset, output will be milliamps. Unless a very large array can be fitted, panels should be considered more as a way of keeping the batteries charged when the boat is unused than as a serious source of power.

Auxiliary generators

These are increasingly carried as they provide the only means of keeping the batteries of most boats charged without frequent recourse to the main engine. Either an inbuilt diesel generator or a portable petrol-driven one may be used. The diesel has the advantage of being permanently available, of producing several kilowatts of power, which may be useful for purposes other than battery charging, and of using the same fuel as the main engine. Sadly, a great number of small diesel generators are not reliable – in an anchorage it is not uncommon to find as many yachts with defective ones as with working ones! As generator size increases, so does reliability. For a yacht over about 14m (46ft), a built-in diesel is probably ideal, but it must have a first-class installation and be conscientiously maintained.

For most yachts a portable petrol generator is probably a better choice. Such units are highly reliable, surprisingly quiet, and relatively cheap. A four-stroke model is much to be preferred to a two-stroke one. Although larger sizes are available, 1 kW is about the maximum size that can realistically be considered portable, but running through a good battery charger, such a generator should enable the batteries to be charged at about 30 amps, and in harbour a couple of hours' running a day will probably be sufficient. In light weather it can be run at sea. Compared to any other auxiliary charging device, portable petrol generators are far and away the most cost effective. Prices vary, but a 1 kW model is likely to cost about the same as one of the larger wind generators or a couple of modest-sized solar panels. It will probably be less than a quarter of the price of the smallest inboard diesel generator. The big disadvantage is having to carry more petrol on board than the outboard needs.

Shore power

The voltages and frequencies used around the Atlantic vary from 50 Hz to 60 Hz and from 110 to 240 volts. It is difficult to devise a simple shore power system or battery charger that can cope with all the possible permutations. Rather than attempt to do so, the best scheme is to set the boat up for the power supply of the home country. If time is spent connected to shore power of a different voltage (frequency is normally less critical), the appropriate transformer can be obtained. It can probably be passed on to a new arrival on departure.

Awnings and forced ventilation

Most Atlantic cruises involve a spell in the tropics, and a yacht that is cool in a hot climate will be much more pleasant to live aboard. Limiting exposure to the sun is important not only for comfort, but also for health reasons. It is therefore worthwhile paying particular attention to awnings and ventilation during preparations for the crossing.

Sailing awnings (biminis)

A permanent awning over the helmsman's position will do much to improve comfort at sea in the tropics, and many people feel that they are essential. The rigid bimini top is more commonly seen aboard American boats than European ones, where a fabric sea awning is more common. Whatever type is chosen, it must not interfere with the working of the sails, and preferably should not obstruct the helmsman's view of the masthead. This is not easy to arrange, particularly in a centre-cockpit yacht. It is worth studying a variety of biminis before designing one's own. Whatever the type it must be removable in heavy weather.

Harbour awnings

For only a single season in the tropics a bimini alone might be adequate, but even for such a short time a proper awning is infinitely preferable. Traditionally, the ideal awning covered the whole deck and certainly went from mast to backstay. This had more to do with keeping a wooden deck cool than protecting the crew from the sun, and aboard a modern, well-insulated yacht, with adequate opening ports and hatches, such a large awning may not be necessary. It is essential, however, that the cockpit, where the crew will spend most of their time in a warm climate, is fully shaded.

The simpler the awning can be, the better. A complicated design will take too long to rig and unrig, and therefore will often not be used. The awning may go over or under the boom; for preference it should not be so high as to need sidescreens, nor be so low as to make movement around the deck awkward. The smaller the yacht, the more likely it is that sidescreens will be necessary, as the height of the awning will be greater, relative to its width. Bamboo spreaders will probably be needed to extend the awning athwartships at each end, and a halyard in the middle will help to stop it sagging. Special telescopic or metal spreaders easily get damaged and do not float.

A secondary use for an awning is to collect rainwater in areas where shore water is hard to come by or is of doubtful quality. An awning will collect a surprisingly large amount of water in a tropical downpour. Plastic pipes can be attached using small plastic through-hull fittings, and should ideally be long enough to reach the tank filler. It may be best to set up the awning and experiment with a hose to discover the natural 'low points' where the pipes should be placed before actually fitting them.

Awnings should be made from a fairly heavy synthetic material – the acrylic used for many sprayhoods is ideal. Light nylon is not satisfactory – sunlight rots it, and much UV light will in any case pass straight through. Because of its light weight, it will rattle in any breeze.

Forced ventilation

The simplest method of forced ventilation when in harbour is by means of windscoops – lightweight sail-cloth triangles, shaped rather like miniature spinnakers, set above each hatch to direct the breeze below. In the Caribbean, during the usual cruising season, there will nearly always be enough breeze for a windscoop to be effective. They should not be made of nylon, as this is liable to rattle in a breeze, and collapse and fill as the yacht swings to an anchor.

In less breezy areas, or during the Caribbean summer, one or more electric fans will make life more pleasant, particularly in the galley. Power consumption may limit running time, however, and this should be checked on purchase. Small solar-powered ventilators are available to get round this problem, but while useful in the heads, or for a boat left closed up and unattended, they cannot be expected to cool the interior significantly.

Mosquito netting

There are very few places in the Caribbean where mosquito nets will be required, particularly aboard a boat that anchors off. However, if visiting Central America, Venezuela, Maine or the Canadian coasts, nets will be needed. There are also plenty of mosquitoes and midges on the West Coast of Scotland. A light wooden frame can be made to fit the washboard area, with nets for hatches set on elastic or Velcro. Anti-mosquito coils are obtainable in the places where mosquitoes are found, but few last throughout the night unless they are of the electric-powered variety. The best defence against mosquitoes is to anchor out.

Dinghies and outboards

Because she will spend so much time at anchor, a good dinghy is essential to the long distance cruising yacht. Either an inflatable or a rigid dinghy may be chosen, and many owners will already have strong feelings on the subject. Much depends on the size of yacht and the number and agility of those aboard. Each type has its advantages and disadvantages.

Rigid tenders are generally easy to row, have a long life, and are unlikely to be stolen. However, hoisting aboard must be simple, particularly as this may be desir-

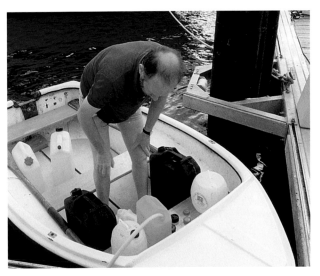

The dinghy will often be used to ferry water out to the yacht at anchor. Photo Georgie McLaren.

able every night in certain harbours. A wooden or glass-fibre dinghy is comparatively easy to repair if damaged and will put up with a good deal of abuse. Deck stowage is likely to be the limiting factor with a solid dinghy. The normal places for it are forward of the mast, an impossibility for most cutters, or amidships on the coachroof, a location only possible in larger yachts. For many, therefore, a rubber dinghy is the only possibility.

The inflatable's main advantage is that, deflated, it takes up little deck room and when on passage it can often be stowed below. It is relatively light and easy to hoist aboard at night, which is just as well as inflatables are particularly vulnerable to theft. If fitted with a solid transom and inflatable keel, an outboard of sufficient power to make the dinghy plane may be used. An inflatable is easier to board from the water than most rigid dinghies, and therefore more suitable for snorkelling or diving expeditions.

The inflatable's drawbacks are that it lacks durability – coral or sharp rocks can rapidly cause damage – and it is difficult to make lasting repairs. Few inflatables row well and, for reasonable comfort, bottom boards or an inflatable floor are needed. Boards can be a struggle to fit. Because of the theft risk (due to the ease with which they can be deflated and hidden) inflatables should be chained and padlocked to a strong point when left unattended.

A relative newcomer to the dinghy scene, at least in sizes suitable for yachts, is the rigid inflatable boat, or RIB. These dinghies have a solid glassfibre bottom and transom, with inflatable tubes forming the sides and providing the buoyancy. The main advantages of a RIB are that a powerful outboard can be fitted, it is easy to board from the water, and it is much less likely to be damaged by coral or rock than a pure inflatable. Its principal drawback is that it is as hard to stow on deck as a solid dinghy. For enthusiastic divers and snorkellers, the RIB is probably the ideal dinghy, provided deck space can be found for it. An occasional coat of wax polish applied to the underside of the dinghy, whether it be rigid or inflatable, will do much to prevent fouling during a lengthy stay in harbour if the dinghy is not hauled out at night.

Whether or not an outboard is carried will depend as much on the type of dinghy used as on personal preference. It should be borne in mind that as anchorages become more crowded so it becomes necessary to anchor further out and, in the Caribbean in particular, there will often be a fresh offshore wind blowing. Almost all cruising yachts do carry an outboard, and with an inflatable dinghy most people consider one essential. As fishermen everywhere use outboard motors it will usually be possible to get one serviced or repaired in even the remotest places, provided that parts for the particular model are available. It is wise to padlock an outboard to the dinghy in some anchorages and, even if the dinghy is left in the water, to stow the engine aboard at night. If at all possible, an outboard should be stowed below during passages. If it must be left on a bracket on the transom, then a waterproof cover is essential.

It is usually an insurance requirement that a dinghy be marked with the parent yacht's name. While this may make recovery easier if the dinghy is lost or stolen, when the dinghy is tied up ashore it does advertise which yachts are probably unattended. A solution is to mark the name on the underside of the dinghy or use the sail number.

Spares and replacements

It is hard to strike the right balance between carrying too few and too many spares. It is obvious that the lack of a simple part can delay a yacht for days or weeks, but it is less apparent that overstocking with unnecessary spares will increase weight and lead to slower passages. A plethora of spares will also make it more difficult to locate the required items in a hurry, and stowage space that could be put to better use will be wasted. The newcomer to ocean sailing is likely to err on the side of caution and carry too much.

Those who have always done their own fitting out will have a better idea of what to take than will those who have relied entirely on a boatyard. The number of items to be carried can be limited to an extent if some standardisation is adopted. Many boats have, for example, six or eight different sizes of shackle in various locations. With a little thought this number might be reduced to three. The same reasoning can be applied to everything from running rigging to bilge pumps. That way, many spares will be interchangeable, with cannibalisation of less important equipment as a possible last resort.

All things mechanical are certain to need servicing, and possibly replacing, during the course of a long cruise. Pumps will need new valves and gaskets; engines will need new fuel and oil filters; and alternators will need new brushes and belts. Hard-working winches will need to be stripped down for cleaning and oiling from time to time and, in this case, spares should include not only internal parts, but also at least one spare handle.

Diesel injector pumps are costly, and cannot be repaired except by experts, so if embarking on a very long cruise it might be wise to carry a spare. A complete set of the moulded rubber hoses that fit the engine is essential, as if they fail there is no substitute. It should not be assumed that the engine maker's recommended list of spares and tools will necessarily include everything needed; it should, however, be a good starting point.

Many ocean cruising sailors do much of their routine work themselves, both for convenience and their own satisfaction. Workshop or user's manuals will be found useful in servicing less familiar equipment and may also be requested by a professional – an electronics engineer will probably wish to consult a circuit diagram, for instance. Facilities for getting reliable work done throughout the north Atlantic have improved dramatically over the last decade and there are few places where it is not possible to find a diesel mechanic or electrician. If the necessary spares are carried it will generally be possible to get them fitted, but obtaining the same items locally may be impossible.

Synthetic sheets and halyards will last for years if not allowed to chafe, but a few hours of careless use may destroy the strength of an important line. A replacement length should be carried for each diameter in use. To suggest carrying enough stainless steel wire to replace any part of the rigging en route would perhaps be a counsel of perfection, but some provision must be made for possible rigging problems. At the very minimum, several 1m (3ft) lengths of wire, together with a plentiful supply of bulldog grips (wire rope clamps), should be carried so that a temporary repair can be made to a damaged wire. It would be preferable to carry (in addition) a length of wire suitable to replace the longest shroud or stay. One or two extra rigging screws and a selection of swageless terminals should also be aboard.

Sail repairs will be routine when ocean sailing, even if the sails are brand new at the start of the voyage. Palm, needles, beeswax and twine, and sailcloth in the weight of each sail, will all be needed. Needles are best stored in a tin containing plenty of grease. If space can be found for one, a sewing machine will save many hours of stitching and should be high on the priority list of the larger yacht. It need not be a special sailmaker's model, although one of those is ideal – a simple hand machine will suffice for temporary repairs.

When deciding what to take and what not to take, consider what one might expect to find in any moderate-sized town and what is likely to be available only in a major city or yachting centre. Ordinary paint, for instance, can be bought in most places, so it is not worth carrying a large supply, whereas antifouling will not be nearly so readily available. Dry cells for torches will be easily found, but the special batteries needed for some cameras may be almost unobtainable.

Thought must also be given to the problems of metric sizes. In the United States and much of the

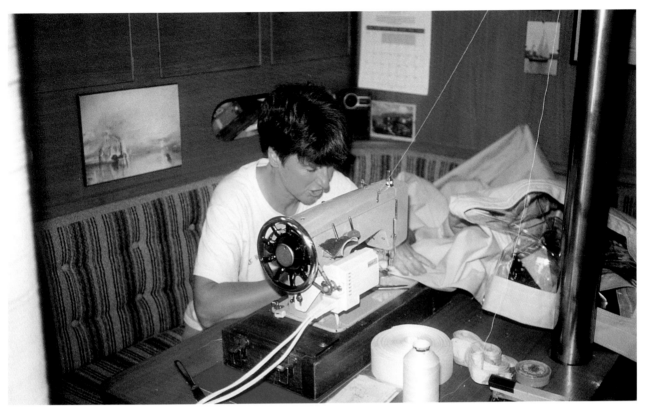

Sail repairs are a fact of voyaging life and, if space can be found for one, a sewing machine will be invaluable. Photo Gavin McLaren.

Caribbean, few items are available in metric sizes, whereas in Europe metrication is almost universal. The difference may be critical for parts for gas and fuel systems and for rigging items. Although the difference may not be obvious, a ³⁄₈in swageless wire terminal may be disastrously inappropriate to 9mm wire, and 6mm compression fittings may not make leakproof joints to ¹⁄₄in copper pipe.

Having decided what to take and what not to take, and accumulated all the items needed, stowage must be carefully arranged and recorded. It is not enough to know that an essential spare or tool is aboard 'somewhere' – the more urgently it may be needed, the more accessible it must be. A few minutes could mean the difference between catching a problem before it can escalate, and being faced with a whole chain of damage and disaster.

The toolbox

Tools must be appropriate to the jobs they will be expected to do, and may need to be bought specially – vane gears, for example, often require Allen keys (hex wrenches) of particular sizes. Almost without exception, good-quality tools are easier to use than inferior

ones and, with reasonable care, will last a lifetime. On a yacht, salt water is the principal enemy of good tools and it is worth making a considerable effort to protect them from it.

The loss of an important tool or part could prove serious, and neither tools nor pieces of dismantled equipment should be left lying about on deck where there is a risk of them going overboard. Aloft, wrist lanyards to prevent tools being dropped are essential. If working on a vital piece of equipment outboard – for example, a vane gear – the dinghy secured beneath it will save the items that will inevitably be dropped. If this cannot be arranged, then some other catch-all should be devised. A sun umbrella, rigged upside-down, is ideal.

Tools are often needed in an emergency and should therefore be readily accessible and in known locations. Few yachts under about 12m (40ft) boast a complete workbench, but well-sited and organised tool stowage is nevertheless essential – and a firmly secured vice is a god-send. In smaller yachts, tool stowage may consist of several boxes, each one devoted to tools of a different type – mechanical, electrical or woodwork, etc. It is a good idea to have a small selection of the tools most often used in a particularly handy stowage. This 'first aid' toolkit might include mole grips, pliers, an adjustable spanner and a couple of screwdrivers.

4 Ocean Navigation

For the transatlantic yacht, the most significant change that has taken place over the last decade has been the advent of the Global Positioning System (GPS). Only two decades ago the majority of yachts making the crossing relied exclusively, once away from the land, on navigation by the sun and stars, and if the sky was overcast the position became increasingly uncertain. The electronic aids available then – Satnav, Loran and Omega – were expensive, bulky, often inaccurate, and required some skill to use successfully. Only Loran is left in operation in some parts of the world, but its future is in doubt.

Today the situation has altered beyond recognition. At the touch of a GPS button, the navigator can read his position, accurate to within a few metres, day or night, rain or shine. If he wishes, the same set will instantly give him his course and speed made good, together with the bearing and distance of his destination; and many other features may be available: all this is in an easy-to-use package no bigger than a paperback book (and often much smaller), whose power requirements are measured in milliamps and which probably cost less

than a week's berthing in most marinas. It is hardly surprising that the yacht without at least one GPS set is considerably rarer than the yacht without an engine.

The GPS can be part of an electronic system operated through a laptop computer using electronic charts, and this is becoming increasingly common even within the traditional cruising fraternity. It would be a most imprudent navigator, however, who did not also have paper charts and written data on board, together with the means to navigate in the event of a total power failure.

There is more to navigation, though, than simply knowing the yacht's position. Other instruments will be needed, and also charts and pilot books. The capabilities and limitations of the GPS set itself must be understood. Although it is still quite possible to cross the Atlantic relying on traditional means alone, this book assumes that a GPS set is carried. The question of GPS failure is considered at the end of this chapter.

The chart table

The most practical chart table in heavy weather is one facing either fore or aft. Ideally, it should be close to the companionway, but not so close that there is much risk of it getting wet. There should be a chart table light; the type on a flexible stalk will enable an area of the chart to be brightly illuminated without disturbing nearby sleepers. There should be some secure book stowage within reach, together with a place where navigational instruments – pencil, rubber, dividers and parallel rulers – and spectacles (if needed) can be safely stowed, and an accurate timepiece must be visible. Nearly as important as the table itself is a secure seat where the navigator can sit safely with all necessary equipment within reach. Using it should not entail evicting another person from their bunk. It will often be necessary to use both hands when navigating and a strap to keep the navigator in his seat may be useful on one or other tack, or when rolling heavily.

Charts must be stored flat as few things are as irritating as a chart perpetually trying to roll itself up while in use. There must be some stowage for charts handy to the table itself; the school-desk type of table with a lifting work surface and stowage within is not ideal, but will serve. A depth of 5cm (2in) will take 100 British Admiralty charts folded once, ie as the majority of them are supplied.

The dimensions of chart tables aboard British yachts have traditionally been dictated by the size of a standard Admiralty chart. Currently this is 71cm deep x 107cm wide (28in deep x 42in wide), and a chart table this size

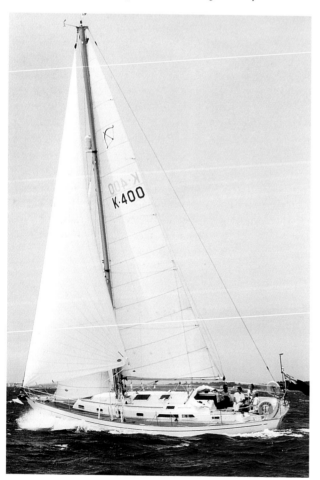

Quiver, *a Bowman 40, is an excellent design for long distance cruising. Photo Anthony Browne.*

has been seen as the ideal – although this is often impossible to accommodate. However, Admiralty charts are increasing in size – in line with European standards – to about 84cm x 119cm (33in x 47in), and this should be considered if building or modifying a chart table. A table size of 84cm x 60cm (33in x 24in) will allow most American or Admiralty charts to be used folded.

Some yachts will use the Admiralty ARCS series of electronic charts which are in the form of CD-ROMs, or other commercial electronic chart systems. Those that do must make arrangements for their use and viewing in a position that is protected from spray, and the chart table may not be ideal for this. ARCS charts and most other electronic systems cover the world, and once the system is installed and set up, it can work out considerably cheaper than buying paper charts; there are also tremendous savings in space and weight. However, it would be most unwise not to carry a reasonable back-up of paper charts and publications.

It should not be thought that the chart table will be wasted space when the yacht is in harbour. Some area apart from the saloon table is invaluable for letter writing and other paperwork, and the chart table will double as a desk, a workbench (for clean jobs), and even a temporary bar.

The log book

An accurate and up-to-date log is no less important than it was in pre-GPS days. Apart from its navigational uses, the log is also a legal document, giving possible evidence in case of a collision or insurance claim. Whether you use a purpose-designed ship's log or a ruled exercise book is immaterial, but in either case allow enough room to devote a separate page to each day at sea.

It is the responsibility of the person on watch to write up the log; in larger crews, where formal watches are not kept during the day, the task may perhaps be allocated to a younger or less active crew member. Two-hourly is the usual interval for regular entries and, as a minimum, the following should be recorded:

1 Time
2 Compass course steered since the last entry
3 Log reading
4 GPS position
5 Wind strength and direction
6 Barometric pressure

The same information should be noted whenever any non-routine entries are made. Which other events are to be recorded should be laid down by the skipper, and a note of them made inside the front cover of the log. As a minimum, the list should include: all changes of course; significant changes in the wind or weather; the running of the engine; any sail changes or reefs taken in or shaken out. Other useful, interesting or memorable events can

also be mentioned, and the odd remark about dolphins or a triumph of cordon bleu cookery will not detract from the log's basic purpose as the official record.

Although not strictly a navigational matter, many skippers use the log each evening to write a brief summary of the day. As well as recording a general impression of the previous 24 hours, this is a good time to note the distance covered and the amounts of fuel and fresh water used and remaining. Such a summary need not be a literary masterpiece but, long after an ocean passage is over, reading it will evoke many memories.

The compass

A reliable, good-quality steering compass is essential, and it should be checked and corrected for deviation before leaving home waters. Do not fall for the fallacy of believing that GPS has rendered this unnecessary. A hand-bearing compass should also be carried, and this can be used to check that the deviation of the steering compass has not altered noticeably. Deviation can change at sea, but this is normally a very gradual process and is not significant during an Atlantic crossing – although on a very long cruise the compass may need to be re-swung. However, a lightning strike, or even a near miss, can cause major changes. Fortunately, deviation can be determined at sea by taking a compass bearing of the sun as it rises or sets. This is compared with the true bearing, which can be easily calculated, or obtained from a simple table. A full description of the procedure is given by Eric Hiscock in *Cruising Under Sail* and is also included in most textbooks on astro-navigation, but it must be appreciated that the method only gives the deviation *for the course being steered at the time*.

Ferro-cement and steel boats, particularly those with steel decks, pose special problems of deviation. Their compasses should be professionally checked and adjusted before departure and at regular intervals during a cruise. Once a year should be the minimum, and for new boats – whose deviation may take many months to settle – more frequently than that.

Barometers and thermometers

An aneroid barometer should be fitted, and checked and adjusted before each ocean passage. A barograph is an attractive and useful instrument, but is bulky and may not, in any case, work well on a small yacht due to the motion. If one is not carried, then the barometer reading must be regularly recorded. In some areas of the Atlantic a thermometer will be useful for checking water as well as air temperature, particularly on the fringes of the Gulf Stream.

GPS receivers

GPS sets calculate position by using signals transmitted from geostationary satellites operated by the United States Department of Defense. A description of the GPS system is found in the manuals provided with most sets. It is sufficient to say here that position is available at all times, worldwide, and to a nominal accuracy of a few metres. This accuracy can be refined to even smaller limits by using Differential GPS (DGPS). The coverage for this service is not yet worldwide, and the range limited to some 300 miles from each DGPS transmitter. The Wide Area Augmentation System (WAASA) produces the same accuracy as DGPS in the United States and is a free service after the initial cost of the receiver; in Europe, the European Geostationary Navigation Overlay Service (EGNOS) will provide the same service as WAASA when it becomes operational. These add-ons to the basic GPS give an accuracy only infrequently needed by the cruising sailor, and although they will warn if there are any uncorrected errors being produced by the system, many will feel that the ordinary GPS set will more than fulfil all their navigational needs.

There are many makes of GPS sets, and the individual maker's handbook should be consulted for details of installation and use. Power may come from the yacht's 12-volt system, or from dry cell batteries, or from either. Some are described as waterproof and a few certainly are. If a set is to be used in the cockpit, however, the manufacturer's specification should be carefully checked as definitions of 'waterproof' vary. All sets will give position in latitude and longitude on the GPS datum, which is WGS 84 – most have the option of selecting other datums. Most sets allow waypoints to be entered, and also give a readout of course and speed over the ground. Almost all sets can give a highly accurate reading of UT – Universal Time, formerly known as GMT. Many can be connected to other electronic instruments, log, compass, wind speed and direction sensors, and to electronic navigation systems, to give a variety of sophisticated readouts.

Occasionally sets are seen that have what may be described as a DR mode, although individual makes will name this mode differently. When it is in operation, the receiver takes no data from the satellites, but instead calculates positions based on the last course and speed made good. It is imperative that if this feature is in use there is a conspicuous indication of the fact. Often, it is automatically selected if satellite signals are lost, which will happen if the aerial or its wiring are damaged. Not realising that this has happened, and that the apparently precise positions displayed are nothing more than electronic guesswork, has caused many groundings.

The ocean passage-maker should select a GPS set that is simple, robust and easy to use. A good-sized screen that can be read in all lights, with large clear figures, substantial buttons set far enough apart, and operating procedures that are logical – all these count for more than the ability to store 1,000 waypoints or remember 100 routes.

Charts, pilots and other publications

Charts

There is no basic difference between the charts required for an Atlantic cruise and those needed for home waters, except perhaps their quantity. Charts can sometimes be bought along the way but, except in major ports, only local stock will be available. For reasons of space and weight (not to mention cost), few yachts carry complete cover for a transatlantic cruise, and so a selection has to be made.

The advantage of ARCS or other electronic charts is that little storage space is needed. A couple of CD-ROMs will cover the whole of the Atlantic, for which several kilos of paper charts would be needed. Availability of ARCS charts may not, however, be as widespread as paper charts; so unless a complete stock is laid in before departure, you should take an up-to-date list of local agents with you (obtainable from a chart agent in the United Kingdom, or by telephoning the UK Hydrographic Office: UK (0)1823 337900).

Before departure, study a copy of *NP 131*, the worldwide *Catalogue of Admiralty Charts*. ARCS charts carry the same numbers as paper charts and are exact electronic copies. The US equivalent source is the *Defense Mapping Agency Public Sale Nautical Charts and Publications Catalogs*, of which Regions 1 to 5 will be relevant to an Atlantic cruise. The Armchair Sailor Seabooks in Newport, Rhode Island (see Appendix D) produces a useful *Atlantic Crossing Checklist* of relevant charts and other publications kept in stock.

Deciding which charts to order can be difficult, particularly if *NP 131* or another suitable catalogue is not readily available to look at. Once the route has been chosen, small-scale passage charts can be selected, with larger scales for the landfalls and inshore work. Very large-scale plans of commercial harbours are generally unnecessary, since these areas are likely to be well buoyed and lit. Harbours likely to be visited by yachts will almost certainly be covered in some detail in the relevant pilot books. Charts relevant to areas in Parts II and III of this book are listed in the relevant sections.

Plotting sheets can be used for working up the DR in the open ocean, where the chart is likely to be on too small a scale for accurate work. Various types are available from chart agents – some cover only a single band of latitude, others are universal and the user constructs the longitude scale appropriate to the latitude he is in, following the instructions on the sheet. This type is preferable. British Admiralty plotting sheet D6018 is recommended as it has clear instructions, will fit easily on a yacht's chart table, and is supplied in pads of 25 sheets.

In the major cruising 'crossroads', yachts that have charts for sale are often found, or it may be possible to borrow charts. In such places, if a full-plan copier is available, charts are often copied. With American charts, and those of some other countries, this may be done freely, but British Admiralty charts and publications are protected by copyright and may not be reproduced without permission. Anyway, working with a copied chart is less satisfactory than with an original and the copying process may well introduce inaccuracies.

Chart datums

The great accuracy of GPS means that the horizontal datum of a chart and positional accuracy of the charted features, something that until now the yachtsman has taken for granted, must now be considered. GPS operates on WGS 84 datum, but charts may be on a completely different datum, which can differ by several hundred metres. Where possible, new editions of charts use WGS 84 and this fact is noted. If a different datum is used, a correction to be applied to GPS positions may be given. If the datum is not specified on the chart, caution should be exercised – particularly if using old black and white charts in feet and fathoms, where discrepancies may be considerable.

It must be remembered that many areas of the world, including parts of the Caribbean, were surveyed before the advent of electronic aids or radio time signals. Latitude and longitude in these areas could only be determined by astronomical means, often using a chronometer that had not been independently checked for months. These surveys are remarkably accurate, but there are sometimes errors, more usually in longitude than in latitude, and these can be as much as half a mile. When making a landfall on a Caribbean island, the date of the survey given on the chart should be checked and the cautionary notes read with care. Although your GPS may be certain where it is, the land you are approaching may not be so sure!

Pilot books and yachtsmen's guides

Ideally, pilots or guides should also be obtained before departure. A careful study of them will help in selecting the route and, if they contain clear plans, it may be possible to dispense with some charts. Unlike charts, pilots and guides are not yet generally available on CD-ROM.

The official publications, the *Sailing Directions* produced by the British Admiralty and the US Defense Mapping Agency, are highly accurate and are updated by regular supplements. They are, however, mainly slanted towards commercial and naval vessels, and this means that many of the harbours and anchorages most suitable for yachts are only briefly mentioned. These books are bulky and expensive, but they do contain a wealth of general information, particularly about climate, currents and tidal streams, which gives a useful background to a cruising area. Not many yachts carry them, but consider borrowing them to study before departure.

Yachtsmen's pilot books vary both in quality and how well they are kept up-to-date. Make sure that the

latest edition is bought, together with any supplements – the better pilots are updated by supplements or amendments annually, but others are not. Some are more like nautical tourist guides than sources of essential navigational information. It will be worth enquiring among people who know an area well for recommendations both as to the best pilot book available and the extent to which it should be trusted. Such pilots and some guides are protected by copyright, and although photocopies are sometimes made (and occasionally offered for sale), this is illegal. Pilot books and guides relevant to areas in Parts II and III of this book are listed in the text and in Appendix B.

Annual publications

Opinion differs among experienced sailors as to how many annual publications need be carried aboard the yacht that is equipped with a good set of reasonably up-to-date charts. Tide tables and tidal stream atlases are obviously a necessity in areas where the tidal influences are great, but are less important for the Atlantic and Caribbean islands. In northern Europe, the Caribbean and North America, a commercial almanac will usually contain the information contained in several official volumes – *Light List*, *Tide Tables* and *Tidal Stream Atlases*. To some extent, the books needed depend on the equipment carried; a yacht with weatherfax and HF transceiver will need the appropriate volumes of the *List of Radio Signals*.

Takapu *has all the hallmarks of a sturdy cruising boat that has sailed many thousands of miles. Photo Peter Knight.*

In the English Channel and its approaches, the tidal range is great and the streams strong. It is essential that a yacht has the necessary tidal information on board for the area before making a landfall in these waters. The same is true, but to a lesser extent, for those bound for the American coast north of the Chesapeake.

Notices to Mariners

Charts, pilot books and lists of lights start going out-of-date even before they have left the printer. Ideally, all should be amended using weekly *Notices to Mariners*. In the United Kingdom these can be consulted at any customs house, obtained on a regular basis from chart agents, or found on www.nmwebsearch.com. In the United States, *Notices to Mariners* are available from the Defense Mapping Agency.

In practice, very few sailors do keep their charts and pilot books up-to-date in this way. To what extent older charts and publications can be relied upon is a matter of judgement. The older the information, the greater the caution that must be exercised before relying on it. It should be remembered that the rocks, reefs and islands generally alter only slowly, but that the works of man, including lights, buoys and other navigational marks, can change overnight.

Gnomonic charts and great circle sailing

The shortest distance between two points on the globe is a great circle. A rhumb line, the straight line on a Mercator chart, goes by a longer route. In practical terms, the difference is negligible except in high latitudes, and the only transatlantic passages where it may be relevant are those between the northern part of the United States and northern Europe. Only in these high latitudes is the saving of distance made by keeping to the great circle route likely to outweigh considerations of finding favourable winds and currents. To plot a great circle, a chart drawn on the gnomonic projection is needed. Details of the procedure can be found in navigational textbooks. GPS receivers usually display course to the destination waypoint as a great circle bearing, although on many sets the rhumb line option can be selected.

Ocean navigation in practice

There is more to ocean navigation than merely switching on the GPS, entering the destination as a waypoint, and then following the set's directions. Although such an approach may work, it offers no protection against mistakes. It would be all too easy, for example, to inadvertently enter 12° 42′ instead of 14° 22′, and not discover the error until land fails to materialise.

The yacht's position must be plotted on the passage chart at regular intervals. In the open ocean this will usually be once each day but, when approaching land or near the Gulf Stream, may need to be done more frequently. In this way, the navigational picture can be seen at once and mistakes are likely to be spotted quickly. Successive daily positions should be heading for the intended spot, be it landfall or turning point, and the distance to go taken from the chart should be the same – within the limits of measurable accuracy – as that calculated by the GPS. If there are discrepancies, then something is wrong and the navigator should find out what it is.

As well as this regular plot, the daily run, as recorded by the GPS, should be compared with the DR worked up from the information in the log. The passage chart will be on too small a scale to do this and a plotting sheet must be used. The two runs, GPS and DR, are unlikely to be the same, the difference being due to either error in the log and/or compass or to the influence of current. If discrepancies are consistently in one direction and of roughly the same size, suspect the former, but before checking the compass ensure that the DR and GPS computations are both using magnetic or true courses. It matters little which, but they must be the same.

As the land is approached the position should be plotted more often, and a larger-scale chart used as soon as the yacht lies within its limits. The DR should be worked up frequently and the current regularly assessed. With GPS, one ought to be certain of the landfall, but it is still possible to be set a long way off the intended track by a wayward current, and currents frequently change significantly near the land. Once the landfall has been made, the normal techniques of coastal navigation take over, and GPS becomes just one of the tools used in the process. Hand bearing compass, echo sounder and the navigator's eyes will be more important. For the reasons mentioned in the section on chart datums, GPS must not be relied on when entering a strange harbour.

The end of an Atlantic crossing is always exciting, even for the most experienced ocean passage-maker. In the euphoria, it should not be forgotten that the period after land has been sighted is likely to be the most navigationally hazardous part of the entire passage, and the one that demands the most care. Celebrations should wait until the yacht is safely berthed.

Equipment failure

All manmade items are fallible and some consideration must be given to the situation should the GPS fail. This might happen for two reasons: the system itself could break down, or the yacht's equipment could become defective.

The first reason, system failure, while theoretically possible, is so unlikely as to be inconceivable. The GPS system was designed to be highly resistant to deliberate attack, let alone accidental failure. All the critical components are duplicated, often several times. There are, for instance, spare satellites in orbit, ready to be switched on should an in-use satellite fail, with others available for launching. GPS was designed to be highly resistant to radio interference, and to be little affected by sunspot activity. It is possible that the system might be sabotaged, but the growing awareness of this threat makes it unlikely, and contingency plans should at least partly fill the gap. Degradation of the signal is, however, possible. Although this is unlikely to pass unnoticed if using DGPS, WAASA or EGNOS, it is something that should always be borne in mind in pilotage waters if using uncorrected GPS.

The likelihood of onboard equipment failure, whether of the GPS set or of the yacht's power supplies, is far higher. Installing good-quality equipment, maintaining the electrical system conscientiously and keeping the batteries well charged, will do much to reduce this possibility, but it is still a real one and provision must be made for it.

The traditional fallback is astro-navigation. This is not the black art that some would make it out to be, but, rather like riding a bicycle, it is a skill that must be acquired by practice rather than just by theory. Equally, it is a skill that, once acquired, is never completely lost. If astro-navigation is to be the fall-back, then a sextant, various books of tables or a dedicated pocket calculator will be required, together with an accurate timepiece. Courses in the subject are available, and there are many textbooks on the subject, some of which are listed in Appendix A.

The alternative to astro-navigation is to rely on back-up electronics. In practical terms this means one, or more, waterproof, hand-held, battery-powered GPS receivers, with the necessary converters to enable them to be run from the ship's power system. With such a set, failure of the main GPS receiver will be little more than an inconvenience. If it is the electrical system that has failed, a hand-held GPS can be switched on once or twice a day to give a position. Used in that way, a set of batteries will last for the duration of the crossing. If this option is chosen, the spare set should be treated like any other piece of emergency equipment, serviced when necessary, tested before departure, and stowed in a dry and secure place. Plenty of batteries should be carried (in case the set is inadvertently left switched on), reserved exclusively for the GPS; they will need periodic replacement, whether used or not.

Astro-navigation has the advantage that it is well proven and that it is independent of any outside agency. Its drawbacks are that the equipment is costly – a good sextant can cost at least twice as much as a hand-held GPS – and that the techniques take time to learn; they also need to be practised at sea before they can be relied upon. In heavy weather it is difficult to achieve accurate results, particularly for the novice. It is not available when the sky is cloudy, a point often overlooked by astro enthusiasts, and on the northern and middle latitude crossings it may be cloudy for many days at a time. Relying on a back-up GPS has the advantages of simplicity, accuracy and indifference to weather conditions. Its drawbacks are that it relies on an outside agency and that, should the yacht be struck by lightning, the back-up set could be destroyed along with all the other electrical and electronic equipment on board (including the astro-navigator's digital watch).

The choice between these two options must rest with the individual. It is a subject on which strong views are often held, not always well-thought-out ones. The following suggestion is made with some trepidation. Those who have experience of using astro-navigation at sea may depend on it as their only back-up system. Those who do not have that experience should carry a reserve GPS set. They may wish to take a sextant and tables, and learn astro-navigation techniques along the way, but they should not count on being able to do so unaided, however many textbooks are carried or courses have been done.

5 Electronics and Communications

Both electronics and communications are highly special-ised subjects and ones in which change is taking place at a great rate. It is not possible here to give more than an overview of the current situation, and to mention some of the general points to consider before installing any electronic equipment. There are excellent books available – many aimed at the less technically minded – covering specific topics and giving comprehensive advice on the choice of equipment, its installation and operation. How-ever, when fitting complicated or interconnected systems, professional help will often prove worthwhile.

Most transatlantic cruisers now fit more, and increas-ingly complex, electronic equipment than a few years ago. Today, gear that used to be confined to the largest yachts is now commonplace. Much of this gear makes long distance cruising more comfortable and convenient, but hardly any of it is essential. Owners must decide what level of comfort and convenience they feel is necessary – this is clearly an individual matter, and what seems an opulent luxury to one yacht may be an absolute essential to another. It should not be forgotten, though, that each piece of equipment must not only be purchased and installed, but must also be maintained, kept dry and provided with the necessary power. Although modern electronics are remarkably reliable, there will inevitably be periodic breakdowns, and getting electronics repaired in faraway places can be frustrat-ing, time-consuming and costly. The most successful ocean voyagers are those who have limited the equip-ment fitted to that which is necessary (to them) for an acceptable, as opposed to the maximum possible, stan-dard of cruising life.

The borderline between electrics and electronics has become increasingly blurred. Many items that would in the past have been thought of as part of the electrical system now contain quite complex electronics – for example, alternators, regulators and battery chargers. Fridge systems will probably contain an electronic controller, and some engine instruments may too. Although the electrical system has been discussed in Chapter 2, the yacht's electrical and electronic systems must be considered together, and if a lot of electronics are to be fitted then the basic electrical installation may need modification.

It is obvious that all electronics take power and that this power will have to be put back into the batteries sometime. What is not so often appreciated is that much electronic equipment needs a comparatively stable supply voltage to run reliably, and this may not be easy to provide. A yacht's battery voltage might vary from 14.2 volts when being charged by a smart alternator, down to 11.5 volts when a heavy load is being taken from it by, for example, a fridge or autopilot. The bigger the battery,

the less will its voltage vary under a given load; a big battery acts as a kind of voltage shock absorber smoothing out the variations. So when fitting electronic items, a larger battery bank may be needed – not only to provide the power, but also to steady the voltage.

The voltage at the battery is one thing, but the volt-age at the equipment is quite another. Every time elec-tricity is squeezed down a wire or through a connection some voltage is lost, and the longer or thinner the wire, or the poorer the connection, the greater will that loss be. It is important, therefore, that sufficiently heavy wiring is used throughout and that all the joints in it are meticulously made. Electricity can leak away to earth through dirt and damp, causing a further voltage drop, so the batteries, switchboard and cabling must be kept clean. If electronic equipment fails to work, or only works intermittently, check that the voltage *at the equipment* is within the manufacturer's specification. Generally, better-quality devices have a greater toler-ance of voltage fluctuations.

Damp, salt-laden air and electronics do not mix well. Not only is salt water a conductor, which causes damaging internal short circuits, it is also corrosive. Salt crystals can attack the circuitry on printed circuit boards with disastrous results. Well-made units, designed for the marine environment, should have cases that fit properly with efficient seals to keep the damp out; cheaper gear is less likely to. Even so, below-decks elec-tronics should be installed where they are unlikely to get wet. Cockpit instruments should be genuinely water-proof. It is worth checking exactly what the manufac-turer means by that word, and that the instruments really will keep the water out when repeatedly drenched, day after day.

Electronics need less maintenance than many items on board, but they do need some. Connections in cabling and aerial runs should be checked periodically to ensure that corrosion has not set in; log and echo sounder trans-ducers and radio earth plates will need occasional clean-ing; log impellers must be renewed at intervals; masthead instruments may need replacement bearings every few years. Many electronic devices contain small internal batteries to retain information in the memory when the equipment is switched off. Although their life may be several years, these batteries do not last for ever and they can normally only be replaced by an expert. So before leaving home waters, have older electronic equipment checked and serviced by a professional. Often this will mean removing it so that it can be tested in a workshop with the right specialist facilities. This gives a good opportunity to ensure that the onboard installation cabling and connectors, normally hidden away out of sight, are in good condition.

Instruments

Echo sounder

This is probably the most useful electronic device aboard. The ocean-going yacht actually spends most of its time within soundings, very often in unfamiliar waters, and a reliable echo sounder is a necessity. A shallow water alarm that can be set to go off when a selected depth is reached is a boon for the shorthanded crew, as long as it is dependable.

For the majority, who have never cruised without one, doing without an echo sounder is nerve-wracking. A lead and line makes a very unsatisfactory substitute, even for those with the skill to use it. For this reason, the echo sounder is one of the few items of electronics for which it is worth carrying a spare. A simple sounder can be bought for under £100. Its transducer can be fitted before departure and the set itself stowed away in the depths of a locker. It will enable the cruise to continue should the main set fail.

Logs

Some sort of log is essential for accurate dead reckoning. Although many voyagers carry a mechanical towed log as a back-up, the electronic through-hull type has significant advantages. If properly calibrated it is more accurate, will measure speed as well as distance run, and may incorporate a trip mechanism. Various types are available. The impeller can be a paddlewheel or a rotator; some logs use sonic or electromagnetic arrangements to measure the water flow, and this has the advantage of eliminating fouling problems. If static for any length of time in the tropics, it is worth withdrawing the log to keep it clean. Some transducers also measure water temperature, and when near the Gulf Stream this is of more than academic interest. A final advantage of the through-hull, as opposed to the towed, log is that it will coexist with a fishing line.

Wind speed and direction

Masthead sensors to measure the apparent wind speed and direction are frequently seen. Provided there is a repeater visible from the helm, the direction indicator may enable a better course to windward to be steered, and also help to prevent an accidental gybe when running downwind. The speed indicator can be informative, but it should be remembered that the wind speed at the masthead is considerably higher than that felt at sea level. Some form of variable damping control is desirable as, particularly in light winds, the movement of the masthead will significantly influence both direction and speed readings. Wind speed indicators are seldom very accurate, but they do provide a yardstick for sail changes.

Integrated systems

These consist of a small, dedicated, computer unit into which information from various sensors is fed. A variety of complex outputs can be calculated and displayed, the range depending on the sophistication of the system. At a minimum, log, wind speed and wind direction data is combined to give true wind angle and true wind speed. If a heading sensor is added (usually a fluxgate compass), then course and wind direction can be given and this information may be supplied to an autopilot. Connecting a GPS receiver will enable – in theory – leeway and tidal stream or current vectors to be computed. Multiple digital readouts and analogue displays can be provided, both at the helm and at the chart table, and alarms can usually be set for wind speed, heading and other functions. The capacity and complexity of an integrated system is limited only by the owner's inclination – and the depth of his or her pocket.

The major drawback is that the failure of a single component may bring the whole edifice crashing down. For example, should an electronic wind direction indicator fail on passage it is unlikely to be more than an inconvenience. But if that failure leads to the loss of all the instrumentation, including the log, echo sounder, autopilot and GPS, then the situation might be serious. For this reason, many very experienced ocean voyagers prefer to have individual, stand-alone, electronic instruments rather than such complex systems.

Navigation aids

Position fixing systems

The almost universal adoption of GPS by commercial shipping and aircraft has led to the demise of most other electronic position fixing systems; Loran is due to be phased out in 2004. The extensive network of coastal DF beacons has been largely dismantled, although a few of the sites are used as transmitters for DGPS. The aeronautical beacons remain, but they are of limited use to the marine navigator.

Radar

Radar sets are increasingly seen aboard cruising yachts. Radar has obvious uses as an aid to collision avoidance in poor visibility or at night and, during the trade wind Atlantic crossing, it will help to spot approaching squalls. It may be of assistance when making a landfall and, in the hands of a skilled user, can enable some unlit harbours to be entered at night. In the north Atlantic, radar comes into its own for those boats planning to cruise in Maine and Nova Scotia where fog is common. It will also be valuable, for the same reason, on the north European coast, particularly in the western approaches to the English Channel. However, sailors should be aware that, under the Collision Regulations, vessels fitted with

Electrical systems are becoming increasingly complex and need to be well installed. As equipment is added, these systems will need modification. Photo Georgie McLaren.

radar are obliged to use it, and use it properly, when visibility is poor; failure to do so might result in an insurance claim being rejected.

Chart systems

The information on charts can be stored electronically and, apart from the Admiralty's ARCS (Admiralty Raster Chart Service) system, there are a number of commercial systems on the market. These have the charts on a CD-ROM or some form of cartridge, which can either be viewed on a PC or dedicated viewer. Most systems are global, but the coverage may not be complete in some instances. There is often provision to feed in GPS positions so that the position of the vessel can be seen at a glance on the screen. Such electronic charting systems have become the norm in most commercial ships, and yachts are following – but in the latter case the systems are much more liable to failure. Electronics and salt water are incompatible bedfellows, and sufficient back-up of paper charts and publications, with the ability to use them, must be at hand.

PCs

A personal portable computer (PC) and printer are now commonplace aboard voyaging yachts. Many skippers keep records of stores, spares and charts in the computer, and it is only a matter of time before books and equipment manuals are also supplied in that format. With the right software, astro-navigation calculations can be performed with ease and tides predicted. A PC can be taken ashore and connected into the telephone system to give access to the internet and e-mail and, increasingly, connected to a radio set to provide a wide range of facilities.

Computers are seldom designed with yachts in mind and are more vulnerable to the effects of life afloat than most electronics. If choosing one specifically for the yacht, physical robustness should be a high priority, and PCs that are at least notionally watertight are available. It is a considerable advantage if both it and the printer can either be run, or have their batteries recharged, directly from the yacht's electrical system rather than via an inverter, but the manufacturer should be consulted about the risk from voltage fluctuations. Some PCs use less than 12 volts, but many use 16 volts – and in this case a small, dedicated inverter will be needed for the PC. Secure, dry stowage will be needed, and every effort must be made to protect parts of the system that are not truly watertight from the effects of damp.

It will generally be impossible to get a PC or printer repaired en route. Probably the best way of trying to deal with any such problems will be to find a fellow sailor who is a computer expert (there are a surprisingly large number in the voyaging community). To give this person any chance of assisting, the most comprehensive manual available should be carried, as should the necessary CDs or floppy discs to enable essential software to be reinstalled. Afloat, it is even more important to make back-up copies of valuable data than it is ashore, as a PC aboard a yacht is much more prone to failure. Only in a very few places will computer consumables be available, so a good supply of printer cartridges, blank floppy discs, etc should be carried.

GMDSS

The Global Maritime Distress and Safety System is now in place almost worldwide. It is a fully automated system relying on dedicated terrestrial and satellite radio to link shore and ships for alerting and any subsequent communications. Each incident is controlled from a Maritime Rescue Co-ordination Centre (MRCC), or a Maritime Rescue Sub Centre (MRSC), which may be hundreds or thousands of miles away from the incident. An incident will be triggered by an emergency DSC transmission, an EPIRB transmission or (at the moment) a distress call on channel 16 or 2182 kHz. All ships over 300 tonnes now have to be fitted with the full GMDSS equipment, and the recommended list for yachts can be found in the GMDSS chapter in *Admiralty Maritime Communications, Caribbean NP 290*.

Within the scope of this book there are now only a few places where the DSC frequency coverage is not yet complete, and watch only maintained on channel 16 and 2182 kHz. It is expected that the changeover will be largely completed in 2003.

While GMDSS now provides a system that immeasurably increases the chances of survival in a marine disaster, it must still be the cruising yachtsman's firm resolve to invoke it only as the last resort.

Communications

The ocean-going sailor needs a radio receiver to obtain weather forecasts. Most also listen to news and other broadcasts, and many wish to be able to communicate with other yachts, with ships, or with those ashore. They may use VHF, HF/MF or satellite radio to do some or all of these things.

Receivers

Whatever other radio equipment is carried it is worth investing in a good-quality, stand-alone receiver with a frequency coverage from 150 to 30,000 kHz. It should be able to receive both ordinary public broadcasts, such as those transmitted by national and commercial radio stations, and single sideband (SSB) transmissions on both the upper and lower sideband (USB/LSB); SSB is generally used for long range communications. The set should be capable of running from either dry batteries or the ship's supply, and several sets of batteries should be carried. Such a receiver can be connected via a suit-

able modem to a PC to enable weatherfax/radiofax to be received. If this is to be done, then a digitally tuned set – one where an exact frequency can be entered via a keypad – should be chosen.

NAVTEX

NAVTEX is an international automated direct printing service providing constant navigational and weather warnings and frequent weather forecasts. It is an integral part of GMDSS and is broadcast in English, and often in the local language too. The receivers are relatively cheap and easy to install; they can have either a direct readout screen or produce the same information on a paper roll. NAVTEX is the most economical means – in terms of cost and power requirements – of receiving continual weather information. The only disadvantage is the limitation of range to about 300 miles from the stations. The European and West African coasts are fully covered almost down to the Cape Verdes, but there is then a long gap in mid-Atlantic until the stations at Curaçao and Costa Rica can be picked up. The Caribbean and the east coast of the United States up to Labrador is fully covered, and there are stations at Bermuda and the Azores.

Weatherfax/radiofax

Once the preserve of large racing yachts, weatherfax, by which synoptic charts, pictorial forecasts and satellite pictures can be received, is now widely used by cruising sailors. Dedicated receivers are available that print out charts on special paper. These are expensive, however, and many yachts use a PC and printer to achieve the same result. The drawback is that unattended operation is often impracticable. Various software and hardware packages are available, and it is worth viewing a selection before choosing a specific one. Radiofax is generally transmitted on HF, and it can be received at long range with virtually worldwide coverage. There are many transmitting stations, and appropriate volumes of *Admiralty Maritime Communications* or *Admiralty List of Radio Signals* need to be consulted for the details of frequencies and times of broadcast.

Transmitters

Yachts may have VHF, HF/MF or satellite transmitters, as well as Emergency Position Indicating Radio Beacons (EPIRBs). The latter are for use solely in distress but the others allow the voyager to make routine communications with ships and shore stations. They too may be useful in an emergency, but no one should embark on a transatlantic passage in the expectation that help can be summoned should things go wrong. Quite apart from any other considerations, in many disasters – fire, hull damage or dismasting – radio transmitters are quite likely to be damaged beyond use.

While receivers may be fitted and operated without restriction, all radio transmitters fitted in yachts (other than those operated by a licensed radio amateur) must be of an approved type, and the operator must be licensed and familiar with GMDSS procedures. The yacht will require a ship station licence as well. Requirements for type approval, and ship and operators' licences, vary from country to country. Operators need to pass an examination on radio procedures – the complexity of the exam depending on the equipment to be used. Most sets on the market will meet the technical requirements, but a secondhand set may not.

VHF

This is widely fitted and will be familiar to most sailors. It is limited to line of sight communications between ships or those with shore stations. Transatlantic voyagers should be aware that the frequencies of some VHF channels (05, 07, 18, 19, 21, 22, 23, 65, 66, 78, 79, 80, 83 and 88) are different in the United States and its environs from the rest of the world. Internationally these channels are duplex, with transmission and reception by ship and shore station on different frequencies. In the United States, they are simplex, with both transmission and reception taking place on the international ship transmitting frequency. They should be referred to with the designator A after the channel number, eg 65 alpha (except for channels 21, 22, 23 and 83, which use the designator CG for Coastguard), but in practice the number alone is usually used in US waters. Modern VHF sets now all have a facility for selecting either the international or US set of frequencies, but it is as well to ask before purchase; the latter will also allow reception of the continuous, dedicated US VHF weather transmissions.

A portable hand-held VHF set should also be carried. This is not only useful for communication with any of the crew ashore, but is extremely valuable in the event of taking to the liferaft. It should be fitted inside a watertight plastic container that allows operation of the set from the outside.

On both sides of the Atlantic, and on the intervening islands, radio and rescue services are now fully integrated into GMDSS. With a few exceptions, all VHF emergency traffic will be conducted on channel 70 DSC off both continents, and constant watch on the previous emergency channel 16 is becoming patchy. It would be worthwhile changing to a DSC-fitted VHF set before the crossing, thus anticipating what will become mandatory in the next few years.

MF/HF and amateur radio

Strictly speaking, Medium Frequency and High Frequency are separate bands. MF runs from 300 to 3,000 kHz, with a maximum range of around 500 miles, whereas the HF band is from 3,000 to 30,000 kHz and can achieve worldwide communications. But MF-only sets are seldom seen today and a combined HF/MF set is the norm; for practical purposes, MF and HF can be considered together and are generally referred to by sailors as HF, divided into marine HF and amateur – or ham – radio. It should be noted that in this context amateur equates to enthusiast rather than to less competent.

Marine HF takes place on specific simplex or duplex frequencies within the marine bands. To operate within these bands a set must meet certain agreed specifications; such sets are referred to as type approved. It is often possible to modify such a set to operate on the amateur bands as well, and this is frequently done. Such a modification, however, means that the set may no longer be used legally on the marine frequencies but, unless it is done, communication with other yachts will be seriously restricted. Using marine HF, calls can be made to other ships and to coast radio stations and the telephone network accessed. With the right equipment, normally a PC and a modem, telex and fax messages can be sent and received and it may be possible to use e-mail. Modern HF sets will be GMDSS compatible and, again, this should be checked before purchase.

Amateur radio operates throughout the amateur bands and not on particular, laid-down frequencies. There are no technical specifications for sets and many amateurs build their own. To ensure that they do not interfere with other radio users, amateurs must pass a considerably more complex exam than marine HF operators before being issued with a licence. A reasonable level of technical knowledge on radio theory and practice is required, as well as the ability to send and receive Morse code on some frequencies, although almost all amateur communications take place using voice. In the United Kingdom, courses are run (usually as evening classes) lasting about six months, although it is possible to study for the exam by correspondence course. Exams are held twice a year. Only qualified amateurs may transmit on the amateur bands, but anyone may listen.

HF sets, whether marine or amateur, must be properly installed to work satisfactorily. They take a good deal of power when transmitting, often up to 25 amps, and are particularly sensitive to a reduction in input voltage – so heavy supply cables are essential here. An insulated shroud or backstay will usually form the aerial and is relatively easily arranged, but providing a good earth for the set and aerial tuning unit is equally important and often more difficult. A wood or glass-fibre yacht will probably need to fit an external ground plate below the waterline and this must be connected to the installation using copper strip (not braid) at least 4cm (2in) wide. In a metal yacht, the hull itself will provide an excellent earth.

HF radio requires some knowledge to use. The frequency chosen must be appropriate for the range required, and different frequencies used by day and by night. Propagation is also affected by sunspot activity.

There are many unlicensed HF users throughout the world, often using indifferent equipment, whose transmissions spill over into adjacent frequencies, and it is common for interference to be so severe that communication is very difficult. Despite these drawbacks, HF, either in the marine or amateur bands, is at present the most popular way for the transatlantic sailor to keep in touch with other yachts and those ashore while on passage. HF sets are relatively expensive. A reasonable installation will cost at least seven times as much as the average VHF set, but it is possible to spend considerably more.

Satellite communications

Once the exclusive preserve of warships and the largest merchantmen, satellite communications are increasingly available to yachts, using the Inmarsat system. For yachtsmen in the north Atlantic the Voice Mini-M and Inmarsat C services will give complete cover. The equipment is sufficiently lightweight to be fitted in the smallest ocean cruiser and power requirements are modest.

Inmarsat Mini-M is much more expensive to buy and operate than C and requires a largish dome aerial. It handles voice communications as well as accepting e-mails through a PC; it has a relatively low rate of data transfer. Once fitted, the yacht has in effect a conventional telephone on board that is free from interference.

Inmarsat C is the popular choice for ocean sailors and is part of the Global Maritime Distress and Safety System (GMDSS). It is a data service that sends and receives telexes and e-mails, and sends (but does not receive) faxes. It automatically receives regular oceanic weather warnings, forecasts and safety messages (but not synoptic charts) for the area that the yacht is in. As part of GMDSS, any automatically generated distress message will be passed straight to the relevant Maritime Rescue Co-ordination Centre. It is still much more expensive than the average HF installation, but prices are coming down.

EPIRBs

Emergency Position Indicating Radio Beacons (EPIRBs) are self-contained devices that can be activated in an emergency to alert the rescue authorities. The original EPIRBs operated on 121.5 MHz, but response to these transmissions will cease in 2009 although the frequency will be retained as a homing frequency in the very much more effective EPIRBs using 406 MHz. These are monitored by the COSPAS/SARSAT satellite system, are an integral part of GMDSS, and any activation of an EPIRB will be reacted to almost immediately anywhere in the world. Some have an in-built GPS that transmits its current position. EPIRBs are literally lifesavers. There are three things that should be borne in mind with this system: the EPIRB should be secured with a hydrostatic switch so that it will release underwater if the yacht sinks before it can be manually released; it must be registered with the national authority (HM Coastguard, Falmouth, in the United Kingdom) so that one's identity and details are known on activation; it must not be switched off if it operates accidentally – instead, every effort must be made to communicate with the nearest Maritime Rescue Co-ordination Centre to inform them.

There are personal EPIRB systems available known as Personal Locator Beacons. These small transmitters can be carried by all crew, and require a receiver in the yacht to pick up the transmissions in the event of man overboard. They are really only useful in yachts with large crews.

SARTs

Search and Rescue Transponders are portable racons intended for deployment in liferafts. They amplify radar signals from searching ships and aircraft to make them more visible to the searcher, and to facilitate homing in on the SART. They can greatly reduce the searching time in bad weather, fog or at night. They are part of the GMDSS, but are still expensive, and some sailors might not regard them as an essential aid.

6 The Crew

Most Atlantic crossings take place as part of a longer cruise. The majority of extended cruising is done by couples, sometimes with children. Guests join from time to time; these are normally friends or relatives who can seldom stay for more than a few weeks and little advice needs to be given about them. But many boats embark crew – who may be neither close friends nor relatives – for the actual ocean passages, and this aspect of an Atlantic voyage needs careful thought. With a happy ship's company consisting of people who know how to live afloat and who enjoy one another's company, a long voyage can be an experience that all will remember with deep and lasting satisfaction. An ocean voyage blighted by friction or argument among those aboard will be miserable.

Recruitment

Crew may either be organised before departure or en route. There is a risk in attempting to do the former too far in advance, as promises are often made by people who are full of enthusiasm – until an attempt is made to pin them down to a firm sailing date. Others may genuinely intend to come, but be prevented by changes in circumstances beyond their control. Before approaching anybody it is best to have the cruise planned in broad outline. To avoid misunderstandings, the following points should be agreed at the outset:

1 Starting date and likely duration
2 Who pays any travelling expenses to or from the points of embarkation and disembarkation
3 What financial contribution, if any, is expected
4 What liability the owner will accept in the event of accident or injury, or for the costs of any changes to, or cancellation of, the arrangements

Once these points have been agreed verbally it will be as well to drop the prospective crew member a note of them in writing. This is not mere pedantry, as he or she may not be joining for several months and memories of the exact arrangements made can fade. Even the best of friendships will be strained by an unexpected demand for a considerable sum of money, or a complete change of itinerary after flights have been booked.

In most countries a yacht's skipper is liable for the costs of repatriating any crew member who leaves the vessel, for whatever reason. In most cases the person will be leaving by prearrangement and will hold an airline ticket, or may be transferring to another yacht. With relatively unknown crew, however, particularly those who have been picked up off the dock, it is a sensible precaution to insist on a deposit to cover the cost of a flight from the furthest point of the cruise to their country of origin. All prospective crew will need valid passports, with visas where necessary, and it is important that these should not expire during the duration of the cruise.

Selecting crew

Actually deciding who to invite is a personal matter on which little advice can be given. Provided that the skipper is competent in all aspects of seamanship and navigation, this person will be entirely free in their choice, be it a young novice crew or experienced older sailors. The important thing is to find people with whom he or she will get along and who will get along with one another, taking account of character and temperament rather than technical knowledge or skill. Even so, one of the crew will have to be the second in command, and they should be competent to replace the skipper in the event of illness or injury; whoever this is must be totally acceptable to the others on board. The only reliable test as to whether people can sail together in harmony is to go for a short trial cruise.

Replacements en route

Crew changes during the course of a cruise may be prearranged, or may rely on finding a suitable person when and where they are needed. The former should be simple enough – many people cannot take the time off work for an entire cruise, but may be eager to join for a limited period. A reasonably firm cruising schedule will allow flights to be booked well in advance, though it must be accepted on both sides that other things may intervene. Absolutely rigid schedules are not practical and will, in any case, ruin a relaxed cruise. Rather than push the pace to reach a particular rendezvous it is better to have a flexible arrangement. The crew can book their flights to or from a particular international airport, but will leave or join the yacht from wherever she happens to be lying at the time. This is particularly necessary in the Caribbean where, for some reason, schedules seem to be especially hard to maintain! Travelling between islands is easy by local airline or by ferry.

The seaports of the world all have, from time to time, itinerants who go from boat to boat trying to thumb a passage to some other place. There may well be good crew among them, but a fair percentage will not be. The really good ones will be snapped up by charter yachts as paid hands, and in most cases only the inexperienced, unknown or unreliable ones will have to rely on casual berths. All in all, taking on casual crew in this way cannot be recommended. If it must be done as a last resort, take precautions. Screen quayside applicants carefully, always ask for references from previous skippers and, whenever possible, take up these references. Examine passports and visas carefully, and insist on the flight deposit already mentioned. Ensure that the crew joins the yacht several days before departure and assists with the storing and preparations, both to get some idea of what they are really like and to find out if they will pull their weight. It is always possible that an unknown crew member may be carrying drugs, and if these are discovered on arrival in port, the consequences may be serious for the skipper as well as the offender.

Training

Forging a group of individuals into a team capable of coping in difficult conditions takes time, and in any case it is impossible to simulate ocean sailing except by making an ocean passage. Assuming that the crew has basic sailing skills, all that remains is to give each person the chance to get to know the particular boat. The sensible skipper will encourage feedback – and even if this person has sailed the yacht for years, will probably find that a fresh viewpoint, based on different experience, is valuable and stimulating and will enable them to improve layout, routines or equipment. That being said, it is the skipper's prerogative to say 'I prefer this particular job done like this', and crew who are not prepared to accept this should find another boat.

Every ship has her own routine – 'different ships, different long splices' – and this should be established as early as possible. Some standardisation is essential to safety: which line goes to which cleat, exactly how to belay a sheet or halyard, where each item of gear is kept. These are not just owners' fads – they could mean the difference between life and death on a dark night.

Ground rules regarding standards of tidiness and cleanliness should be established early. There is no need for this to be done formally, but it is easier to nip problems in the bud rather than have to recover the situation when things are getting out of hand. One person's belongings constantly left lying about, for example, or a galley habitually left for the next watch to clean up, will lead to discord and resentment. A good skipper will be aware of these and similar problems and will sort them out firmly, but diplomatically.

It would be ridiculous to suggest that the skipper should make a formal daily inspection in a small boat, but they should check over the whole yacht both on deck and below at least once a day. This will give the skipper an opportunity to keep an unobtrusive eye open for any incipient crew problems. Praise is also impor-

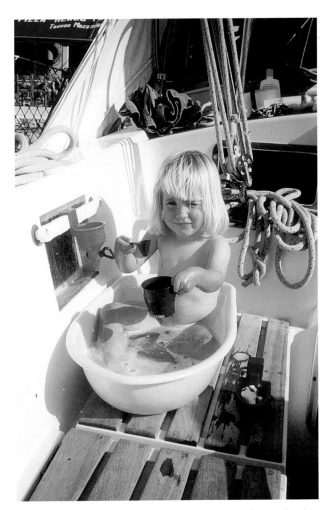

In a warm climate the cockpit makes a perfect bathroom for the liveaboard child. Photo Liz Hammick.

tant and should be given where it is due. Few things are as dispiriting to a hardworking crew as to have their efforts go apparently unnoticed.

Division of responsibilities

The small size of the average ocean cruiser's crew demands that each member should have some particular skill – or preferably several – and so, for both efficiency and to encourage a sense of involvement, a division of responsibilities is essential. One person, usually the skipper, will be in charge of navigation. The only other area that is usually an individual responsibility is the galley. Even if the actual cooking is shared on a rota basis, one person should oversee the catering and storing. Regular food is fundamental to the efficiency and morale of the whole ship's company, yet there are few more difficult tasks than cooking interesting meals at sea in a small boat. With a large crew there may well be a full-time cook who will not keep any watches at all. In a smaller yacht, if one person is prepared to do all, or the majority of, the cooking, the remainder of the crew should count themselves lucky – and be ready to do the washing-up. Certainly any such person should be suitably rewarded – perhaps by exemption from some of the night watches.

Friction aboard

A happy ship's company is so well worth achieving that no effort should be spared in the attempt. The skipper must not only maintain a good relationship with each person on board, but must also try to prevent disputes arising between crew members. Should these occur he will often be called on to arbitrate, an unenviable task in which it is seldom possible to satisfy all parties.

Crew problems may arise in port as often as at sea, perhaps more so. The common challenge of actively sailing a small yacht will often paper over minor cracks, but when this goal is removed they can reappear. It is also in port that differences in personal habits become most significant – preferred times of rising, eating and turning in, sociability towards fellow sailors, consideration over the use of a dinghy on which others also depend. Regular routine maintenance must be carried out, and if friction is to be avoided it must be made quite clear from the start what the crew are expected to do. One solution is for the mornings to belong to the ship and for work on board to be carried out then, while the afternoons are kept for relaxation.

It is hard to define a happy ship, but it is possible to tell one the moment you step aboard. Common factors appear to be a sound ship, a competent, fair and considerate skipper, well-thought-out organisation and good communication – in both directions – between the skipper and the crew, and among the crew themselves. Above all, there will be willingness by all on board to do just a little more for the yacht and for those around them than they have to.

The skipper

The role of the skipper depends, to a large extent, on the formation of the crew – a family crew will not view the skipper in the same light as a crew composed of semi-strangers. They, in turn, will have a different attitude to that of friends who have sailed together for years. Some couples, who have cruised together for a very long time and who are both equally experienced and competent, may truly be co-skippers, but they are rare. Normally one person must be in charge and be prepared to shoulder the responsibility not only for the safety of the boat and all those aboard, but also to a large extent for their happiness as well.

The idea of doing an 'apprenticeship' as crew before aspiring to skippering one's own yacht across an ocean no longer prevails, and nowadays most first-time transatlantic skippers have no more experience of the passage than their crews. Only a fool feels no apprehension at the start of an ocean voyage – and although, with experience, this reduces, it should never vanish entirely. A good crew will understand that the skipper has more on his or her plate than they do and will allow for it. They will expect their leader to appear calm and confident, but will be uneasy if this is overdone. Only the most experienced skippers can appear completely relaxed and at ease in all circumstances. For others to attempt to emulate them will not inspire confidence in the crew – quite the reverse in fact.

It is for the skipper to set the tenor of life aboard, and this person can do this more by example than by any other means. The problem of incompatibility in a small ship's company is often the result of inexperience – living at close quarters is an art that does not come easily to all. For every cruise that has been marred by one selfish individual, there have been many others so rewarding that the experience binds the participants together for the rest of their lives. This will not happen without a good skipper. If things do not turn out so happily, the skipper should remember that there are no bad crews, only bad skippers – and learn from their mistakes.

7 Provisioning

Provisioning for a long Atlantic cruise, which is to include several ocean passages, is less difficult that it was even a decade ago. The range of foods available in most places has increased markedly. Even quite small European villages are likely to have a reasonable food shop, while in the larger ports, where major stocking-up is likely to be done, there will be a selection of supermarkets. In the Caribbean islands the facilities are not quite so good, but here too the range available is quite adequate – and only a yacht with a very large or demanding crew will find provisioning difficult. In North America major storing can be carried out at almost any harbour, although here, because supermarkets are normally out of town, it may be necessary to organise transport.

Regardless of whether or not the task of cooking is to be shared among the crew, calculating and buying food stores is best done by one person. They must not only take into account the length of time the boat is expected to be away, but also have some idea of the stowage space available, what can be bought en route and the limitations of the galley equipment – as well as the individual likes and dislikes of those on board.

There has been a great advance in recent years in the quality and variety of dried or dehydrated foods, and crews in long distance ocean races use them almost exclusively. This may not be the choice of the more sybaritic cruiser, but a selection of such foods should be carried if only for use in emergencies or unexpectedly lengthy crossings.

Storing before departure

There is a major difference between storing up at home for an Atlantic cruise, the first leg of which may be only a few days across the Bay of Biscay or out to Bermuda, and storing for a specific passage such as the Atlantic crossing. Before leaving home is the time to lay in those items that are likely to be expensive or simply unavailable elsewhere: instant coffee, tea bags, bread mix and yeast extract fall into this category, as would favourite branded products. This is also the time to stock up on 'national' foods, be it British Branston pickle and tinned steak and kidney pie or American peanut butter and jelly. Within reason, buy as much of these products as can be stowed. However, avoid over-stocking staples that can be found almost everywhere – bread, flour, sugar, pasta, rice, canned fish, canned fruit and vegetables and fresh eggs. A couple of weeks' supply of all of these will be ample initially for most boats – perhaps a little more if the first passage is to be a long one.

Provisioning for ocean cruising is time-consuming, and allowance must be made for this when planning the trip. Photo Michael Beaumont.

Storing for a single passage

Calculating the stores needed for a specific passage is more complicated. The first step is to establish how many meals there will be each day, and the type of food to be eaten at each. For example, some crews prefer a cooked breakfast, some are happy with cereals and toast, and some eat no breakfast at all, but have a larger and earlier midday meal. If possible, the whole crew should be consulted but, if it is very large, the skipper will have to lay down a policy for everyone. Eating habits will almost certainly change at sea, and a generous allowance of nibbles such as biscuits (both sweet and savoury), chocolate bars and sweets will seldom be wasted. Having estimated what might be consumed on any given day, it should not be difficult to expand this to cover the entire passage, allowing an extra 50 per cent for unforeseen delays. Some people like to do a dummy run in home waters: laying in and then living off stores for a one-week cruise to check if anything has been forgotten. Much depends on the experience of the person in charge of catering – few people used to running and feeding a household will need this kind of reassurance.

Food can help to provide variety and boost morale during a long passage, and it is a good idea for the caterer to lay in some luxury items for notable occasions or celebrations. Unobtrusive enquiries before departure can be made to see if any crew member will celebrate a birthday or other anniversary during the trip so that a surprise special meal can be cooked on that day. Some crews like to have a celebratory dinner to mark the halfway point. A good caterer will plan for these and similar events, and the ability to produce something out of the ordinary when the occasion demands will be much appreciated.

Provisioning in different areas

Storing up for a long passage will be easiest if done at a port of some size as the choice will be better and the prices cheaper than in smaller places. The distance to the main source of supply and the convenience of the berth are also considerations. The ports listed in Part III are capable of meeting most needs unless stated otherwise. Even so, it may be useful to have a broad indication as to what each area is likely to offer.

The Iberian peninsula is noted for the quality of its fruit and vegetables and is an excellent place to stock up on Mediterranean produce such as pasta and olive oil. Canned fish and seafood of all kinds are another speciality. For British yachts, mainland Portugal has supermarkets stocking a surprisingly large range of English foods. Gibraltar offers a full range of the best of British and Spanish provisions as well as being largely duty free. Both Madeira and the Canaries have excellent supermarkets, making stocking up for a long passage a positive pleasure. The local markets are good

too, but beware that in the larger ones some of the apparently fresh fruit and vegetables may have been chilled, which harms the keeping qualities. Arrive early in the day and check the items buried deep down in the displays; if these are icy cold, then the produce will not keep well. In the Cape Verde Islands, which are both dry and poor, little is available – and even the staples mentioned above may be difficult to find. If stopping there before the tradewind passage, arrive with the yacht already stocked up with basics.

In the Caribbean, both the quality and variety of food available has improved markedly over recent years, and a mixture of modern supermarkets, smaller stores and the excellent local markets can provide for almost every need. Those islands that are mountainous, and therefore have plenty of rainfall (Grenada, St Vincent, St Lucia, Martinique, Dominica, etc), produce excellent fruit and vegetables, while those that are generally lower and drier (Antigua, St Maarten, the British Virgin Islands, etc), generally do not. In addition to local produce, the French islands are noted for the range and quality of imported foods such as cheese and pâté. In the British Virgin Islands most food is imported, and fresh vegetables with good keeping qualities are difficult to find. The American Virgin Islands and the Bahamas can supply most of the products available on the American mainland.

The quality of food available along the eastern seaboard of the United States and Canada is well known, though owing to the wide use of freezers it may be difficult to find tinned meats. There is a greater likelihood that fruit and vegetables will have been chilled than in less sophisticated areas, but a little asking around may well lead you to a farmers' market where real fresh produce can be found.

Although supermarkets in Bermuda are well stocked, nearly all food is imported, thus making this probably the most expensive place to stock up in the north Atlantic; it is also extremely difficult to find produce that has not been chilled. All in all, it is best to avoid a major restock in Bermuda.

The Azorean islands vary, with the best provisioning at Horta in Faial, Angra do Heroismo in Terceira, and Ponta Delgada in São Miguel – towns that also have good markets. Basics such as bread, fish and some fruit and vegetables are available on all the islands, but imported foods may not be. Dairy products are widely available and good cheese is made.

Non-perishables

Aboard the smaller yacht every cubic inch of space available will be pressed into use for the storage of food and other essentials. The purist, and certainly the owner of a very small yacht, will go to great lengths to keep weights as low as possible, but if tins are to be kept in the bilge they should have the contents marked in indelible pen and their labels should be removed. This is to prevent them clogging bilge pump strainers, and should be done even in a boat whose bilge is normally bone dry as, if a lot of water comes aboard unexpectedly, her bilge pump will be vital.

The galley itself should include a ready-use locker for coffee, tea, sugar, salt, etc, and many cooks also like to keep a day or two's supply of other food handy in order to avoid scrabbling in lockers after dark or in heavy weather. If, as is usually the case, bulk stores are spread around the boat, then some kind of system will be needed. By far the most efficient, and essential if more than one person is doing the cooking, is to have a notebook showing where each item will be found and, in the case of tins and packets, how many are on board. A pencil stub tied to the notebook, reinforced by dire threats from the caterer, should ensure that each individual item is crossed off as it is used.

Some non-perishables will of course be bought in bulk, and it may be possible to negotiate a small discount on tins bought by the case. However, always test unknown brands before buying in quantity. Avoid the 'giant economy pack'. It may not fit the boat's lockers and, once opened, unless its contents can be used quickly, they will probably go bad. Dry stores may be bought in bulk and decanted into smaller airtight containers for use as required. This is also true of margarine, available in large square containers from which a table tub can be refilled. Some margarines seem to keep almost indefinitely, and to retain a semi-solid state even without refrigeration, whereas butter, even in tins, is best avoided unless the boat has adequate refrigeration.

Along with edible non-perishables it may be convenient to include those 'housekeeping' items without which the cruise will not be a happy one. In the galley: kitchen towel, detergent (dish soap) and surface cleaners. Elsewhere: washing powder, bleach or the equivalent, and toilet rolls. Though the last can be bought everywhere, the quality in some countries leaves much to be desired.

Fresh stores and storage

The length of time that fresh stores will keep depends both on their quality and the care with which they are stored. Sound potatoes, carrots and onions will last for a month-long voyage even in tropical latitudes, provided they are picked over regularly and any suspect ones removed. Fresh eggs will also last for a month without treatment, but not if they have been chilled at any time. There are various methods of preserving eggs that have been chilled and, unless certain otherwise, assume that they have been chilled. Coating with Vaseline (petroleum jelly) certainly works, and eggs treated in this way will last for at least six weeks. Untreated eggs should be turned twice a week to prevent their shells from drying out and the yolks from settling.

Fruit is less predictable. Green tomatoes will ripen gradually in a warm atmosphere, and do not need daylight. Nearly all citrus fruit will keep for weeks if not months, providing a useful source of vitamin C. Lemons keep well if wrapped in foil. A hand of green bananas will be inedible for several days, but will then all ripen at once. Hard green cabbage will last for the crossing, and will form the basis of a reasonable salad or coleslaw. Some voyagers grow sprouting seeds during long passages; this is probably not necessary for health, but it is fun, particularly for children, and easy to do. Fresh greenstuffs such as mustard and cress or alfalfa will be welcome in the latter part of the crossing, as will crispy bean sprouts.

If faced with unfamiliar local produce in West Indian markets, the local ladies will generally be delighted to advise, and it may also be worth buying a book on Caribbean cookery.

Fishing

While it would be most unwise to depend on catching fish for food, they can nevertheless provide welcome variety – and some yachts fish regularly on passage with great success. Others using similar gear never catch anything. A fishing line will need to be both strong and easy to grip, and heavyweight gloves may be useful. If towing a line for long periods it is common practice to run a few turns anticlockwise around a winch before making up the inboard end. Any pull on the hook will cause the winch to spin, alerting the crew immediately. Ideas on suitable lures vary – the polished spoon can work well, others prefer to camouflage the hook among strips of coloured polythene cut from carrier bags. Special lures can also be bought. If a large fish has been landed and is thrashing around, a little neat spirit poured into the gills will kill it immediately; alternatively, a hard blow on the head with a winch handle may be easier.

Many cruising areas are nature reserves where fishing is either restricted or banned. Spear fishing is forbidden in the Tobago Cays, parts of Antigua, the Virgin Islands and Bermuda among other places, although local people may be allowed to fish by traditional methods, usually traps or pots. In the Bahamas a fishing permit is needed and fishing of any sort is prohibited in the Exuma National Park. The local cruising guide should give the details.

Towing a lure on ocean passage is generally safe, but owing to the prevalence of ciguatera poisoning in parts of the West Indies, fishing should not take place there without seeking local advice. Ciguatera is caused by a toxin derived from dinoflagellates found on coral and seaweed, eaten by fish, and passed along the food chain from small to bigger fish and to man when he eats many common larger fish. It causes nausea, vomiting, abdominal pain and diarrhoea and can lead to paralysis and death. The only cure is to make the sufferer vomit to empty the stomach. If there is any doubt about fish caught locally only eat small portions of any predatory fish such as kingfish, tuna, dorado, barracuda, snapper and parrot fish – and never any fish offal. The barracuda, a long, evil-looking beast with a powerful jaw and large teeth, is the only menacing fish likely to be met when snorkelling, when it can be unnerving – though seldom actually dangerous.

In the tropics there may be the bonus of flying fish landing on deck during the night, and displaying a light will tend to attract them. Even so, there are unlikely to be enough to provide a substantial breakfast – except perhaps for the singlehander.

Liquid refreshment

The subject of drinking water and tankage has already been covered in Chapter 2. Choice and quantity of non-alcoholic beverages will, of course, depend on the tastes of the crew. Carbonated drinks are generally available everywhere; the diet or sugar-free varieties are the most thirst quenching. Fruit juice, either in cans or increasingly in cartons, can be found in most places, but concentrated fruit squash is much rarer.

A yacht may be allowed to embark bonded stores – duty-free alcohol – before leaving for a long voyage. In the United Kingdom this procedure is no longer worthwhile unless large quantities are involved – at least five cases of spirits – as the fixed charges, fees for attendance of customs officers, delivery charges, etc have been increased over time. The procedure is in any event tedious: a special sealed locker must be provided, and the stores may not be used until beyond EU waters.

Most sailors prefer to experiment with the local produce as the cruise progresses. Iberia produces wine, port, sherry and brandy (all for sale in the Canaries, which are a duty-free zone); 'Madeira' comes in a range from very dry indeed to rich and creamy. In the Caribbean, rum is of course the staple and there are many varieties to sample. The French islands (Martinique, Guadeloupe, St Barts and St Martin) are good places to stock up with wine or brandy. In the United States, spirits (liquor) are reasonably priced by European standards and good wines are produced. Imported alcohol is more expensive, and Scotch Whisky particularly dear. Bermuda appears to sell everything, at a price, while the Azores offer Portuguese brands in addition to locally made wines. Beer, either in bottles or in cans, is available almost everywhere.

The Mechanics of Ocean Cruising

In addition to his responsibility for the boat, her equipment and her crew, the skipper of any small vessel must deal with all her day-to-day affairs, from coping with officialdom to changing the clocks and organising the watch systems. The following is a mixed bag of reminders and suggestions.

Watchkeeping systems

A happy voyage depends to a great extent on establishing a daily routine. As well as ensuring that all the necessary work gets done, it must also be a routine with which all those on board can live with for weeks at a stretch. This applies as much to singlehanders, who must work out for themselves whatever compromise between sleep and watchkeeping they feel they can live with. Whatever the size of the crew, be it one person aboard a small cruiser or 16 on a maxi racing machine, the energy and resilience of those aboard is a finite resource that must not be squandered.

Though the watch system must take account not only of the sailing, but also of the daily chores such as navigation, cooking and ongoing maintenance, its prime objective must always be to ensure the safe conduct of the ship. Ideally this entails having enough manpower on deck to deal with whatever needs to be done without calling those below, but as few cruising yachts will have more than one person on watch at a time this may not

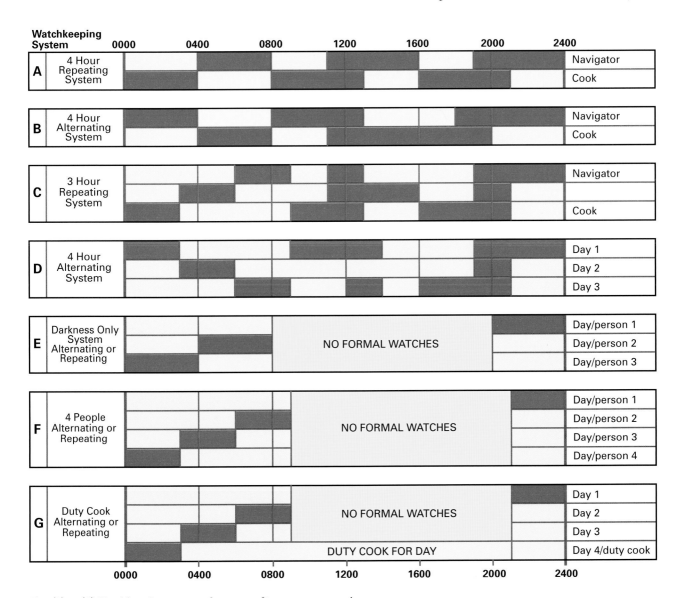

Fig 1(A) to (G) Watchkeeping systems for crews of two or more people.

always be feasible. In bad weather or in extreme cold, one hour on deck steering by hand may be as long as even a strong, fit person can stand. In such conditions the yacht with a crew of three or less will depend heavily on a powerful and reliable self-steering gear, and it is essential that it should be equal to the task.

Many watchkeeping systems have been evolved for small boats. How long the watches should be is a matter of choice. If it is necessary to helm continuously, not many people will manage more than two hours even in good conditions, and less time would be preferable. If it is possible to leave the helm, even for only a short spell occasionally, perhaps by using the autopilot for five minutes every half-hour, then this period can be considerably extended. The watchkeeper will then be able to move around, to visit the heads or prepare a snack. In a warm climate, with a good self-steering system, a watch of six hours in the open ocean may be quite acceptable – at least during the day – and for a two-handed crew will give the off-watch time for a worthwhile period of rest. If there are more than two aboard, then it should not be necessary for watches to be more than four hours.

The watchkeeping routines that follow have stood the test of time, but they are not the only ones. They will, however, give you an idea of some of the factors to consider when planning.

Watch systems for two people

1   A straightforward system of three- or four-hour watches with extended periods to provide a two-hour overlap twice a day at mealtimes. This is convenient where one person does all the cooking and the other all the navigation, as each person is on watch during the same period each day – Fig 1(A).
2   As above, but not considering overlap periods as part of a watch. This allows the times each person is on watch to alternate between one day and the next, pro-

viding some variety aboard those boats where both navigation and cooking are shared equally – Fig 1(B).
3   A straight three hours on and three hours off, starting at noon. Some people like the regularity, and the body adapts to a three-hour sleep rhythm.

Watch systems for three people

1   An adaptation of either (1) or (2) above with watches carried on day and night – Fig 1(C) and 2(D).
2   Formal watches during the hours of darkness only. It will still be necessary for someone to keep a lookout during the day, but this may be on a volunteer rather than a duty basis – Fig 1(E). This will only be suitable in the open ocean, and who has the lookout responsibility must be clearly defined.
3   A straight three hours on and six hours off, but on call for the last three hours. This can be timed for the cook to be on call at mealtimes.

Watch systems for four or more people

1   Again a straight three- or four-hour system, either permanently or just at night. Assuming that only one person is normally on watch at any time, this will effectively mean the crew spending most of the night in their bunks, so sleep during the day is unlikely to be more than the odd nap – Fig 1(F).
2   If one person is doing all the cooking for a larger crew, they deserve a suitable reward, possibly exemption from the unpopular 0000–0400 watch or even exemption from watches entirely. This is also feasible if cooking is alternated, with a full night's sleep being awarded to the day's cook – Fig 1(G).

In general, the more people there are aboard the easier it will be to organise a system that not only meets the watchkeeping requirements, but also allows time for relaxation, hobbies and some feeling of community among the crew – a regular 'happy hour' before supper is often popular. With a very small crew it is possible to barely exchange a word with the others aboard for days at a stretch, apart from a few minutes on handing over the watch and a brief period at mealtimes.

With any crew of more than two it is important to keep the noise level at the change of watch as low and as brief as possible, particularly at night. Most skippers sleep with half an ear open, and to be regularly disturbed while off watch will do nothing for their alertness in the long term, or probably their temper.

Falmouth is the first English port of call for many transatlantic sailors. The Royal Cornwall Yacht Club has provided a warm welcome for over a century. Photo Anne Hammick.

It must be clearly understood who is 'on call' should assistance be needed on deck. On some yachts this will always be the skipper, on others the person due on the next watch. Though it must depend ultimately on the capabilities and experience of the crew, the skipper should beware of having their sleep so broken that they have no reserves of energy should a real emergency arise. Bad weather or a sudden crisis can disrupt the watch system with little or no warning, and it will usually be the skipper who will have to bear the greatest load when this happens.

Ship's time

It is best to alter the ship's clocks periodically during the course of an east/west (or west/east) crossing, both to avoid a major alteration on reaching land and to keep some resemblance of normality on board – it is disconcerting to watch the sun rise at 0200 or to eat the evening meal at 2300. The time change is one hour for every 15° of longitude, the clocks being put back when heading west, and forward when heading east. The change need not be made slavishly on crossing an imaginary line in the ocean, but rather when convenient and the difference split between two watches.

When writing up the log it must be crystal clear what time zone is being used. To avoid confusion, two columns can be used, one with UT and one for ship's time.

Paperwork

Documentation

Requirements vary from country to country and it makes sense to carry anything one might possibly be called upon to produce. In most cases original documents will be needed, although it is useful to have several sets of photocopies on board, with a further set at home in case the originals are lost. Not all the documents listed here will be examined in every country, but items 1-6 will be regularly required.

1   Valid passports for everyone on board, with visas as necessary. If the crew are multinational it must be remembered that some may need visas for a particular country, while others will not. Neither passports nor, if possible, visas should expire during the course of the cruise.
2   RYA or International Certificate of Competence, at least for the skipper.
3   Crew list. Normally everyone aboard should be listed as crew rather than passengers, as some countries levy high fees for charter yachts or other passenger-carrying vessels.
4   Certificate of Registry, or Small Ships Registry Certificate. American yachts should have national, as opposed to state, documentation. For British yachts, both full and Small Ships Registry need to be renewed periodically; if possible, ensure that this will not happen during the cruise.
5   For European yachts, evidence of VAT status – either that tax has been paid or that the vessel is exempt, most often on grounds of age (yachts launched before 1985). The correct document is the Single Administrative Document or SAD, in practice Copy 8 of the multi-part Form C88, which is used throughout the EU in connection with the movement of goods. Although a full Certificate of British Registry gives the date when the vessel was first registered and may be accepted as evidence of age, all European customs officials will recognise the SAD.
6   Clearance papers from the previous port of call. In certain countries, notably Spain and the Canaries, these can be difficult to obtain. A dated receipt for, say, fuel may be a useful alternative.
7   Stores list, which should differentiate between opened and unopened items. In practice, very few countries are interested in stores other than alcohol, although fresh fruit and vegetables should always be mentioned, as these may have to be destroyed to prevent the spread of pests.
8   Cruising permit (issued to visiting yachts in the United States, Canada and some Caribbean islands), if applicable.
9   VHF and other radio licences/operator's certificates as applicable.
10   Insurance papers – a few marinas will not allow boats without at least third party insurance to berth. It helps if a certificate in the language of the countries visited can be obtained.
11   Bill of Sale.
12   World Health Organisation Yellow Card, plus Bills of Health or Pratiques acquired en route. Few countries now demand a Bill of Health, but a sudden epidemic could alter the rules overnight.
13   Charter documents, if applicable.
14   For British yachts, Ensign Warrant, if applicable.

Preparations for arrival

The last few hours of an ocean voyage may be among the most demanding of the entire passage for the skipper, and the practical aspects of making a landfall are covered in Chapter 4. However, while the crew can often relax as soon as the anchor is down or the yacht secured, few officials allow the skipper to do so before dealing with the formalities. For this reason, it is worth making a few preparations in advance – ideally, the day before the landfall.

Check through the entry procedures for the country to which you are going, not least to ensure that the port for which you are heading is an official port of entry. Check whether it is necessary to report by radio before entering harbour. In most places the skipper should go ashore to report as soon as the yacht is secured, but occasionally he or she – and the rest of the crew – must remain on board until the officials visit. If unsure, another yacht in the anchorage may be able to advise.

Collect all the documents needed and make out a crew list with full names, dates and places of birth, and passport numbers. Some people carry photocopied crew lists but, though this can obviously do no harm, it must be updated to keep track of any crew changes – a computer can be useful here. Different countries demand different information, and many insist that the details should be written on their own printed forms. Make a list of dutiable stores, especially wines and spirits, and check that it is correct. If you have medical drugs aboard there should be an accompanying certificate from a doctor, naming the patient and stating the quantity of each drug. Apart from the documents, in many places things will go quicker if the skipper remembers to take their own ballpoint, a supply of carbon paper, some blank paper for making notes, and a phrase book if applicable. Some cash is likely to be needed; this should preferably be in the local currency, but US dollars are usually acceptable. The more weary the skipper, the greater the chance of something being forgotten – and the more irritating the chore of returning for it.

Finally, hoist the national ensign if it has not been worn at sea, and have both the Q flag and a courtesy ensign ready to hoist on entering territorial waters. Not surprisingly, yachts flying an incorrect, tattered or upside-down courtesy ensign are unlikely to be welcomed with open arms.

Hoisting the courtesy ensign and the Q flag before arrival. Photo Mark Scott.

The ship's stamp and modern equivalents

It was once fashionable to have a ship's stamp – sometimes a small drawing of the boat together with name, home port, and perhaps a registered number or radio call sign – with which to adorn customs documentation. However, times have changed, and officials in nearly all countries are now professionals who will be unimpressed by such things. Keep the rubber stamp for books and letterheads.

A more useful item is a boat's 'business card' with similar information, plus the skipper's or owner's mailing address, and/or small adhesive address stickers. It is also possible to obtain adhesive-backed prints bearing a coloured photo of the boat and her crew together with brief written details. These look impressive in visitors' books and may even make suitable small gifts for local people.

Books and miscellaneous paperwork

Bibliographies devoted to various topics will be found in the Appendices. While it is not suggested that every single volume should be carried, there are some that can claim to form the nucleus of every yacht's bookshelf. For lighter reading, most yachts carry many paperbacks, especially on long passages, exchanging them either with other yachts or in one of the book-swaps to be found in most of the larger harbours.

Most boats also carry some non-nautical reference books. A dictionary and an atlas will be useful, as well as the compact editions of other reference books that would normally be used at home. Tourist guides to the places being visited will enhance the enjoyment of the trip, as will books about the flora and fauna. Comprehensive reference works, including complete encyclopaedias, are now available on CD-ROMs, and some yachts carry these as well.

Letter writing is a favourite occupation with many people, so airmail paper and envelopes (preferably with self-sealing flaps that won't stick until intended) will be needed. Notebooks, both lined and plain, take up little space and will find a multitude of uses, as will a pad of tracing paper. Plenty of pencils, pens, coloured felt-tips, erasers and adhesive tape complete the stationery locker.

Money

There is much to be said for obtaining some currency for each country to be visited before arrival. About £50 or US$100 worth will suffice. Dues normally have to be paid on arrival and, although US$ are acceptable for this purpose, in most places the rate of exchange may be exorbitant. A quantity of the local currency will also be useful for small purchases until a bank can be visited. In Europe, except for the United Kingdom, Channel Islands and Gibraltar, the common currency is

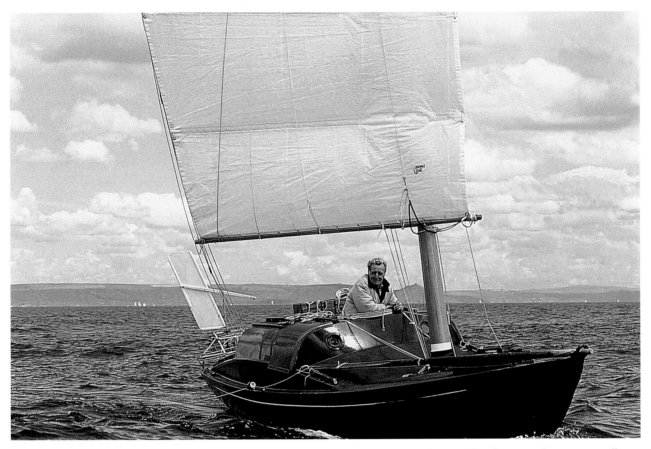

Small boats continue to make Atlantic crossings. The famous converted Folkboat Jester *has completed many such passages – all singlehanded with the indomitable Michael Richey.*

the euro. The currency in use in each country is noted at the head of each port section in Part III.

The almost universal acceptance of Visa and Master-Card by banks has largely solved the problem of obtaining cash during an extended cruise. Increasingly they can be used in shops as well. Automatic teller machines (ATMs) continue to spread to even the smallest islands. Where these are not available, it is safe to say that if there is a bank, it will be able to issue cash against one or other of these cards. It is sensible to carry a selection of cards of both types and not to keep all of them together, so that the loss or theft of a handbag or wallet will not be completely disastrous. Obtaining replacement cards abroad is a fraught process. For this reason, some experienced skippers refuse to use ATMs (which can retain cards) at all, but instead use the bank itself and, if you are following their example, a passport will be needed for identification. Cash can also be obtained with traveller's cheques and some cruisers carry these as a fallback.

In the United States, Visa or MasterCard is almost essential. Cash is sometimes not welcome, and occasionally not even accepted. A card will certainly be required to hire a car or book an airline ticket.

Many yachts carry a concealed reserve of cash against an emergency. There is no doubt that this can sometimes be an advantage – an immediate offer of a cash payment might prevent a salvage claim, for example. If deciding to do this, the cash – preferably in US$ –

should be split into reasonable-sized amounts and hidden separately. Never tell anyone where this cash is hidden, or even that it is aboard.

Insurance

Marine

Whether or not to insure is a personal decision, but if one considers the size of a third party claim that might have to be met in the event of an accident involving others, protection against this risk seems highly desirable – especially as it is relatively inexpensive. It is difficult (but not impossible) for yachts sailed by two or even three people to get comprehensive insurance, and the benefits of having such cover may have to be balanced against the undesirability of being forced to carry extra crew or carry third party insurance only.

Companies are much more likely to provide cover if they believe that the proposed cruise has been properly planned and sensibly thought out. This is something that should be discussed with insurers or brokers at an early stage. Evidence of careful preparation, a well-found and properly equipped boat, thorough research into the most sensible itinerary, and plans to deal with problems gives the best chance of convincing an underwriter that a particular proposal is an acceptable risk.

Willingness to accept a high excess (deductible) will demonstrate that trivial claims – which are as administratively expensive as major ones – are not being contemplated. However careful one's preparations, though, it will still be extremely difficult to obtain insurance cover for the Caribbean during the hurricane season. If insurance can be arranged, it is important to remember that a fundamental principle of all marine insurance is that you should act at all times with the same caution that you would adopt if you were uninsured.

Medical

A standard medical insurance policy may or may not protect you while cruising, and this should be checked and the cover amended if necessary. Europeans should complete a form E111, which entitles them to free, or reduced-cost, emergency treatment in EU countries. Private medical fees are high in the West Indies and the United States compared with Europe, though many West Indian islands have free health schemes based on the UK National Health model, and in some islands reciprocal arrangements for free treatment have been established with the United Kingdom and with some other EU countries. Medical attention in the United States is very much more likely to be prompt if evidence of US-valid medical insurance is produced at the outset.

The law

Very few cruising sailors have any dealings with the authorities in foreign countries, other than with customs and immigration officers. Other officials are generally only met when a problem arises – a lost or stolen item, a navigational mishap, or a dispute with a local tradesman or fisherman. In these circumstances, people are seldom at their coolest or most rational and it is easy for misunderstandings to arise.

By and large, officials of all the countries around the north Atlantic are co-operative, fair and honest. Of course there are exceptions, but they are rare and, should they arise, the visiting sailor can do little but go elsewhere. Before we are too quick to criticise, though, we should remember that we are – to the countries we visit – tourists; and it is hardly surprising that our problems sometimes appear to be less significant to the authorities than those of local working people. We should also bear in mind that there are some crews who behave badly, who ignore regulations, who leave without paying their bills, or who show contempt for local people. So we should ensure that we are not in this category.

The golden rules are: abide by the regulations; be meticulous in declaring items that might possibly be restricted or prohibited; infringe as little as possible upon the local community; respect their customs and ideals – even if they do not accord with your own; care for the local environment; treat officials, who have a job to do, honestly and considerately; avoid political discussions; eschew drugs. Above all, we need to remember that we are where we are by choice and that we are visitors. The treatment other visitors receive will depend, in part, on *our* behaviour. We need to make sure we leave a clean wake.

Clothing

An Atlantic cruise calls for a variety of clothing. Some of the northern routes are in near-Arctic temperatures, though for the majority of cruising people the whole object of the exercise is to reach the tropics.

If starting from a northern area, waterproof clothing will probably be in daily use at sea. Once the tropics are reached it may be put away for several months, but will be needed again on approaching home waters. Good-quality oilskins (foul weather gear) are essential. They need a rinse in fresh water and careful storage when not in regular use – if they are just crammed into a locker and forgotten, they will certainly be in poor condition when next needed.

In the tropics, clothes will be light and few in number, but they will need frequent washing. It is a pleasant habit to keep a set of clean clothes tucked away for arrival – a freshwater shower will be a much higher priority than getting the laundry done, and one's first trip ashore for several weeks will be more enjoyable in clean clothes. A reasonably clean and tidy crew will also make a better impression on customs or immigration officials than a dirty and dishevelled one.

Almost anything will pass on the beach, but in the Caribbean toplessness for women is generally not accepted except in remote areas, or the French islands. It is possible to cause offence by failing to conform to local standards of dress in public places, restaurants or shops. Except in the most informal bars, men will be expected to wear a short-sleeved shirt, while women in overly skimpy blouses or shorts may attract undue attention. In any case, looser clothing or a cotton skirt may well be cooler. Only in a very few places will men be expected to wear a collar and tie or jacket when dining ashore.

Protection from the sun is a high priority. Although darker complexions will acclimatise more quickly than fairer skins, it is generally accepted that over-exposure to the tropical sun is harmful. Covering up should be the rule rather than the exception, and a wide-brimmed hat will do much to help. Guests who fly out to the tropics from the northern winter should take particular care, as a bad case of sunburn will ruin what should be an ideal holiday.

Suitable footwear should not be forgotten. Although many people prefer bare feet on deck, it is dangerous to walk ashore without shoes – broken glass, sea urchins and the fallen fruit of the manchineel tree (common on Caribbean beaches) can all cause painful injuries. Shoes are considered a part of normal dress in nearly all areas, and many restaurants will not serve barefooted customers. Lightweight sandals are both practical and cool, but flip-flops are dangerous on board. Most voyaging sailors do a lot of their exploring on foot and so comfortable walking shoes are important.

Stowage of clothes

Each person aboard should have some completely private stowage space, much of which is likely to be devoted to their clothes – no one should be expected to live for weeks out of their luggage holders. In larger lockers, not provided with shelving, generous use of polythene bags, preferably of the self-seal variety, will provide protection from damp and keep some semblance of order. Ideally, the only shared locker should be for oilskins, though in many yachts this will also have to double as a hanging locker for whaever tidy clothes are carried. Protect the latter with plastic sacks or purpose-made zipped clothing bags. Unprotected clothing allowed to swing incessantly backwards and forwards in a hanging locker during an ocean passage is likely to emerge with conspicuously threadbare patches where it has chafed against the bulkheads.

Firearms

Very few experienced voyaging sailors have firearms aboard, not only because they are of little use, but also because the inconvenience they cause far outweighs any possible benefits they might conceivably have. In most countries firearms will be impounded on arrival and not returned until departure; this will normally have to be done at the port of arrival and thus not be available while in the country.

Apart from their possible use to scare away sharks, it is hard to envisage a use for firearms at sea. Pirates or drug smugglers, who might theoretically pose a threat to a yacht, are unlikely to be deterred by the weapons that it would be feasible for her to carry aboard. In those countries where firearms may be retained on board in harbour, the authorities will need to be satisfied that they are secured in a proper stowage, and if this is done they will not be readily available. It would be a rare situation aboard a yacht, however unpleasant or frightening, when the use – or threat of use – of firearms would not make matters worse. In this context, a Verey or flare pistol needs a firearms certificate in the United Kingdom and Europe before it can be carried on board. However, it may not be acceptable as safety equipment in other countries; it is easier to rely on less lethal but just as effective and acceptable safety pyrotechnics.

Pests

These fall into three categories: waterborne, airborne and land-based. Of the waterborne pests, owners of wooden yachts should be concerned about both teredo worm and gribble, and although protection is provided by antifouling paint, it needs to be in perfect condition to give complete immunity. Almost every yacht collects a crop of goose barnacles during a trade wind crossing, principally in the splash zone above the waterline on the quarters, but these do no harm and can be removed at the end of the passage.

Airborne pests include flies, mosquitoes and occasionally wasps. The best protection is to anchor well off and ensure good ventilation at all times – see Chapter 3. Experience suggests that the vast majority of mosquito bites are sustained while ashore, particularly around dusk.

Anchoring off will also give protection against many land-based pests, other than those unwittingly brought aboard in food or boxes. In some areas, including the Caribbean, rats may make their way on board a yacht with lines ashore, and once they are established they are very difficult to get rid of. They can do a phenomenal amount of damage in a short time, chewing through food containers, wiring and plastic hoses, including those attached to open seacocks. Should a rat take up residence aboard, resist the temptation to poison it – it is likely to retreat into an inaccessible place, normally under a water tank in the bilge, to die with fragrant consequences. Either a trap, or a cat, left aboard the sealed and deserted yacht overnight is an infinitely preferable solution. The pretty little rope guards sold in some chandlers, or improvised protectors made from plastic funnels, may look impressive, but are completely ineffectual. To do any good, a conical rope guard that will defeat a determined rat – and there is no other kind – needs to be made of metal and be a minimum of 2m (7ft) in diameter, hardly practical for the average cruiser.

Weevils are difficult to avoid, since they are generally brought aboard in the food in which they are later found. However, they are less prevalent than used to be the case, although they are still occasionally found in flour, rice or pasta bought in the islands.

Cockroaches are the most unpleasant of the insect pests if they are allowed to gain a firm hold. Preventatives include avoiding lying alongside, careful examination of all foods brought aboard, especially fruit and vegetables, and a complete ban on cardboard cartons on board as these frequently harbour eggs. If such cartons must be embarked, then they should be thoroughly sprayed with insecticide, inside and out, before being taken below. Frequent use of one of the sprays available should be routine to catch any stray intruder that may get aboard. If a yacht *does* become infested, the best solution is to use boric acid, a white powder, which can be obtained from chemists on special order. A couple of pounds of this costs little, and it is worth laying in a supply before departure. If needed, it is best used undiluted – and not mixed with condensed milk or sugar, as is sometimes suggested. A generous sprinkling in all the areas that roaches frequent is necessary. Typical places are behind the headlining, around the cooker, in the backs of cupboards and drawers, and behind books. The treatment should be repeated frequently and will take around a month to be fully effective. If this is not done, and the yacht becomes seriously infected, professional fumigation of the yacht in a port with these facilities will be needed.

Communications with home

Almost all cruisers need to keep in touch to some extent with friends and relatives in their home country. Most will have some affairs that need to be attended to as well, even if only an arrangement for the credit card bills to be paid and mail to be forwarded.

The telephone system around the north Atlantic is now excellent and it is possible to make direct-dialled calls practically everywhere or to use mobiles when near to land. Local phone cards can be bought, and using the local telephone system is cheaper than using mobiles. Fax facilities are becoming increasingly widespread, and it is worth considering installing a fax machine at the home base. The use of e-mail has now become usual almost everywhere. This can be accessed by using internet cafés, taking a laptop computer ashore and connecting to the local telephone network, or by using HF or satellite radio. Prior arrangements need to be made with an appropriate server if using the ship's radio (and this is expensive), but it does mean that messages can be sent or received at sea.

Mobile phone coverage has increased enormously in recent years and there are few places in the scope of this book within range of shore transceivers where they cannot be used. Prior arrangement will need to be made with the phone company to extend the contract to other countries.

The use of mobile phones in coastal waters has led to the demise of most coastal radio stations, and the facility to make link calls through them is now very patchy. Details of countries that still provide local radio VHF and MF services other than the emergency frequencies can be found in *Admiralty Maritime Communications NP 289* and *NP 290*.

For many voyagers, mail still remains a principal way of keeping in touch and is the only way to transmit packages and parcels. Mail may be sent *poste restante* (general delivery) to post offices in most towns, to be collected on arrival – but the time that it will be retained varies from country to country. Some marinas, yacht clubs and harbour offices will hold mail for visiting yachts. Local pilot books should give details. Mailing addresses for the ports in Part III are given in the text.

9 Safety

Crossing an ocean aboard a seaworthy yacht carries no more inherent risk than coastal sailing – and, in many ways, less. On an ocean passage there is no risk of grounding, heavy weather is less hazardous in deep water, and the chance of collision is much reduced. However, equally, the option to seek shelter at the onset of bad weather is removed and, should something serious go wrong, assistance is unlikely to be available. Even if help can be summoned it will probably take a considerable time to arrive. On an ocean voyage the yacht is on her own and the crew must rely entirely on their own resources in the event of difficulty. It is not the purpose of this book to teach basic seamanship, and before contemplating an Atlantic passage the skipper should be satisfied that he and his crew are equal to most eventualities, that he knows how his boat should be handled, and how she will react in all circumstances.

The chance of meeting bad weather is always present, and must be faced. Fire, collision, man overboard and, to a large extent, gear failures are avoidable, but will have to be dealt with should they occur. The possibility of illness or injury cannot be ignored, and both skipper and crew should be aware of any ailment to which they might be prone. However, a well-prepared boat in the hands of a competent and resourceful crew has no more reason to encounter problems while crossing the Atlantic than while crossing the English Channel or the Florida Straits. In particular, those who have cruised extensively in the unforgiving waters of northern Europe or New England, with their strong tides, heavy traffic and frequent bad visibility, should be well equipped to deal with whatever the open ocean can throw at them.

The deck: design features

Moving about the deck of a small boat at sea has been likened to trying to walk on a wet, sloping roof in an earthquake. It is surprising how few of us fall off. Good design, the sensible provision of handholds, and plenty of points to clip on to are essential. The larger the yacht, the easier will be the motion and the more stable the deck. It should also be drier, and although the risk of being physically washed off the deck of any yacht is only really present in extreme conditions, a wet deck is more slippery than a dry one and a soaked crew member is more likely to make a careless mistake. But, whatever the size of yacht, moving around the deck at sea will always require care. It is as easy, and in some ways easier, to fall overboard in light weather, when one is relaxed and off guard, than it is in heavy weather when the dangers are obvious and every precaution will

be taken. The camber of the deck of a good ocean cruiser should not be too extreme; excessive camber may make the weather deck more or less level when the vessel is heeled, but the lee deck will be untenable. It should be possible to move all around the deck in the worst conditions, even if only on hands and knees.

A solid toe rail is essential, though deep bulwarks combined with low freeboard, such as grandfather's boat had, are a mixed blessing, often scooping up water and holding it there. Guard rails also provide some protection, but they must be strong enough to take the weight of a heavy person thrown right across the deck. This is not easy to arrange, particularly in a small yacht where the structure may not be equal to that sort of strain without reinforcement. Stanchion sockets must be securely attached – through-bolted to a wooden or glassfibre hull with adequate backing plates, or welded to a metal one.

Plastic-covered, stainless-steel wire can have hidden defects beneath the surface and it is better to use bare wire even though this is less pleasant to fall against. Pre-stretched polyester line, very little thicker than covered wire, is equally strong, and any defect will be obvious; but it is very liable to chafe where it passes through the stanchions, and for this reason is best avoided. Wire guard rails may be secured either by lashings or by small bottlescrews. The former can be cut quickly, but are subject to chafe and need frequent checking. If bottlescrews are used, then there should be some way of disconnecting the guard rail in a hurry – a properly moused pelican hook will serve.

If dodgers (weather cloths) are fitted there must be a gap of at least 10–15cm (4–6in) between them and the deck. Otherwise, if a big sea comes aboard, they may carry away – possibly taking guard rails and stanchions with them. Dodgers should be secured with elastic cord rather than with rope for the same reason. Some skippers remove them completely at the onset of bad weather, or they can be brailed up to avoid the risk of damage.

Pulpits must be strong beyond all question. A man working at the stemhead must both feel, and be, completely safe. It should be possible to move all over the deck from one handhold to another without ever having to let go with both hands – hand rails along the entire length of the coachroof on each side are very desirable. Waist-high stainless-steel rails either side of the mast give valuable support to a person working at its foot.

Finally, the deck and coachroof surfaces must provide as good a grip when wet as when dry, for bare feet and for seaboots. GRP decks often have a diamond pattern moulded in, but with an older yacht this may have become worn and ineffective and some form of commercial non-skid deck covering or non-slip paint may be required.

Heavy weather

Although the prospect causes much apprehension, it is a fact that most people cross the Atlantic, especially by the more southerly routes, without ever experiencing truly severe weather. Gales, with winds of 35 to 45 knots, occur relatively frequently north of about 40°, but storms, with gusts reaching 60 knots, are rare except during the winter months in high latitudes. Even so, the possibility of a deep depression or out-of-season hurricane is always present, and only a fool would set off on an ocean crossing unprepared for heavy weather.

The best tactics to employ in severe conditions depend to a large extent on the yacht herself and on the number, strength and skill of those aboard. Few people will deliberately seek out a gale before departure in order to test out their theories and, in any case, ocean seas are very different, and far easier to deal with, than those in confined waters. However, if the opportunity arises, experimenting with using the trysail, heaving-to, lying a'hull and running under bare poles, with or without warps, even in force 6 to 7 (25 to 30 knots), will give a good idea of how the boat will behave in stronger winds.

There are many excellent books on the subject of coping with bad weather at sea, notably *Heavy Weather Sailing* by K Adlard Coles, revised by Peter Bruce, the standard reference work on the subject. Accounts by less experienced yachtsmen facing heavy weather are also worth reading, as they will describe the situation from the perspective of those experiencing a gale for the first time.

While it is impossible to prevent solid water coming aboard any yacht, steps must be taken to ensure that it will disappear again as quickly as possible, and that it does not find its way below. A cockpit filled with sea-water can seriously affect a boat's trim and stability, making her much more susceptible to the next wave. Large drains are essential and, if fitted with strainers, these must be cleared regularly. In practice, the violent movement generated by seas likely to come aboard will often throw much of the water out the same way it came in.

The importance of a solid bridgedeck and strong washboards has already been mentioned in Chapter 2, along with the need to be able to secure locker lids. Doghouse and coachroof windows are a source of weakness aboard some yachts, and should be provided with plywood covers for temporary repairs in the event of breakage. GRP yachts with small, aluminium-framed windows of toughened glass are less likely to be at risk. It is essential that the glass is secured by more than just the rubber seal, which should only be there for water-tightness. While aesthetically unpleasing, the transparent slabs bolted to the outside of a coachroof as windows

are probably stronger than the structure itself, provided that they are not too large. They are, however, prone to leak unless bedded on generous amounts of good-quality sealant.

The hazards of a knockdown, and particularly the danger posed to the crew by heavy, unsecured fittings flying about below, are well known. Few yachts these days carry inside ballast, but if there is some it must be immovable. Batteries must be secured so that, even if the boat is rolled right over, they cannot move either. The gimbals for the stove must be of the closed variety, preferably backed up by bolts. Make sure that lockers containing heavy tools, cutlery or glassware cannot empty their contents. This is hard to achieve and, if knocked down, you will certainly wonder how on earth some of the items managed to get where they did.

Many knockdowns occur after the worst of the weather has passed, when the seas are still big but the wind has begun to moderate. This is particularly true if a front has gone through and the wind direction changed significantly. If the boat is undercanvased she will be more at the mercy of rogue waves than if she has the power to answer the helm quickly. Increasing sail early runs counter to the natural inclination of a tired crew to take life a little bit easy for a while and ensure the worst really *is* over, but it is a point worth remembering.

An ocean gale is an awe-inspiring spectacle, but it is much less dangerous than one in confined waters. It is sensible to have one's first brush with bad weather in deep water, with plenty of sea room and as far from a lee shore as possible. This is not quite as silly as it sounds. Although the weather for a landfall must, by and large, be taken as it comes, the departure time, and therefore the weather, can be selected. Leaving with a favourable forecast gives the opportunity to get well clear of the land, and preferably off the continental shelf, before bad weather can reach you. Both boat and crew will have had a chance to settle down, and from then onwards they will be able to take bad weather in their stride.

Although never pleasant, heavy weather is much worse in anticipation than in actuality, but until one has had a brush with it the prospect is particularly alarming. Once experienced, the terrors it holds will be much reduced. Until then it is worth remembering that for every account of disaster in bad weather there are literally thousands of small yachts, often with quite inexperienced crews, who have come through similar weather unscathed, but with heightened confidence in themselves and in their yachts.

Lightning

One facet of bad weather that worries many people, more for the damage it causes than any immediate threat, is being struck by lightning. Although comparatively rare, it does occur from time to time and little can be done to prevent it. Some yachts have lightning conductors fitted, usually in the form of heavy copper strapping from the masthead straight down through deck and kingpost to the keel, terminating in a large grounding plate. If you are considering fitting one, then professional advice should be taken.

A less expensive step is to shackle short lengths of chain to the shrouds and backstay when lightning threatens. They should be of sufficient length to stay immersed whatever the motion. The chain can be passed through a piece of plastic pipe to save the topsides.

The effects of a lightning strike are likely to be severe. There is a distinct possibility of structural damage – aluminium mastheads can be melted or split, and if the charge leaves through a skin fitting it may be destroyed. If it exits via an encapsulated keel, then a section of the GRP can be blown off. It is likely that most of the electronic equipment aboard will be destroyed, whether powered by the ship's supply or by batteries, and whether in use at the time or isolated. The damage may be obvious – in some cases instruments will virtually explode, or be blown from their mountings – or it may not be apparent until the equipment is tested. Alternators and their regulators are not immune to damage, but it seems that starter motors are less vulnerable. The main electrical system will also probably suffer, and many yachts need complete rewiring following a strike. Even if the wiring is undamaged, individual light bulbs are likely to blow, either immediately or within the next few days. Fluorescent light fittings are almost certain to be destroyed. Surprisingly, injuries to the crew are rare.

There may be other, less obvious damage as well. Very high currents may affect rigging terminals and insulators, and current passing along the propeller shaft has occasionally damaged internal gearbox components. A large compass error will probably be induced. A yacht that has been struck should have a thorough survey as soon as possible.

On an ocean passage the consequences for a yacht dependent on electronics for navigation will be serious, as a hand-held GPS carried as a back-up is quite likely to be destroyed along with the main set. In theory, objects completely enclosed in a metal container are protected from lightning by the Faraday Cage effect, but the authors know of no case where this has been demonstrated at sea. At least one highly experienced voyager, a doctor of physics to boot, puts his back-up GPS in the oven if lightning is about, but he has fortunately not had his caution put to the test. Such a measure might prevent damage to a GPS set and can do no harm – provided the cook remembers it is there!

Gear failure

Prevention is better than cure. Routine inspection for chafe should be made every day, and careful checks made before, during and after each passage to ensure that both standing and running rigging are in good order. All seacocks and pumps should be worked period-

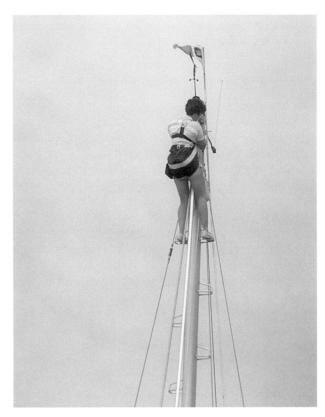

It is vital that a check aloft is made before each ocean-going passage. Photo Gavin McLaren.

ically, and all machinery given regular tests to make certain that it will function when needed. See Chapter 2.

Emergency steering

Any wheel-steered yacht should carry an emergency tiller for use should the linkage to the wheel fail, and a tiller-steered boat should carry a spare tiller (unless the fitted one is so strong as to make breakage genuinely impossible). Often, the point of attachment of a tiller to the rudder is a weak link, particularly if a large amount of material has been cut away from the rudder stock to accommodate the tiller; if this is the case, then some reinforcing plates may be needed. Other forms of steering – a sweep over the stern, towing buckets or warps, or simply balancing the sails – should be experimented with.

Collision

About 95 per cent of collision avoidance depends on three things: a good lookout, bright navigation lights, and an efficient radar reflector. The other 5 per cent is down to sheer luck. Yachts do occasionally hit semi-submerged debris that the most conscientious lookout could not hope to spot. However, hitting debris is not necessarily very serious, particularly to a relatively slow-moving boat, and many ocean cruisers have received a loud and unexpected thump without any real harm to the hull beyond a few scratches or chipped gelcoat.

Collision with a ship would be another matter, and there is little doubt that from time to time yachts are lost in this way. The risk factor is, in reality, extremely low when well offshore and away from fishing grounds, but it does exist. The continental margins are much busier, which adds to the potential problems inherent in any landfall. Wherever the yacht is, a good lookout is the best defence, with white flares ready to hand at night. If fitted, radar gives a powerful protection, and some sets will sound an alarm if a contact reaches a pre-set range.

Although the risk of being run down is ever present and vigilance should never be relaxed, electronic aids may help. Warning devices that sound an alarm if a radar signal is detected are useful. Radar reflectors of the octahedral type should be hoisted in the catch-rain position, but the majority of experienced cruising skippers prefer the cylindrical reflectors, often permanently mounted on a mast bracket. The different types vary in their efficiency (a favourite topic with sailing magazines), and before fitting one some research should be undertaken into the different makes available. A radar transponder, which detects an incoming radar signal and transmits a response to enhance the echo on the screen, requires continuous power to operate and is expensive, but virtually guarantees that a yacht will be detected. It should be remembered that none of these devices is the slightest use against a ship that is not operating radar, and in the open ocean some ships do not do so, at least by day. The standard of visual lookout has regrettably declined with the reduction of manning standards in commercial shipping, and there are many anecdotes of ships passing close with apparently no one on the bridge. This fact therefore stresses the need for a conscientious and regular lookout on all yachts, which are obviously far more vulnerable to damage than commercial shipping in the event of a collision.

Oil rigs

At present, there appear to be fewer exploratory oil rigs stationed in the western approaches to the British Isles than was the case in the past, but the occasional fixed rig may still be encountered. They may also be found off the coasts of Nova Scotia and Cape Cod (see Chapter 18), or may occasionally be met under tow. Fixed rigs should be shown on up-to-date charts, while newly established ones are listed in *Notices to Mariners*.

In fact, it would be extremely difficult to collide with an oil rig unless no watch at all was being kept. They present a confusing sight at night – a mass of lights visible from far off in clear weather, either alone or in groups, with the chief hazard being the many unlit buoys marking the ends of mooring cables. Rigs on the move are attended by several tugs, whose long towlines will be largely submerged and therefore invisible. Night or day, fixed or moving, oil rigs should be given a very wide berth. International regulations require all vessels to keep 500m (0.25 miles) away from rigs, but at least a mile would be preferable.

Whales

There have been a number of well-publicised accounts of yachts having close encounters with whales, and those on ocean cruises see whales at some stage. However, in very few cases does a collision or any direct contact take place. The very rare attacks that do occur are usually by a frightened or injured creature. Otherwise, the danger is of running into a whale dozing on the surface, usually at night and, as with floating debris, the faster the yacht is going the greater the likelihood of serious damage.

Whales are curious and, like dolphins, may approach a boat for no apparent reason; they are only likely to react violently if startled. If there are whales in the vicinity and you suspect they may not be aware of your presence, start the engine but keep the revolutions low; running the echo sounder may also help.

Fire

Serious fires on cruising yachts are very uncommon, but the consequences of a major fire on an ocean passage might be disastrous and so adequate precautions must be taken.

Galley fires

The most common cause of fire in the galley is attempting to light a paraffin pressure stove without adequate priming. Fuel spillage, either of paraffin or alcohol, is another possible cause and, though neither of these fuels is volatile, wood or fabric soaked in either of them will burn vigorously. It is not enough just to mop up any spillage – the area should be washed with detergent to emulsify paraffin or to dilute and render alcohol harmless. Carelessness with bottled gas is more likely to cause an explosion than a fire. Careful installation and maintenance, together with safe operating procedures, are the best way to guard against this risk (see Chapter 2). Galley fires have also been started by the ignition of hot fat or cooking oil – deep fat frying should never be risked at sea, and is unwise even in harbour. Petrol should always be stowed on the upper deck, and generators and outboards should always be filled where any spillage can be washed directly overboard.

Engine fires

Engine compartment fires are particularly dangerous as they can take hold unnoticed and become well established before anyone is aware of them. Although the engine itself is unlikely to burn, most engine compartments contain a good deal of inflammable material, including the fuel coming into the engine. It is essential that the engine space is kept clean and, in particular, that any sound insulation material is not allowed to become saturated with oil or fuel. This can happen gradually over a long period and such insulation will probably need eventual replacement. Fire in the engine compartment is most likely to be started by an electrical short circuit, a ruptured fuel line, or inflammable material touching an unlagged section of an exhaust pipe.

An engine fire will almost certainly flare up, possibly explosively, if the engine hatch is opened – thereby admitting oxygen. The ideal way to combat such a fire is with a permanently installed extinguisher within the compartment, operated either automatically or manually by remote control. Since the operator will not be near the fire, a powder or CO_2 extinguisher may be chosen; Halon extinguishers are no longer legal (as from the end of 2003). An alternative is a hole in the casing, normally closed with a flap or plug, through which a hand-held extinguisher may be discharged. There must be a means of shutting off the fuel supply without opening the engine compartment covers.

Electrical fires

The chances of an electrical fire are greatest on boats where additional loads have been added to the system without the wiring being upgraded. Overloading may result in overheating, and poor connections producing heat and possibly sparks, either at the switchboard or elsewhere. Starter motors, alternators and electric anchor windlasses consume or generate very high loads and call for wiring and circuitry of the highest standard. Fuses or breakers of the correct rating must always be used – keep a list of the values and never replace a fuse with one of a higher rating. Batteries generate explosive gases when being charged and must have adequate ventilation.

Smoking

Careless smoking can be a fire hazard and is banned below decks on many yachts, although this is usually by personal preference, rather than for safety, reasons. If smoking is allowed in the cockpit, care must be taken that a lighted end does not fall into an open locker or get flipped into the dinghy (a particularly common failing among non-sailing guests). Smoking in one's bunk is as foolish and dangerous afloat as it is in bed when ashore.

Firefighting equipment

An adequate number of fire extinguishers should be carried – the minimum is three, but more are preferable. There are various types, but dry powder extinguishers are the best choice. Although they make a lot of mess, so does a fire. They should be shaken regularly to prevent the contents of the extinguisher from settling. CO_2 is very effective in confined spaces because it denies the fire oxygen, but is dangerous to the operator for the same reason. Water is a very effective extinguisher, is available in large quantities and can be used on most fires. The

exceptions to this are fat- or fuel-based fires or those involving mains voltage electricity which may be present if an inverter or HF radio is involved. A fire blanket is effective for smothering a small fire and is particularly appropriate in the galley. It must be accessible without having to reach over the stove itself.

Siting of extinguishers

This is important. There must be extinguishers on both sides of any point at which a fire might start so that, wherever the crew may be, it will be possible to tackle the fire with the right equipment. There should be an extinguisher adjacent to each hatch, one immediately available to the cook, and one close to the engine compartment. You should not be parsimonious with fire extinguishers. If a fire does break out, no one will complain that there are too many of them.

Finally, it should be remembered that a big fire is simply a little fire that nobody put out. The golden rule is to tackle any fire, however small, instantly, using all the means available.

Lifesaving equipment

Liferaft

A conventional liferaft will need servicing by an approved centre before departure and possibly at intervals throughout a longer cruise. Liferafts can now be bought with a three-year servicing period. It is well worth watching the raft being inflated and getting to know how it works and what equipment it contains. Most service centres are happy for owners to do this. Do not be tempted to pull the cord at home. Not only is the canister or valise likely to be badly damaged, but the valve will probably freeze as the pressurised CO_2 expands (if used at sea, the water dissipates the chill). At the testing centre the sealing gasket is first removed, and the raft then inflated by air pump.

Some of those who cruise prefer a sailing tender as a liferaft, and the 'Tinker' range from J M Henshaw (Marine) Ltd is available with CO_2 bottles and an inflatable canopy for this purpose. Except in a very small yacht, such a liferaft should be in addition to, rather than combined with, the dinghy in everyday use. It is not reasonable to expect such a vital piece of equipment as the liferaft to put up with the hard use that a yacht's tender gets.

Among the dedicated rafts various options are available, including different types of container, single or double floors, and more or less comprehensive emergency packs. The ocean-going yacht will obviously require the full pack. When the raft is serviced, extra gear can (within reason) be added to the pack. Items to consider include: any vital medications; reading glasses if needed; a hand-held watermaker; a 121.5 MHz EPIRB for homing; a hand-held VHF radio, and possibly a SART. If there is room, extra water should also be included. In addition to this pack, an emergency 'grab bag' should be assembled and kept accessible. Suitable contents include: extra water; foil survival blankets; flares; heliograph; fishing gear; sunscreen; additional antiseasickness pills; glucose tablets. Some skippers also like to include ship's papers, passports, some cash and credit cards.

Lifebuoys

Two fluorescent lifebuoys, both equipped with automatic lights and one attached to a danbuoy, should be within reach of the helmsman and ready for throwing overboard. The combination should also have a small drogue attached to slow down any drift once in the water. The danbuoy pole will need a brightly coloured flag on top with a counterweight to keep it upright. The whole assembly must be carefully stowed so that danbuoy, lifebuoy, light, drogue and connecting line can be deployed instantly without fouling.

Danbuoy, lifebuoys, harnesses and lifejackets all benefit from having reflective tape stuck on them for location in the dark. Some materials do not hold their reflective quality indefinitely, so make sure that those in use at the start of the voyage are in good order and replaced as necessary.

There are a few dedicated man overboard lifesaving systems that are capable of being deployed in an emergency very much quicker than the usual lifebuoy/danbuoy/light combination.

Desirable as any of these measures are, the important principle is prevention of an overboard occurrence. The chances of recovery in a shorthanded cruiser in the open ocean are small.

Flares

It makes sense to carry plenty of flares, particularly of the parachute type – it is said that the first draws attention, the second confirms it wasn't an illusion, and the third provides the opportunity to take a bearing. An ocean cruising yacht should carry at least a dozen, together with orange smoke markers, hand-held red flares, and hand-held white anti-collision flares. A supply of white parachute rockets will greatly help the search for a man overboard at night. They should never, however, be used to warn of an impending collision situation at night, despite the advice given in at least one chandler's catalogue. They will simply serve to surprise and distract the bridge crew of the approaching ship, who are unlikely to realise that they were launched from a yacht close ahead.

Personal safety gear

Harnesses

Losing a person overboard is one of every skipper's worst nightmares, and rules must be established as to when harnesses are worn. The skipper must lay down whether a harness is mandatory whenever one person is on watch alone, or only at night, or only if leaving the cockpit, or only in bad weather. Whatever the rules, they must be adhered to. Wearing a harness without getting snarled up takes a little practice, and an inexperienced crew would be wise to accustom themselves to working in harnesses before needing to do so in anger.

Most harnesses are manufactured to nationally approved standards, and each person should be respon-

In strong winds and fast sailing, a harness is essential for the helmsman. Photo Jill Vasey.

sible for adjusting and stowing their own. The safety line is as important as the harness itself. It should be about 2m (7ft) long, with a clip at each end, and preferably one in the middle also. In cooler climates there is much to be said for the harness being built into an oilskin jacket, but during a trade wind passage, or in the Caribbean, you may sometimes need to wear a harness without wanting the additional warmth and weight that such a jacket provides.

A harness is no stronger than its point of attachment. Several through-bolted eyes will be needed in the cockpit, with one for the helmsman and another within reach from inside the companionway, together with webbing jackstays running along the sidedecks. (Although webbing has a shorter life than wire, it is safer as it provides a stable surface if trodden on.) The crew must know what points can be used to clip onto when working forward or at the mast. Shrouds should never be used, because – in the event of a knockdown – a person clipped to them may find themselves at the spreaders.

Lifejackets

Very few adults routinely wear lifejackets, but every cruising yacht should carry enough for the maximum number that may ever be on board. A lifejacket should support a heavy person with their head out of the water, and turn them face up even if unconscious. It should be equipped with a whistle, and possibly an automatic light that will activate when immersed.

Regulations in some countries require lifejackets to be carried in the dinghy when going ashore (leaving the problem of what to do with them once landed), and non-swimming guests should always be encouraged to put one on.

Personal lights and flares packs

There are some excellent personal strobe lights available, operating from a single dry cell and fully waterproof. They may be kept in a pocket or worn around the upper arm. When switched on they give a very bright intermittent flash that would be hard to miss, even at some distance, and would certainly help to locate a person overboard. Several types of miniature flares are also small enough to fit in the pocket, and could prove invaluable at night or in high seas. Personal locator beacons also exist, but they require special gear aboard the parent craft to track them and are generally only suited to large, fully crewed yachts.

Man overboard

Every boat should have a drill to recover a person in the water, and this must reflect both the boat's handling characteristics and the capabilities and physical strength of the crew left aboard. The situation on an ocean

passage will be identical to that when sailing close to the coast except for two factors. The first is that there will probably be a large swell, which will make spotting the man in the water much more difficult. The second is that the boat may be under downwind rig at the time, and consequently more difficult to manoeuvre quickly.

Not much can be done about the swell except to ensure that the danbuoy is launched as quickly as possible. The downwind rig problem can be overcome, but a well-thought-out routine will be needed and it must have been rehearsed beforehand to have any chance of success. For the shorthanded crew the engine will be used and, despite the urgency, it is vital to check that there are no lines in the water before starting it. In the haste to lower or furl sails, it is likely that there will be. When the boat is turned she will probably pitch and roll heavily, and solid water may come aboard, washing loose ropes overboard; they must be secured as well. It is far quicker to jettison a towing log rotator or water-driven generator impeller than to recover them.

Once the man has been located he will have to be got back on board, possibly a bigger problem than finding him. The routine used in coastal waters will serve equally well in the ocean, but it must have been practised.

The overriding principle for all man overboard situations is that they should not be allowed to occur in the first place. A properly planned cockpit and deck incorporating non-skid surfacing and plenty of handholds, together with sensible rules on when harnesses are to be worn, are the best ways of keeping the crew on board where they belong. No one should be in any doubt that should they go overboard, particularly at night or when running in strong winds, their chances of survival are poor.

Illness and injury

Cruising is a remarkably healthy way of life and serious illness or injury is rare. By far the most common ailment, which affects most people at some time or other, is seasickness. Fortunately, this is usually a passing phase, and after a couple of days most people recover and become immune for the rest of the voyage. Of the various remedies on the market, Stugeron (cinnazarine) seems to be the most effective of the pills. Hyoscine patches worn behind the ear, from which the drug is absorbed through the skin, are also worth considering.

Medical and dental check-ups before departure are an obvious precaution, and while a chronic condition should not necessarily prevent anyone from crossing the Atlantic, it is only fair for the rest of the crew to know the details. A good supply of medication or drugs will be needed, and these should be accompanied by a doctor's certificate to show to customs officials. Many years ago it was the fashion for the ocean-going sailor to have his or her appendix removed before departure, but unless it has already given trouble, this seems overcautious. It is worth remembering that during the typical Atlantic cruise a yacht will only be out of reach of help for a very small proportion of the time.

Accidents are much more likely to happen ashore than in the familiar environment on board, particularly if sensible precautions are taken against burns and scalds while cooking in heavy weather, and against accidental gybes. However, the risk *is* there, and everybody should have some knowledge of first aid. There should also be a good book, such as *The Ship's Captain's Medical Guide*, on the subject on board (see Appendix A). If fitted with HF radio or Inmarsat, medical advice can always be obtained with a Pan call, and also when within VHF range of a shore station.

The first aid kit

A really comprehensive first aid kit should be carried. As well as plenty of remedies for common ailments, cuts and bruises, sunburn and minor aches and pains, it will need to have sufficient gear to cope with serious emergencies at sea. It should include strong painkillers, several types of antibiotics (necessary as some strains of infection respond better to one kind than another), plenty of wound dressings, sutures or steristrips, and adequate burn dressings. Treatments for eye or ear infections or injuries should not be forgotten. Your own GP or other medical professional will be able to give more comprehensive advice, and in any case many items in the first aid kit will have to be obtained on prescription. There should be a basic dental kit, sufficient to apply a temporary replacement filling or to deal with a broken tooth.

If the cruise will take in any areas where malaria is present, then the appropriate prophylactic drugs will be needed. Parts of central and northern South America may be affected, and advice should be sought. The normal courses of inoculations for travellers should be organised well before departure, as some will need a booster dose some time after the initial injections.

Blood transfusions

With the increasing spread of the HIV virus (AIDS) in some parts of the world, the possible need for a blood transfusion – or even the stitching of a relatively minor injury – is a growing worry. The best way of approaching the latter problem is to carry a traveller's pack of sterile equipment, including needles and syringes (available from larger chemists).

Blood transfusions pose more of a difficulty. It is not possible to carry an emergency supply of blood or plasma aboard because of the controlled storage conditions necessary. If speed is not of the essence, British subjects abroad can usually be supplied with blood from the United Kingdom. Another possibility might be for one member of the crew – or indeed a volunteer from another yacht – to donate blood for the immediate use of the patient. It will be far preferable for him or her to be transferred, if at all possible, to an area where adequate precautions against the virus are taken. Blood Transfusion Centres will be able to offer more detailed advice, and to identify the countries where the risk of infection during medical or dental treatment is high.

Security

Although the matter of security when sailing in foreign waters is often brought up by those who have not done so, this subject is not generally among the primary concerns of those who have. Accounts of crews being injured, or even murdered, aboard their yachts receive a great deal of publicity, not least because such incidents are so rare. The stories are often embellished in the retelling, and it is not uncommon for a minor scuffle with a petty thief to develop within a few weeks into a tale of piracy, kidnapping and murder. It is very hard to sort out the fact from the fiction, and even what is reported in the media is often incorrect.

What is certain is that very little violent crime against sailors actually takes place around the north Atlantic. Of course there are areas where the risk is greater – any major city or seaport will have places where a stranger will be vulnerable. But in the yachting harbours themselves, assaults are extremely rare, and the risks for the average cruiser are considerably less than they would be if they stayed at home.

Some theft, however, occurs pretty well everywhere, at home as well as abroad, and in both cases there are two kinds of thief. The serious one will steal valuables, for which there is always a ready market, while the petty thief picks up any trifle left within reach. The first kind will take outboard engines and rubber dinghies, and has even been known to unscrew winches and vane gears from yachts left unattended. The second variety will take the oars or rowlocks from a dinghy on the beach, or a coil of rope left on deck and within easy reach. Neither sort of thief is likely to resort to physical violence unless extremely frightened. Sensible precautions include never leaving the boat unlocked, stowing valuables below and, in some areas, chaining up both dinghy and outboard when ashore, and hoisting them aboard at night. It is regrettable, but a fact, that other sailors – rather than local people – are responsible for much of the theft from yachts.

Piracy at sea is also another favourite topic for discussion before departure. In fact, piracy in Atlantic waters is almost unheard of – what little there is being totally confined to those areas in which drug smuggling is rife and that are best avoided anyway. There have been no cases in the Caribbean for decades.

PART II

PASSAGES AND LANDFALLS

10   The North Atlantic – Background

Routes, seasons and timing

Among the many things that go to make a successful ocean cruise, two are essential. One is to be in the right place at the right time, the other is to move in the right direction. It is an over-simplification, but a useful one, to think of the north Atlantic as a giant roundabout always turning clockwise. The ocean currents revolve in a clockwise direction and the weather systems (though not always the local winds) do too. Both have their centre south-west of the Azores. By keeping within the limits of a favourable wind and current system, a yacht may cover extra miles, but the sailing will be far more pleasant. She will probably reach her destination more quickly than those who take what appears, at first glance, to be a more direct route.

No matter where you begin your Atlantic cruise, hop onto the roundabout and let it help you on your way. From America or Canada, head east during the summer; from northern Europe, head south in summer or early autumn; from Madeira or the Canary Islands, wait until mid-November or December and make for the trade wind zone (perhaps with a stop in the Cape Verde

	JAN	FEB	MAR	APR	MAY	JUN	JUL	AUG	SEP	OCT	NOV	DEC
The British & European Coasts					▓	▓	▓	▓	▓			
Southwards in the Eastern Atlantic					▓	▓	▓	▓	▓	▓	▓	▓
The Madeiran, Canary & Cape Verde archipelagos	▓	▓	▓	▓					▓	▓	▓	▓
The Trade Wind crossing	▓	▓	▓	▓							▓	▓
The South Atlantic (Cape Town to Caribbean)	▓	▓	▓	▓							▓	▓
The Caribbean	▓	▓	▓	▓							▓	▓
The Bahamas & Florida	▓	▓	▓	▓						▓	▓	▓
North from the Caribbean			▓	▓	▓	▓	▓					
The North American coastline (Northern States)						▓	▓	▓	▓			
Transatlantic in the middle & northern latitudes						▓	▓	▓	▓			

Fig 2 Where to be and when. Green areas indicate best times for cruising or passage-making.

Islands) before heading west. From the West Indies, go north or north-west in the late spring. Fig 2 shows, in simplified form, the best times and seasons for each cruising area or ocean passage. Detailed information will be found in the relevant chapters.

Winds and weather

Winds and weather in the north Atlantic are dominated by the permanent high pressure in mid-ocean and by the relatively low pressures surrounding it. Winds tend to blow clockwise and slightly outwards from the high. This is true for the eastern side of the ocean to around 45°N, and for the trade wind latitudes north of about 10°N and on towards the Bahamas and Florida. There are modifications elsewhere, for the land mass of North America, the warm Gulf Stream and its confluence with the cold Labrador Current result in unstable conditions in that region. These give rise to the typical weather patterns of the British Isles – a succession of lows that form over the western north Atlantic and are then propelled east or north-east towards Europe. Each of these depressions creates its own wind system in its immediate locality – anticlockwise around the low. In spite of this, the whole area from west to east, in the forties and fifties of latitude, is known as 'the Westerlies', indicating that the wind blows from that quarter more often than not. Gales are frequent in this area, though they are generally less common and less severe in summer. Details of some regional weather forecast transmissions will be found in Appendix G.

Hurricanes

Tropical revolving storms, or hurricanes, occur on the western side of the north Atlantic, chiefly during the summer months. As the old rhyme has it:

> June, too soon
> July, stand by
> August, come she must
> September, remember
> October, all over

But this is not entirely accurate, and Fig 3 gives the average number of hurricanes per month. These are only average figures, however, and from year to year there may be considerable variations.

Although each individual one is small in area, perhaps as little as 100 miles across, hurricanes are among the most destructive forces of nature, on a par with earthquakes and volcanic eruptions in terms of the devastation they cause. Sustained winds can reach 135 knots, with gusts far in excess of that, and the seas will be huge; if the storm passes very close, the wind direction will shift rapidly and a lethally confused wave pattern will result. When a hurricane reaches land, the surge associated with

it may temporarily raise the sea level by as much as 3–4 m (10–13ft). Even large commercial ships encountering such storms are often damaged and sometimes lost. Yachts, whether at sea or in the snuggest harbours, will be fortunate to survive the direct passage of a hurricane. Therefore, one of the most important considerations in planning an Atlantic passage or cruise is to avoid the hurricane area during the season. If this cannot be achieved, then time spent in the risk area should be during the months when storms are least likely.

The advent of weather and oceanographic satellites means that much more is now known about tropical storms. They form both east and west of the Caribbean islands chain. Those that form to the east usually have their origins hundreds, or even thousands, of miles out into the Atlantic. Occasionally, in mid-season, a hurricane will form much closer to land, sometimes even between Barbados and the main island chain, and there is likely to be very little warning of such a storm. Hurricanes that form in the Caribbean basin do not usually affect the Windward or Leeward Islands, but may track over Florida and the Bahamas. The energy that generates and sustains a hurricane is drawn from the seawater beneath it; a very broad generalisation is that the warmer the sea in any year, the more frequent and more severe hurricanes are likely to be. Very small temperature changes – as little as 1° or 2°C – are significant, and it is likely that even minimal global warming will affect the frequency and severity of tropical storms.

Hurricanes are closely monitored and tracked and their movements forecast. These forecasts may not be entirely accurate and will certainly not be accurate enough for a yacht to move from one island to another in time to avoid the centre of the system. Fast-moving storms tend to behave more predictably than slow-moving ones.

Some characteristics of hurricanes in the north Atlantic will help with passage planning and cruise timing. Storms hardly ever pass south of Grenada; only very occasionally (once in five to ten years) do they affect the east coast of the United States north of Cape Hatteras, and by then they are losing their tropical characteristics and are usually more akin to a normal (but none the less severe) winter storm system. However, even a distant

Fig 3 Hurricane months in the Caribbean.

brush with a hurricane by a yacht in the Gulf Stream may prove disastrous as a result of the enormous and steep seas that may form where the current runs against the wind.

In general, the following advice will minimise the chances of experiencing a hurricane:

1 Bound for the Caribbean, do not leave the Canaries or Cape Verdes before the middle of November.
2 If remaining in the Caribbean for the summer, be south of Grenada by the beginning of June.
3 If sailing directly to Europe, leave the Caribbean by mid-May; if going via Bermuda, leave earlier to allow for time spent there. Whether bound for Europe or for the north-eastern United States, leave Bermuda by early June.
4 If transiting the Bahamas and the US Intracoastal Waterway northwards, be north of Cape Hatteras by the beginning of June.
5 Monitor the forecasts regularly when on passage between late May and November. (See later in this chapter.)

Hurricane holes and harbours

Many Caribbean islands have harbours commonly known as hurricane holes. These traditional refuges for shipping, unlike many local anchorages that are often wide open to the west, are sheltered from all directions. Over the years many, but not all, ships using them have ridden out hurricanes.

Recently, however, the belief has grown that yachts too can safely remain in the Caribbean during the summer provided that they stay in one of these so-called 'safe' harbours. Island governments, anxious for the economic benefits that visitors bring, have encouraged this idea; yachtsmen, eager to remain in the Caribbean for more

than one season, are only to ready to believe it. Unfortunately, it is a myth. In even the most secure hurricane hole a well-prepared yacht, with several heavy anchors out and with plenty of space around her, or moored among the mangroves, may simply be overwhelmed and destroyed by the forces generated in a hurricane.

Lately the situation has become worse, due to the vast numbers of yachts in the Caribbean. During a storm alert, hurricane holes become impossibly crowded. Often these are large charter fleets, hastily and inadequately anchored and then abandoned. Once a few of these start to drag, fouling other yachts, the situation becomes hopeless. For those berthed in marinas, things are little better. Often the storm surge floats pontoons, complete with boats attached to them, off their securing piles.

Despite the initial appearance from the chart, most of the US Intracoastal Waterway is not a safe place in which to weather a hurricane either, as much of the land area it runs through is only a few feet above sea level. The marinas are particularly vulnerable to the surge already mentioned. To make matters worse, the lifting bridges that cross the waterway will cease operating well before a storm arrives, so as to allow residents to evacuate the areas at risk. Yachts will therefore be unable to move away from the dangerous zone.

Before deciding to stay in the Caribbean during the summer, the risks and consequences of a hurricane should be calmly and carefully considered. Of some one thousand yachts in the lagoon at St Maarten – long considered one of the safest of hurricane holes – over 800 were sunk or wrecked during Hurricane *Luis* in 1995. Not all of their crews survived. The strength of the wind was over four times greater than in the 'hurricane' that devastated southern Britain in 1987. In the face of such forces, the sailor is completely powerless to influence events.

It should be noted that most insurance companies now exclude cover for loss or damage to yachts that remain in the Caribbean during the hurricane season.

Yachts piled up on the beach in the lagoon at St Maarten following Hurricane Luis. *Photo Malcolm Page.*

Those considering doing so should check the specific details of their policies.

Fog

When a south or south-west wind moves warm moist air across the cold Labrador Current, fog becomes widespread on the coast of Maine and in the region of the Grand Banks. It is most prevalent in spring and summer, and can be expected on about ten days in each month. All of the coastal areas on the eastern side of the north Atlantic, from Norway southwards, are subject to fog.

British and European sailors who tend to associate fog with light winds or calms should be aware that this is often not the case in the western Atlantic, where fog may be accompanied by steady winds of 25 knots or more.

Ice

North Atlantic icebergs form by 'calving' from Greenland's glaciers, and are then carried south by wind and currents. They are almost totally confined to an area north of 40°N and west of 40°W, though stray bergs have very occasionally been found south or east of this; they are most widespread between March and July. The

International Ice Patrol locates the position of bergs and gives radio reports.

Ocean currents

There is a close but complex relationship between prevailing winds and ocean currents. That currents will be set up wherever the surface water is continually blown in one direction is fairly obvious, but that this should in turn give rise to coastal currents may be less so. Basically, the mass of moving water must go somewhere on reaching the continental margins, and is generally deflected towards the 'intake' area of the next major wind-driven current.

Thus the north-east trade wind gives rises to the North Equatorial Current, flowing east to west across the Atlantic between about 10° and 25°N. This creates a head of water in the Gulf of Mexico and the Caribbean Sea, which emerges through the Strait of Florida and, named the Gulf Stream, flows in a north-easterly direction until it meets the Labrador Current flowing south around Newfoundland and Nova Scotia. This causes the Labrador Current to divide: one part forcing a passage down between the Gulf Stream and the American coast,

Plan 1 *General direction of current flow in the north Atlantic.*

and the other turning eastward and combining with the Gulf Stream to form the North Atlantic Current.

The North Atlantic Current, urged on by the prevailing westerly winds, eventually meets the obstruction of the continent of Europe. Again it divides, one stream going north of Scotland, and the other being deflected southeast and then south to form the Azores Current, the Portuguese Current and finally the Canaries Current. This in turn feeds the embryonic North Equatorial Current to complete the giant circle. In addition there are local features, such as the currents flowing into the English Channel, the Bay of Biscay and the Mediterranean, but these have little importance beyond their own margins.

When a current flows past a continental coastline its course tends to be orderly, but in mid-ocean, or on encountering islands in its path, its track may split or become very ragged at the edges. In some places there are well-documented changes of course, due to land masses, and there are areas in which eddies or countercurrents occur predictably. The study of these can be important because parallel courses only a few miles apart may be in waters moving in opposite directions. When this happens the choice of the right track can make a significant difference to the day's run.

The Gulf Stream is carefully monitored by the US Coast Guard, and their 1600 and 2200 UT weather forecasts from NMN in Portsmouth, Virginia (see pages 66 and 67) give the coordinates of the West or Cold Wall (the line of demarcation between the Gulf Stream and the Labrador Current flowing along the US coast), the speed and position of the middle of the Gulf Stream at various latitudes, and the position of major established eddies. That this service is considered to be necessary emphasises that the stream cannot be accurately predicted – it has to be observed and reported.

Sources of information

Until fairly recently there was no single volume of route-planning information specifically for yachts. When the classic *Ocean Passages for the World* talks about sailing vessels it means 'those able to stand up to, and take advantage of, the heavy weather to be found on many of the recommended routes'. Although this applies to few cruising yachts, the book contains good background information on the weather systems of the world.

Detailed information regarding prevailing winds and currents, percentage frequency of gales and calms, wave and swell heights, hurricane tracks, icebergs and fog is presented on the Admiralty *Routeing Charts* (BA Chart 5124 monthly numbers 1–12), and the US *Pilot Charts* DMA Pilot Chart 16, quarterly, three months in each). These charts, which are similar in form, are compiled using reports from merchant vessels, naval units and weather ships collected over a long period. While they can only show the average, they give an excellent basis for timing and route planning.

Much the same information, presented visually on monthly charts with explanatory text, but in a more handy size and format for the yacht with a small chart table, is to be found in the *Atlantic Pilot Atlas* compiled by James Clarke. This covers the north Atlantic and Caribbean in considerable detail, and the south Atlantic and Mediterranean in more condensed form.

World Cruising Routes by Jimmy Cornell adopts a similar approach to *Ocean Passages for the World*, but is aimed specifically at cruising yachts and describes each passage individually. In addition, the regional weather and currents for each ocean and cruising area are discussed, together with tactics to be adopted should a tropical storm be met at sea.

Charts

Charts will need to be bought over a period of time. Basic ocean-passage charts (see plan 2) will be useful for reference in the early stages of planning and again later for plotting daily positions at sea. As each section of the intended route is studied, the relevant passage planning charts will be useful – lists are included in each chapter. These small-scale charts carry little detail, and it will not matter if they are months, or even a few years, out of date by the time the cruise starts.

No attempt has been made to provide a comprehensive list of all paper and electronic charts available for each area. Far too many are published, and in any case needs will vary according to the route chosen. First plan the itinerary – where it is intended to stop, where coastal passages will be made, which are the possible ports of refuge in the event of bad weather or emergency. Only then should a current chart catalogue be consulted and an order placed. Plenty of time should be allowed for the order to be filled, but large-scale charts should not be collected until shortly before departure. This is particularly important in the United Kingdom where charts should be corrected up to the date of sale, less so in the United States where uncorrected latest editions will normally be supplied. Although there are chart agents throughout the world, many of them only carry local stock.

Ocean passage charts

Coverage	Admiralty	US
Northern N Atlantic	4011 (1:10,000,000)	121 (1:5,870,000)
Southern N Atlantic	4012 (1:10,000,000)	120 (1:6,331,100)
Gnomonic (Great Circle)	5095 (1:13,500,000)	17 (Variable scale)

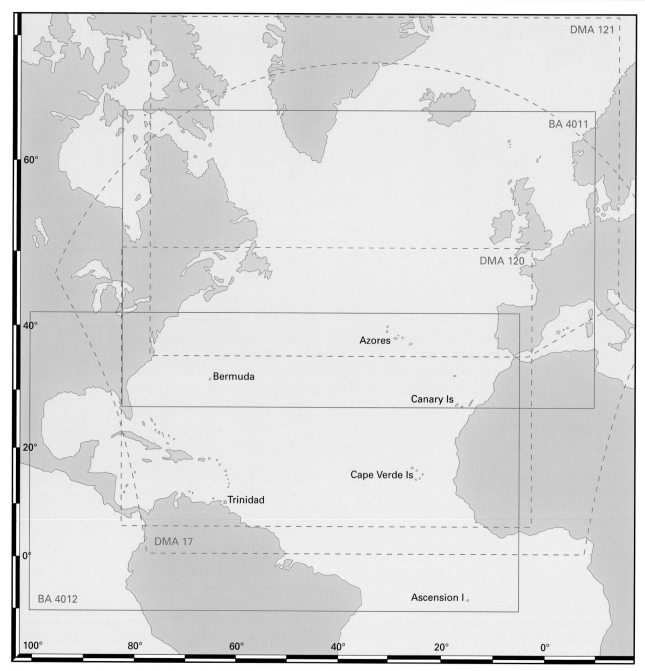

Plan 2 *Passage planning charts for the north Atlantic (Admiralty in continuous lines, US DMA in broken lines).*

Pilots, guides and sailing directions

Pilots and guides fall into two distinct types – official publications intended primarily for use by naval and commercial shipping, and those written purely with the yachtsman in mind.

Chief among the former are the *Sailing Directions* published by the British Admiralty, the US Defense Mapping Agency and the Canadian Hydrographic Service. Each volume of these comprehensive books covers a specific area, and contains a wealth of detailed information on the climate, the coast and the harbours. Every danger to shipping is described and every harbour detail is covered, but only those relevant to big

ships. Little information specifically for the yachtsman is included. They are kept reasonably up to date by periodic supplements. They are expensive, and it is probably not worth any but the largest yachts carrying them.

Much more useful to yachts are the pilots and guides written specifically for them. The margins of the north Atlantic are particularly well covered by such books and a list will be found in Appendix B. However, it should be remembered that these privately researched guides vary dramatically in their content and accuracy. Only the better books are updated by supplements from the publishers, and many of them continue to be sold long after time has rendered them inaccurate.

Pilots applicable to each area are listed at the end of the relevant chapter.

Weather forecast transmissions

Weather forecasts for the coastal regions of the north Atlantic are comprehensive. Almost every country broadcasts forecasts for shipping in some form. General details of the more useful ones appear in Appendix G. The remainder of this section gives brief information on ocean forecasts, which are much less readily available.

The only voice forecast that covers the complete trade wind crossing from Europe is that broadcast by Radio France Internationale at 1140 UT daily on the following AM (A3E) frequencies:

6175, **11700**, 11845, 15300, **15530**, and **17575** kHz

Those frequencies in bold type broadcast the forecast for all the areas on plan 3. The remainder broadcast a selection relevant to the frequency reception area. The forecast is read clearly in French; it may be advantageous for non-French speakers to record it for translation. This transmission also covers much of the area crossed by mid-latitude passage-makers. The remainder, on the west side of the ocean, is covered by the American High Seas forecast. This is broadcast from several stations – probably the most easily received is that transmitted by the US Coast Guard Portsmouth, Virginia (call sign NMN). There are up to eight different times and five frequencies and the *Admiralty List of*

Radio Signals, Vol III, Part 2, NP 283, will need to be consulted for the details.

The area covered is the Atlantic north of 3°N and west of 35°W, together with the Gulf of Mexico and the Caribbean Sea. Any hurricane warnings will be transmitted before the forecast. In addition, some broadcasts include a Gulf Stream analysis. This forecast is read by a computer-generated voice synthesiser, which takes some getting used to. Again, a tape recorder will be helpful.

The Antilles Emergency and Weather Net on 3.815 Mhz every day at 1030 UT and 2230 UT has all sorts of weather information from the Caribbean islands.

Other forecasts are available to yachts fitted with weatherfax/radiofax, or those with a receiver, laptop and printer suitably adapted to receive the broadcasts and weather maps from seven stations in the United States, Canada, Morocco and the United Kingdom. NAVTEX weather broadcasts are available when within about 300 miles of the stations on both sides of the Atlantic.

Any yacht equipped with HF or satellite radio, or with the ability to receive weatherfax/radiofax, should carry the five relevant *Admiralty Maritime Communications* or *Admiralty Lists of Radio Signals*. See Appendix G page 238 for details. These contain complete details of all weather and safety broadcasts. Yachts with only VHF may likewise find them useful as they also contain details of the NAVTEX broadcasts together with all the harbour and marina frequencies, telephone numbers, websites and e-mail addresses on both sides of the Atlantic.

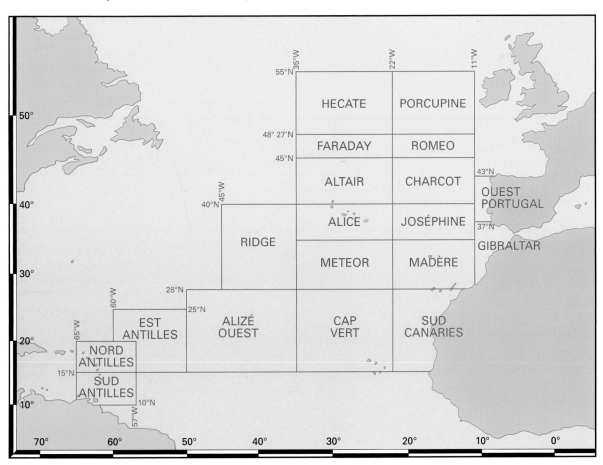

Plan 3 *Radio France Internationale weather forecast areas.*

Amateur forecasts

Several amateur or 'ham' nets transmit useful weather information. Only licensed amateur operators may transmit on these nets, but all sailors may listen and useful information can be obtained. Nets come and go, but the following three are long established. All frequencies are USB (J3E).

1 The **Transatlantic Maritime Net**, run by Trudi in Barbados (call sign 8P6QM), broadcasts at 1300 UT on 21.400 kHz USB (J3E). Yachts throughout the Atlantic check in, giving positions and actual weather conditions. If it is available, a translation of the Radio France weather forecast is broadcast at around 1330 UT. This net is most useful for those crossing west on the trade wind route. It may not operate for certain periods during the hurricane season.

2 The **Caribbean SSB Weather Net** run by David from the yacht *Mistine* (call sign ZHBJ5). He has nets at the following times (all UT) and frequencies: 1230–1300, 8140; 1300–1330, 12359; 1330–1400, 16531.

3 **Herb's Net.** Herb Hilgenberg, call sign VAX498 (but more commonly known as *Southbound 2*), broadcasts on 12359 MHz starting at 2000 UT. This gives a detailed forecast to each boat that checks in; those who are only listening will gain much useful information and may well find that a forecast is given for a boat close to their position. To check in, call via e-mail HeHilgen@aol.com giving your planned route; a donation is usually asked for.

Traffic Separation Schemes (TSS)

In many areas where shipping is heavy – particularly around headlands, where a number of major routes converge, and in constricted waters – IMCO Traffic Separation Schemes have been set up. Typically they consist of two lanes down which vessels pass port-to-port, a central separation zone, and usually an inshore traffic zone. The rules governing separation schemes are detailed in the *International Regulations for Preventing Collisions at Sea*, but as far as yachts are concerned the most important points are as follows:

1 As far as possible, avoid crossing traffic lanes, but if obliged to do so cross on a heading as nearly as practicable at right angles to the general direction of traffic flow. (It should be noted that it is the heading rather than the ground track that is to be at right angles to the traffic flow.)

2 Use inshore traffic zones whenever possible.

3 Do not impede the safe passage of a power-driven vessel following a traffic lane.

Traffic Separation Schemes are often monitored by coastguards or other official bodies, usually by radar, and sailors have been prosecuted for ignoring the regulations. The Traffic Separation Schemes that yachts might encounter going across the Atlantic are: off Lands End, off Ouessant, off the north-west corner of Spain, off Cape St Vincent, in the Gibraltar Straits, around Cuba, and the many along the east coast of the United States and Canada.

11 The British and European Coasts

Regional weather

The Atlantic coast of Europe reaches from 36°N at Gibraltar to the Arctic Circle and beyond, the vast majority of yachts staying south of 60°N. The cruising season around the coasts of the United Kingdom and France runs from May until early October, extending later into the year as you progress south.

From the latitude of northern Spain northwards, winds blow predominantly from between south-west and north-west, although winds from other directions are common. The weather pattern is unstable, and sailors used to the more settled summer conditions found off the east coast of the United States may be startled by how quickly conditions can change. The BBC shipping forecasts covering the area are generally reliable.

The Bay of Biscay has long had a reputation for particularly unpleasant weather, dating back to the days of the square-riggers and beyond. While this may not be entirely deserved during the summer months, setting off across Biscay too late in the year is unwise. To risk catching a gale without sufficient sea room and before the crew have settled into their stride is a poor way to start any long cruise, and it is best to plan to reach Spanish waters by the end of August.

A large area of low pressure forms annually over the Iberian Peninsula in early summer, dominating weather patterns until late autumn. The western edge of this depression gives rise to the Portuguese trades, northerly winds that blow parallel to the coast in a band some 100 miles wide. These winds are most reliable from July through to September or October, and may be augmented near the coast by strong sea breezes, sometimes giving rise to strong or even gale force winds for a short time in the afternoon.

If making a diversion into Gibraltar, the wind may be more variable in both strength and direction after passing Cape St Vincent and, on reaching the Strait of Gibraltar, be blowing either straight in or straight out. There is a constant flow of current from the Atlantic into the Mediterranean, due to the high rate of evaporation in the confined area of the Mediterranean Sea. The speed of this current is affected partly by the tide, which retards or accelerates it, and partly by the wind. In moderate weather there is no difficulty in beating into Gibraltar, but against the *levanter* (the local name for a strong easterly wind) it may be impossible for a small yacht to make much progress, due to the steep seas kicked up by wind against current. In that case, shelter may be sought in one of the Spanish ports westward of the Strait. A strong westerly or south-westerly wind, which reinforces the current, can make it difficult for a yacht to get out from Gibraltar and into the Atlantic. Even a very slight easing of the wind strength does, however, make an immediate and remarkable difference, and as soon as this happens good progress may be made by hugging the Spanish coast as far as Tarifa, after which the strength of the current falls off rapidly.

Once clear of the coasts of Spain and Portugal, the chances are that a breeze from a northerly quarter will be found to take the yacht towards the Madeiran archipelago or towards the Canaries.

Currents

The North Atlantic Current divides in two before reaching the British Isles, one part running up the west coast of Scotland towards Scandinavia and the other deflected south-east and then south past the Iberian Peninsula. Smaller branches enter the English Channel and Irish Sea. The relatively warm water of what was previously the Gulf Stream provides a moderating influence on temperatures in western Europe, which tend to be much less extreme than those inland.

The Portuguese Current, again part of the vast clockwise circulation of water in the North Atlantic, runs in a generally southerly direction from Cape Finisterre to the Canary Islands where it becomes known as the Canary Current. It is reinforced by the constant flow through the Strait of Gibraltar mentioned above.

Tides and tidal streams

Both tidal range and strength of stream vary a great deal along the Atlantic coast of Europe. Greatest spring range among the relevant ports listed in Part III is the 6.1m experienced at Brest, while the least is the 1.1m found at Gibraltar. However, ranges of 12m may occur in some areas, notably around the Channel Islands and the adjacent French coast and in the Bristol Channel.

These great ranges naturally give rise to strong tidal streams, which are generally much more significant to the sailor than is the current. On the coast of the British Isles and France tidal streams regularly reach speeds of 3–4 knots, while in the famous 'Alderney Race' between the Channel Islands and the Normandy peninsula the flood can exceed 9 knots. Tidal streams can be especially strong off headlands, with heavy overfalls. If these are marked on the chart it is particularly important to keep clear of them, but tide rips and overfalls can occur off most headlands and one must always be prepared for

Plan 4 *Prevailing winds and currents off the coast of Europe for August. Winds are coloured pink, currents in dark blue. Based on information from the* Atlantic Pilot Atlas.

this. Strong winds against the stream will aggravate the situation and can create dangerous conditions. Conditions may moderate significantly when the tide turns.

Details of tidal ranges, streams and races will be found in the various local nautical almanacs.

Approach and landfall

Approaching the European coastline there is always the chance of strong onshore winds and poor visibility. If the yacht's position is uncertain the best action may be to heave-to and await an improvement before closing the coast, even with GPS.

The network of marine DF beacons is being discontinued. The few of those still operating have reduced ranges; some broadcast DGPS information. There are many aero DF beacons, but these are not positioned to be of much use to the mariner. Most fog sound signals

have also ceased. A landfall in thick weather without GPS positions confirmed by other means, based on DF information alone, should now only be attempted in a real emergency. In general, navigation aids are well maintained and can be relied upon.

The Scottish coast

Boats making direct for Scandinavia, and passing round the north of Scotland, should have no problems provided they are well clear of Rockall (57°37′N 13°41′W). The St Kilda Island group and the Flannan Islands, 40 miles and 20 miles off the west coast of the Outer Hebrides, should be well clear to starboard, but Sula Sgeir (59°06′N 6°11′W) and North Rona (59°08′N 5°50′W) could be close to the route and are hazards to be avoided in thick weather. Both are now lit.

The passage through the Pentland Firth, between the north Scottish coast and the Orkney islands, should not be attempted in strong winds or poor visibility. Shelter can be sought in the lee of Lewis by passing round the Butt of Lewis, and Stornoway on the east side is an official entry port with good facilities.

If the prevailing or forecast conditions make it inadvisable to approach the mainland coast, then seek shelter on the east coast of the Outer Hebrides. Under no circumstances should the Sounds of Harris or Barra be attempted by a stranger in other than ideal conditions. If approaching the southern end of the islands, pass at least 3 miles clear of Barra Head to avoid the strong tidal stream and heavy overfalls. The best haven in the south is Castlebay, Barra. When anchoring in Scottish waters, beware of kelp. A heavy anchor should be used – see page 15.

The Irish coast

A landfall on the south Irish coast is generally straightforward. If making for Crosshaven in Cork Harbour under deteriorating conditions, shelter can be found at several places on the south and south-west coasts. North of Mizen Head, identifying the coast by eye can be difficult. If approaching Castletown in Bear Haven on the north side of Bantry Bay, ensure that the correct bay is being entered. South of Mizen Head, Crookhaven is safe in almost any weather and anchorage can also be found at Baltimore. The Old Head of Kinsale gives a lee to the entrance to Kinsale Harbour where there is an anchorage and marinas.

The English coast

If making for Falmouth or Plymouth, the Bishop Rock lighthouse marking the south-western extremity of the Scilly Isles is the traditional first landfall in good visibility. There can be strong tidal streams off the Bishop Rock, and overfalls on the Pol Bank, 3 miles to the south-west. There may also be strong streams off Lizard Point and heavy overfalls extending to the south for 3 miles or

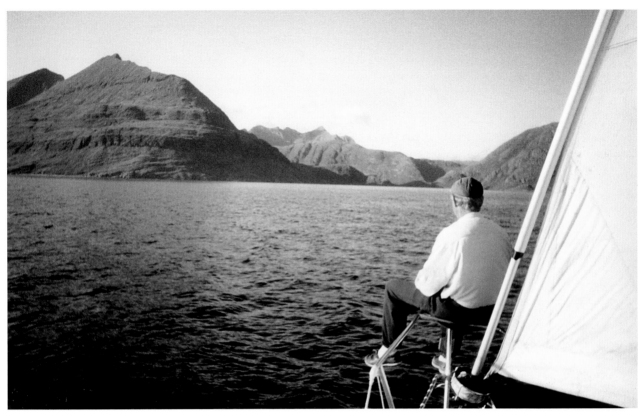

The west coast of Scotland in good weather is a wonderful cruising ground. Ayesha *approaches the Cuillins in Skye.
Photo Ashley Crawford.*

more. Give these points a wide berth, and in strong south-westerlies make no attempt to close the coast until well round the Lizard, when a course for Falmouth can be shaped northwards in the lee of the land.

There is often considerable shipping in the vicinity of the Lizard, though there is no longer a formal separation zone off the headland. In addition to traffic up and down the English Channel, vessels may also be altering course for Falmouth or Plymouth. The whole situation can be very confusing, especially at night, with the addition of brilliantly lit fishing vessels, often working in fleets and occasionally in pairs. In heavy or thick weather it is safer to keep well clear to the south until able to turn north towards Falmouth and cross the traffic at right angles.

The English Channel

The English Channel has one of the world's highest concentrations of ship traffic, and it is essential to maintain a good lookout and to proceed with great caution if visibility is poor. Most of the traffic is concentrated on two main routes, one on the northern side running from the Scilly Isles and Land's End towards the Dover Strait, and the other on the southern side, rounding Ushant and the Casquets before again heading east to the Dover Strait. Each of these corridors carries two-way traffic. There are also ferries sailing between England and France, and coastal trading vessels, fishing boats and yachts continually on the move. If at any time after entering the English Channel weather conditions or bad visibility make it

advisable to seek shelter, it will generally be found safer to close the English coast rather than the French.

The French coast

The north-west coast of France (the Brittany peninsula) is a particularly dangerous coast to approach in thick or heavy weather because of the many offlying rocks, strong tidal streams and, particularly during summer, the likelihood of encountering fog. There is heavy shipping in the separation lanes off Ushant, a turning point where ships often alter course. The Traffic Separation Scheme is 35–40 miles wide and lies to the north-west of Ushant. It is important to study an up-to-date chart before approaching this area.

The many dangers are well marked but it is essential to have adequate visibility, a suitable chart, an awareness of the tidal streams, and a reliable and accurate position before closing this coast. If the weather is thick and the marks cannot be identified with certainty, it is far safer to stand well off the land, clear of the strongest tidal streams and shipping lanes, and either await fairer weather or proceed elsewhere.

If making for Cherbourg or further east it is perfectly feasible to proceed up the English Channel in heavy weather if the wind is fair. However, conditions may be uncomfortable as Channel seas tend to be short and steep, particularly when there is a strong tidal stream running against the wind. The streams increase in strength as the Channel narrows towards the Cherbourg peninsula and they can have a marked effect on both

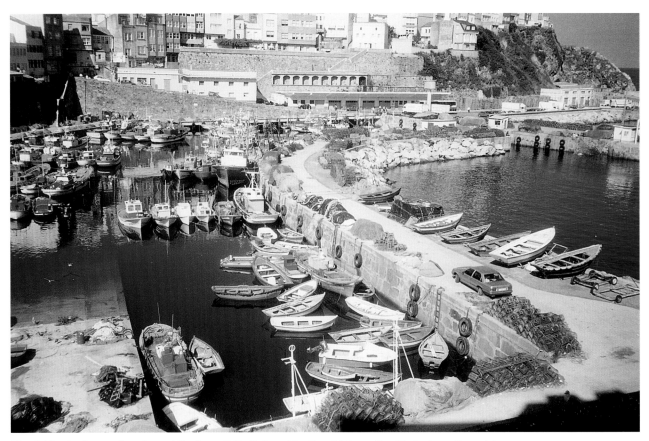

The fishing harbours of north-west Spain are full of interest for the visiting sailor. Photo Anne Hammick.

progress and sea state. There is a Traffic Separation Scheme in mid Channel to the N of the Channel Islands and the Casquets.

The Spanish and Portuguese coasts

The coast of Iberia is in some ways safer than that of northern Europe, with relatively few outlying rocks or tidal races. However, this is balanced by heavy shipping and frequent poor visibility, both prevalent along a narrow band relatively close inshore. Sudden northerly gales are another feature of the area. It may be best to keep well offshore until on the approximate latitude of your landfall, before crossing the shipping lanes and approaching the coast at right angles. There is much commercial fishing, often by large sea-going trawlers that may travel at speed to and from the fishing grounds, and are not always known for the efficiency of their lookout.

Formalities

Both customs and immigration regulations and the formality with which they are applied varies from country to country within Europe. Throughout the United Kingdom, France and Portugal the paperwork is taken seriously on both arrival and departure. In Spain the attitude is usually more relaxed. Generally speaking, European officials treat sailors very fairly, a situation that will only be maintained so long as the attitude is mutual.

All those ports listed in Part III are official entry/exit ports. Traditionally, once within the territorial waters of any country the Q flag had to be flown and clearance obtained as soon as possible, but nowadays most authorities will accept that, in stress of weather, a vessel may have to shelter in the nearest available haven before moving to an official port of entry. In some places, where smuggling or gun-running are not unknown, a yacht entering a remote harbour or anchorage may be treated with suspicion – to allay these fears, always contact the authorities, even if only the local police, by radio, telephone or in person.

Changes within the structure of the EU have made the situation more complex. In theory, there is complete freedom of movement of goods and people between the member states of the Union, but both the United Kingdom and the Irish Republic have exemptions to retain immigration controls. Some officials take the view that the freedom of movement applies only to the goods and nationals of EU countries, others take the more liberal view that once cleared into any EU country, you are cleared into the Union as a whole. There is little consistency between the interpretation of the rules by different states, and sometimes even by different officials within states. One certainty, however, is that full clearance procedures must be completed at the first EU port visited. After this, non-EU-flagged yachts, or those with non-EU citizens aboard, are advised to arrive in each EU country at a reasonable-sized port, to fly a Q flag, and to immediately enquire what formalities, if any, should be completed. Neither the Channel Islands,

Gibraltar nor the Canaries are part of the EU and full formalities must be completed when departing for, or returning from, them.

There is a universal ban on the import of hard drugs, and many countries look carefully at prescribed medicines, which are best accompanied by a letter from the prescribing doctor. Import of fresh meat is forbidden in some European countries, as are growing plants and some fresh vegetables. All countries place restrictions on the import of alcohol and tobacco for personal use. All firearms, including flare guns, must be declared and failure to do so will incur very heavy penalties, particularly in the United Kingdom.

There are very strict regulations in the United Kingdom and Irish Republic regarding bringing animals of any kind into the country, and if planning to do so it is *essential* to contact the authorities at the intended port of arrival well in advance. The anti-rabies laws are taken very seriously indeed and any breach will inevitably lead to the destruction of the animal and a heavy fine for the owner. In recent years, though, there has been some relaxation in the United Kingdom of the quarantine requirements for dogs with embedded microchips.

Facilities

Depending on where the boat is lying, facilities may be anything from top class to non-existent. All European harbours described in Part III have good facilities, and full details for each harbour will be found in that section of this book.

Sailing directions and yachtsmen's guides

In addition to the publications mentioned in Part I, there are many yachtsmen's guides for the Atlantic coast of Europe and outlying islands. These, together with a selection of almanacs, tide tables and tidal stream atlases, are listed in Appendix B.

Relevant ports covered in Part III

1	Cork Harbour/Crosshaven, Ireland	page 120
2	Falmouth, England	page 124
3	Plymouth, England	page 127
4	Brest, France	page 131
5	La Coruña, Spain	page 133
6	Bayona, Spain	page 136
7	Leixões, Portugal	page 139
8	Lisbon, Portugal	page 142
9	Lagos, Portugal	page 146
10	Gibraltar	page 148

12 Southwards in the Eastern Atlantic

The trend of the prevailing wind and current systems of the eastern Atlantic is southwards, in tune with the wishes of most European sailors. Thus, most cruising yachts leaving Europe head in this direction, by a variety of routes. There is a wide choice of possible departure and landfall points, and while those chosen are both typical and popular, there should be little difficulty in interpolating for other passages.

Passage	Approx distance
Falmouth to Madeira via the coast of Iberia	1,300 miles
Falmouth to Madeira direct	1,250 miles
Falmouth to the Azores	1,200 miles
Azores to Madeira	500 miles
Madeira to the Canaries	240 miles
Canaries to the Cape Verde Islands	850 miles

Passage planning charts

Latitudes	Admiralty	US
60°20′N–48°20′N	4102 (1:3,500,000)	102 (1:3,500,000)
50°30′N–34°40′N	4103 (1:3,500,000)	103 (1:3,500,000)
38°50′N–8°20′N	4104 (1:3,500,000)	104 (1:3,500,000)

In addition to the small-scale charts listed above, many large-scale charts are published by the Portuguese and Spanish hydrographic offices as well as the British Admiralty and the US Defense Mapping Agency.

Falmouth to Madeira via the coasts of Spain and Portugal

This is one of the pleasantest ways to start an Atlantic circuit cruise. It avoids overlong passages in the initial stages, takes in an attractive and interesting cruising area, and meshes perfectly with the seasonal weather patterns.

A yacht intending to depart from British shores before mid-August has time in hand to wait for a good forecast to cross the Bay of Biscay and may spend an enjoyable month or six weeks cruising in Spain. Landfall can be made anywhere along the north coast where there are many unspoilt ports and stunning scenery. The rias in the north-west corner are a cruising area in their own right and, south of Bayona, ports are spaced at intervals of 50 miles or less down the Portuguese coast. Allowing a couple of weeks for the latter and a further week or ten days on passage to Madeira or the Canaries, the yacht will arrive there around the end of October and allow another month to explore the area and get organised for the Atlantic passage. This is so near to the ideal that it is well worth aiming for if at all possible.

If time is limited, two choices are open. The better one is to sail south in the summer and leave the yacht in some safe port for collection later in the year. Lagos or Vilamoura are the most obvious, while further east in Spain many new marinas have opened in the last few years. Gibraltar, although further from the route to the Canaries or Madeira, offers advantages to English speakers. There is little chance of finding room to leave a yacht in Funchal or Porto Santo in Madeira. There are several harbours in the Canaries where an unattended yacht might be left – see Part III or consult *Atlantic Islands*. Early booking will be essential and charges are likely to be high.

The alternative is to leave the English Channel late in the year and run the gauntlet of the autumn weather. This is a poor second choice as the incidence of gales in Biscay increases from an average of one day a month in August to nine in November. The detailed long-range forecast will dictate departure timing, and consideration should be given to sailing from Falmouth to south-west Ireland to await suitable conditions. This increases the amount of sea room in the Bay if caught out. Leaving Falmouth after the end of September should only be considered by a strongly crewed larger yacht, able to make a fast passage between the depressions.

When crossing the Bay of Biscay, fishing vessels are likely to be met and when approaching the northern coast of Spain there may be some shipping heading to and from such ports as Bordeaux and Brest. If the passage includes a diversion into Gibraltar, a yacht returning westwards will encounter a high concentration of traffic in the Strait. This fans out as soon as the narrowest part is passed, with the merchant shipping dividing into three main streams. One goes westward to Cape St Vincent, one coastwise to the south, and one in the general direction of Madeira and the Canaries. There will, in addition, be large numbers of fishing craft. In 24 hours most of this will be left behind, and little more will then be seen until the main north/south Atlantic shipping lane is crossed, west of the longitude of Cape St Vincent.

The 500-mile passage from the Portuguese coast towards Madeira is usually a pleasant one, often carrying the north-easterly winds to one's destination. The first island to be seen will probably be Porto Santo, and if planning to visit in normal conditions it will be best to do so at this stage and avoid the beat back from Madeira.

Falmouth to Madeira direct

Although the direct course from the English Channel to Madeira passes close to the Spanish coast, if the passage is to be made direct it will be worth making enough westing to remain a safe distance off this potential lee shore. The greatest concentrations of traffic will also be found near the coast, an area known for its poor visibility. By staying 50–100 miles offshore, you should escape both these problems while still receiving the full benefits of the northerly Portuguese Trades and Portuguese Current.

Falmouth to the Azores

This passage might be the first stage of a transatlantic voyage by the middle latitudes, a dog-leg on the way down to Madeira or the Canaries and the trade wind

passage, or the outward part of a return cruise from England to the Azores. Timing will probably depend largely on the purpose of the voyage, but any period between late May and early August would be suitable.

Unless you particularly want to visit Spain or Portugal en route, in which case headwinds will probably have to be faced on the westward passage to the Azores, it is best to keep as near the rhumb line as conditions permit. The current sets south-east and prevailing winds are likely to be between south-west and north-west. The Azores high will probably be encountered en route, and in the early summer may extend as a ridge a considerable distance to the north-east of the islands. As much fuel as possible should be carried.

Azores to Madeira

A pleasant passage can be anticipated, with winds between north-west and north-east backed by a favourable current. There is generally good visibility and relatively little shipping. Though there may be a temptation to linger in the Azores, it would be wise to leave before the middle of September.

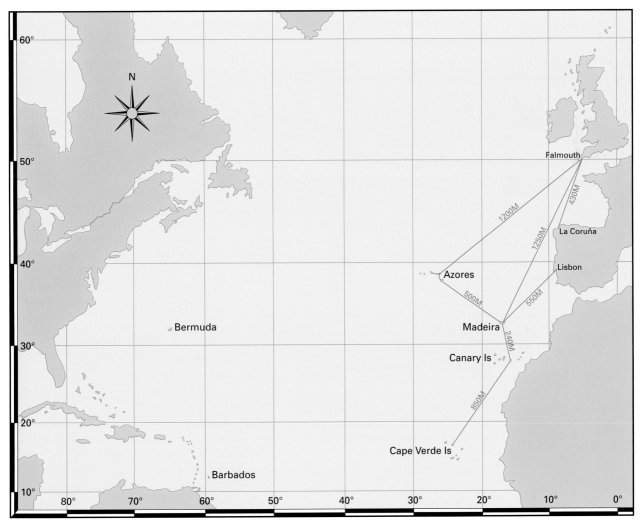

Plan 5 *Typical routes in the eastern Atlantic.*

Near Bayona in north-west Spain lie the Islas Cies, with fine sandy beaches providing for the Caribbean-bound sailor a foretaste of the pleasures to come. Photo Alfredo Lagos.

Madeira to the Canaries

This passage may be made at any time of the year, but the chances of increased wind and decreased visibility will be greater from November onwards. The south-going current is relatively constant. If intending to cruise the Canary Islands it makes good sense to head for the eastern end of the group; if planning only a brief stopover before the Atlantic passage, keep further west. The passage from Funchal to Santa Cruz de Las Palmas lies close to the Ilhas Selvagens or Salvage Islands (see Chapter 13), known for the unreliability of their lights, and unless conditions are perfect, it would be wise to keep well off.

Canaries to the Cape Verde Islands

It is debatable whether this passage should not be considered as part of the trade wind route, since many yachts pass near the Cape Verde Islands after leaving

the Canaries whether they stop or not. For European yachts it may also be their first passage made mainly under downwind rig.

Both current and winds are likely to be favourable, with the latter becoming more reliable as you progress south. However, as the wind picks up, so visibility will decrease. This is the *harmattan*, a dust-laden wind from West Africa, which often reduces visibility to a few miles or less. Even though the sky may be clear and the horizon apparently sharp, the latter may actually be much closer than it appears. Until the advent of satellite-based surveys, the positions of the islands were incorrectly charted by as much as 3 miles. Even the latest charts of this area may be significantly in error and a good lookout is even more important than usual.

13 The Madeiran, Canary and Cape Verdean Archipelagos

Regional weather

Although the Madeiran, Canary and Cape Verdean archipelagos cover a stretch of ocean more than 1,000 miles from north to south, prevailing weather conditions are much less varied than would be the case further north. All lie in the path of the north-east trades, the main difference being that whereas Madeira and the Canaries may be influenced by the southern edge of winter depressions, in the latitude of the Cape Verde Islands the north-east trades hold almost total sway, with the only real variation being in wind strength. Within the Canary Islands a yacht may encounter sudden and gusty increases in wind, typically around the south-west and south-east coasts of the higher islands. These 'acceleration zones' can be quite distinct and may produce an increase from less than 5 knots to 25 knots or more within a few hundred metres. Mention has already been made of the *harmattan* wind, which blows off the African continent south of about 20°N and can carry dust up to 500 miles offshore – or occasionally right across the Atlantic Ocean to the Caribbean. This is not so much a distinct wind as the visual result of any breeze blowing at 20 knots or more over a period of several days, and can thus be anticipated with reasonable accuracy. Whether or not visibility appears to be bad, if the wind is above 20 knots *harmattan* conditions should be suspected – clear skies and an apparently firm horizon, out of which islands or other vessels may materialise when only a few miles distant.

Currents

Madeira and the Canary Islands lie squarely in the path of the south-west-setting Canary Current, which swings somewhat further westward by the latitude of the Cape Verde Islands. In summer the influence of the Equatorial Counter Current may set up south- or south-east-setting eddies between 10°N and 15°N, but by November or December these have retreated south of 10°N. As in all areas, an ocean current averaging 1 knot or less may, when constricted between islands, run at considerably greater speeds.

Tides and tidal streams

Tidal rise and fall in the area is relatively slight, the mean spring range decreasing from 2.2m at Porto Santo to 0.8m in the Cape Verde Islands. Even so, tidal streams in the Cape Verdes can run strongly between the islands, and may reach over 3 knots when combined with the current.

Approach and landfall

Landfall will most often be made from northwards and should present no particular hazards. With the exception of one or two of the Cape Verdes, all the islands are relatively high, some excessively so, and Tenerife in particular may sometimes be seen from 50 or 60 miles away. The vast majority of yachts making the trade wind passage leave from either Madeira, one of the Canary Islands or the Cape Verdes, and the passages between the groups are covered in the previous chapter. Each area has its advantages and disadvantages, and all offer some interesting cruising in their own right.

The Madeira group

This group comprises Madeira Grande, Porto Santo lying some 30 miles to the north-east, the two Ilhas

Plan 6 *Prevailing winds and currents of the eastern Atlantic, Madeira to Cape Verdes for November. Winds are coloured pink, currents in dark blue. Based on information from the* Atlantic Pilot Atlas.

Desertas, and the isolated and rocky Ilhas Selvagens just over 150 miles south on the course between Funchal and the western Canaries. Only Madeira and Porto Santo are regularly visited by yachts, though both the other groups have fair-weather anchorages.

First sight of the Madeiras is likely to be of the conical peak of Porto Santo. This is a most satisfying landfall, rising as it does in solitary grandeur, visible in daylight at a distance of 40 miles or more. The islands are well lit.

If planning a stop at Porto Santo it is wise to do so first to save beating back. It is an official port of entry. There is a large harbour with room for several dozen yachts to anchor, visitors' moorings (these may be unreliable and should be used with care) and a small marina. Provided the wind stays in the north-east, an excellent anchorage can be found off the sandy beach between the harbour and the old town pier. (Anchoring west of the pier is now prohibited.) Porto Santo is well worth a visit, and if the marina at Funchal is full – often the case in October and November – then it is preferable to remain at Porto Santo than to use the exposed and uncomfortable anchorage at Funchal.

To most yachtsmen Madeira effectively means Funchal (see page 151), as although there are a number of other possible anchorages none offer remotely comparable facilities. The harbour is well lit and the town quite unmistakable, making it possible to enter at any hour of day or night. It is, however, a busy harbour, and in addition to the normal commercial traffic and fishing craft there are often cruise ships on the move.

Many yachts spend a month or more in Funchal, either rafted alongside in the small marina or anchored off (note the caution on page 152), while their crews explore the island. It is arguably the loveliest of any visited on the standard Atlantic circuit and, once outside the tourist area round Funchal, is remarkably unspoilt. Local buses provide a cheap and entertaining way to travel.

Funchal has several large supermarkets and an impressive fruit and vegetable market, with a fish market next door. It is a reasonable place to stock up for the transatlantic passage, but prices in the Canary Islands may be cheaper on many items, and the selection better. The international airport on the south-east coast makes crew changes simple and, if conditions are settled, it may be easiest to anchor off the nearby town of Machico and save on taxi fares.

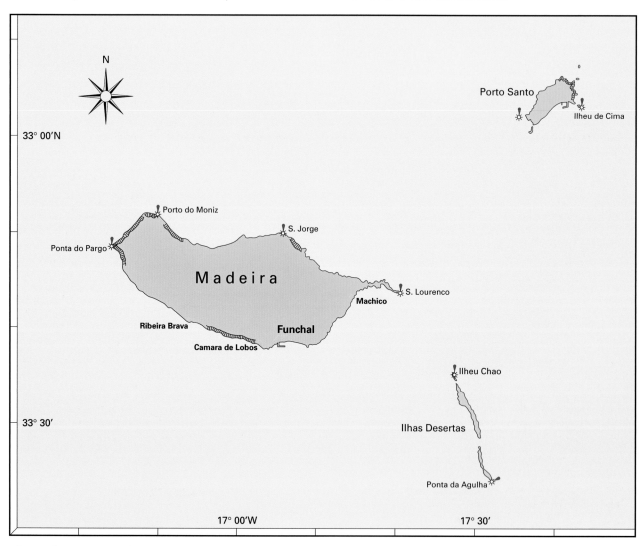

Plan 7 *The Madeiran archipelago.*

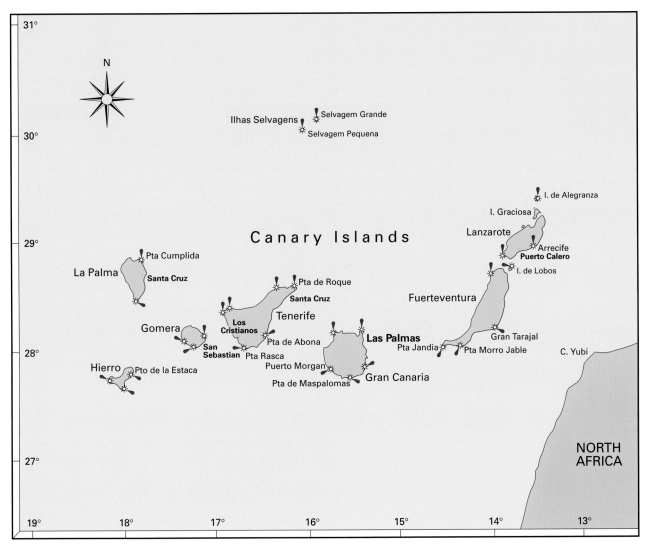

Plan 8 *The Canary Islands.*

The Canary Islands

The Canaries have become popular with yachtsmen over recent years. As well as attracting those en route to the Caribbean the islands have developed as a cruising ground in their own right, with increasing numbers of yachts based locally, together with a rapidly growing charter fleet. Although there are now many more yacht harbours and marinas than previously, some popular small ports have closed to visitors. Pressure on facilities is intense, especially in the autumn. At that time the cruising sailor may have difficulty in finding a secure berth or anchorage, particularly in the more popular areas.

Approaching from the north, the 3,717m (12,195ft) volcanic peak of Tenerife will be seen from a great distance in clear weather, often complete with a scattering of snow despite being less than 300 miles from the tropics. Those yachts only planning to pause briefly in the Canaries should make for the western end of the archipelago; for those intending to cruise the islands, it is logical to make a landfall further east, either at Lanzarote or the small island of Graciosa which lies off its north-eastern tip.

The harbours detailed in Part III are good places to stock up for an Atlantic crossing, but are by no means the only ones. Excellent-quality fruit and vegetables are available almost everywhere, and even smaller towns generally have at least one supermarket.

The annual ARC rally currently leaves from Las Palmas, Gran Canaria, where there is a large marina, good anchorage and excellent facilities, but becomes very crowded in November. Whether the mushrooming development of tourist resorts is felt to be a plus or a minus, one by-product is that air communications are particularly good in terms of both frequency and value.

The Canaries, technically a military province of Spain, are not part of the EU and time limitations that may be placed on non-EU, yachts remaining in the Union should not apply. The islands are a duty-free zone and therefore a particularly good place to embark beer, wine or spirits.

The Cape Verdean archipelago

Due to poor facilities and lack of available information, the Cape Verde Islands were visited by few cruising yachts until the early 1990s. However, this has changed,

The popular port anchorage at Baía do Tarrafal, Ilha de Santiago, in the Cape Verdes, seen on one of the few cloudy days of the year. Photo Anne Hammick.

and now more yachts enjoy the practical advantage of shortening the transatlantic passage by nearly a third – the distance to Barbados is under 2,000 miles, compared with 2,700 miles from the Canaries, and as the islands are well within the trade wind belt a direct course can usually be steered on leaving them.

Entry into the group is restricted to three ports – Baía de Palmeira on Ilha do Sal, Porto Grande/Mindelo on São Vicente, and Porto da Praia on Ilha de Santiago – and this regulation must be followed or otherwise you run the risk of substantial fines. Ilha do Sal is the most windward of the islands and has the international airport; it would be the one to choose if entry is to be followed by a cruise around the islands. São Vincente is easily identified, lies at the westen end of the group, has a secure anchorage and some shopping and other facilities; it would be the one to choose if visiting the group to top up before the crossing.

Throughout the Cape Verdes, maintenance of navigation aids is poor and even the major lights cannot be relied upon. Information about changes in light characteristics takes a very long time to reach the Hydrographic Offices of other countries. Do not trust even the most recent charts to be entirely accurate.

The chief appeal of the Cape Verdes lies in the fact that they are largely undeveloped, and nearer in spirit to Africa (from which much of the population originally came) than to Portugal, the colonial power before independence in 1975. They are also very poor, and for this reason precautions should be taken against petty theft. Tourism is still a fairly new concept, but there have been

recent efforts to expand this and cruise ships call at São Vincente. The local people are always friendly – if sometimes overly curious.

Storing facilities are not good and all food except fresh fish is expensive, making it wise to do the bulk of stocking up for the transatlantic passage in Madeira or the Canaries. Good drinking water may also be hard to come by in the dry, northern islands. The southern chain is generally wetter, and both water and fresh stores may be more readily available.

Few visitors remain indifferent to the Cape Verdes. Most are fascinated; a few cannot reconcile themselves to the poverty, dirt and lack of facilities. In comparison, the Caribbean islands will seem like the centre of civilisation. Try to visit before the situation changes.

Formalities

Customs and immigration formalities differ between the groups. The Madeiran group, being Portuguese, takes paperwork seriously and it is necessary to clear in and out of each island – sometimes each anchorage. In theory, the advent of the EU should mean fewer formalities for yachts entering Madeira from EU countries, but the theory may not always match the practice.

The Canaries are not part of the EU, but usually the relaxed Spanish attitude is taken and formalities are at a minimum. It is wise to obtain some sort of documentary evidence of leaving to present to the customs on

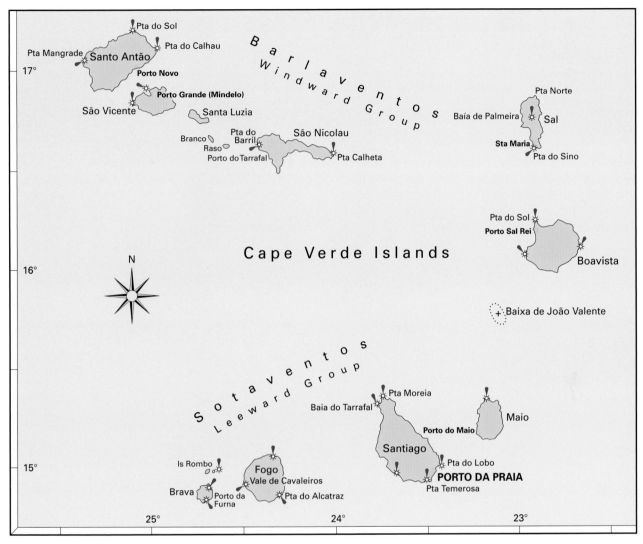

Plan 9 *The Cape Verdean Archipelago. Based on a plan in* Atlantic Islands.

arrival in the Caribbean – a marina receipt or similar document will normally be sufficient to establish that the yacht has recently crossed from Europe.

The Cape Verdean authorities take customs (and particularly immigration) seriously and have recently imposed restrictions on ports of entry, hefty entry payments and fines for any transgressions, which hardly match the intention of promoting tourism. It would be worthwhile contacting the Cape Verdean embassy beforehand if intending to visit, to find out the latest policy.

For full details, see Part III, port information.

Sailing directions and yachtsmen's guides

In addition to the official publications mentioned in Part I, one yachtsmen's guide covers the entire area while another two describe individual island groups. See Appendices A and B, pages 227 and 229, for publishers' details.

Relevant ports in Part III

<table>
<tr><td>11</td><td>Funchal, Madeira</td><td>page 151</td></tr>
<tr><td>12</td><td>Harbours in the Canaries</td><td>page 154</td></tr>
<tr><td>13</td><td>Porto Grande (Mindelo),
São Vicente, Cape Verdes</td><td>page 161</td></tr>
</table>

14 | The Trade Wind Crossing

While for European yachts the trade wind Atlantic voyage generally receives the bulk of the anticipation and planning, it is often the most trouble-free passage of the entire circuit. This crossing has not been nicknamed the 'milk run' for nothing. There are a number of possible routes in terms of departure, arrival and distance, but all run pretty well parallel and are governed by the same prevailing conditions. For that reason, they will be taken together rather than separately.

Passage	Approx distance
Madeira to Antigua	2,900 miles
Canaries to Barbados	2,700 miles
Cape Verdes to Barbados	1,900 miles

Passage planning charts

Latitudes	Admiralty	US
Southern North Atlantic	4102 (1:10,000,000)	102 (1:6,331,100)

It is important to remember that magnetic variation alters as you cross the Atlantic, from approximately 7°30′W in Madeira and the Canaries to 13°W in the vicinity of the Cape Verdes, 18° in the middle, and around 14° 30′ in the Caribbean islands. All these values are changing gradually, not necessarily at the same speed. The chart will therefore show nothing but the true compass rose, plus isogonic lines linking the places that have the same amount of variation, and details of annual change. It is worth calculating and applying these accurately, as even a few degrees of error can produce a sizeable divergence over several days' run.

Plan 10 *Typical trade wind routes.*

Timing

The majority of yachts make the trade wind crossing in November or December to give the maximum time in the Caribbean. Before mid-November hurricanes are possible and the winds are likely to be unreliable. However, there is no good reason why this passage should not be made in January, February or even later, and some of the fastest crossing times have been recorded at this time of year. In general, the later the crossing, the stronger the winds are likely to be.

The trade wind belt

Whichever departure point is chosen, the objective is to get well into the belt of the established north-east trades as soon as possible. The northern limit of this belt varies with the seasons – from about 30°N in summer to 25°N in winter – and also from year to year. For those without large reserves of fuel it is usually a mistake to head west too soon and to risk getting caught in the 'light 'n' variables' that predominate towards the centre of the Atlantic's massive high pressure system. Even when established, the trade wind, contrary to popular belief, does not always blow from the same quarter or at the same strength. Sometimes it does not blow at all, and the crew who do not experience a day or two of mid-ocean calm are fortunate. It is, however, less fickle than winds in many other parts of the world. Its strength rarely exceeds force 6 (25 knots) and averages at nearer force 4 (15 knots).

Bound for the Caribbean, Wrestler *runs fast under double-head-sail rig in the north-east trades. Photo Anne Hammick.*

As mentioned, the northern limit of the trade wind belt varies each year. On occasions the trades become established almost as far north as the Canaries, and yachts staying near the direct route to the Caribbean make fast passages. A position of 25°N 25°W is often quoted as being the point to make for, and in some years this is good advice – in other years it may be necessary to go much further south to find the trades. A good general rule is to head south-south-west on leaving the Canaries, aiming to pass some 150–200 miles north-west of the Cape Verde Islands, only turning west when the trades have definitely been encountered and the

Plan 11 *Prevailing winds and currents of the southern north Atlantic for December. Winds are coloured pink, currents in dark blue. Based on information from the* Atlantic Pilot Atlas.

A safe arrival in the Caribbean. Juliet approaches St Lucia from the south. Photo Margaret Honey.

yacht is at least 200 miles south of their northern limit. Once certain that you are well within the trade wind belt, a course can be shaped for the chosen landfall.

When the trades are fully established the sky is usually speckled with small clouds, like puffs of steam from an old-fashioned railway engine. Any large mass of cloud, lower and darker than the rest and coming up astern, is likely to denote a squall. At best, this may give the ship a welcome burst of speed; at worst, it might make it necessary to shorten sail. Sometimes these squalls bring a sharp downpour of rain, occasionally with thunder and lightning, though the worst of these thunderstorms seems to take place to the north of the trade wind route, and one is often a spectator (and thankfully only that) at an impressive but reassuringly distant display.

Ocean currents and swell

The Canary Current, as it approaches the Cape Verde Islands, changes its course and changes its name. It turns increasingly westward and becomes known as the North Equatorial Current. Both movement and reliability tend to increase throughout the winter season, though speed at any given point cannot be predicted.

Even an apparently calm ocean is seldom totally without swell, which may suddenly increase for no apparent reason. Usually it arises from a storm many thousands of miles away and is in itself harmless, though if running down from the north Atlantic, as commonly happens, may catch a yacht under running sails on the beam, causing her to roll horrendously. When sizeable swells and locally created seas oppose each other, troublesome crests will be created, some of which may come aboard.

If skirting the windward side of an island at the end of a transatlantic passage, making generous allowance for current and leeway takes on particular importance. More than one yacht has driven ashore because forces that had contributed to forward progress during the downwind passage, and therefore went largely unnoticed, were ignored on altering course onto the wind.

Caribbean approach and landfall

The traditional island on which to make landfall after a trade wind crossing is Barbados, not least because it lies more than 80 miles to windward of the rest of the archipelago, and to call later would involve a long and tedious beat into the trade wind. The island is well worth a visit, with good shopping and other facilities. Details of the capital, Bridgetown, will be found in Part III.

Other popular islands on which to make landfall are Antigua, Martinique, St Lucia and Grenada. Boats coming from the south Atlantic usually opt for Grenada or Trinidad. Suitable ports of entry on each of these islands are included in Part III.

Although few Caribbean islands are well lit in terms of navigational aids, considerable ambient light is produced by airports, hotels, domestic and street lighting. This is particularly true of Barbados, Martinique and Antigua, though all three are fringed by windward reefs, which could prove hazardous in poor visibility. Usually the weather is clear, and heavy rain – which is the only thing likely to cut down visibility – will normally be in the form of short-lived squalls, which soon move away.

Many people, years after returning from a one-year Atlantic circuit, remember the trade wind crossing as the high point of the entire cruise. For most, it will be the longest ocean passage they ever make. It is as well that it is also usually one of the most enjoyable.

15

The Caribbean Island Chain (Windward and Leeward Islands)

For many Europeans, the chance to spend time cruising the Caribbean islands provides the main incentive for an Atlantic crossing. Situated as they are in the trade wind zone and within the tropics, their waters afford some of the world's best sailing conditions.

were brought over from Africa in the seventeenth and eighteenth centuries to work in the sugar plantations.

Nearly all the islands have small museums, but one in St John's, Antigua, is particularly notable for its comprehensive collection of pre-Columbian artefacts.

History

Although the (misnamed) West Indies are often thought of as having been discovered by Columbus, recent archaeological research has proved the existence of much earlier human occupation. The Caribs, who were in possession of much of the Caribbean before the Europeans took over, represented the second or third wave of Indian emigration from South America. In most of the islands, they were wiped out within a few hundred years, but some still live in a reserved territory on the windward side of Dominica. The vast majority of the local people today are descended from the slaves who

Trade winds

Although trade winds dominate Caribbean weather, there are subtle but important variations throughout the cruising season. From December until early April the winds are remarkably constant in both strength and direction, averaging about 15–20 knots out of the east or north-east. However, force may increase dramatically in sudden squalls (usually, though not invariably, signalled by an advancing line of purple-grey clouds), or where the trade wind funnels down valleys or around the ends of islands. From time to time, the entire Caribbean experiences a winter with lighter winds than

Plan 12 *Prevailing winds in the Caribbean islands for January. Based on information from the* Atlantic Pilot Atlas.

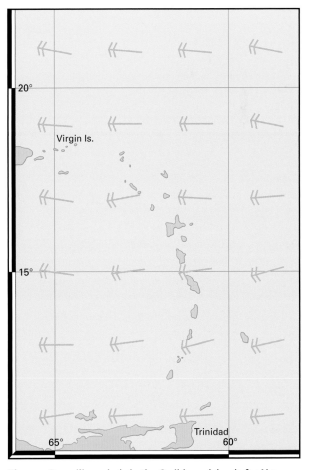

Plan 13 *Prevailing winds in the Caribbean islands for May. Based on information from the* Atlantic Pilot Atlas.

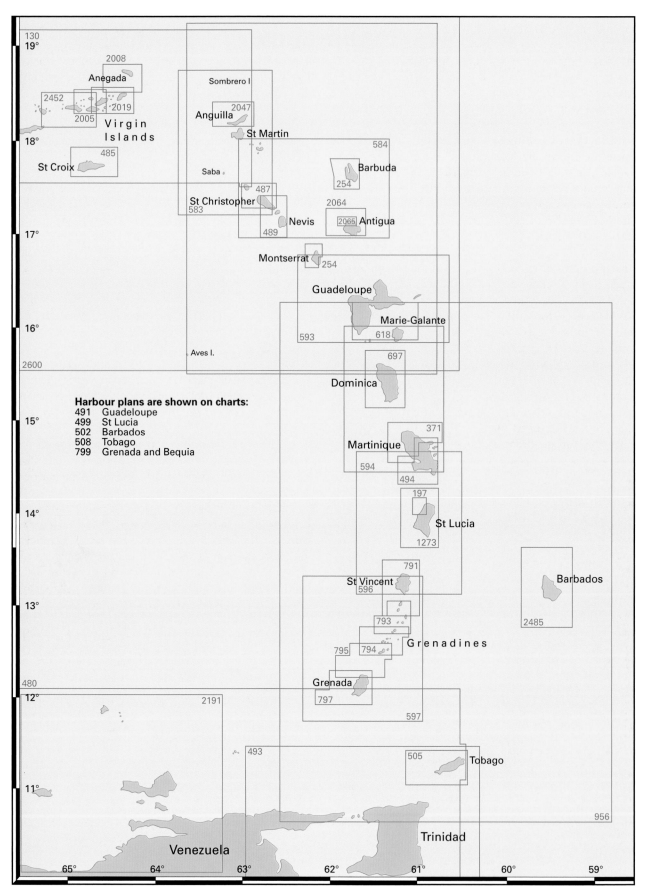

Plan 14 *British Admiralty charts for the eastern Caribbean. Based on Admiralty publication NP 131.*

normal. There is a local tradition that winds become stronger in late December and early January, the so-called 'Christmas winds'. It may be necessary to adapt the itinerary to suit the prevailing conditions.

From mid-April to the beginning of the hurricane season in June or July (see Chapter 10) the winds become less consistent. Antigua Race Week, held at the end of April, is renowned for producing everything from flat calms to gusts resulting in knockdowns, quite often on consecutive days. By May the winds will be definitely lighter, particularly in the northern part of the area. As they moderate they also veer slightly, swinging from north-east through east to slightly south of east, a definite boon for yachts leaving the islands for the United States or Bermuda.

Even when the open water trades are blowing strongly, calms often lurk in the lee of the higher islands – effectively all those of any size between Grenada and Guadeloupe. To make progress under sail, one must either keep as close inshore as is safe – ideally within a few tens of metres of the land – or else pass at least 5 miles offshore. Neither of these methods is guaranteed to find the wind, though, and sometimes the route to windward of an island is the only way to achieve reasonable progress under sail.

Conversely, it is easy to ghost or motor towards the end of an island forgetting that once out of the lee, the flat water and gentle breeze may suddenly be replaced by very boisterous conditions with gusty winds and an ocean swell. This change can occur within a few boat lengths. During the day, the deteriorating conditions can usually be seen ahead, but at night they can be a hazard and it may be wise to reduce sail in anticipation while conditions are light.

Current and swell

The North Equatorial Current sets westward between the islands, often attaining a knot or more. Though tidal streams may increase or decrease the rate of flow, they are seldom strong enough to overcome it completely. It is easy to overlook this and find that you have been set a long way to leeward when sailing between the islands.

Navigation and pilotage

Except for Barbados, which lies to the east of the main archipelago, each island is within sight of its immediate neighbours and navigation can be mostly by eye if so minded. Navigation aids are few, their maintenance is often poor, and they cannot be relied upon. What buoyage there is throughout the islands follows the IALA B system (red right returning). There are some cardinal marks.

Night sailing is often hazardous due to the number of fish-pot floats to be found even well offshore, and often clustered particularly thickly in the approaches to many anchorages. These floats may be of glassfibre or plastic, white or coloured, or simply be stoppered bottles or chunks of expanded polystyrene. Others may be the old traditional bamboo floats, 2m (6–8ft) long, and sometimes waterlogged and floating a few inches below the surface. All of these are hazards when you are moving under power. Under sail they are less of a menace, but can still wrap themselves around an exposed rudder or freewheeling propeller. At night, small fishing boats seldom show navigation lights and may be completely unlit. Any lights that are displayed are unlikely to be in accordance with International Regulations!

Anchorages

To those used to ever-changing winds and strong reversing tidal streams, it may go against the grain to anchor in a position protected through only half the compass or less. However, due to the constancy of the trade winds, the islands afford a reliable lee on their western coasts and many of the traditional anchorages are quite open in this direction. The best afford shelter from both the wind and swell, but this is not always the case and

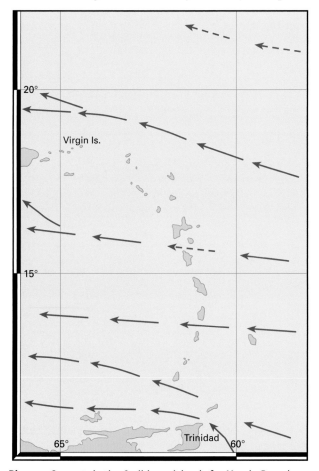

Plan 15 *Currents in the Caribbean islands for March. Based on information from the* Atlantic Pilot Atlas.

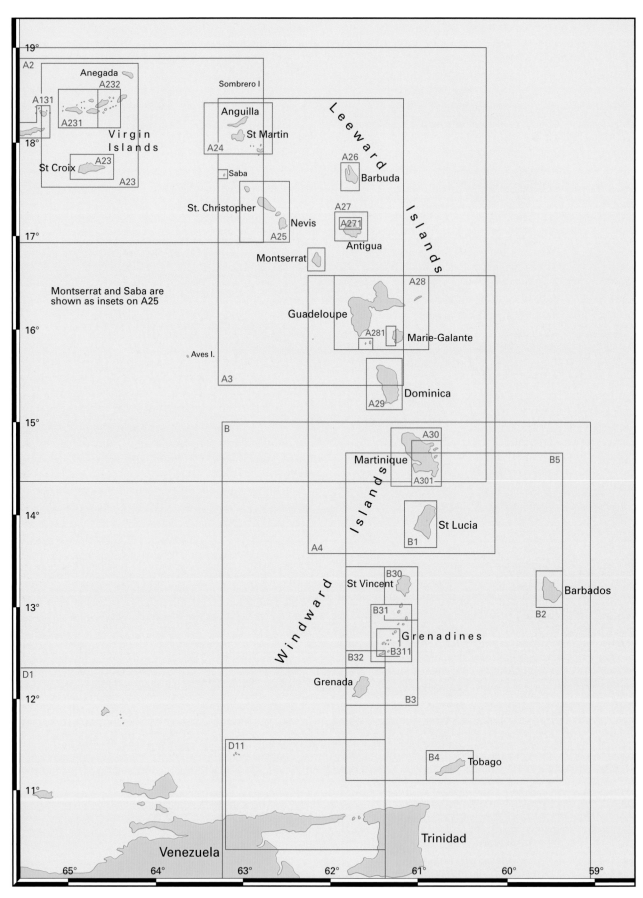

Plan 16 *Imray-Iolaire charts for the eastern Caribbean. Based on information from Imray Laurie Norie & Wilson.*

quite often a certain amount of rolling may have to be endured. This is particularly true of those anchorages chosen more because of shoreside convenience than actual shelter, such as Carlisle Bay, Barbados, and the anchorages off St Pierre, Martinique and Roseau, Dominica – all worth visiting for different reasons.

Formalities

On approaching land, allow time to brush up your knowledge of the entry procedure for the particular island to which you are going. All are different. Except for the French, Dutch and American islands, most have been granted their independence and nearly every island that was formerly a British possession is now a country in its own right, with its own national colours. For the visiting yacht, this means a lot of different courtesy flags as well as a lot of formalities.

Nearly all the islands take entry and clearance procedures seriously. The authorities will wish to see clearance papers from the last port of call, and failure to produce these may result in being turned away until they are produced – and will probably lead to a fine as well. In some islands there is only one port of entry, in others there are several. All the ports listed in Part III are official entry ports.

Procedures vary from island to island and sometimes from year to year. Local pilot books give specific details, but in general the following principles should be adhered to. Ensure that the correct courtesy ensign and the Q flag are being flown before arrival, together with the yacht's ensign. After anchoring or berthing, the skipper alone should go ashore and complete the formalities.

If arriving at night it may be possible to delay this until the following day, but in most islands it is preferable to arrive and depart during office hours. Arriving at other times may incur 'overtime' charges, even though the actual formalities are completed during office hours.

The skipper should take with him the clearance papers from the last port, the ship's papers and the passports of all on board, together with any necessary visas. There may be several authorities to visit (customs, immigration and perhaps the harbour authority) and numerous forms to complete, usually in duplicate or triplicate; taking a few sheets of carbon paper can speed the process. There will probably be some charges to pay, both on entering and clearing, so some cash in the appropriate currency should be carried, though US dollars are normally accepted. Fees are usually modest and it is unreasonable to expect officials in a small office to be able to deal with large-denomination banknotes. Firearms and ammunition must be declared and on most islands they will be impounded; they will have to be collected on departure from the port of entry, which is not always convenient. If any crew members are leaving the yacht during the visit, this should be stated on entry. There will almost certainly be some formalities to be completed before the authorities will accept that they have left, or will leave, the country legitimately and are not attempting to become unauthorised immigrants. Often valid airline tickets must be produced, and passports endorsed. Failure to comply with these regulations will cause considerable problems when the yacht comes to clear out.

Generally speaking, the authorities on the islands are fair and tolerant in their treatment of yachts. However, the officials, quite reasonably, expect to be taken seriously. It will be considered discourteous if the visitor presents himself at customs wearing clothing more

Sun, sand and crystal-clear water. Visions of such perfect Caribbean anchorages may be the first steps in the plans for an Atlantic crossing. Photo Anne Hammick.

appropriate for the beach than a government office, and officers may refuse to deal with him. Rudeness and incivility will lengthen the procedures, and impatience will certainly be counterproductive. Deliberate deceit or attempted bribery is likely to lead to arrest.

The sailor who deals with the officials in the islands in the same honest and fair manner that he would adopt towards the same officials in his own country is likely to encounter few problems. It is worth remembering that you are a visitor, and no country is obliged to admit you. Officials have considerable powers to make life difficult for sailors, so it is unwise to antagonise them.

Formalities in the US islands

Foreign yachts must clear into and out of the US Virgin Islands and Puerto Rico as they would in any other country. Views vary between officials as to whether it is necessary to complete formalities if travelling directly between them, and it is sensible to enquire before departure. In theory, once cleared into Puerto Rico (but not the USVI), you may sail directly to the mainland United States without clearing, but it would be sensible to clear out of Puerto Rico in case an unscheduled stop needs to be made en route. The USVI are considered a single group, and clearance is not necessary when travelling between islands.

Although access to the United States by airline is relatively formality free, all foreign visitors (except Canadians) arriving in the country *by yacht must be in possession of a valid visa. This also applies to Puerto Rico and the USVI.* Visas should be obtained from the US embassy in your own country, as in the Caribbean they can only be issued in Trinidad, Barbados and Nassau. It should be noted that even 'indefinite' visas now expire after ten years and must then be renewed. Arriving without a visa will lead to a fine.

Regulations for US-flagged yachts and nationals entering and leaving Puerto Rico and the USVI are currently under review. Enquiries should be made before leaving the mainland United States, or on arrival.

Currency

In most of the islands from Grenada to Antigua the Eastern Caribbean dollar (EC) is used, currently pegged to the US dollar at a rate of EC$2.40 to US$1. The only ex-British island to have its own currency is Barbados, with a dollar roughly equal in value to the EC dollar, but not acceptable outside Barbados. All the French islands use the euro, as does Dutch St Maarten, where US dollars are also accepted; in both the US and British Virgin Islands the US dollar is the official currency.

In point of fact the US dollar is acceptable throughout all the English-speaking islands, and if a price seems particularly reasonable check that you have not been quoted in US dollars. Most confusion is sheer misunderstanding on both sides, but occasionally the less scrupulous may ask for payment in US dollars and then attempt to give change, dollar for dollar, in EC dollars.

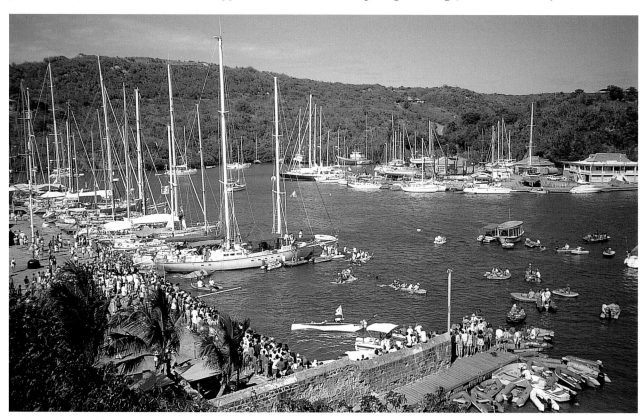

Nelson's dockyard in English Harbour, Antigua, seen here during the festivities of Sailing Week, is one of the Caribbean's most famous cruising rendezvous. Photo Anne Hammick.

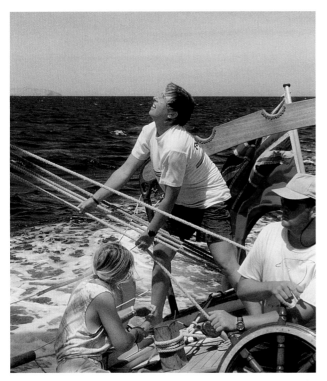

Blue skies, sunshine and steady winds make Caribbean sailing a delight. Photo Michael Beaumont.

All but the smallest islands have banks, usually the national bank of that particular country, and often a branch of a major international chain as well. Cash can normally be obtained using either Visa or MasterCard. The acceptance of these cards as payment for services is growing fast and it is as well to carry both. Passports are likely to be required to cash traveller's cheques or to obtain cash with a card, but automated cash withdrawal machines are becoming more widespread on all the bigger islands.

Facilities

Services and facilities for sailors throughout the eastern Caribbean are excellent, largely due to the ever-growing charter boat and tourist industries.

All islands other than the very smallest now have reasonable food shops, many have large supermarkets, and most sport bustling local produce markets that not only offer variety and good value, but are great fun to visit. Hotels, restaurants and cafés of all persuasions and prices have mushroomed, though many of the best are among the old-established.

Boatyard facilities have also improved dramatically, and throughout the region yards capable of hauling and carrying out repairs abound. Most will be busy during the cruising season, and in particular it may be necessary to make an advance booking for a haulout in St Lucia around the end of the ARC rally, and in Antigua before or during (and after!) race week. It is possible that a

European yacht on a one-year circuit of the north Atlantic might get away without hauling for antifouling, but the ban on TBT paints has made this unlikely. Even with frequent swimming to scrub, fouling on the homeward passages would likely be severe.

The best facilities for major repairs or maintenance are in St Maarten, Antigua and St Lucia. Of these, St Maarten has the advantage of minimum customs formalities for the importation of spare parts, a process that at present is tedious and expensive on the other two islands.

Medium- and large-scale charts

The Caribbean islands are particularly well covered by medium- and large-scale charts with, in addition to those published by the British Admiralty (plan 14, page 86) and the US Defense Mapping Agency, the Imray-Iolaire series of yachtsmen's charts (plan 16, page 88) and French publications covering Martinique, Guadeloupe, St Barts and St Martin.

Sailing directions and yachtsmen's guides

In addition to the official publications mentioned in Part I there are numerous yachtsmen's guides to the Caribbean. Very few cover the entire area, and as each approaches its locality in a different fashion there is much to be said for carrying several. See Appendices A and B, pages 227 and 229, for publishers' details.

Chart packs

Maptech chart kit: No 10, The Virgin Islands
CYC Charts Series 1–4. Virgin Islands to Grenada, including Barbados

Relevant ports in Part III

14	Chaguaramas Bay, Trinidad	page 164
15	Prickly Bay, Grenada	page 168
16	Bridgetown, Port St Charles, Barbados	page 170
17	Rodney Bay, St Lucia	page 174
18	Fort de France, Martinique	page 177
19	English Harbour/Falmouth Bay, Antigua	page 180
20	Road Town, Tortola and Virgin Gorda Yacht Harbour, British Virgin Islands	page 184

The Bahamas

The Bahamas, together with the adjoining Turks and Caicos Islands, form an extensive chain of rocky islands surrounded by coral reefs and sandbanks. They extend from about 21°N to 27°30′N and from 71°W to 79°W, covering an area of more than 5,000 square miles, much of it with depths of less than 1.8m (6ft). Columbus made his first landing in the New World at San Salvador in 1492. The archipelago is best cruised from east to west. Both prevailing winds and currents set this way, and for much of the day the sun will be aft, enabling water colours indicating shoals and coral heads to be most easily read.

Caution

Although in the past the Bahamas have had an unenviable reputation for violent crime, the situation has improved markedly over recent years and in this respect the area is probably now no more hazardous to yachts than any other. Much of the problem in the past was concerned with drug smuggling, but this has now been controlled chiefly through surveillance by US government agencies. The US Coast Guard continues its surveillance, and officers frequently board and search private yachts in the course of their work. This is a routine matter that should be accepted as such, and is almost invariably carried out politely and professionally. The Coast Guard has authority from the Bahamian government to search all vessels within their waters, regardless of nationality.

Weather and currents

Prevailing winds are easterly, with a northerly component from October to January or February, and an increasingly southerly trend from June until September. May is the transition month when cold fronts from North America cease and frontal waves from the tropical Atlantic begin. These may cause local but intense weather systems between the Virgin Islands and the Bahamas, and the Bahamas themselves often experience at least one severe storm during May. Several different weather forecast transmissions cover the area and these

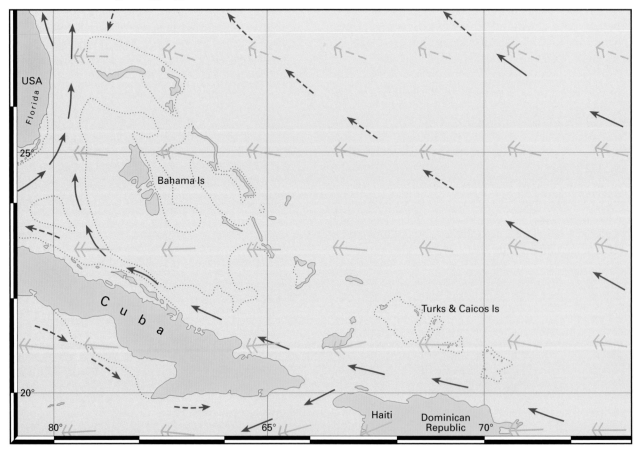

Plan 17 *Prevailing winds and currents in the Bahamas for May. Winds are coloured pink, currents in dark blue. Based on information from the* Atlantic Pilot Atlas.

should be listened to with care. The Bahamas lie squarely in the hurricane belt and it would therefore be very wise to plan to be out of the area by early June.

A north-west-going current averaging about 0.5 knots follows the trend of the Bahamas until it merges with the Gulf Stream north of the islands. In places it may run with considerably greater speed, setting onto and across shoals and reefs, and is one more good reason for avoiding passage-making after dark. In the NW Providence Channel currents are unpredictable and much influenced by the wind. In the Florida Strait the Gulf Stream runs at 3.5 to 4 knots in midstream, rather less at the edges, and if heading for Miami or Fort Lauderdale allowance must be made.

Navigation and pilotage

The shallow waters dotted with coral heads and sand-banks, combined with unpredictable currents and tidal streams, all call for what is known locally as 'eyeball navigation'. It cannot be emphasised too strongly that errors in these waters may be dangerous and that the greatest care must be exercised. Yachts drawing more than 1.5m (5ft) will be constrained in the areas they can visit.

Charts are frequently out-of-date or inaccurate, and markers and beacons few and far between. Those with most experience advise as follows:

1 Avoid night passages if possible, but if you do find yourself at sea at nightfall, heave-to in open water to await daylight.
2 Navigating from east to west, try to make passages across shoal waters before noon, with the sun at your back so that you can see the submerged coral heads.
3 Avoid inter-island passages from west to east, to windward with the sun in your eyes. If forced to go in this direction it may well be better to make an ocean passage.
4 Remember that tides and currents may not only be stronger than indicated, but may set in the opposite direction to that which is forecast. Take local advice whenever possible, especially among the skippers of fishing and inter-island trading craft.

Formalities

Clearance must be obtained at an official entry port – prior to that, a yacht may sail through the islands but cannot anchor overnight. The Q flag should be hoisted 3 miles off and, in theory, everyone is expected to stay aboard until officials come out to grant clearance. In practice, it will be necessary to go ashore and complete formalities. A cruising permit will be issued, which remains valid for up to six months. There are severe penalties for not observing clearance formalities.

Firearms must be declared and kept locked away until departure. Animals need valid rabies inoculation certificates.

Facilities

The Bahamas has its own currency, the Bahamas dollar (B$). This is at par with the US dollar, which is also widely accepted.

Facilities depend almost entirely on where you are. At Nassau on New Providence Island they are excellent, with several marinas and chandleries catering for the yacht owner plus several large supermarkets. The same is true of Freeport on Grand Bahama Island and also in the Abaco group. However, some of the outer islands are fairly basic – right down to those that are no more than a sand bar supporting a few palm trees. Consult one of the cruising guides.

Sailing directions and yachtsmen's guides

In addition to the official publications mentioned in Part I, there are a number of yachtsmen's guides and chart books available. See Appendices A and B, pages 227 and 229, where they are listed by area for recommendations and publishers' details.

Chart packs

Maptech chart kit: No 9, The Bahamas
Explorer Chart Books: The Near and Far Bahamas

17 North from the Caribbean Islands

Most cruising yachts leave the Caribbean in April or May, in order to be well north before the start of the hurricane season in June. The incidence of hurricanes in that month is in fact very low (see Chapter 10), but departure in good time enables yachts to reach their next cruising ground on the North American coast, or make the transatlantic passage back towards Europe, at the best time of year.

Yachts heading for America may follow the Bahamas to Florida, sail direct to some point further north, or make the passage via Bermuda. A few of those returning to Europe will sail directly to the Azores, but most will also call at Bermuda, and then visit the Azores before making their final landfall in the British Isles or mainland Europe. These latter passages are dealt with in Chapter 21. Wherever yachts are heading, nearly all will be aiming for higher latitudes in which summer cruising can be undertaken and tropical storms avoided.

Passage	Approx distance
Virgin Islands to Florida via the Bahamas	1,000 miles
Virgin Islands to Morehead City, North Carolina	1,200 miles
Virgin Islands to Bermuda	850 miles
Antigua to Bermuda	940 miles
Bermuda to Newport, Rhode Island	650 miles
Virgin Islands to the Azores (recommended route)	2,500 miles

Passage planning charts

Coverage	Admiralty	US
BA to 42°N	4012 (1:10,000,000)	
US to 45°N		120 (1:6,331,100)
To 45°N and 60°W	4403 (1:3,500,000)	108 (1:3,500,000)

Virgin Islands to Florida via the Bahamas

This route cuts ocean passage-making to a minimum, linking as it does with the Intracoastal Waterway running parallel to the eastern seaboard of the United States. However, with depths throughout much of the Bahamas no more than 1.8m (6ft), it calls for meticulous navigation, and both charts and cruising guides will need to be studied with care. See Chapter 16 for further details of the Bahamas.

If time is limited or draught prevents passage through the Bahamas themselves, a second possibility is to sail up the Atlantic side of the chain until Eleuthera is abeam, then pass through the NE and NW Providence Channels and across the Strait of Florida to Miami or Fort Lauderdale.

Both these passages should enjoy favourable winds and currents, though the latter are unpredictable and have caused the loss of more than one yacht. Winds between April and June are predominantly easterly at 10–15 knots, becoming south-easterly as the season progresses. Unsettled weather is most likely to be encountered during May.

The US Coast Guard monitors all vessels entering US waters, and it is possible that a yacht will be boarded at sea and searched.

Virgin Islands to Beaufort, North Carolina

This should be another largely downwind passage, with south-easterly winds veering into the south and a 2.5-knot current following the trend of the coast. If sailing the rhumb line course in May or June there is an outside chance of encountering a hard blow, but a far greater likelihood of experiencing calms – particularly during the mid portion of the passage. Plenty of fuel should be carried. The alternative is to sail a dog-leg, shaping a course to a point near 28°N 37°W before swinging northwards, in order to avoid the edge of the central Atlantic high pressure system with its associated light winds and calms.

If taking the direct route towards Beaufort, North Carolina, care should be taken to allow for the effects of the Gulf Stream. If set too far to the north it will be hard work indeed to return against both wind and current.

Virgin Islands to Bermuda

Bermuda lies almost due north from the Virgin Islands at just short of 65°W, and is well within the possible path of early season hurricanes. Therefore, this is another passage that should be completed before mid-June.

Plan 18 *Typical routes north from the Caribbean.*

Departing from the Virgin Islands in May or June, south-easterly trade winds should aid the initial stages of the passage. However, as progress is made northwards winds are likely to become less reliable, with a high probability of light variables or calms later in the passage. Occasionally a late-season *norther* may come through, but this is unusual after mid-April. Winds associated with cold fronts generally blow up sharply from the north-west, veering through north, east and south to finally blow themselves out in the south-west.

A north-west-going current of about 0.5 knots can be expected until within 100 miles of Bermuda, after which it will vary in both speed and direction. Plenty of fuel should be carried, some of which should be earmarked for the final approach. Although Bermuda has a bad name as a landfall because of the extensive coral reefs that surround it, yachts coming from the south have the least difficult approach (see Chapter 19).

The passage between the Virgin Islands and Bermuda traverses the western edge of the Sargasso Sea – technically, this is not a sea at all, but the static area around which the vast north Atlantic current systems sweep. Large carpets of brown Sargasso seaweed will be encountered, and towed and impeller logs are likely to be frequently fouled.

Antigua to Bermuda

This is very similar to the above, but typically it is sailed slightly earlier in the season by yachts departing at the beginning of May after Antigua Week. Winds are likely to be easterly or even north of east on departure, to some extent offsetting the advantage of leaving from a point further to windward. They are likely to veer south of east as progress is made northwards, becoming light and variable. The skipper with a schedule to maintain should carry plenty of fuel.

Bermuda to Newport, Rhode Island

Although Newport has been chosen, as it is a frequent destination, remarks for this passage apply equally if bound for any destination north of New York. The route lies within the hurricane belt, making a landfall by the end of June highly desirable. Winds in that month are likely to be south or south-westerly for much of the passage, though should a cold front move eastward off the American continent, strong west or north-west winds, often accompanied by driving rain, can be expected. Particularly unpleasant seas will be produced where the wind runs against the Gulf Stream. They may become dangerous.

Currents are likely to be variable until around 35°N where the full force of the Gulf Stream will be met. Between Bermuda and Newport this sets east or north-east at up to 1.5 knots. The width of the main stream varies from a mere 20 or 30 miles to 300 or more. The advent of oceanographic satellites means that its position can be determined with considerable accuracy, and as changes from day to day tend to be small, it is worth studying the latest Gulf Stream chart before leaving Bermuda. Those with weatherfax receivers can obtain updates en route.

The last 100 miles or so of the passage will be affected by the cold Labrador Current, which flows past Newfoundland and Nova Scotia, and continues south-west along the coast before petering out around the latitude of the Chesapeake. The northern edge of the Gulf Stream, where it meets the cold Labrador Current flowing south-west, is typically marked by a wall of fog. In June and July visibility of less than 2 miles can be expected for more than 20 per cent of the time in the later stages of the passage. If heading north of Cape Cod, fog is almost certain to be encountered.

Virgin Islands to the Azores

The direct distance from the Virgin Islands to the Azores is about 2,200 miles, whereas the recommended route adds some 300 to 400 miles. This is because the great circle course passes through the large area of high pressure that dominates the central Atlantic and where light and variable winds are almost guaranteed. It should only be attempted by yachts able to make good progress in very light winds. Even those whose sailing performance is sparkling in these conditions – a small minority of ocean cruisers – should carry fuel for at least 1,000 miles as areas of absolute calm may extend for several hundred miles.

The more usual procedure is to shape a course to pass within 200 to 300 miles of Bermuda before swing-

Plan 19 *Prevailing winds and currents in the western Atlantic for June. Winds are coloured pink, currents in dark blue. Based on information from the* Atlantic Pilot Atlas.

ing north-eastwards. Exactly how far to continue before heading east is open to argument, and will depend both on the conditions for the year and the preferences of those aboard – sail the rhumb line after reaching 35°N and run the risk of prolonged calms, or keep going to 38°N or 40°N in search of stronger winds and a faster passage? See Chapter 21 for more details on the later part of this route.

Even those taking this more traditional route are likely to encounter some calms and so plenty of fuel should be carried. In some years, this passage may take a yacht with limited range under power as much as 35 days. When it is calm it is likely to be extremely hot. Water consumption will be noticeably greater than on previous passages and this should be allowed for.

Weather and currents

The continent of North America has a coastline stretching from the Tropic of Cancer to the Arctic Circle, though few yachts venture beyond 60°N. Regional weather patterns, and particularly temperature, vary accordingly.

One of the few generalisations that can be made is that, during the summer cruising season, winds generally blow either offshore or parallel to the coast. Thus strong onshore gales, familiar to the European yachtsman, are seldom a problem. A more frequent hazard north of about 40°N is poor visibility, caused by the cold Labrador Current bringing arctic water south in a narrow stream almost to the latitude of Cape Hatteras. As the cold water encounters the warm air, it literally steams, giving rise to the notorious fogs of the Newfoundland Banks, Nova Scotia and Cape Cod. Unlike poor visibility around British or European coasts, which is often associated with high pressure and therefore light winds or calms, thick fog allied with winds of 20–30 knots is not unusual off the American and Canadian coasts.

Visibility is at its worst in summer, with a 20 per cent likelihood of less than 2 miles in all areas north of Block Island, increasing to a 40 per cent likelihood off Nova Scotia and Newfoundland. Yachts without radar are at a definite disadvantage in these waters, and those planning to cruise the area will save themselves anxious hours by fitting a set.

Further south, the warm Gulf Stream parallels the coast, running at up to 4 knots in the Florida Strait but slowing as it fans out into the Atlantic. When strong northerly winds oppose the north-east-going current, particularly vicious seas can form, which have been responsible for the loss of more than one yacht. Satellite surveillance now enables the position of the stream and its associated eddies to be known with accuracy. Details are broadcast by radiofax and voice.

Plan 20 *Prevailing winds and currents off the North American coastline for July. Winds are coloured pink, currents in dark blue. Based on information from the* Atlantic Pilot Atlas.

Plan 21 *Iceberg limits and percentage likelihood of less than 2 miles visibility off the North American coast for July. Based on information from the* Atlantic Pilot Atlas.

Ice

The Labrador Current is also responsible for carrying icebergs south past Newfoundland, but only very occasionally do bergs reach as far south as 40°N before melting. They are seldom encountered east of 40°W or west of 60°W, their range being most widespread in April and May and shrinking throughout the summer. The occasional rogue berg, or growler, which comes further south is usually well tracked and its position broadcast. There can be a concentration of bergs east of Cape Race, where the big ones go aground on the Grand Banks. As the season progresses and the icebergs begin to melt, they float off and move further south, finally reaching the northern edge of the Gulf Stream where they disperse and melt completely. Ice is therefore most prevalent in the northern and eastern parts of the Grand Banks early in the year and on their southern side later on. The International Ice Patrol co-ordinated by the US and Canadian Coast Guard services broadcasts daily reports of the location and drift of bergs.

Tides and tidal streams

Tidal influence varies enormously along the North American coast, from a bare 1.3m in Florida to the massive 15m tides of the Bay of Fundy. The appropriate tide and tidal stream tables should be consulted.

Approach and landfall

Conditions on approaching the coast will be dictated to a great extent by the specific latitude and area chosen. It is not possible to cover all feasible landfalls, but those on the east coasts of the United States and Canada are dealt with in a general sense below. More information can be found for the ports in Part III. A suitable pilot book should be consulted for full details of individual ports.

Much of the US eastern seaboard is fringed by a wide and relatively shallow continental shelf, with depths of 36m (119ft) or less being found 50 miles offshore in many areas. Depths then drop off very suddenly to 3,000m (10,000ft) or more, and in bad weather very confused seas can result. It is important not to get caught in this area by the onset of heavy weather on approaching the coast, and equally important to make offing as rapidly as possible on departure in order to get into deep water before there is any chance of meeting heavy weather.

The main problem on approaching the Canadian and northern US coasts is the high incidence of fog, and the fact that it can be prolonged. It therefore may not be practical to stand off and wait for conditions to improve; you must be prepared to continue and enter port in bad visibility.

Cape Race and the east coast of Newfoundland are within the iceberg zone in the early part of the season. This, combined with fog, will call for great caution when approaching this coast. The coasts of Nova Scotia and the United States can generally be regarded as being to the west of the iceberg zone.

The Grand Banks and the waters off Nova Scotia are popular fishing grounds for fleets of trawlers and coastal fishing boats. A sharp lookout should be maintained for them, and also for both nets and lines of pots marked by floats, which may be found well offshore. The gear itself will be submerged, and thus the buoy is the only danger. The increasing reliance on radar by shipping means that merchant vessels seldom reduce speed much in poor visibility, even though small craft may not be spotted on the screen. The main concentrations of shipping may be expected off Cape Race, the approaches to Halifax, the Nantucket Light Vessel, and to the north of Cape Cod where the routes to Boston and the Cape Cod Canal will be crossed.

Newfoundland

St John's is the nearest port to Europe and full details of approach and entry are given in Part III. Cape Race (46°39'N 53°04'W) may be used as a landfall by those on the northern or great circle routes. Virgin Rocks and the nearby Eastern Shoals, lying 100 miles east of Cape Race, are a potential hazard on the approach.

Offshore, the current sets southerly at about 1 knot, but runs westerly around Cape Race. There can be a strong northerly eddy off the south coast of Newfoundland. If close inshore, beware of the tides and the possibility of being swept into the bays along the southern coast. Many wrecks have occurred in fog on the southeastern and southern coasts of Newfoundland, owing to the indraught or to the current setting north-eastward.

Nova Scotia

Sable Island (43°55'N 59°50'W) lies just under 100 miles off the coast of Nova Scotia and must be given a wide berth – it is a graveyard for ships with strong and unpredictable currents and shoal water. In the southern part of Nova Scotia a strong indraught has been reported in the vicinity of Cape Sable. Oil rigs may be encountered in the area. Halifax is the recommended port for entering Nova Scotia and full details will be found in Part III.

Nantucket Shoals

Many yachts on passage from Europe or coming up from Bermuda make landfall at the Nantucket Shoals Lanby (40°30'N 69°26'W), 50 miles south-east of Nantucket Island with its offlying shoals. Probably the majority continue to Newport, Rhode Island, for which harbour and final approach details will be found in Part III. Nantucket Shoals Lanby carries a 13-mile-range light standing 13m (43ft) above sea level, and is also equipped with a horn. Care must be taken in the vicinity of the Lanby as it also marks the separation zone for the shipping lanes in and out of New York (see Chapter 10).

The Nantucket Shoals, which stretch more than 30 miles south-east of Nantucket Island, have a least depth of 1.25m (4ft) and break in bad weather. Strong tidal streams set over the Shoals, and though they can be crossed in calm weather via the marked channels this is not advised. In any case, only a slight deflection to the west of the rhumb line will be needed if heading for Newport, and none at all for Block Island or further west. If heading northwards, the choice is between clos-

The US Intracoastal Waterway provides a sheltered and convenient route between Chesapeake and Florida. Photo Georgie McLaren.

One of the many lifting bridges along the US Intracoastal Waterway. The fixed bridges have a clearance of at least 20m (65ft). Photo Gavin McLaren.

ing the coast at Buzzards Bay and traversing the Cape Cod Canal, or heading north-east from the Lanby to shape a course between Nantucket Shoal and Georges Bank, where oil rigs may be encountered.

Cape Hatteras

While Cape Hatteras (35°15′N 75°31′W) may be broadly defined as a target area for yachts coming west from Bermuda or north from the Windward or Leeward Islands or Bahamas, its coastline is highly dangerous, with many offlying banks and strong and unpredictable currents. Cape Hatteras itself deserves to be given a wide berth.

A popular route for northbound yachts is to join the Intracoastal Waterway at Beaufort, North Carolina, passing through the Sounds inside Cape Hatteras en route to the Chesapeake Bay. The principal requirement when making the approach is to avoid the Lookout Shoals.

Southbound yachts should either stand well offshore around Cape Hatteras, or enter the Chesapeake and thence the Intracoastal Waterway at Norfolk, Virginia.

Formalities: Canada

Arrival should be made at an official port of entry, and if possible you should notify them by VHF. Otherwise the skipper should go ashore alone to contact customs and immigration. The usual paperwork and details are required, together with (for a foreign yacht) an intended itinerary and approximate departure date. In the case of a number of countries, including the United Kingdom, a cruising permit can then be issued, removing the need to clear again at subsequent ports. Firearms must be

declared on arrival, but most single-shot weapons are permitted. Animals must have valid rabies vaccination certificates, but even so are not allowed ashore and will have to remain on board.

Formalities: the United States

Yachts entering the United States should be aware that US customs agents handle both yachts and large ships. There is no simplified procedure specifically for yachts.

It is necessary to clear in at a designated port of entry. Normally, clearance is carried out at any public access berth (such as a municipal pier or marina dock), or at a yacht club jetty. If in doubt, the local Coast Guard will advise on procedure. Yachts are expected to seek clearance immediately upon arrival, and most foreign yachts are then boarded for inspection. While US customs agents have been known to board yachts at sea, this is very rare. A Coast Guard boarding at sea has nothing to do with inward customs clearance, which must still be completed after arrival.

Unless the entire crew are US citizens, an immigration officer will normally accompany a customs officer to the arrival inspection. Ship's papers, clearance from the previous port and a crew list will be required. The United States is one of the few major countries for which nearly all nationalities (including all Europeans) must have a visa. While fresh perishable foods (especially fruits and vegetables) may not be imported, it is rare for agriculture inspectors to visit yachts unless animals are aboard.

Firearms must be registered upon arrival, and only hunting and sporting firearms may be brought in without restriction. Individual state firearms' laws also apply, and these may be more restrictive. Animals do not need rabies certificates if arriving from rabies-free countries, but will otherwise require them, and rabies does exist in some of the Caribbean islands. Pet birds will be put into quarantine. There are also restrictions on various animal products from declared endangered species – few yachts are likely to have furs aboard, but many people may have bought souvenirs of tortoise or turtle shell jewellery, scrimshaw on whalebone or ivory, or simply have picked up some coral.

Yachts of most nationalities, including those from Britain and northern Europe, may apply for a cruising permit. This remains valid for up to a year, and exempts the yacht from further clearance while in US waters. A condition of the cruising permit is that yachts notify US customs when they move from one customs port sector to another. While penalties for failure to do so are very rare, notification is simple and may be made by calling the toll free phone number 1 800 973 2867.

US-registered yachts returning home must also report arrival to customs, but are less likely to be boarded for inspection, unless the yacht has a foreign crew. There is no specific requirement for US vessels to clear outwards, though it may be wise to do so since the authorities of most other countries will wish to see evidence regarding date and port of departure.

The US Coast Guard

Confusion can sometimes arise over the role and responsibilities of the US Coast Guard, which has a much wider brief than the British service of the same name.

Whereas the British Coastguard is largely land-based, the US Coast Guard is very active afloat. Its responsibilities include policing its own and nearby international waters for drug smugglers (in the course of which private yachts are frequently boarded and searched), the maintenance of navigational aids, and generally ensuring that all vessels proceed in an orderly manner. Unlike Britain, where lifeboats are the responsibility of the Royal National Lifeboat Institution, in the United States the Coast Guard also runs its own search and rescue vessels and aircraft. They will respond if a vessel is in immediate danger, but where there is no risk to life or craft, the Coast Guard will usually turn the job over to private contractors for commercial assistance – which is likely to be expensive.

The US Coast Guard monitors VHF channels 16 and 22A, the latter being their working channel. Except in an emergency, initial contact should be made on 22A. European yachts should note that it is illegal to call the Coast Guard (or anyone else) on channel 16 solely for a radio check.

The Coast Guard is also responsible for small craft safety, and if your boat is boarded by them they are likely to inspect the safety equipment carried. The list of requirements includes several items not normally found aboard European yachts. In theory, foreign yachts are governed by exactly the same regulations as US-registered ones; in practice, a reasonable approach is usually taken and, provided the authorities are not antagonised, a well-equipped ocean cruiser should have few problems.

Sewage disposal

The Federal government has charged the US Coast Guard with the inspection of sewage disposal arrangements on yachts. The rules in US waters are an amalgam of Federal, State and local regulations. Many yacht harbours have been designated 'No Discharge Areas', where disposal of even treated sewage is strictly prohibited. Local harbourmasters or State marine police are

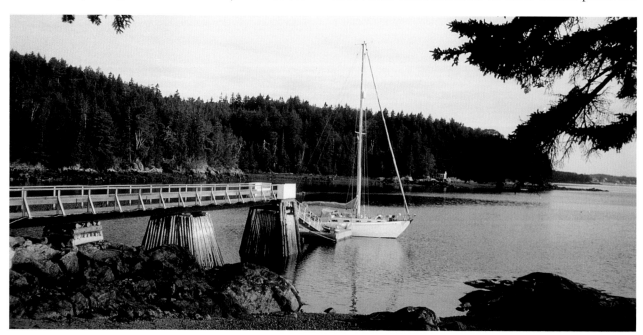

Maine, the best summer cruising ground on the US east coast. Photo Georgie McLaren.

usually responsible for enforcing the regulations. The usual recourse for visiting yachts is to fit a valve at the heads, in order that sewage can be pumped directly overboard when offshore and into a holding tank in harbour. Holding tanks can be emptied via a deck fitting at pump-out stations at many marinas and yacht clubs, or the tank may be discharged overboard when the yacht is well clear of the harbour. Heads without holding tanks must show evidence of being secured from use while in harbour – it has been suggested that a cable tie securing the discharge seacock in the shut position would suffice.

Facilities

Facilities in the United States equal the best to be found in the world. The larger yachting centres of Canada are not far behind. Equally, both countries still offer cruising grounds with dozens of miles between loaves of bread!

All those harbours detailed in Part III have good facilities for yachts, though many of the best-known yachting centres are outside the scope of this book. Local cruising guides should be consulted.

Sailing directions and yachtsmen's guides

In addition to the official publications mentioned in Part I, a list of the current almanacs, yachtsmen's guides and chart books for the North American coastline will be found in Appendices A and B, pages 227 and 229.

Chart packs

Maptech chart kits:
   No 2, Canada to Block Island
   No 3, New York to Nantucket
   No 4, Chesapeake and Delaware
   No 6, Norfolk to Jacksonville
   No 7, Florida East Coast

Maptech compact chart kits:
   Cape Sable to Clearwater
   Jacksonville to Miami
   Florida Keys

Richardson's chartbooks:
   Long Island Sound to Hell Gate NY
   Narragansett Bay to Cutty Hunk and Block Island
   Buzzards Bay, South Cape and the Islands
   Cape Cod Canal to Kettery, Maine

Relevant ports in Part III

21	Fort Lauderdale, Florida, USA	page 187
22	Beaufort/Morehead City, North Carolina, USA	page 190
23	Norfolk, Virginia, USA	page 193
24	Annapolis, Maryland, USA	page 196
25	Newport, Rhode Island, USA	page 200
26	Rockland, Maine, USA	page 204
27	Halifax, Nova Scotia, Canada	page 208
28	St John's, Newfoundland, Canada	page 212

19 Bermuda

Bermuda is Britain's oldest colony and is self-governing. It has its own currency, the Bermuda dollar, which is on a par with the US dollar. Its economy is closely linked to the American tourist trade, and the two currencies are interchangeable. The islands consist of a low-lying group of small coral islets, many of which are joined by causeways, surrounded by extensive reefs.

Weather and currents

Weather in Bermuda is influenced by the position of the Azores high, the Gulf Stream, and the weather systems on the eastern seaboard of the United States. Winds typically box the compass during the year, being generally westerly from December through until April, backing into the south around May, and gradually swinging through south-west, west and north from September onwards. In June and July, when the majority of yachts pass through, an average of 15–20 knots may be expected, though a sudden increase to 30 or 40 knots may accompany the passage of a frontal wave moving from the American coast. The islands lie well within the hurricane belt (see Chapter 10) and passage-making yachts should endeavour to be out of the area by the end of June. Temperatures vary from around 17°C (62°F) in February to 28°C (82°F) in August.

Currents in the vicinity are unpredictable, though a northerly set is the most common. The islands lie within a few hundred miles of the eastern wall of the Gulf Stream, which frequently sets up large eddies, and though currents seldom exceed 0.5 knots, they may reverse direction within a matter of days.

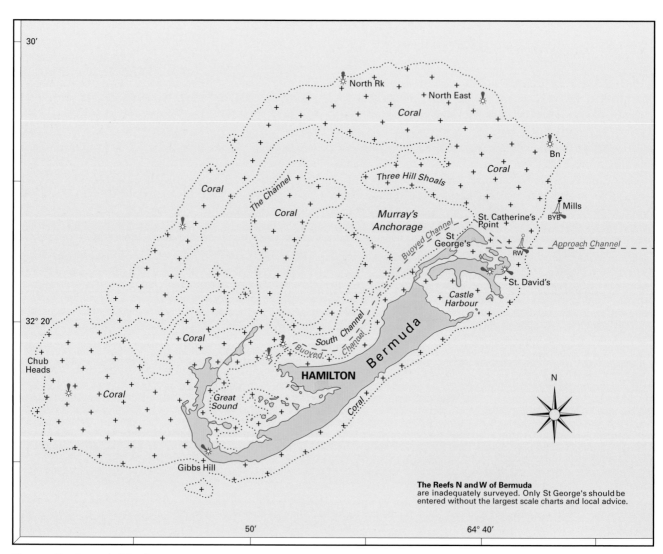

Plan 22 *The Bermuda islands.*

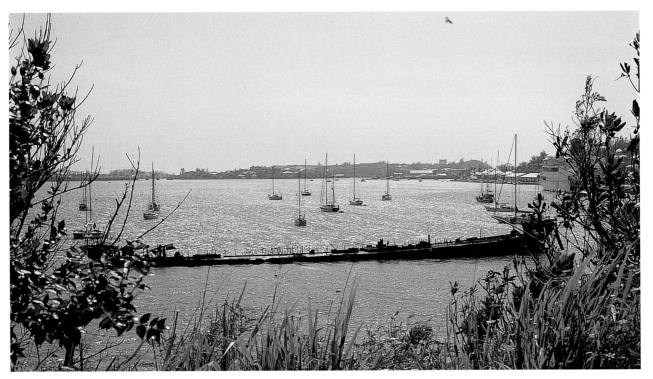

Yachts in St George's Harbour, Bermuda, with some old sailing ship wrecks lying north of the yacht anchorage.
Photo Anne Hammick.

Approach and landfall

Due to the reefs that extend up to 10 miles off the north-east, north and west coasts of Bermuda, the only safe approach is from a position south or south-east of the group. Here the coast is very steep-to, with the 200m (650ft) sounding lying within 1 mile of the coastline in places. There is also a local magnetic anomaly, which may increase the variation by up to 6°.

Yachts will be called by Bermuda Harbour Radio on VHF channel 16 as they approach the islands. This station can often be received as far as 50 miles south of Bermuda. Details of equipment carried must be given, including the serial numbers of EPIRBs on board, so it is as well to have this information to hand. Channel 16 should be monitored throughout the approach to St George's as the harbour will be closed during the movement of large cruise liners through the narrow cut at its entrance.

Details of the approach and entry to St George's Harbour will be found in Part III.

Formalities

Although reduced in recent years, clearance charges at Bermuda are higher than those of most other countries around the Atlantic. Entry must be made at St George's – full details will be found in Part III. The Q flag should be flown when entering and until pratique has been granted, after which boats may proceed to Hamilton or elsewhere. St George's must again be visited for clearance out prior to departure.

Visitors are normally allowed to remain for an initial period of three weeks, but if a longer stay is desired application must be made to the Department of Immigration. If any crew members are leaving or joining in Bermuda, then the immigration authorities should be contacted well in advance, preferably several months. Various forms must be completed, and without them it is unlikely that a single airline ticket to the island can be obtained.

Firearms, including flare pistols and spear guns, must be declared and may be impounded until departure or placed under seal aboard. Medically prescribed drugs must also be declared. There are severe penalties for the possession of illegal drugs.

Facilities

Bermuda is a sophisticated island with all manner of shopping facilities for both the tourist and the yacht owner. All slipping and repair services are available, and bonded stores may be obtained prior to departure. However, almost everything is imported, making food and other stores extremely expensive. Services are priced to match. Canned foods are available, but variety may be limited as great reliance locally is placed on chilled and frozen foods. For the yacht without refrigeration this creates a problem, since chilling fruit or vegetables badly impairs their keeping properties. It may be possible by asking around to find a source of locally laid eggs which have been neither washed nor chilled, and some locally grown vegetables.

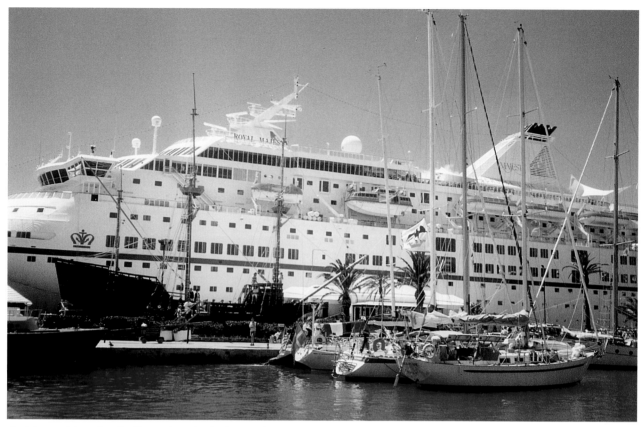

Cruising yachts and cruise liners share the harbour at St George's, Bermuda. Photo Georgie McLaren.

Sailing directions and yachtsmen's guides

In addition to the official publications mentioned in Part I and a section in *Reeds Nautical Almanac: Caribbean Edition*, a 20-page information sheet is published bi-annually by the Bermuda Department of Tourism (PO Box HM 465, Hamilton HM BX, Bermuda). This gives detailed information on buoyage and navigation, clearance, facilities, etc and will be sent free on request. If intending to cruise Bermuda and its surrounding reefs, a copy of Edward Harris's *Yachting Guide to Bermuda* will be invaluable. See Appendices A and B, pages 227 and 229, for publishers' details.

Relevant port in Part III

29 St George's, Bermuda   page 215

20 The Azores Group

The Azores form an autonomous region of Portugal (and are thus within the EU), where Portuguese is spoken with an accent that varies from island to island. Currency is the euro.

Compared with other island groups in the Atlantic, the Azores are thinly spread. The nine islands lie in three distinct groups stretching over more than 300 miles of ocean, and show surprising diversity in terms of both landscape and populace. All are of volcanic origin, and ancient *caldeira* craters are a feature of nearly every island. Only Pico retains its original cone, with the dramatic 2,351m (7713ft) summit being visible at 50 or 60 miles in clear weather.

Several new harbour developments are taking shape throughout the islands, and though naturally intended primarily for the use of local people, visiting sailors will also benefit. Until recently only Horta on Faial and Ponta Delgada on São Miguel could be regarded as safe under nearly all conditions, but the completion of an extensive double breakwater at Praia da Vitoria on Terceira has added a third harbour to the list. A yacht marina is operational in the northern part of the bay and offers the usual facilities. There are also many less well-protected bays and harbours where a yacht can lie at anchor in settled conditions.

The Azores have long been regarded by most yachtsmen simply as a convenient place to break the Atlantic passage, and their merits as a cruising ground are largely overlooked. If at all possible, at least two or three weeks should be spent in the islands, not all of them in Horta.

Weather and currents

During the sailing season, effectively from June until mid-September, the climate is dominated by the Azores High. In most years this becomes strongly established,

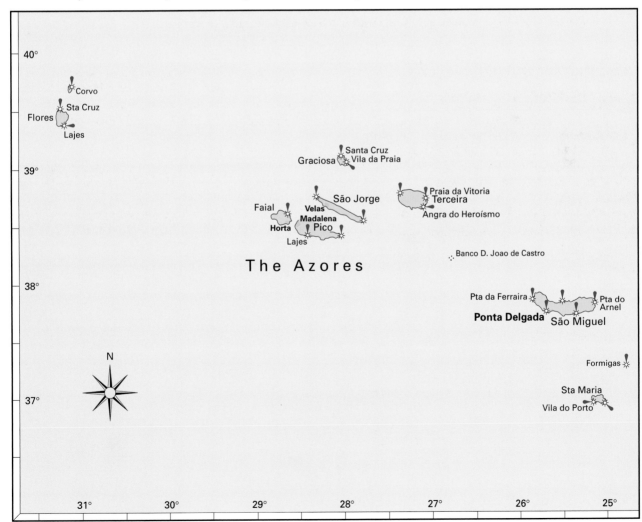

Plan 23 *The Azores archipelago.*

resulting in prolonged periods of light winds or calms, but sometimes the High remains weak so that windier, more changeable weather predominates as it does during other seasons. Winds between south-west and north are the most common throughout the year, but almost every other direction is likely to be experienced at some time. As in Atlantic Europe, south-easterly winds usually foretell an approaching front. There is a 6 per cent likelihood of calms between June and August, decreasing to 4 per cent in September.

Summer temperatures typically rise to around 23°C, though heatwaves can occasionally produce a sizzling 30°C for days at a time. However, nights can feel chilly, particularly to those who have spent the previous months in the tropics.

Visibility is generally good, though southerly winds may produce hazy conditions that limit the field of view to 5 miles or so while still apparently giving a sharp horizon. This is particularly common around the western islands of Flores and Corvo. Like the *harmattan* in the Cape Verdes, it can be most misleading.

The Azores are affected by that branch of the North Atlantic Current setting south-east towards the Iberian coast, which later becomes the Canary Current. Flow in open waters seldom exceeds half a knot, but this may double around the ends of the larger islands and, when ocean and tidal currents combine, races may form. Ocean swell can be a factor when picking an anchorage, as it frequently runs in from the west even when winds are light. For this reason, the majority of Azorean harbours are on south or east-facing coasts.

Tides and tidal streams

Tidal range is relatively small throughout the Azores and nowhere exceeds 1.8m. However, streams can run with surprising speed and may reach 2 knots in the Canal do Faial between Faial and Pico. Tides set north or north-east on the flood, south or south-west on the ebb.

Approach and landfall

Approach to the Azores is straightforward, and neither Flores nor Faial, the two most popular landfall islands for transatlantic yachts, have any serious outlying hazards. The usual course is to skirt their southern coasts, and if approaching Faial in darkness it should be noted that the Vale Formoso lighthouse at its western end is widely regarded as being considerably less powerful than stated, with a range of nearer 5 miles than the claimed 13 miles. Yachts approaching from Europe often make landfall on São Miguel which again is steep-to.

Buoyage (such as it is) follows the European IALA A system, which is the opposite to that found in North America and the Caribbean.

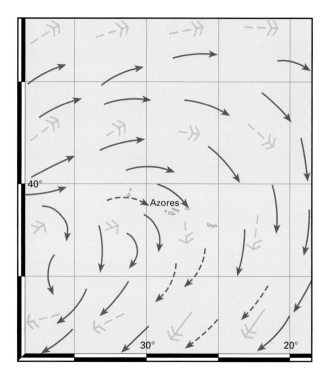

Plan 24 *Prevailing winds and currents round the Azores for July. Winds are coloured pink, currents in dark blue. Based on information from the* Atlantic Pilot Atlas.

Formalities

Entry and departure formalities have eased somewhat with the advent of the EU, but yachts must clear in and out at one of the following three ports: Horta (Faial), Praia da Vitoria (Terceira) or Ponta Delgada (São Miguel). The usual ship's papers and passports will be required and the process still takes some time.

A Portuguese courtesy flag should be flown, and many visiting yachtsmen like to hoist the blue, white and gold Azorean flag beneath it.

Facilities

Although repair and other facilities for yachts have improved considerably over recent years, the islands remain relatively unsophisticated in this respect. Almost any work needed on a yacht *can* be done, but it may be a time-consuming and expensive process. By far the best facilities are at Horta and at Ponta Delgada, both of which have small but well-run marinas with helpful, English-speaking staff who would almost certainly assist with recommendations and/or translation as necessary. Further details of both these harbours will be found in Part III. Mid Atlantic Yacht Services, although located in Horta, can deal with problems in all the islands and may prove the best initial contact if in difficulties or needing repairs.

Food shopping has improved considerably over the past decade, though many of the smaller towns still offer

Horta, Faial, in the Azores has a popular marina and many facilities. Photo Georgie McLaren.

little more than the basics. Most islands have markets and the fresh produce is excellent – both temperate and tropical fruit and vegetables thrive, and seasonal gluts of plums and figs may test the toughest digestion. Particularly good cheese is also produced, notably on Pico and São Jorge. A major re-stock can be achieved at Ponta Delgada, Horta, or Praia da Vitoria, where there are supermarkets and a full range of food shops.

Relevant ports in Part III

30 Horta, Faial, Azores   page 219
31 Ponta Delgada, São Miguel, Azores   page 223

Sailing directions and yachtsmen's guides

In addition to the official publications mentioned in Part I, there are two yachtsmen's guides to the archipelago. See Appendices A and B, pages 227 and 229, for publishers' details.

Transatlantic in the Middle and Northern Latitudes

There is a wide variety of possible routes if sailing from the United States or Canada to the United Kingdom and Europe, some of which break the voyage at one or more of the mid Atlantic island groups. Probably the majority of cruising yachts elect to take the voyage in stages. Others make the passage direct, usually keeping further north. It is broadly true to say that eastward routes tend to keep further south so as to make maximum use of the North Atlantic Current. It is certainly more pleasant to cross the northern Atlantic from west to east than vice versa, with a good chance of favourable winds for most of the passage. Yachts heading westwards must either stay well north and face the likelihood of severe weather, or remain further south in the hope of lighter weather, but at the expense of mileage lost to the current.

Inevitably, many of the following remarks that refer to one passage will also apply to others with a similar departure point or landfall. It is therefore suggested that readers should study all those passages taking a similar or parallel course, in addition to the one they actually intend to sail.

Passages eastwards	Approx distance
USA to Bermuda	650 to 700 miles
Bermuda to Horta, Azores	1,820 miles
Newport, Rhode Island to Horta, Azores	1,980 miles
Halifax, Nova Scotia to Horta, Azores	1,635 miles
St John's, Newfoundland to Horta, Azores	1,240 miles
Horta, Azores to Falmouth, UK	1,250 miles
Ponta Delgada, Azores to Spain or Portugal	750 to 820 miles
Ponta Delgada, Azores to Gibraltar	960 miles
Newport, Rhode Island to Falmouth via the mid-latitudes	2,940 miles
Halifax, Nova Scotia to Falmouth via the mid-latitudes	2,600 miles
Newport, Rhode Island to Falmouth via the great circle	2,850 miles
St John's, Newfoundland to Falmouth via the great circle	1,900 miles

Passages westwards	Approx distance
Falmouth, UK to the Azores – see Chapter 12	1,200 miles
Horta, Azores to Bermuda	1,820 miles
Bermuda to Newport, Rhode Island – see Chapter 17	650 miles
Falmouth to Newport, Rhode Island via the mid-latitudes	2,940 miles
Falmouth to Halifax, Nova Scotia via the mid-latitudes	2,600 miles
Falmouth to Newport, Rhode Island via the great circle	2,850 miles
Falmouth to Halifax, Nova Scotia via the great circle	2,390 miles
Falmouth to St John's, Newfoundland via the great circle	1,900 miles
Falmouth to Newport, Rhode Island via the Northern Route	2,870 miles
Falmouth to Halifax, Nova Scotia via the Northern Route	2,230 miles
Falmouth to St John's, Newfoundland via the Northern Route	2,050 miles

Note: Many of the above distances are approximations, due to the wide variety of possible routes.

Passage planning charts

Coverage	Admiralty	US
Northern north Atlantic	4011 (1:10,000,000)	121 (1:5,870,000)
Southern north Atlantic	4012 (1:10,000,000)	120 (1:6,331,100)

It is important to note that magnetic variation differs as you cross the Atlantic, rising to more than 20° of westerly variation near 50°W. The amount of variation fluctuates slowly, rates varying from place to place. Ocean passage charts show isogonic lines, linking places with equal variation, and also give details of annual changes.

Plan 25 *Prevailing winds and currents between 30° and 60°N for June. Winds are coloured pink, currents in dark blue. Based on information from the* Atlantic Pilot Atlas.

Weather patterns

Except in the immediate vicinity of Bermuda, the passages discussed in this chapter lie between 35°N and 60°N. Those routes in higher latitudes, perhaps visiting Greenland or Iceland en route to Norway, are the preserve of the experienced sailor and should be carefully researched using the relevant *Sailing Directions* and *Admiralty Routeing Charts* or *US Pilot Charts*.

The latitudes in which crossings are most often made are dominated by the prevailing westerly and south-westerly winds, created by low pressure to the north and the mid-Atlantic high pressure system to the south. This typically stretches from Bermuda to the Azores throughout the summer, but in some years may remain further south than usual, allowing the passage of depressions also to veer unusually far south. Less frequently, associated cells of high pressure not only form, but persist, further north, giving light winds and calms over large areas for weeks at a time. Thus while some features – such as fog – tend to be true of a particular area or latitude at all times, others may shift their area of influence from one year to the next. Whereas the movements of the trade wind belt can be forecast with a fair degree of accuracy, weather affecting all crossings in the middle and northern latitudes is less predictable.

Short-term weather over the entire area is dominated by the west-to-east passage of Atlantic depressions, as they move from North America towards Europe. These give rise to those rapidly changing conditions familiar to European sailors: south-east winds veering into the south-west, together with a falling barometer as the depression approaches, a period of south-westerlies, and heavy rain as the warm front passes, followed by a sudden shift into the north-west as the cold front comes through – often accompanied by sharp, squally showers, but soon clearing to give blue skies and clear visibility.

Not only do Atlantic depressions generally move more slowly in summer than in winter, but almost without exception they are much less intense and generate correspondingly less powerful winds. Thus by far the best season for all transatlantic crossings north of the Atlantic high pressure system is between mid-May and mid-August.

Unfortunately, visibility off the coasts of Canada and the northern United States is at its worst in the summer, and the iceberg limit is also at its greatest extent (see Chapter 18). However, these drawbacks are far outweighed by the almost certain promise of lighter winds (from a 10 per cent plus chance of winds over 35 knots on any one day between October and April, down to an average of only 1 per cent in July). Naturally, the chance of encountering a gale is always greater in northern latitudes than further south. Although it is rare for a hurricane to track beyond 40°N 60°W, the possibility should be borne in mind and careful attention paid to weather forecasts.

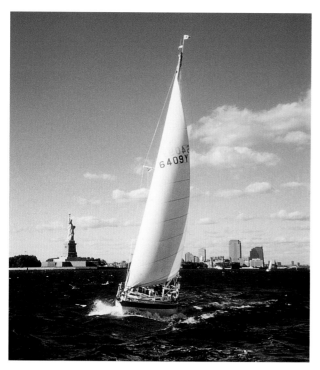

Celadus leaves New York outward bound. Photo Liza Copeland.

Ocean currents

The northern north Atlantic is dominated by the vast clockwise circulation described in Chapter 10. The Gulf Stream sets north-east in a clearly defined band off the North American continent, continuing to flow east or slightly north of east at around half a knot over much of the ocean between 35° and 55°N, by which time it is known simply as the North Atlantic Current. On reaching about 20°W this current splits, one arm continuing past Scotland towards Norway, and the other setting south-east and then south off the coasts of Spain and Portugal. Minor branches flow into the English Channel and Bay of Biscay.

The only major exception to the generally east-going circulation is the Labrador Current, which sets south or south-west down the coasts of Canada and the northern United States (see Chapter 18). From 50°W westwards the interface between the Gulf Stream and the Labrador Current is known as the Cold Wall and is normally very noticeable because of the change both in water temperature and in colour – the cold Labrador Current is light green, whereas the warm Gulf Stream is a deep blue. However, there will not be a sharp and unbroken dividing line at all times – rather, bulges and eddies where the warm and cold waters mix.

United States to Bermuda

Departure can be made from whichever US port is most convenient and a direct course normally sailed. In order to clear the Bermuda area before the onset of the hurricane season, many yachts make the passage in May, when south-westerly winds of 15–25 knots alternate with stronger winds from the north or north-east. When these oppose the Gulf Stream, dangerous seas can be created. By June, the incidence of northerlies is less, but the chance of an early-season hurricane must be considered.

Plan 26 *Typical routes eastwards in the middle and northern latitudes.*

The further north the departure point, the more windward work is likely to be called for, and it may be worth diverging from the rhumb line course in order to cross the Gulf Stream as quickly as possible, having made additional westing while still in the Labrador Current. Although the *Routeing* and *Pilot Charts* show the Gulf Stream in this area as running at an innocuous 1–1½ knots, many observers have experienced much higher rates, together with eddies and offshoots totally uncharted and inexplicable. For comfort – and also for safety – avoid crossing the Stream in a strong northerly wind.

The corridor between Bermuda and the US coast is a favourite hurricane track, those later in the season tending to run further inshore than early-season hurricanes, which (though far less likely to start with) have a statistically greater chance of approaching Bermuda itself. Hurricane forecasting has become a fine art, and if you leave the US coast with a favourable forecast, although there is no guarantee of reaching Bermuda unscathed, neither is there any reason to be caught unawares. Both speed and track become more predictable than is the case earlier in the hurricane's existence and the meteorologists should give enough warning for evasive action to be taken. Although a hurricane can occur any time between June and November, the worst period is from July to September. For that reason, departure eastward from Bermuda should be made by mid-June.

Details of approach and landfall on Bermuda will be found in Chapter 19. St George's Harbour is covered in Part III.

Bermuda to the Azores

There are two choices regarding this passage. The first is to head north-east after departure until 38°N or 40°N is reached, before turning due east for the Azores. Unless a major cell of high pressure has formed much further north than is usually the case, this should put you firmly into the belt of the westerlies. There is also a good chance of a favourable current. The disadvantages are an increased distance to sail, and the fact that gales are common in these latitudes, particularly in May and June.

The alternative is to sail a course much nearer to the great circle, though it would still be wise to make some northing early on. On this route the likelihood of calms is considerably greater, but the chance of gales is correspondingly less. The current will also be much less predictable, particularly in the earlier stages of the passage. Although the general trend of the North Atlantic Current in this area is between east and south, giant eddies may form, setting at up to half a knot in almost any direction and frequently altering from day to day. Plenty of fuel may be needed if the passage is not to be a slow one. Choice of route will depend on the size of yacht and the strength and priorities of her crew.

The Azores are well known for the extensive calm that often surrounds them and, if possible, enough fuel should be kept in reserve to motor the last 100 or so miles. Details of the approaches to the islands are given in Chapter 20, and entry details for the harbours of Horta and Ponta Delgada in Part III.

Plan 27 *Typical routes westwards in the middle and northern latitudes.*

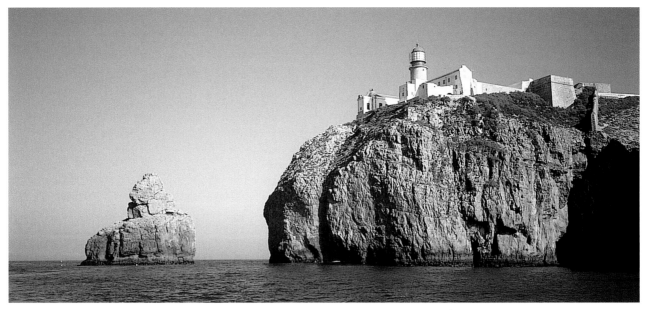

The south-west corner of Europe at Cape St Vincent en route to Lagos and Gibraltar. Photo John Lawson.

United States or Canada to the Azores

This is most likely to be the choice of yachts leaving from the Chesapeake Bay or further north, and much of what has been said under the previous two headings will apply equally to the direct route.

From south of New York it should be possible to sail a great circle course, and enjoy favourable winds and currents most of the way. From further north the standard procedure is to head south-east to make a good offing and get well clear of the Labrador Current with its attendant fogs. Once around 40°N a direct course can be shaped for the Azores, though some skippers may prefer to continue a little further south. The first part of the passage will be within the hurricane zone, and it would be wise to be east of 55°W before mid-June.

Azores to northern Europe

It is often necessary to leave the Azores under engine, and if fuel is limited the wind is most likely to be found first by motoring due north. Even if leaving with a good wind, every opportunity should be taken to make northing until at least 45°N, aiming to cross it near 20°W. A direct course from this position should make the most of the east-going current (and avoid the south-east set towards Iberia) and there is a reasonable chance of favourable winds. In some years it may be necessary to work even further north before reaching the westerlies – it is worth listening to the BBC shipping forecasts even before the area covered is reached as the Atlantic synopsis may be useful.

If at all possible, landfall should be made before the end of August. The south-western approaches to the English Channel – and the rest of northern Europe for that matter – are notorious for the severe gales that often come through early in September. If entering the English Channel in such a gale, which is almost certain to come up from the south-west and later veer into the north-west, by far the best harbour to make for will be Falmouth, tucked behind the shelter of the Lizard peninsula. Details of both Falmouth and Plymouth will be found in Part III.

Azores to Iberia or Gibraltar

There are two likely reasons for heading east from the Azores. Crews from northern Europe who are in no particular hurry may choose to break the passage homewards on the coast of north-west Spain, waiting there for a good forecast before crossing the Bay of Biscay. Others may be planning to cruise the west coast of Iberia before heading east to Gibraltar and thence into the Mediterranean.

Whatever the reason, there is a good chance of this being a pleasant passage, with northerly winds and a south-going current, both of which are apt to be quite strong. As the chance of north-easterlies increases on closing the coast, it would be wise to keep well to windward of the intended destination, to avoid a last minute slog against both wind and current. If continuing direct to Gibraltar, after rounding Cape St Vincent the current will tend towards the Straits as there is a permanent flow into the Mediterranean caused by the high rate of evaporation in that warm area. Winds may be variable.

There is certain to be considerable shipping off the coasts of Spain and Portugal, where poor visibility may also be encountered – see Chapter 11. There is also heavy traffic through the Straits of Gibraltar, where a Traffic Separation Scheme is in force.

United States or Canada to Europe via the mid-latitudes

The mid-latitudes, as far as this passage is concerned, may be defined as a track passing south of Sable Island and the Newfoundland Grand Banks but well north of the Azores high pressure system. If the yacht is lying west of Cape Cod, the choice is either to sail south of the Nantucket Shoals or transit the Cape Cod Canal and leave from further north.

In either case, to reduce the time spent in fog and avoid possible icebergs, make for the vicinity of 40°N 50°W – point P on plan 26. Up-to-date weather and ice reports may make it possible to shift this point further north and reduce the distance to be sailed, but the track may then coincide with the main shipping routes which it is preferable to avoid. If ice has moved particularly far south, it may be necessary to continue south of point P.

From point P, a great circle course can be sailed for most European destinations. Winds will be predominantly westerly, but may veer right around the compass as depressions pass through. West of 30°W, up to 1 knot of north-easterly current may be experienced, but both the strength and northerly component diminish further east.

Those remarks regarding landfall made in the section above entitled 'Azores to northern Europe' apply equally to this passage, and to the following one.

United States or Canada to Europe via the great circle

From anywhere in the north-eastern United States the great circle route to northern Europe runs close past the coast of Nova Scotia (well inside Sable Island) and thence to Cape Race on the south-east tip of Newfoundland. The winds are likely to be fair, but there can be a high incidence of fog and there will also be the weak adverse Labrador Current on this part of the route. St John's Harbour, 60 miles north of Cape Race, makes a good final port for provisions and stores. An up-to-date ice report should also be obtained.

From Cape Race or St John's, a great circle course can be shaped. Icebergs and/or fog may have to be contended with until around 40°W (crossed on this route at about 49°N), but east of 40°W normal north Atlantic conditions can be expected with a predominance of fair winds and current. Unfortunately, the Atlantic depressions spawned off Nova Scotia also favour the great circle route on their way to north-west Europe, and there is a good chance of at least one severe gale if crossing this far north. Larger seas may also be expected for much more of the passage than if crossing further south.

Passages westward

Any passage westward in the higher latitudes involves a lot of windward sailing and adverse currents with, in the latter stages, the chance of meeting ice and the certainty of fog on and to the west of the Grand Banks. For this reason few cruising sailors opt to sail directly from northern Europe to Canada or the United States, more often going via the Azores and possibly Bermuda. The direct routes are largely the preserve of entrants in the single-handed races run from Plymouth, United Kingdom to Newport, Rhode Island, who are in the main experienced sailors well able to decide their own routes and prepared to take their chances with the weather. Whatever route is chosen, gale-force headwinds may be met repeatedly as depressions track past, and at least some progress will be lost to the current.

A potential problem further south is the outside chance of encountering a hurricane – see 'United States to Bermuda' above. Weather forecasts should be monitored carefully, particularly later in the season, and the yacht should be readied to take evasive action if necessary. Ideally, landfalls on the American coast south of 40°N should be made before the end of June.

Azores to Bermuda

The route from Europe to the Azores (see Chapter 12), and thence either to Bermuda or direct to the United States, is the summer choice of most cruising sailors. Though headwinds and an adverse current are inevitable for much of the passage, it will at least be warm, and yachts with a good range under power may consider taking the rhumb line or great circle course along the ridge of high pressure that normally lies between Bermuda

Calm weather in mid-ocean between Bermuda and the Azores. Photo Georgie McLaren.

and the Azores. Extensive calms and flat to glassy seas can be expected on this route, and it will be very hot.

Yachts with less range under power would be wise to head due west, at least until beyond 50°W, only ducking further south if the forecast indicates that reliable winds are likely to be found – certainly both timing and route planning for this passage are easier than they used to be due to better weather forecasting. If departing from Horta, a long-term forecast can usually be obtained from the marina office.

It must be remembered that Bermuda lies well into the hurricane belt, as does the area between Bermuda and the North American mainland. The passage should be timed accordingly.

Details of the approaches to Bermuda will be found in Chapter 19, with St George's Harbour covered in Part III. Onward routes are considered in Chapter 17.

Azores to the United States or Canada

Unless the destination is very far north, the first part of this route will be much the same as if heading for Bermuda. The best plan is to remain at around 38°N until south or south-east of your landfall in order to minimise time spent in fog. A high proportion of headwinds and adverse current can be expected, and plenty of fuel, stores and water should be carried. Details of approach and landfall are given in Chapter 18, but the remaining sections of this chapter are also relevant.

Europe to the United States or Canada via the mid-latitudes

This passage follows much the same route as its reciprocal from west to east. Its objectives are also largely the same – to keep well north of the Azores high pressure system, but south of the Grand Banks and Sable Island. If the destination is west of Cape Cod the Nantucket Shoals should either be left well to starboard, or landfall made north of the Cape and the passage continued close down the coast and through the Cape Cod Canal.

Exactly what route is taken in order to reach 40°N 50°W – point P on plan 27 – will depend on individual choice. The shortest will obviously be the great circle, but many cruising sailors will opt to keep further south in the hope of avoiding some of the strong headwinds likely to be found near 50°N. However, heading too far south early on risks becoming caught in the calms that so often surround the Azores – it would be wiser to keep at least 300 miles north of the islands. Whatever

latitude is chosen, this passage will be largely to windward with an opposing current.

While point P is quoted as a suitable point from which an onward course can be shaped to the final destination, this could be altered in the light of up-to-date ice reports. While the temptation will always be to get out of the opposing Gulf Stream and into the favourable Labrador Current as soon as the ice situation permits, this also means heading into the worst of the fog.

Europe to the United States or Canada via the great circle

To sail the great circle from your departure port to Cape Race at the south-western extremity of Newfoundland will be the shortest route in terms of distance, but not necessarily the fastest option – and certainly not the most pleasant. Winds will be mainly from between north-west and south-west, and there is a high probability of heavy weather as Atlantic depressions track towards Europe. Landfall is likely to be made in poor visibility (Cape Race has a 40 per cent incidence of visibility under 2 miles in July) and, from 40°W onwards, ice may be encountered.

Europe to the United States or Canada via the northern route

This cold, windy route is largely the preserve of entrants in various transatlantic races – and most cruising people would probably consider them welcome to it. The object is to go north of the succession of lows, which track across the Atlantic from west to east, in the hope of picking up easterly winds on their northern perimeters. A typical point to head for is 55°N 30°W, after which a great circle can be shaped to Cape Race, Newfoundland, and beyond, giving Sable Island a wide berth. It is likely to be cold and the weather heavier than on the more southerly routes, but offers the potential of a fast passage. This is not guaranteed, though, for if the lows pass unusually far north, bitter headwinds will be encountered.

The latter part of the voyage goes straight through the centre of the fog and iceberg zones, and many competitors in the transatlantic races have spoken of sudden and unnerving sightings. There is also a considerable amount of traffic, both merchant ships and fishing vessels, making radar extremely useful. Jock McLeod, an intrepid singlehander with many ocean races to his credit, has this to say about the northerly route: 'It could be described as a long thrash to windward with a permanently foul tide, and should not be undertaken lightly.'

PART III

PORT INFORMATION

Selection

The following ports have been selected primarily as being suitable for landfall or departure, and most also have reasonable facilities for yachts. No attempt has been made to cover all viable harbours, for which local cruising guides should be consulted. Where possible, ports have been chosen which, with due caution, may be approached and entered even in bad conditions. With the sole exception of Annapolis, Maryland, USA all are official ports of entry.

Coordinates

The coordinates given for each port, rounded to the nearest half degree, correspond with the lines of latitude and longitude shown on the appropriate port plan. However, users of GPS and other electronic position fixing systems should be aware that there may occasionally be a considerable discrepancy between the charted position of a feature and that given by their instrument. This is particularly true in the Cape Verde Islands and parts of the Caribbean.

Bearings, where given, are in true from seaward.

Local time

Local time (LT), in relation to Universal Time (UT), is quoted for each port. In many places, including Great Britain, clocks are advanced during the summer months. The dates when this operates are decided by the government of each country and may vary from year to year. The times quoted are therefore subject to the appropriate adjustment for local 'summer' time if applicable.

Tides

Tidal heights quoted are Mean Level above Datum, as listed in the *British Admiralty Tide Tables NP 202*. All heights are given in metres.

Charts

For most ports only British Admiralty and US Defense Mapping Agency paper charts are listed, together with the Imray-Iolaire Caribbean series where applicable and Canadian charts for Nova Scotia and Newfoundland. Others, sometimes on a larger scale, may be produced by the hydrographic office of the country concerned, but are often difficult to obtain. Chart numbers, both paper and electronic, change from time to time with the publication of new editions and an up-to-date catalogue of charts should be consulted before placing an order.

Where a chart is listed twice with different scales, this indicates a relevant larger-scale insert on a chart of an overall smaller scale.

Buoyage

The IALA A system (red to port, green to starboard, plus cardinals) is standard in European waters, including the Azores, Madeira and the Canaries. The IALA B system (green to port, red to starboard, plus cardinals) is used throughout American waters, as well as Bermuda and the Caribbean, though few cardinal buoys will be found.

Chartlets and harbour plans

The chartlets and harbour plans in this book should not be used for navigation: they are intended only to illustrate the text. In many areas developments are taking place that could render information out-of-date at any time. Current charts, pilot books and yachtsmen's guides should be consulted before attempting to enter any harbour for the first time.

Caution

Ocean cruising sailors should be aware that maintenance of navigation aids is poor in some areas, and even major lights may sometimes be out of service for long periods. Where a change is notified, it may also take several months for it to appear in *Notices to Mariners* and therefore on newly bought charts. If approaching in darkness and in any doubt at all about entry, it is always prudent to stand off until daylight.

Mailing addresses

It is always wise to arrange mailing addresses in advance, though in most cases mail will be held for all yachts. *Poste restante* is used in Europe, General Delivery in American-influenced areas, and the words 'Please hold for arrival' can do no harm. Wording should be kept clear and simple, without titles or honorifics, and the sender's address always given on the envelope (though by no means all uncollected letters will be returned).

Duty-free imports

Many countries allow yacht equipment or spares for a visiting foreign yacht to be imported duty free. It is always wise to enquire about current regulations concerning paperwork, labelling and notification before despatch, and any such parcel should be clearly labelled 'STORES FOR VESSEL IN TRANSIT' (unless other wording is specified locally). Personal imports are nearly always subject to duty.

1

Crosshaven, Ireland
51°48'.5N 8°17'.5W UT

Springs: 4.1m		Range 3.7m	
Neaps: 3.2m		Range 1.9m	
Flag: Republic of Ireland		Currency: Euro	
Tel/fax – Country code: 353, Area code: (0) 21			
Charts	Admiralty		US
General	2424	(1:150,000)	35400 (1:150,000)
Approach	1765	(1:50,000)	35424 (1:50,000)
Harbour	1777	(1:12,500)	35421 (1:12,500)

General

On the south coast of Ireland and 60 miles east of Fastnet Rock, Cork Harbour is one of the world's finest natural harbours and a busy commercial port. Crosshaven on the Owenboy River is on the west side within the entrance and is the centre for yachting in the estuary. It is the home of the Royal Cork Yacht Club, the oldest yacht club in the world, and three marinas; it offers good shelter in all weathers. It is said that Sir Francis Drake once evaded a superior Spanish force by taking his fleet of ships up the Owenboy River to Drake's Pool.

Buoyage follows the European IALA A system.

Approach

The distinctive promontory known as the Old Head of Kinsale [Fl (2) 10s 72m 25M] lies some 15 miles south-west of Cork entrance and is easily identified if closing the coast from the south or south-west. On approaching Cork Harbour itself, landfall marks are a 24m (80ft) high hammer-headed water tower about 1.5 miles east of Roche's Point, and a high chimney with red and white horizontal bands and vertical red lights north-east of Corkbeg Island which shows clearly beyond Roche's Point. A pillar buoy marking safe water is situated some 5 miles south of the entrance.

Dangers in approaches

Pollack Rock with a least depth of 7.6m (25ft) lies 1.25 miles east-south-east of Power Head, itself 3.25 miles east of the entrance to Cork Harbour. The rock is buoyed and covered by a red sector of Roche's Point light. Daunt Rock, with a least depth of 3.5m (12ft), which breaks in bad weather, lies nearly 5 miles south-south-west of Roche's Point. This rock too is buoyed [Fl R (2) 6s] and covered by a red sector of Roche's Point light.

Radio

Cork Harbour Radio monitors VHF channel 16, working channels 12 and 14. The Royal Cork Yacht Club and Crosshaven Boatyard both monitor channels 16 and M(37) during working hours.

Entrance

Entry is between Weavers Point and Roche's Point, on a heading slightly west of north. At this point the entrance is about 0.8 miles wide, narrowing to 0.5 miles between Fort Meagher and Fort Davis. There are two well-buoyed channels divided by Harbour Rock, but as this has a least depth of 5.2m (17ft), both buoyed channels and leading lights (two sets) can normally be ignored by yachts. Rock ledges extend up to 180m (600ft) offshore on either side. Two rocks, the Cow – which always shows – and the Calf – which dries 1.3m (4ft) – extend 180m south of Roche's Point.

Tidal streams can run strongly in the entrance, reaching 2 knots at springs, though the strength of the ebb can be somewhat lessened by keeping to the west side of the channel.

On reaching Fort Meagher, allow at least 180m clearance around Ram's Head before altering course north-westwards for the Owenboy River, passing close to the green cone buoy which marks the east end of the spit dividing the west channel from the Crosshaven channel. The leading line/lights then lead into the Crosshaven channel, which is narrow, and no liberties should be taken with buoyage or unlit perches. If approaching at night and unfamiliar with the area, it is wise to anchor and await daylight, although most of the buoys are lit.

Anchorage and moorings

There is no good anchorage in the lower river, which is crowded and has cables and numerous old chains fouling the bottom, but a mooring may be available through the Royal Cork Yacht Club or Salve Marina Ltd. Drakes Pool, 1.5 miles up the river, offers secure anchorage in 2–4m (7–13ft) in delightful surroundings, but has no facilities.

Berthing and marinas

There are three marinas, progressing upstream. The Crosshaven Boatyard (tel: 4831161, fax: 4831603) with 20 visitors' berths; 40m (130ft) maximum, 4m (13ft) draught. Salve Marina (tel: 4831145, fax: 4831747) will accommodate visitors up to 30m (100ft) and 3.5m (12ft)

COBH

Cobh Road

Spit Bank

Fairway

East Channel

Haulbowline Island

Spit Bank

Outer
Anchorage

West Channel

Spike
Island

2F.G.Vert

Chimney
152

51° 50'N

Corkbeg
Island

Black Rk

Oil
Refinery

Flare

Fl.R.5s

Lough Beg

Fl.G.5s

Ldg.Oc.5s
Dognose

Fort Davis

Ldg. Lts. 252°

Ldg.Oc.R.5s

Fort Meagher   Ram's Head

CROSSHAVEN

Red

QFl

BY

Mast

Weavers Pt   Fl.R

The
Sound

N

Fl.R.2.5s

Fl.G.10s   Fl.G.5s

Roche's Pt   Tr.

Fl.WR.3s30m
20/16M

51° 47'

Red

White

08° 19'   Depths in Metres   08° 15'W

Plan 29 *Cork Harbour.*

draught. The largest, at the Royal Cork Yacht Club (tel: 4831023, fax: 4831586), will accommodate up to 20m (66ft) and 3m (10ft) draught. All are on the south side of the river. The least depth in the Owenboy channel up to the Royal Cork Yacht Club is 2.3m (8ft), but there are deeper parts beyond, up to Drake's Pool.

Formalities

Entry requirements may be waived in the case of an EU-registered yacht arriving direct from another EU coun-

try (including the Azores), but if in any doubt it would be wise to check the procedures with customs. In the case of a non-EU registered vessel, or if arriving from a non-EU country or with non-EU nationals aboard, hoist the Q flag on closing the land. Customs and immigration may be contacted by telephone (0214 831222), through any of the marina offices, or via the police station situated across the road from the Royal Cork Yacht Club.

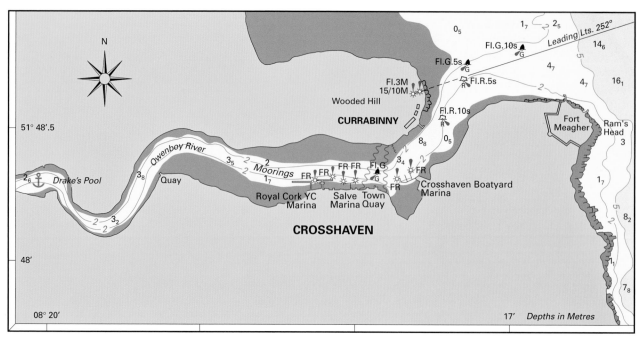

Plan 30 *Crosshaven, Ireland.*

Facilities

Boatyard The Crosshaven Boatyard has a 40-tonne travel lift, covered and open boat storage areas, and can handle most repairs and maintenance, including rigging. Salve Marina call in a mobile crane if required.

Engineers Salve Marina and Crosshaven Boatyard.

Sailmaker UK McWilliams Sailmaker (tel: 831505, fax: 831700) just outside Crosshaven are the only sail-makers/repairers in the area and will collect and deliver.

Chandlery At Crosshaven Boatyard and several in Cork.

Yacht club The Royal Cork Yacht Club is the oldest in existence, having been founded in 1720. It has a fine clubhouse overlooking the river and an established reputation for hospitality to visiting sailors.

Crosshaven looking east down the Owenboy River. The Royal Cork Yacht Club and marina can be seen on the right. Roche's Point lighthouse is in the background (top right). Photo Kevin Dwyer.

Diesel From Crosshaven Boatyard and Salve Marina; petrol by can from garage.

Water At all three marinas and the town quay.

Electricity At all three marinas.

Bottled gas Camping and Kosangas from Power's shop in Crosshaven.

Showers At the Royal Cork Yacht Club.

Laundry/laundrette In Crosshaven.

Banks One in Crosshaven and many in Cork.

General shopping Butcher, post office, general stores and chemist in Crosshaven, but a full range in Cork some 19km (12 miles) away; supermarket 6km (4 miles) on bus route to Cork.

Restaurants/hotels Several locally and in Royal Cork Yacht Club; a wide choice in Cork and the surrounding countryside.

Medical services Hospitals in Cork.

Communications

Mailing address C/o any of the marinas (name + Crosshaven, Co Cork, Republic of Ireland) by prior arrangement.

Post office In Crosshaven.

Telephones At the yacht club and elsewhere; mobile coverage good.

Bus/rail services Buses to Cork, linking with the rail network.

Ferry services Car ferry to Swansea in South Wales and to Roscoff in Brittany.

Taxis Crosshaven Cabs (tel: 0214 832138).

Air services Cork airport, with flights to the United Kingdom and the Continent about 16km (10 miles) distant. Train from Cork to Limerick for Shannon airport and transatlantic flights.

2

Falmouth, England
50°09'N 5°03'W UT

Charts		Admiralty	US

Springs: 5.4m   **Range** 4.6m

Neaps: 4.3m   **Range** 2.2m

Flag: British (Red Ensign)   **Currency:** £ sterling

Tel/fax – Country code: 44, **Area code:** (0) 1326

Charts			Admiralty	US
General	2665	(1:150,000)	36140	(1:200,000)
Approach	154	(1:35,000)	36181	(1:75,000)
			37041	(1:35,000)
Harbour	32	(1:12,500)	37042	(1:12,500)

General

Falmouth is the most westerly of the larger English Channel ports and is convenient for departure and landfall for passages south and west. It is one of the finest natural harbours in Europe, with much sheltered deep water and several inlets and creeks. There are sometimes shipping movements (tug assisted) entering and leaving the harbour and dock area, and also some commercial fishing. The entrance is well marked and safe under all conditions.

Approach

After passing the Lizard [Fl 3s 70m 25M] the only danger is the group of rocks known as the Manacles, clearly marked on the chart and with an East Cardinal buoy to seaward. An easterly wind combined with a flood tide can produce a race between Black Head and the Manacles on the direct course to Falmouth. In these conditions, after rounding the Lizard, head towards the Lowland Buoy in about 50°N 5°W and thence east of the race towards Falmouth. Lobster pot marker buoys may be encountered anywhere in the area, either singly or in attached strings, and may be found well offshore.

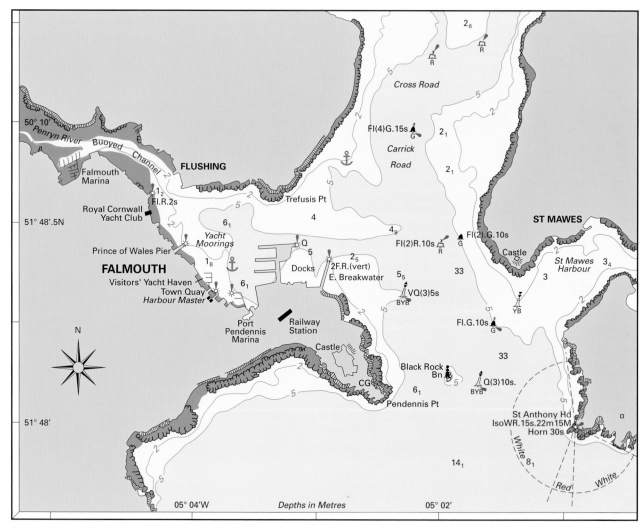

Plan 31 *Falmouth, England.*

They are often poorly marked and constitute a hazard to a yacht under power, particularly at night.

Radio

Falmouth Harbour Radio monitors VHF channel 16, and uses 11, 12 and 14 as working channels. The harbour launch *Killigrew* operates on channel 12. All three marinas monitor channel M (80).

Entrance

The entrance is passable under all conditions – even with a southerly gale and ebb tide a yacht can enter in safety, if not comfort. The main channel lies between St Anthony Head and the East Cardinal buoy marking the unlit Black Rock Beacon, and should be used after dark. In daylight a yacht can safely pass either side of Black Rock with an offing of 100m (330ft).

There is local racing in Carrick Road on two or three afternoons each week in summer. This is taken very seriously, particularly by the skippers of the gaff-rigged Falmouth Working Boats, and it would be most unwise to cut through the racing fleet.

Anchorage and moorings

The main yacht anchorage is in the south-west of the harbour off the Town Quay, though anchoring too close to the docks is prohibited (see plan 31). Holding is generally good in firm mud, though there are a few soft patches, and protection is adequate. In northerly winds more shelter may also be found east of the moorings that run between Flushing and Trefusis Point.

The Royal Cornwall Yacht Club (tel: 312126, fax: 211614) has six visitors' moorings able to take up to 12m (40ft). The Harbour Commissioners (tel: 312285/ 314379, fax: 211352) have 18 moorings (with green pick-up buoys) in the northern part of the harbour – some able to take yachts up to 24m (80ft). A detached island pontoon, to which yachts raft up, is normally in place from April until early October.

Land at either the Visitors' Yacht Haven or the Royal Cornwall Yacht Club.

Berthing and marinas

There are three marinas in Falmouth and one just up the river at Mylor.

Falmouth harbour looking NW with Pendennis Point and the docks in the right foreground. The Penryn River leads left up to Falmouth Marina. Photo Crown Copyright MOD 1999/2000.

The Visitors' Yacht Haven (tel: 312285, fax: 211352), run by the Harbour Commissioners, can accommodate yachts up to 15m (50ft) length and 2.5m (8ft) draught. This is probably the most convenient for the transient, as it has all the facilities and is in the middle of the town.

Falmouth Marina (tel: 316620, fax: 313939), with about 330 berths, is situated about 0.7 miles up the Penryn River. The approach channel carries a minimum of 2.0m (7ft), as does the marina, which can accept yachts up to 25m (83ft) by arrangement; the river is buoyed, but the dredged channel at the marina is narrow and the beacons must be followed. Secure to the clearly marked reception pontoon until directed to a berth by marina staff. Falmouth Marina accepts some liveaboards and is a pleasant marina in which to winter. There is a supermarket close by.

Port Pendennis Marina (tel: 311113, fax: 311116), a marina village development with space for a few visiting yachts, lies in the southern part of the harbour between the docks and the town. The marina basin, containing about 60 berths, is enclosed within a single tidal barrier with access for about half the tide. The outer section has a 3m (10ft) draught limit, and can accommodate boats up to 50m (165ft) or more, and keeps space for visitors; it has all the facilities except fuel, and is at the end of the main street where there are many shops.

Formalities

Entry requirements are waived in the case of an EU-registered yacht arriving direct from another EU country (including the Azores).

In the case of a non-EU registered vessel, or if arriving from a non-EU country or with non-EU nationals aboard, hoist the Q flag at sea and telephone customs on 0345 231110 immediately on arrival.

Facilities

Falmouth has excellent facilities for yachts, and is a good place to make final preparations for an Atlantic crossing. All the following companies are in or near Falmouth itself, others are situated elsewhere on the estuary:

Boatyards/engineers There are many: Falmouth Boat Construction (tel: 374309, fax: 377679) across the water at Flushing can haul boats of up to 25m (83ft) into a covered work area; though not a boatyard as such, Falmouth Marina (tel: 316620, fax: 313939) has a 30-tonne travel lift and a large area of hardstanding; Challenger Marine, Penryn (tel: 377222, fax: 377800), which can crane up to 12 tonnes; and finally Pendennis Shipyard (tel: 211344, fax: 319253) in the docks, which will cope with the largest mega-yacht.

Electronics Sea-Com Electronics Ltd, in Falmouth Marina (tel: 210031).

Riggers Falmouth Boat Construction Ltd (tel: 374309, fax: 377679), and the Boat Store Chandlery in Falmouth Marina (tel: 318314).

Sailmakers SKB Sails (tel: 372107, fax: 373792) and South West Sails (tel: 375291, fax: 376350), both in Penryn, and Penrose Sailmakers (tel/fax: 312705), who also specialise in traditional sails.

Chandleries Marine Instruments (tel: 312414, fax: 211 414) on the waterfront in Falmouth; the Boat Store (tel: 318314) at Falmouth Marina, and Challenger Marine on the Penryn road. Millers Maritime Bookshop (tel: 314542, fax: 318024) carries a good stock of cruising guides, etc.

Admiralty chart agent/compass adjusters Marine Instruments.

Yacht clubs The Royal Cornwall Yacht Club welcomes visiting yachtsmen and has a dinghy landing, showers, a bar and an excellent restaurant (tel: 311105). Closed on Monday.

Diesel Falmouth Marina and the Visitors' Yacht Haven. The fuelling barge Ulster Industry is usually moored south-west of Trefusis Point.

Petrol The Visitors' Yacht Haven, or by can from a filling station directly behind Falmouth Marina.

Water On pontoons at all marinas, or by can from the Royal Cornwall Yacht Club.

Electricity On the pontoons in all marinas.

Bottled gas Falmouth Marina, the Visitors' Yacht Haven, Marine Instruments and elsewhere.

Showers At all marinas and the Royal Cornwall Yacht Club.

Laundry/laundrette At all marinas, and in the town.

Banks Several, with ATMs.

General shopping Good, and anything lacking can generally be found in Truro about 16km (10 miles) away.

Provisioning Several supermarkets, including one close to Falmouth Marina and a large Asda at Penryn.

Restaurants/hotels Dozens, at all levels.

Medical services Falmouth Health Centre (tel: 317317) or Treliske Hospital in Truro. Many doctors, dentists and opticians.

Communications

Mailing addresses C/o Falmouth Marina, North Parade, Falmouth, Cornwall TR11 2TD; Port Pendennis Marina, Falmouth, Cornwall TR11 3YE; Falmouth Harbour Commissioners, 44 Arwenack Street, Falmouth, Cornwall TR11 3JQ or the Royal Cornwall Yacht Club, Greenbank, Falmouth, Cornwall TR11 2SW, all by prior agreement.

Fax services At Falmouth Marina (fax: 313939).

e-mails Falmouth Marina – markD@premiermarinas.com.

Post offices Several.

Telephones Numerous, both coin and card operated. Mobile coverage is good.

Bus/rail services Buses to Truro and other nearby towns. Trains to Truro for connections to London, etc.

Taxis No problem.

Car hire AVIS, Truro (tel: 01872 262226).

Air services Daily flights to London from Newquay airport about 48km (30 miles) away.

3 Plymouth, England

50°21'N 4°09'.5W UT

Springs: 5.5m		Range 4.7m	
Neaps: 4.4m		Range 2.2m	
Flag: British (Red Ensign)		Currency: £ sterling	
Tel/fax – Country code: 44, Area code: (0) 1752			
Charts	Admiralty		US
General	442 (1:150,000)		37070 (1:200,000)
Approach	1267 (1:75,000)		37043 (1:75,000)
			37046 (1:75,000)
Harbour	30 (1:12,500)		37044 (1:12,500)
	1901 (1:5,000)		37045 (1:5,000)

General

Plymouth is one of England's larger maritime cities, with excellent facilities for yachtsmen; it also has good communications. Local yards and suppliers are accustomed to meeting the needs of long distance voyagers of all nationalities. Plymouth is a busy naval, commercial and fishing port, but this does not conflict with the yachtsman's needs.

Approach

The Eddystone Lighthouse [Fl (2) 10s 41m 20M] marks a small area of drying rocks 10 miles south-south-west of Plymouth. It is conspicuous by day or night and can be passed on either side at a distance of 500m (0.3 miles). Rame Head and Penlee Point to the west of the entrance, and the Mewstone to the east, are prominent features. In clear weather, the high land of Dartmoor to the north-east and the radio masts on Staddon Heights on the eastern shore of the Sound assist identification. The gunnery range to the east of the entrance at Wembury is no longer operational.

Radio

Plymouth is under the jurisdiction of the Queen's Harbour Master – call Longroom port control on VHF channel 16, transferring to channel 14. Devonport Naval Dockyard up the Hamoaze works on channels 13 and 73, and the ferry terminal at Millbay Docks on channels 12, 14 and 16. All the marinas monitor channel 80. Sutton Harbour lock monitors channel 16 and works on channel 12.

Entrance

Plymouth Sound is nearly 2 miles wide at its entrance, over half of this being blocked by a detached stone breakwater. Although the breakwater is lit at both ends it would not be impossible for a stranger entering in bad conditions to spot the large fort in the middle, mistake it for one of the ends, and run up on the breakwater. The Western Channel can be used in all conditions, though gales from a southerly quarter may cause sizeable breaking seas off the breakwater end. Thereafter the recommended approach lies north-east across the Sound, leaving Drake's Island to port. The whole area is very well buoyed.

Bridge Channel to the west of Drake's Island makes a convenient short cut if heading for the Mayflower Marina and is marked by two large lit beacons at the north and south ends.

Anchorage and moorings

There are no protected anchorages convenient to the city itself, though quiet anchorages and good shelter, depending upon wind direction, can be found in Cawsand Bay to the west of the detached breakwater, Jennycliff Bay beneath the prominent Staddon Heights radio masts, and Barn Pool to the west of Drake's Island (trip line needed). It is also possible to anchor off The Hoe, as shown on plan 32, but it is rather exposed. The Tamar and Lynher Rivers afford some interesting exploring and many protected but remote anchorages. There are very few moorings available to visitors,

Plymouth looking NNE. Queen Anne's Battery Marina and the Royal Western Yacht Club are seen to the right with Sutton lock (left upper centre) and Sutton Harbour Marina (upper left). Photo Trevor Burrows.

Plan 32 *Plymouth, England.*

though the Royal Western Yacht Club has a few to the south of Queen Anne's Battery.

Berthing and marinas

There are four large marinas in the Plymouth area, plus several smaller ones:

1 Longest established is the Mayflower International Marina (tel: 556633, fax: 606896), which can take deep-draught yachts up to 30m (100ft). About 30 of its 270 berths are reserved for visitors. The staff are helpful, and facilities and security excellent, but without transport it is some distance from the city and shops. Tidal streams run strongly across the approach, and in severe south-westerly gales the marina can become uncomfortable.

2 Queen Anne's Battery Marina (tel: 671142, fax: 266297) on the northern shore of the Cattewater can take yachts up to 45m (150ft) and 4.5m (15ft) draught, with 50 of its 240 berths reserved for visitors. A passenger ferry crosses to the Mayflower Steps in the historic area of the city, or you can walk via the Sutton Harbour lock gate. Several major races, including those organised by the Royal Western Yacht Club of England, begin and/or end using the marina. There are clear written rules for the marina and, among other things, long-term living aboard is not permitted.

3 Sutton Harbour Marina (tel: 204186, fax: 205403) is entered via a 24-hour access lock (see 'Radio', above) situated north of the entrance to Queen Anne's Battery Marina. There is a floating pontoon inside the lock, which is floodlit at night. The marina is very convenient to the old city with its restaurants, shops and nightlife, and as a result its two dozen or so visitors' berths are often occupied. Sutton Harbour Marina is unsuitable for vessels of more than about 15m (50ft) overall.

4 Plymouth Yacht Haven Bay Marina (tel: 404231, fax: 484177) lies opposite Queen Anne's Battery on the south bank of the Cattewater at Mountbatten, and is the newest of Plymouth's larger marinas. It is dredged to 2.25m (7ft) throughout. There is a regular ferry service across the Cattewater to the Barbican.

Of the smaller marinas, Millbay Marina Village (tel: 226785), on the eastern side of the entrance to the old Millbay Dock opposite the Brittany Ferries terminal, is a residential development with berthing for property owners. There is limited space for visiting yachts, and berths may occasionally be available if arranged in advance.

Torpoint Yacht Harbour (tel: 813658), on the west bank of the River Tamar, largely caters for annual berthholders, but may sometimes have a vacant pontoon berth available, length 12m (40ft), draught 2m (7ft), and moorings for larger boats. Southdown Marina (tel/fax: 823084) in Millbrook Creek, running south-west from the Hamoaze, largely dries and is unlikely to be suitable for visitors.

Formalities

Entry requirements are waived in the case of an EU-registered yacht arriving direct from another EU country (including the Azores).

In the case of a non-EU-registered vessel, or if arriving from a non-EU country or with non-EU nationals aboard, hoist the Q flag at sea and telephone customs on 0345 231110 immediately on arrival.

Facilities

Many historic voyages have begun or ended in Plymouth, from the time of the Pilgrim Fathers onwards. It is hard to imagine anything a yacht might require that could not easily be found.

Boatyards/engineers Mashford Brothers Ltd at Cremyll (tel: 822232) is the largest yacht yard with slip facilities and the capacity to service yachts up to 250 tonnes, 37m (122ft) LOA, 7.0m (23ft) beam and 3.5m (12ft) draught. There is a 25-tonne travel lift plus boatyard facilities at Mayflower International Marina; a 20-tonne travel lift and facilities at Queen Anne's Battery Marina, and a 65-tonne travel lift at Plymouth Yacht Haven. Harbour Marine (tel: 204186) is situated in Sutton Harbour; it has a 25-tonne travel lift and many repair facilities.

Plymouth looking ESE with Mountbatten peninsula and breakwater in foreground. Plymouth Yacht Haven Marina beyond in the Cattewater. Photo Trevor Burrows.

Independent yards include A Blagdon (tel: 561830) on Richmond Walk near the Mayflower International Marina and Bostons (tel: 4407265) in Oreston Creek to the east of Plymouth Yacht Haven.

Electronics Waypoint One (tel: 661913) at Queen Anne's Battery; Plymouth Marine Electronics (tel: 227711) and SM Group (tel: 662129), both at Sutton Harbour.

Sailmakers Ösen Sails (tel: 563666) near to Mayflower Marina; Andrew Hooper at Holbeton (tel: 830411) and Westaway Sails at Ivybridge (tel: 892560) will collect and deliver to all marinas.

Chandleries Seven or eight, including at least one at each of the larger marinas.

Admiralty chart agent The Sea Chest, Queen Anne's Battery (tel: 222012), which also has a wide selection of new and secondhand books.

Yacht clubs Royal Western Yacht Club of England (tel: 660077) occupies upper floor rooms at Queen Anne's Battery; the Royal Plymouth Corinthian Yacht Club (tel: 664327, fax: 256140) has premises at the east end of The Hoe. Both are very welcoming to visitors.

Weather forecast Posted daily at the larger marinas. See *Admiralty Maritime Communications NP 289* and *RYA Weather Forecast G5/02* for full details of all radio and other forecasts.

Diesel/petrol All larger marinas and at Mashfords Boatyard

Water All marinas.

Electricity All marinas.

Bottled gas Mayflower International, Queen Anne's Battery and Plymouth Yacht Haven marinas, and in the city itself.

Showers All marinas.

Laundrettes Mayflower, Queen Anne's Battery and Plymouth Yacht Haven marinas, and in the city itself.

Banks All major British banks, with ATMs.

General shopping Excellent, as befits a major city, but only possible with transport or a taxi from Mayflower Marina.

Provisioning Excellent, but as above for general shopping. There is only one major supermarket (Sainsbury's) actually in the city.

Restaurants/Hotels Numerous, at all prices; Mayflower has a small restaurant on site, as does Plymouth Yacht Haven; Sutton Harbour is adjacent to the Barbican area, which has many cafés and restaurants.

Medical services Derriford Hospital (tel: 777111) is a fully equipped area hospital on the city outskirts; Nuffield Private Hospital is in the same area (tel: 775861). Many doctors, dentists and opticians in the city.

Communications

Mailing addresses C/o Royal Plymouth Corinthian Yacht Club, Madeira Road, Plymouth PL1 2NY; Royal Western Yacht Club of England or Queen Anne's Battery Marina, both at Queen Anne's Battery, Plymouth PL4 0LP; Mayflower International Marina, Ocean Quay, Richmond Walk, Plymouth PL1 4LS or Plymouth Yacht Centre, The Quay, Mountbatten, Plymouth PL9 9TF, all by prior arrangement.

Fax services At Mayflower International (fax: 606896) and Plymouth Yacht Centre marinas (fax: 484177).

Post offices Several.

Telephones At all marinas and in the city; good mobile coverage.

Bus/rail services Local bus services, coaches and mainline trains to London and elsewhere.

Ferries Services to Roscoff, Brittany and Santander, in northern Spain.

Taxis Numerous private firms.

Car hire All major agencies.

Air services Plymouth airport, with regular services to London, the North, the Channel Islands, the Republic of Ireland and the Continent.

4 **Brest,** France

48°23'N 4°29'W UT + 1

Springs: 7.5m	Range 5.9m		
Neaps: 5.9m	Range 2.8m		
Flag: France	Currency: Euro		
Tel/fax – Country code: 33, Area code: (0) 2			
Charts	Admiralty		US
General	2643	(1:200,000)	37320 (1:150,000)
Approach	798	(1:60,000)	37328 (1:50,000)
	3427	(1:30,000)	
Harbour	3428	(1:15,000)	37325 (1:15,000)
			37326 (1:7,500)

General

Brest has long been one of France's primary naval bases, no doubt partly due to its protected and easily defensible position inside the relatively narrow Goulet de Brest some 10 miles from the open sea. The Rade de Brest makes an interesting cruising ground, though some parts are reserved for naval use, with the movement of yachts restricted and anchoring prohibited. Brest is a large city of considerable historic interest, with excellent facilities.

Approach

When entering from the west or south-west, align the light towers of Pointe du Petit Minou [Fl (2) WR 6s] with Pointe du Portzic [Oc (2) WR 12s] on 068° to leave the well-marked Plateau des Fillettes shoal to starboard. In daylight this shoal can be left to port, but good clearance must be allowed around the Pointe des Espagnols where a wreck on a rock close to the north-east is marked by a white beacon.

Radio

French coastal stations do not answer an initial call on VHF channel 16 unless it is a Mayday call. The commercial port working channel is channel 12, with channel 74 used in the military port. The Marina du Moulin Blanc may be contacted on channel 09, 0800–2000 (0900–1200 and 1400–1900 on public holidays).

Entrance

On approaching Pointe du Portzic, the city, together with the large naval and commercial port complex, will be seen some 2 miles beyond. Yachts are not welcome in the naval port, but may berth in the Port du Commerce. However, they may prefer to continue the further 3 miles to the Marina du Moulin Blanc, on the eastern edge of reclaimed land near the mouth of the Elorn River and 1 mile below the two bridges. The marina is approached via a narrow dredged channel with a minimum of 2m (7ft), and the buoyage should be observed.

Anchorage and moorings

There are many sheltered anchorages within the Rade de Brest, but not adjacent to the port of Brest itself where anchoring is generally either forbidden, or the water too shallow.

Berthing and marinas

The Marina du Moulin Blanc (tel: 980 22002, fax: 984 16791) is a large marina complex with more than 1,300 berths, of which 100 are reserved for visiting yachts of up to 30m (100ft). A central breakwater divides the marina into two parts, with reception, fuelling and visitors' pontoons on its northern side. The *Capitainerie* (harbour office) is near the root of this breakwater.

Formalities

It is not necessary for a yacht registered in the EU to report to customs if arriving from another EU country, but failure to do so implies a formal declaration that the vessel complies with all the detailed customs and health regulations. Non-EU-registered yachts, those arriving from a non-EU country or those with non-EU nationals aboard should report arrival without delay. All yachts must carry some form of registration and insurance, and it is important that these documents are originals and in-date. Officials may visit yachts, sometimes boarding at sea.

Facilities

Boatyard With 14-tonne travel lift and 6-tonne crane at the Marina du Moulin Blanc.
Engineers/electronics At the marina and the Port du Commerce.
Sailmaker At the marina and the Port du Commerce.
Chandlery At the marina and the Port du Commerce.
Chart agent At the Port du Commerce.
Weather forecasts Posted daily at the harbour office. See *Admiralty Maritime Communications NP 289* and *RYA Weather Forecasts G5/2002* for full details of those available.
Diesel/petrol At the marina.
Water On pontoons at the marina.
Electricity On pontoons at the marina.
Bottled gas At the marina, and many places in the city (Camping Gaz only available).

Plan 33 *Brest, France.*

Ice At the marina.
Showers At the marina.
Laundry/laundrette At the marina.
Banks Currency exchange available at the harbour office, and many banks in the city.
General shopping Shops of all varieties in the city.

Provisioning Grocery store in the marina, large super-market on the road into Brest, plus many others.
Restaurants/hotels Restaurant in the marina complex, plus many others.
Medical services Good, as befits a large city.

Communications

Mailing address C/o Port de Plaisance du Moulin Blanc, 29200 Brest, France, by prior arrangement.
Post office In the city.
Telephones Kiosks at the marina and in the city.
Bus/rail services Frequent buses into the city (although the marina lies 5km (3 miles) beyond the Port du Commerce, it is little more than 1 mile from the city by land). Trains from Brest to Morlaix, Rennes and Paris.
Taxis/car hire Agency at the marina, plus bicycle hire.
Air services Twice-daily flights to Paris (not Sundays). Guipavas airport 10km (6 miles) from the city centre.

Looking north to Marina du Moulin Blanc, Brest. Photo SHOM.

5 La Coruña, Spain

43°21'.5N 8°23'W UT + 1

Springs: 4.2m	Range 3.9m	
Neaps: 2.8m	Range 1.2m	
Flag: Spain	Currency: Euro	
Tel/fax – Country code: 34, Area code: (9) 81		
Charts	Admiralty	US
General	87 (1:1,000,000)	37034 (1:300,000)
Approach	1111 (1:200,000)	37505 (1:156,800)
Harbour	1114 (1:25,000)	37506 (1:25,000)

General

La Coruña is a major city of Galicia with roots going back to Roman times, and although the newer parts of the city are largely commercial, the older quarters are very picturesque and well worth exploring. La Coruña is a busy fishing and commercial port, also visited by cruise ships, and facilities are generally good.

The main yachting facility is situated inside the north-west end of Dique de Abrigo, the major breakwater protecting the harbour just below a conspicuous double tower.

Of the four marina pontoons, the northern two are administered by the Sporting Club Casino, the southern two by the Real Club Náutico, an arrangement that can occasionally cause confusion. Pontoons have now been placed in the Dársena de la Marina just to the west of Castillo de San Antón, and this alternative is nearer to the town and the shops.

Approach

Yachts on passage southwards across the Bay of Biscay may make landfall anywhere on the coast between Pta Estaca de Bares [Fl (2) 7.5s 99m 25M] nearly 40 miles to the north-east of La Coruña and Islas Sisargas [Fl (3) 15s 108m 23M] just over 20 miles to the west. An even better landfall would be Cabo Prior [Fl (1+2) 15s 105m 22M], about 10 miles north of La Coruña entrance. The Torre de Hércules [Fl (4) 20s 104m 23M], which stands on the peninsula to the west of the harbour, was originally built by the Romans and is the world's oldest operational lighthouse. There are various banks and shoals in the approaches which, although not of depths to trouble yachts, can cause the seas to break severely in bad weather. In these conditions approach is best made from the west, on a bearing of no more than 145° on the Torre de Hércules until the prominent Punta Mera leading line on 109° can be picked up, which leads inside the offlying banks; the Punta Fiaiteira leading line on 182° will then lead in close to the south-east end of Dique de Abrigo.

Radio

La Coruña port control operates on VHF channels 12, 16 and 70. Both sections of the marina monitor channel 09. Port control – tel: 34 (9)81 227402/223220, fax: 34 (9)81 205862.

Entrance

The entrance is straightforward by day or night. Dique de Abrigo is a solid affair, visible from some distance and lit at its eastern end. The tall, white double tower near its root houses the port authorities as well as a restaurant with spectacular views. A floating breakwater some 200m (660ft) long lies off the Castillo de San Antón, running on an axis of 065°–245°. It is intended to protect the marina from wash, but is low in the water and may be difficult to see, particularly at night.

Anchorage and moorings

There are a limited number of mooring buoys controlled by the two yacht clubs – consult the appropriate club boatman. It is also possible to anchor further out, in about 12m (40ft) over mud. However, there is little shelter from winds from the south-east sector, holding is patchy, and a trip line advisable. There appears to be no objection to landing by dinghy on the marina pontoons, whether on a mooring or anchored off.

Various other anchorages exist in the Ría de la Coruña, but none are convenient to the city.

Berthing and marinas

As stated above, there is a relatively small marina shared between the Sporting Club Casino (tel: 209007, fax: 213953) and the Real Club Náutico (tel: 207910, fax: 203008). A few of the 250 or so berths are reserved for visitors. Parts of the marina are shallow and rocky, including the fuel berth which has just 1m (3ft) alongside. Berthing in both sections is either bow- or stern-to, with a holding-off line provided. Yachts longer than about 15m (50ft), and more than 2.5m (8ft) draught, should seek a berth in Dársena de la Marina.

Formalities

In theory it is not necessary for a yacht registered in the EU to report to customs if arriving from another EU country unless there are non-EU nationals aboard, and in any case formalities in Spain have always been relaxed. However, it can do no harm to check in, and non-EU-registered yachts should report arrival without delay. Enquire at the yacht club as to current procedure.

Plan 34 La Coruña, Spain.

Facilities

Boatyard With 25-tonne travel lift at the Real Club Náutico.

Engineers/electronics Enquire at the Real Club Náutico.

Sailmaker Toldos Jar, at Calle Merced 40–42, a taxi-ride across the city.

Chandlery Yacht chandlery at Regata, at Pasio Dársena, 13 Bajo; larger items obtainable from Effectos Navales Pombo on Avenida Primo de Riveira.

Yacht clubs The Real Club Náutico (tel: 207910, fax: 203008) and Sporting Club Casino (tel: 209007, fax: 213953) both have premises by the marinas.

Weather forecasts La Coruña NAVTEX station is identification letter D; the range of the station is about 300 miles, but reception is not very good in the port;

24-hour forecasts at 0950, 1150 and 2150 UT on VHF channel 26 (in Spanish).

Diesel/petrol In the marina.

Water At marina berths.

Electricity At marina berths (220 volt, 50 Hz).

Bottled gas Camping Gaz readily available in the city. Calor Gas and propane cylinders must be taken to a plant some miles to the south for refilling.

Showers In both clubs.

Laundry/laundrette In the Real Club Náutico.

Banks Many in the city, with ATMs.

General shopping Excellent, but a fair walk unless in Dársena de la Marina.

Provisioning For a major stock-up it may be worth

Looking NW towards the marina at La Coruña. Dique de Abrigo Ii, at its eastern end, is seen in the foreground. Photo Anne Hammick.

taking a taxi to the hypermarket outside the city. Otherwise, there is good provisioning in the city, with a particularly good fruit, vegetable and fish market.

Restaurants/hotels Many and varied.

Medical services Hospital outside the city.

Communications

Mailing addresses C/o the main post office (the *poste restante* office has a separate entrance around the back) or at the Real Club Náutico by prior arrangement.

Post office This imposing building is on the main thoroughfare leading past the Dársena de la Marina.

Telephones At the marina and throughout the city. Mobile phone coverage good.

Bus/rail services Local buses, trains to Madrid and elsewhere.

Taxis/car hire No problem.

Air services The airport at Santiago de Compostela about 60km (38 miles) away handles many international flights. La Coruña airport is close to the port and handles internal flights, with occasional ones to the United Kingdom in the summer; otherwise, all destinations can be reached from La Coruña via Madrid.

Bayona, Spain
42°07'N 8°51'W UT + 1

Springs: 3.5m		Range 3.0m	
Neaps: 2.7m		Range 1.3m	
Flag: Spain		Currency: Euro	
Tel/fax – Country code: 34, Area code: 986			
Charts	Admiralty		US
General	3633	(1:200,000)	51100 (1:200,000)
Approach	2548	(1:42,000)	–

General

A medium-sized town, Bayona is one of the most popular and useful harbours on this coast for the cruising sailor. It can be entered in all weathers by day and night and the shelter is good – except in easterlies, which are rare. The security in the marina is good and a yacht can be left here with confidence. The surrounding area is attractive, with some pleasant walks, and the town contains many old buildings. The city of Vigo lies less than 8 miles away as the crow flies (though considerably further by road), and any requirement that cannot be satisfied in Bayona can probably be met in Vigo.

Bayona was Columbus's first Iberian landfall on his return from the Caribbean in 1493 aboard the *Pinta*, after a less than warm reception in the Azores.

Approach

Approach may either be made from the north, passing inside the Islas Cies and with Cabo de Home and Punta Robaleira [Fl (2) WR 7.5s 25m 11/9M] to port, or from the west, to the south of the Islas Cies and leaving the Islote Boerio (or Agoeiro) [Fl (2) R 8s 21m 6M] to port.

If coming from south of west, Cabo Silleiro [Fl (2+1) 15s 83m 24M] may be the landfall, but it should be noted that the lighthouse is situated nearly 1 mile south of the headland of the same name, from which offlying rocks extend some distance northwards.

Radio

The Monte Real Club de Yates, which runs the marina, monitors VHF channel 06.

Entrance

If approaching from inside the Islas Cies, the intrepid may wish to try a passage, known as the Canal de la Porta, which leads between Monte Ferro and the easternmost of the three Estelas islands. However, it shoals to 0.9m (3ft), so a large-scale chart will be needed.

Most sailors will prefer to use the main entrance, leaving Las Serralleiras [Fl G 4s 9m 6M] – and its atten-

Bayona, looking SW with the marina in the foreground. Monte Real Club de Yates is on the right with the anchorage on the left. Photo Anne Hammick.

Plan 35 *Bayona, Spain.*

dant buoys marking the western extremity of the Islas las Estelas – well to port. The leading lights then bear 084°, with the front one, Cabezo de San Juan, being on a shoal almost in the centre of the bay. In daylight, both Pta del Buey and the breakwater head can be left close to starboard.

Anchorage and moorings

The yacht anchorage, which has excellent holding, is to the south and south-west of the mole, outside the mooring buoys. The fairway leading to the fishermen's mole south of the marina should be left clear. The moorings are administered by the yacht club – consult their berthing master. The club does not like dinghies from anchored yachts being left tied to its pontoons, but there is generally space to leave a dinghy on the pontoons at the fishermen's mole.

Berthing and marinas

The marina pontoons are administered by the Monte Real Club de Yates (tel: 986 355234, fax: 986 355061). The reception and fuelling berths are on the south side of the main jetty, and though much of the marina is occupied by local boats the berthing master is usually

able to arrange a visitor's berth. There are two berths available up to 35m (116ft), but there are draught restrictions in some parts of the marina.

There are sometimes pontoons placed on the inner side of Dique de Abrigo, where there are no facilities – but no charges either.

Formalities

In theory it is not necessary for a yacht registered in the EU to report to customs if arriving from another EU country and crewed only by EU nationals, and in any case formalities in Spain have always been relaxed. However, it can do no harm to check in, and non-EU-registered yachts should report arrival without delay. Enquire at the yacht club as to current procedure.

Facilities

Boatyard Repair facilities and a 17-tonne travel lift at the Monte Real Club de Yates. For major work, try Astilleros Lagos, Avda de Eduardo Cabello 2, 36208 Vigo (tel: 232626, fax: 291833), a family-run boatyard with a high reputation for quality and where good English is spoken.

Engineers/electronics Some facilities at the yacht club, but for major work it may be necessary to go to Vigo.

Chandlery There are two in Bayona and a major chandlery in Vigo.

Yacht club The Monte Real Club de Yates (tel: 355234/ 355576, fax: 355061) occupies an imposing building overlooking the marina and bay. It has a large and comfortable bar and a good restaurant.

Weather forecast Posted daily at the yacht club.

Diesel/petrol Fuelling berth on the south side of the marina main jetty, but access may be tidal limited for the deeper-draught yacht.

Water At marina berths.

Electricity At marina berths (220 volt, 50 Hz).

Bottled gas Camping Gaz available in the town.

Ice At the yacht club.

Showers In the basement of the yacht club.

Laundry/laundrette One road back from the waterfront.

Banks Several in the town, with credit card facilities.

General shopping Usual medium-sized town facilities.

Provisioning Several small supermarkets, plus a fresh produce market. Adequate for replenishing supplies.

Restaurants/hotels Numerous. The Parador, a hotel converted from the Castillo de Monte Real, has attractive walks, a restaurant and a bar – all are open to non-residents.

Medical services A clinic near to the marina; nearest hospital is in Vigo.

Communications

Mailing address C/o the Monte Real Club de Yates, Bayona, Galicia, Spain, by prior arrangement.

Post office In the town.

Telephones Booths at the yacht club and in town; mobile coverage is reasonable.

Bus/rail services Buses to Vigo, linking with railway.

Taxis/car hire Enquire at the yacht club.

Air services National airport at Vigo, or international flights from Santiago de Compostela (about an hour away).

7 Leixões, Portugal

41°11'N 8°42'W UT

Charts	Admiralty	US
General	3634 (1:200,000)	51100 (1:200,000)
		51120 (1:200,000)
Approach	3254 (1:50,000)	51109 (1:50,000)
Harbour	3254 (1:10,000)	51109 (1:15,000)

Springs: 3.2m   **Range** 3.0m

Neaps: 2.4m   **Range** 1.3m

Flag: Portugal   **Currency:** Euro

Tel/fax – Country code: 351, Area code: 22

General

Leixões, with its well-protected entrance, is a good port of refuge that can be entered in almost any weather (the other refuge ports are Cascais and Nazaré). There is a small marina in the northern corner of what is otherwise a rather grim oil, fishing and general commercial port. Inevitably, it can sometimes be rather dirty.

Leixões lies only a few miles north of the ancient city of Porto (Oporto) on the Rio Douro, the approach to which can be dangerous in onshore winds or swell.

Approach

Compared to the coastline further north, the area around Leixões is somewhat featureless. The oil refinery 1.5 miles to the north is a good mark by day or night, with the powerful Leça light [Fl (3) 14s 57m 28M] lying between it and the town. South of Leixões, the city of Oporto can be seen from well offshore.

Radio

The Radar Station controls navigation within 18 miles of the port approaches, working on VHF channels 11, 12, 13, 16, 19 and 60. Port control uses channels 61, 64, 79 and 80. Channel 13 is used for navigational safety. The marina monitors channel 62. Harbour Authority – tel: 351 22 995 3000; the Marina – tel: 351 22 9964895.

Entrance

If approaching from the north, harbour regulations state that vessels must give the northern breakwater a berth of at least 1 mile. Not all fishing boats observe this, though there are dangers 200m (660ft) to its seaward side. During westerly gales the swell at the entrance may be heavy, but this is lost once within the breakwater. Head for the middle of the passage between the two inner moles on about 355°. At night, the breakwater light may be difficult to identify against the bright shore lights, but from south of Leixões the Leça light on 350° leads through the inner moles. The marina mole has been extended and is now lit.

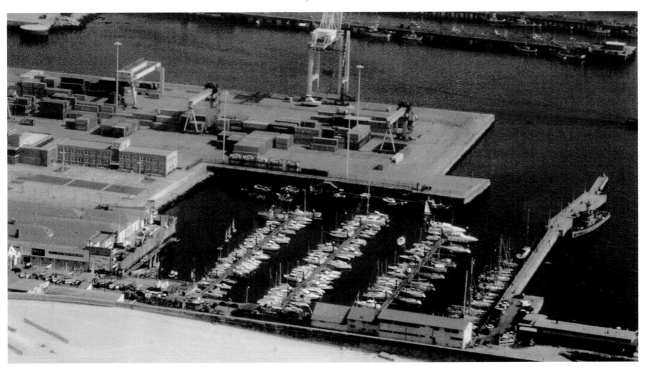

Leixões marina looking SE. Photo Anne Hammick.

Plan 36 *Leixões, Portugal.*

Anchorage and moorings

It is possible to anchor in the angle formed by the marina's south-west wall and the main breakwater in 4.0m (13ft) or less.

Berthing and marinas

The Marina Porto Atlântico (tel: 996 4895, fax: 996 4899) occupies the old fishing harbour in the northern corner of the main harbour. The south-east facing entrance is less than 50m (165ft) wide. All its 250 berths are normally occupied, but space will probably be found – secure to the reception pontoon (to starboard on entry) and visit the marina office on the north mole (open 0900–1830 daily, or 0900–2000 from mid-June to mid-September). Berthing is either bow- or stern-to with a holding-off line provided.

Formalities

Although the advent of the EU has led to a lessening of the previous strict formalities exercised by the Portuguese, all foreign yachts are still (2003) expected to report their arrival, and their movements once within the country, to the relevant authorities. In this instance visit the marina office, taking passports, ship's papers and insurance documents. The Administração do Portos do Douro e Leixões occupies the upper floor.

Facilities

Boatyard/engineers/electronics Practically any repair can be made at the larger yards, though this is geared more to fishing vessels than yachts. There is no travel lift at the marina itself, only a 6.5-tonne crane.

Sailmaker Near the airport, about 6km (4 miles) away; ask for details at the marina.

Yacht clubs The Clube Vela Atlântico (tel: 995 2725) and Clube Náutico de Leça (tel: 995 1700) overlook the marina.

Diesel On the south-west wall of the marina.

Petrol By can from filling stations.

Water On the marina pontoons.

Electricity On the marina pontoons (220 volt, 50 Hz).

Bottled gas Camping Gaz available in the town.

Showers Unisex showers in the marina building, otherwise at the Clube Vela Atlântico.

Banks In the town, most with credit card facilities.

General shopping Reasonable, but better in Oporto.

Provisioning As above. There is a market at Matosinhos, best reached by taxi.

Restaurants/hotels The Clube Vela Atlântico serves meals, but there is much more choice in Oporto.

Medical services Best to go to Oporto if possible.

Communications

Mailing address C/o the Marina Porto Atlântico, Molhe Norte, Leça de Palmeira, 4450 Matosinhos, Portugal, by prior arrangement, or at the main post office.

Post office/telephones In Leixões.

Bus/rail services The 44 and 76 buses run from near the marina gate into Oporto, and link with the rail network at Leça de Palmeira and Oporto.

Taxis Readily available.

Car hire In Oporto, or can be arranged through the marina office.

Air services Oporto International airport lies about 6km (4 miles) north-east from Leixões.

Lisbon, Portugal
38°41'.5N 9°12'.5W UT

Charts	Admiralty	US
General	3635 (1:200,000)	51150 (1:300,000)
Approach	3263 (1:25,000)	51142 (1:75,000)
Harbour	3264 (1:25,000)	51143 (1:15,000)

Springs: 3.8m   **Range** 3.3m

Neaps: 3.0m   **Range** 1.5m

Flag: Portugal   **Currency:** Euro

Tel/fax – Country code: 351, **Area code:** 21

General

Lisbon has been the capital of Portugal for more than 700 years. It occupies a splendid site on the north bank of the Rio Tejo (River Tagus), which allows sizeable ships to berth in front of one of the main squares. It is an intriguing city with Arabic undertones and a history of seafaring and exploration. The maritime museum (just inland from the Tôrre de Belém) is particularly fascinating and not to be missed.

Provision for yachts visiting Lisbon is improving rapidly, and any remaining shortcomings are more than compensated for by the sheer interest of berthing in the heart of one of Europe's more handsome capital cities.

For those not wanting to make the 10-mile journey upriver to the city there is perfect shelter, and most facilities, in the new marina at Cascais. This, too, would be a safer option in strong south-west winds, when the outer part of the North Channel can become dangerous – especially on the ebb.

Approach

If making landfall from north or west, the high cliffs of Cabo da Roca [Fl (4) 18s 164m 26M] are likely to be the first indication that the latitude of Lisbon has nearly been

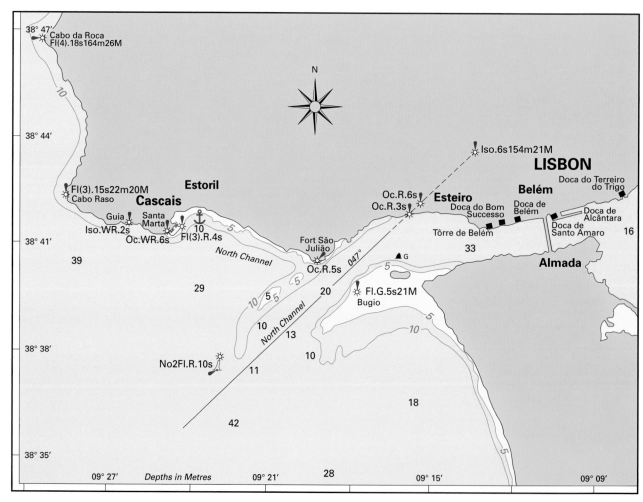

Plan 37 *Lisbon, Portugal.*

reached. Some 5 miles further south, the lower headland of Cabo Raso [Fl (3) 15s 22m 20M] is rounded to port, with the town of Cascais soon becoming visible. The marina is just round the point at Santa Marta and there is a large and pleasant anchorage off it in settled conditions, but open to the south and south-west.

Radio

Call Lisboa port control on VHF channel 16, and working channels 12, 13, 61 and 64. The Harbour Police broadcast navigational and storm warnings on channel 11. Cascais Marina is on channels 16 and 62.

Entrance

The Rio Tejo is entered between Fort São Julião on the north bank and Fort Bugio to the south-east. The main channel lies on a bearing of about 050° from No 2 buoy, or follow the leading lights at Esteiro up on 047°. Do not be tempted to cut Fort Bugio too close or turn too soon – the edge of the banks are marked by lit starboard-hand buoys; the best water and least ebb stream is found near the northern bank. Tidal streams run at 3 knots at springs (more on the ebb after heavy rain), and in strong south-westerly winds the outer part of the main channel in the vicinity of No 2 buoy can be dangerous.

There are shallow passages that cut the corner off to the east of Bugio, but these are not recommended unless you have a large-scale chart, the right state of the tide, settled weather and no swell. Once inside the mouth, the Rio Tejo is deep with no unmarked hazards. The Ponte de 25 Abril suspension bridge leading to Almada on the south bank has a clearance of 70m (230ft), so is unlikely to worry most yachts.

Lisbon: Tôrre de Belém.

Anchorage and moorings

There is no yacht anchorage convenient to Lisbon itself, though there are a number of possible areas further upriver where it widens into the Mar de Palha (literally 'Sea of Straw', or reeds). A large-scale Portuguese chart would be needed to proceed this far upstream.

Berthing and marinas

There are currently five marinas in Lisbon, not all of which accept visitors, with a sixth one further east. Brief details of all of them are given below.

All the yacht harbours are built inside old commercial docks – so be prepared for the tidal set across their

Cascais marina in the approaches to Lisbon, looking NW. The anchorage is to the right of the marina. Photo Anne Hammick.

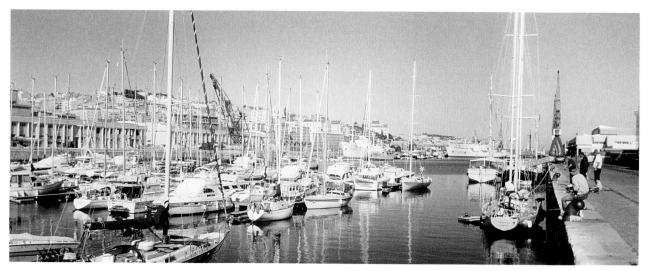

Doca de Alcântara in the centre of Lisbon, looking NE. Photo Anne Hammick.

often narrow entrances. Not only will it set the yacht sideways, but it may also tend to slew her round during those seconds when the bow is in the calm water of the entrance and the stern still in the moving river.

Taken from west to east, those docks used by yachts comprise:

1   The Doca do Bom Successo (tel: 21 392 2011), just upstream of the ornate (and largely original) Tôrre de Belém – which is floodlit at night. It is small and crowded, maximum length 12m (40ft), depths are claimed as 3.0m (10ft); the entrance is not lit; fuel and water are available.

2   The Doca de Belém (tel: 21 363 1246), just beyond the striking monument to Prince Henry the Navigator, which is also floodlit. There are unlikely to be any spaces for visitors, but fuel is available. It has been reported as dredged to 3.5m (12ft).

3   The Doca de Santo Amaro (tel: 21 392 2011, fax: 392 2038) is just east of the suspension bridge; it is also crowded with local boats, and it is unikely that you will find a space. It is reported as dredged to 4m (13ft) with a soft and muddy bottom. It is very noisy because of the constant traffic passing on the bridge overhead, and as a result of the many surrounding bars and night spots.

4   The Doca de Alcântara (tel: 21 392 2048, fax: 392 2038) – which contains over 200 berths and is being expanded – is currently the first place you should try as berths are reserved for visitors. The dock itself is more than 0.5 miles long, with the yacht berths at the west end. It is entered about 1 mile upstream of the suspension bridge via an entry channel crossed by a swing bridge. This is usually permanently open, but the situation might change. There is a waiting pontoon nearby. Until recently it was a purely commercial dock and is still used by ships of considerable size – for this reason, it can sometimes be oily. The pontoons are equipped with fingers and have water and electricity, but fuel is not available here. The depths are considerable and the largest yachts can be accommo-

dated alongside the wall. Security is adequate, via a gated fence, and the area is quietly commercial.

5   The Doca do Terreiro do Trigo, which is also known as the Marina Aporvela (tel: 21 887 6854, fax: 887 3885), is considerably further upstream near the old part of the city, just beyond the Doca de Marinha – which is reserved for naval use. It is run by the Portuguese Sail Training Organisation and, although normally occupied by their vessels, it may occasionally have space for a few visiting yachts. It was reported as being very shallow (drying at datum, but very soft mud) in 2000. It is close to the historic Alfama district, which is probably the only reason for going there.

6   The Marina Expo is 7 miles above Tôrre de Bélem and 1.5 miles below the new Vasco da Gama bridge. The entrance is 300m (0.2 miles) to the north of the red flashing CR6 buoy and is not lit. The marina has the usual facilities, but is only really convenient for the remaining attractions of the Expo 98 site, including the aquarium. There are over 500 berths, with a few up to 50m (165ft).

Cascais

The marina, built in 1999, has 650 berths in depths up to 6m (20ft); many are kept for visitors. There is berthing for large yachts over 40m (130ft) outside on a pontoon in depths of 7m (23ft). The east breakwater end extends north-east underwater, and a wide sweep outside the buoys marking it should be taken on the approach. The marina has all the facilities needed, including a 70-tonne travel lift, fuel, water, electricity and a small supermarket on site, with full provisioning possible nearby in Cascais town. There are frequent and swift train communications with Lisbon, and the international airport is less than one hour away.

The anchorage off the town is good in sand and mud, but is being encroached by small-boat moorings and is open to the south and south-west – although the marina now offers further shelter.

A new but smaller marina at Oeiras, halfway between Cascais and Lisbon, should be completed in 2003.

Formalities

The advent of the EU should in theory mean fewer formalities for EU-registered yachts arriving from another EU country, but all foreign yachts should report their arrival to the relevant authorities. All that is now necessary is for the skipper to report to the marina office with the usual papers and passports on arrival and fill in a standard form.

A port control launch may intercept the yacht while entering Lisbon and officials come aboard. It would be as well to have all necessary paperwork to hand. This does not exempt the skipper from the normal clearance once berthed.

Facilities

Boatyards/engineers/electronics Good facilities are available in Lisbon, though two of the yards, Estaleiro Venancio at Amora and Estaleiro Jose Gouveia at Porto Brandao, are on the south bank of the Tejo. There are many others – ask marina staff or enquire at the Associação Naval de Lisboa at the Doca de Belém, where there is a boatyard with a travel lift and also a scrubbing grid.

Sailmaker Velamar in Rua do Giestal, or enquire at the marina office.

Chandlery J Garraio, Avenida 24 Julho 2 (tel: 347 3081), and Godhino, both in the Cais Sodre area near the Estoril train terminal.

Charts The Instituto Hidrografico (tel: 395 5119/5124, fax: 396 0515), Rua das Trinas 49 (the shop door is on the side of the building, on Rua Garoa de Orta), publishes Portuguese charts and pilots. Also, Godhino and Garraio (see above), or G Vieria, Travessa do Carvalho 15-1, 1200 for US DMA charts.

Yacht club The Associação Naval de Lisboa has premises overlooking the Doca de Belém. Aporvela, the Portuguese Sail Training Association, have their headquarters at the Doca do Terreiro do Trigo.

Weather forecast A five-day forecast is available, in English, from the Lisbon meteorological office on tel: 848 3961, for a small charge. Daily forecasts are posted in all the marinas.

Diesel Not available at either the Doca de Alcântara or Doca de Santo Amaro. The Shell wharf on the south bank about 1 mile below the suspension bridge will serve larger yachts requiring reasonable quantities.

Water In all the marinas.

Electricity In all the marinas (220 volt, 50 Hz).

Bottled gas Camping Gaz is readily available in Lisbon. Calor Gas bottles may still be filled at a depot behind the Expo site.

Showers At the Doca de Belém and Doca do Terreiro do Trigo, plus a shower block between the Doca de Santo Amaro and Doca de Alcântara that is shared by both marinas.

Laundry/laundrette Several in the city.

Banks Many, with credit card facilities. Banking hours 0830–1200 and 1345–1430.

General shopping Excellent.

Provisioning Very good – there are several large supermarkets in the city, one within five minutes' walk of the Doca de Alcântara, and a hypermarket on the road to Cascais (you will need taxis there and back).

Restaurants/hotels Many and varied. Some bars and restaurants feature live *fado* singing.

Medical services The British Hospital, Rua Saraiva de Carvalho 49.

Communications

Mailing address Probably best c/o the Doca de Alcântara, 1300 Alcântara, Lisbon, Portugal, by prior arrangement, though there is an entire building adjacent to the main post office given over to nothing but *poste restante*.

Internet and e-mail services There are many internet cafés to be found.

Post office/telephones Many. Stamps can be bought at any shop displaying the green *correio* sign.

Bus/tram/rail services Frequent buses and trams between the Belém area and central Lisbon. Trains to Cascais every 30 minutes via Belém and Estoril. The revamped metro is efficient, but the city centre stations are hard to find.

Taxis/car hire No problem.

Air services Lisbon has an international airport in the north-east part of the city, to which it is linked by buses, rail and metro.

9 Lagos, Portugal
37°06'N 8°40'W UT

Springs: 3.4m	Range 2.8m	
Neaps: 2.6m	Range 1.2m	
Flag: Portugal	Currency: Euro	
Tel/fax – Country code: 351, Area code: 282		
Charts	Admiralty	US
General	89 (1:175,000)	51160 (1:300,000)
	–	51155 (1:150,000)

General

Lagos is a small town with an active fishing fleet, some excellent beaches much favoured by tourists, and a first-class marina founded in 1994. The entrance is shallow (2.3m (8ft)) and should not be attempted in strong south-east winds. In these conditions, Portimao (also with a new marina), 7 miles to the east, would be preferable. Lagos is a secure place to leave a yacht and it has good communications.

Approach

Lagos is 17 miles east of Cape St Vincent and 7 miles west of Portimao. It lies 1.5 miles north of Ponta da Piedade, and has an indented and rocky coast; its small beaches are appreciated by tourists and sailors alike. There are no offlying dangers outside the 5m line. A safe approach to the entrance is between 350° and 280°.

Radio

Harbour control operates on VHF channels 11 and 16, 0900–1200 and 1400–1700 Monday to Friday. Marina de Lagos operates on channels 16 and 62, 0800–2200 in the summer. English is spoken.

Entrance

The entrance is straightforward between the two breakwaters, but a bar forms outside them from time to time. The approach should be made with a close eye kept on the state of tide and the echo sounder. Once inside, the channel and the marina carry at least 3m (10ft).

Anchorage and moorings

In westerlies, an anchorage may be found outside between the breakwaters and Ponta de Piedade, or to the north-east of the breakwater ends off Praia de San Roque in hard sand.

Berthing and marinas

The Marina de Lagos lies about 0.75 miles from the entrance (tel: 770210, fax: 770219). Go alongside the long pontoon on the east side below the offices, and before the footbridge, to complete formalities. Visitors are not welcome in the fishing harbour to starboard on the way up. The footbridge will open on request on channel 62 between 0800 and 2200, but stays closed 15

Plan 38 *Lagos.*

minutes either side of train arrival or departure times.

The bridge has a limiting width of 11m (36ft). There are always berths for visitors – boats up to 30m (100ft) overall and 3m (10ft) draught.

Formalities

All formalities are handled at the marina office, which lies just above the reception pontoon below the footbridge. A careful if discreet watch is kept on the movement of all yachts on the Algarve coast due to the activities of drug smugglers from North Africa.

Facilities

Boatyard In the fishing harbour, where they are able to haul boats in a hydraulic cradle (up to 14 tonnes or 15m (50ft) LOA) for scrubbing or for other work. A travel lift in the marina has been planned for several years, but has been slow to materialise.

Engineers At the boatyard. They are agents for a number of international firms.

Electronics and radio At the boatyard, and also Bluewater Yacht Services Lda (see below).

Sailmaker Enquire at the marina office.

Chandlery Several, including Bluewater Yacht Services Lda on the upper floor of the marina office complex.

Yacht club The friendly Clube de Vela de Lagos is situated near the entrance at the root of the west breakwater.

Diesel Fuel pumps on the reception pontoon during office hours; cash only.

Water At all berths and at the fuel pontoon.

Electricity At all berths, with a variety of voltages available.

Bottled gas Camping Gaz is available from the hardware shop near the railway station, and from some of the chandlers.

Ice At the fuel/reception pontoon.

Showers A shower block is adjacent to the marina office complex.

Laundrettes Near to the shower block.

Banks In the marina complex, and also many, with ATMs, in the town.

General shopping There are many tourist and general shops in the town.

Provisioning Excellent, either from the small shops in the marina complex, the many shops in the town, or from an enormous supermarket near the road bridge north of the marina.

Restaurants/hotels A great many of all sizes, prices and qualities.

Looking SSE down onto Lagos with the marina in the foreground and the fishing harbour and boatyard beyond. Photo Anne Hammick.

Medical services In the town, including a private hospital that also deals with dental problems.

Communications

Mailing address C/o Marina de Lagos, Apartado 18, 8600 Lagos, Portugal, by prior arrangement.

Fax services At the marina office (fax: 770219).

Post office In the town.

Telephones Several booths around the marina basin, which will accept either money or cards. Mobile coverage is good.

Rail service Lagos is at the west end of the rather slow Algarve coastal line: 90 minutes to reach the airport.

Taxis/car hire No problem, obtainable through the marina office.

Air services Faro International airport is 50 minutes by taxi, 90 minutes (but very much cheaper) by train.

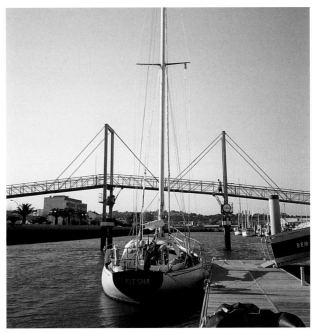
Lagos: the reception pontoon looking north to the footbridge. Photo John Lawson.

Gibraltar,
36°8'.5N 5°22'W UT + 1

Springs: 1.0m		**Range** 0.9m		
Neaps: 0.7m		**Range** 0.4m		

Flag: British (Red Ensign)

Currency: Gibraltar £ and GBP

Tel/fax – Country code: 350, **Area code:** none

Charts	Admiralty		US	
General	92	(1:400,000)	52040	(1:300,000)
	773	(1:300,000)		
Approach	142	(1:100,000)	52039	(1:100,000)
Harbour	1448	(1:25,000)	52043	(1:15,000)
	144	(1:10,000)		
	45	(1:3,600)		

General

Gibraltar is a British colony, self-governing, through an elected House of Assembly. It has withstood a number of Spanish sieges, but since 1985 the border with Spain has been open on both sides. Tourism is the major industry, though its importance in banking and as a tax haven is growing. The population is an ethnic mixture of all the Mediterranean races as well as British, and while English is the official language, much Spanish is also spoken.

Though somewhat off the beaten track so far as the average Atlantic cruise is concerned, Gibraltar is a good place for major repairs or to lay up, particularly for those with a limited command of foreign languages. It is also considerably quicker and easier to get imported items through customs in Gibraltar than in many other places – yacht equipment sent from abroad addressed to the yacht and marked 'Ship's Stores In Transit' will normally be admitted duty free, though personal imports are usually subject to duty. It may actually be cheaper to have equipment flown in than to buy locally.

Approach

The Rock of Gibraltar is quite unmistakable from both west and east. After dark, the Aeromarine light flashes the letters GB in Morse from high on the rock itself [R 10s 405m 30M], with the sectored Europa Point light [Iso W 10s 49m 19M, Oc R 10s 15m and FR 44m 15M] near its southern tip. The airport, just to the north of the customs berth and two of the three marinas, is also well lit.

Gibraltar Bay has deep water everywhere except for the offshore reefs on its western side, from Pta Carnero to just south of Algeciras. Depths in the area north of the airstrip (where a new, Spanish-owned marina has recently been completed) also shelve gradually.

Radio

Port control operates on VHF channels 06, 12, 13, 14 and 16; channel 12 is the Gibraltar Bay working channel. Marina Bay operates daily on channel 71, 0830–2230, with fewer hours in winter. Sheppard's Marina also operates on channel 71 (working hours only). Queensway Marina operates on channel 73, 0830–2145, with fewer hours in winter. Queen's Harbour Master controls the military port on channel 08.

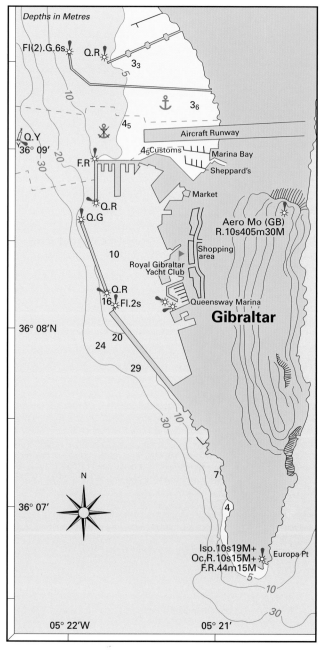

Plan 39 *Gibraltar.*

Entrance

If making for one of the two northern marinas, head north-east into Gibraltar Bay past the long breakwaters of the naval and commercial port. The airport runway will be seen ahead – both Marina Bay and Sheppard's Marina lie in the angle formed between the North Mole and the runway. Note that before securing at either marina, yachts must first call at the reporting station on the North Mole (*see* 'Formalities' below).

If heading for Queensway Quay Marina, pass between the south mole and the detached mole (both lit), from which the marina entrance (also lit) will be seen about 650m (0.5 miles) ahead. This entrance can be confusing if approached for the first time after dark, as two long floating pontoons produce a very distinct 'S' bend (an attempt to keep swell out). If berthing at Queensway Quay Marina, the requirement to first visit the reporting station is waived and formalities can be completed at Queensway (*see* 'Formalities' below).

Anchorage and moorings

It is possible to anchor north of the runway, but note the prohibited areas shown on the plan. Holding is good in 4–5m (13–17ft) over sand. As the border runs close north of the runway, most of this anchorage is actually in Spain.

Berthing and marinas

Three marinas serve Gibraltar, the northern two being long-established, while Queensway Quay is relatively new. All tend to be full and it is wise to telephone in advance. Otherwise, contact via VHF on approach.

1 Marina Bay (tel: 73300, fax: 42656) is the largest of the three with about 200 berths – maximum boat length 70m (230ft), maximum draught 4.5m (14ft). The reception berth is alongside the office towards the outer end of the main pier – office hours are 0800–2230 daily. Proof of insurance will be required.
2 Sheppard's Marina (tel: 75148/77183, fax: 42535) was established in 1961 and is very much a working boatyard with comprehensive repair and maintenance facilities – maximum boat length 30m (100ft), least depth 3.5m (12ft). Arrivals berth alongside the pontoon extending south-west from the main pier. Many of its 140 berths are bow- or stern-to without finger pontoons. Office hours are 0900–1255 and 1430–1800, weekdays only.
3 Queensway Quay Marina (tel: 44700, fax: 44699) opened in 1994 as part of a rather attractive wharf-side development – maximum boat length 35m (116ft), least depth 3.5m (12ft). It has the advantage over the older marinas of greater distance from the dust and noise of the airport, and of being barely a five-minute walk from the town centre. The staff are noted for being particularly helpful and friendly. Problems with swell entering the marina in westerly

gales have led to the dog-leg entrance described above, and the re-siting of the main pontoons from a north/south axis to an east/west axis; this appears to have done the trick. Office hours are 0830–2145 in summer, with fewer hours in winter.

Formalities

Gibraltar is not a part of the EU and all yachts must observe the formalities. If making for Marina Bay or Sheppard's Marina, yachts must first call at the reporting station (Waterport Wharf) on the north mole opposite the western end of the airport runway. The station flies the Q flag by day, has an illuminated sign at night, and has a berthing pontoon. Visitors to Queensway Quay Marina may complete customs formalities by fax from the marina office. In both cases, normal particulars of vessel and crew will be required. Any crew member leaving the yacht, whether to move ashore, to another vessel or to leave by air, must be reported by the skipper to the police and the crew list amended accordingly. The same applies to any new arrivals on board. Yacht departures are notified to the marina office, which informs the relevant authorities. Quarantine restrictions no longer apply to animals aboard yachts, though they should be declared on arrival.

Facilities

Boatyards Gun Wharf Ltd (further south from Queensway Marina inside the main commercial harbour) can handle vessels up to 200 tonnes. It has an excellent reputation, but is not cheap. Sheppard's Marina has a 40-tonne travel lift and a 10-tonne crane, and permits DIY work. Cammell Laird Gibraltar at the south end of the harbour can handle the largest mega-yacht.

Engineers/electronics At Sheppard's Marina and elsewhere.

Sailmakers There are none in Gibraltar. The nearest is at Malaga, Mainland Marine Management Services (tel/fax: 353 952 499113; e-mail: mainlandmarine @terra.es), who may be willing to collect and deliver.

Chandleries At all three marinas. Delivery from the United Kingdom takes between three days and three weeks on a speed = cost ratio.

Chart agent Gibraltar Chart Agency Ltd, 11A Block 5, Watergardens (tel: 76293, fax: 77293).

Yacht club The long-established Royal Gibraltar Yacht Club (tel: 78897) welcomes visiting sailors as honorary members while in port.

Weather forecast Posted at the marinas, and broadcast on the English-language radio stations. Navtex: Tarifa (G).

Diesel At the Shell jetty near the customs office and at Queensway Marina.

Water At the Shell jetty and at marina berths.

Bottled gas Camping Gaz exchanges in Marina Bay and Sheppard's.

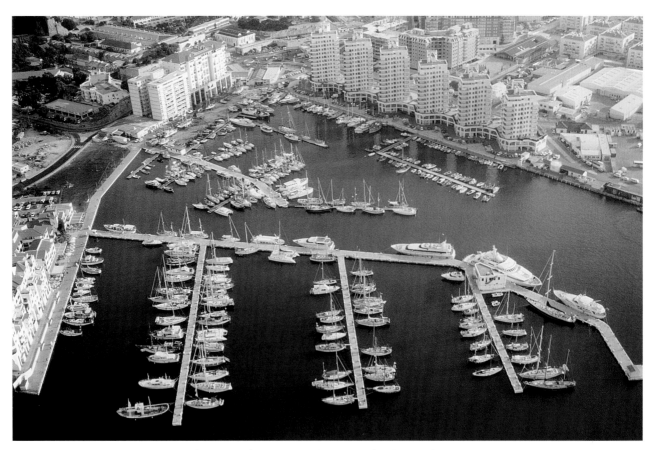

Gibraltar: looking SE over Marina Bay (foreground) and Sheppard's Marina (background). The customs reporting pontoon is on the quay to the right just out of the photo. Photo Anne Hammick.

Ice At the marinas.

Showers At the marinas.

Laundry/laundrette At Marina Bay and Queensway Marina, and in the town.

Banks At Marina Bay and in the town, with ATMs.

General shopping A wide range of shops, many shutting between 1300 and 1500.

Provisioning Several supermarkets, including a vast Safeway opposite Sheppard's Marina. Also, shops specialising in Spanish and Mediterranean foods.

Restaurants/hotels Wide choice at all prices.

Medical services St Bernards Hospital (casualty, tel: 73941); Health Clinic, Casement Square (tel: 78337/77603). Reciprocal arrangements with the NHS.

Communications

Mailing addresses C/o the Post Office; Marina Bay Complex Ltd, PO Box 80, Gibraltar; H Sheppard & Co Ltd, Waterport, Gibraltar; or Queensway Quay Marina, PO Box 19, Gibraltar – all requiring prior arrangement.

Public telephones Convenient to all marinas; some marina berths have telephone points. Mobile phone coverage is good.

Taxis Plenty.

Car hire Several rental firms; cars may be taken into Spain.

Buses Buses to La Linea, where connection may be made with the Spanish bus and train services.

Ferries Twice weekly to Tangier.

Air Several flights daily to the United Kingdom and also to Tangier and Morocco. There are no flights to or from Spain.

11 Funchal, Madeira
32°37'.5N 16°54'.5W UT –1

Springs: 2.4m	Range 2.0m	
Neaps: 1.8m	Range 0.9m	
Flag: Portugal	Currency: Euro	
Tel/fax – Country code: 351, Area code: 291		

Charts	Admiralty		US	
General	3132	(1:125,000)	51261	(1:150,000)
	3133	(1: 125,000)		
Approach	1831	(1:150,000)	51263	(1:10,000)
Harbour	1689	(1:7,500)	51263	(1:5,000)

General

Funchal is a favourite harbour with many ocean cruising sailors, and as a result it is very crowded – especially during the autumn. The city of Funchal is somewhat touristy, fed by the many cruise liners that visit, but the island itself is quite beautiful and well worth exploring.

There has long been talk of building a second yacht marina – most probably at Machico in the eastern part of the island, though possibly at an unspecified location west of Funchal.

The island of Porto Santo lies 30 miles to the north-east and it may be tempting to go there first when coming from that direction. There is a small but well-sheltered marina on the south coast of Porto Santo, with adequate provisions, but there are not the facilities to be found in Funchal.

Approach

Most yachts will approach from the east around Pta de Garajau, which is topped by a huge statue of Christ that is floodlit at night. The city and harbour are unmistakable by day or night, and Funchal Bay has deep water everywhere.

Radio

The port authority operates on VHF channels 11, 12, 13 and 16; intership traffic channels are 06 and 08; the marina monitors channel 62.

Plan 40 *Funchal, Madeira.*

The marina at Funchal, Madeira, looking east.

Entrance

This is very straightforward, though it would be unwise to cut the end of the main breakwater too close. If entering at night there are a great many shore lights, which could cause confusion, but on the other hand the ambient light will be helpful in spotting unlit mooring buoys or anchored yachts.

Anchorage and moorings

Yachts may anchor to the south or south-east of the marina in a somewhat exposed position, untenable in strong onshore winds when the only adequate shelter would be inside the marina. Depths of 10m (30ft) or more are found close inshore and the holding is poor in places. A First World War wreck lies directly off the easternmost of the two small river mouths some 400m (0.25 miles) east of the marina, and the area should be avoided.

Caution: Particular care must be taken if anchoring, as the prevailing north-easterly wind eddies around the mountains and frequently blows parallel to the south coast – generally from the west, but occasionally from the east. If combined with an onshore sea breeze during the afternoon, this will take on a southerly component, which will not only swing yachts through 360° each day, but may also set them ashore should they drag.

Berthing and marinas

The construction of a marina (tel: 232717, fax: 225524) in the mid-1980s was much welcomed by visiting sailors, and the administration has improved in the last few years. Four jetties with finger pontoons provide berths for around 160 local craft, but visiting yachts lie along-side the southern wall, frequently eight or ten abreast. Being in a commercial harbour, oil and debris may gather in the marina.

Formalities

Madeira is part of Portugal and therefore also part of the EU. In theory, this should mean fewer formalities for EU-registered yachts arriving from another EU country, but as of 2002 all foreign yachts were still required to report their arrival to the relevant authorities. These are conveniently situated together in a small office at the end of the south breakwater; the process takes about ten minutes. They should be visited again before departure.

Facilities

Boatyard/engineers/electronics Varadouro São Lázaro is situated close to the west of the marina and has a 25-tonne travel lift; it can cope with most repair work in all materials.

Ramp/drying grid Inside the mole to the west of the marina; it is capable of handling yachts up to about 11m (36ft) and 2.0m (7ft) draught.

Sailmaker Enquire at the marina office.

Chandlery There are three, one of which is in the marina; catalogued items take a few days from Lisbon.

Compass adjustment If wishing to check the yacht's compass:

1 The eastern end of the breakwater and the eastern end of the harbour office are in line on a bearing of true north.

2 From a position east of the breakwater, the lamp standards are in line on a bearing of true west.

Yacht club The Clube Naval do Funchal (CNF) has its clubhouse 2 miles west of Funchal at Quinta Calaca – visiting sailors are welcomed.

Weather forecast Posted daily in the window of the Capitania do Porto office and at around noon in the marina office. Navtex: Porto Santo (P).

Diesel and petrol At the western end of the marina wall, 0900–1600 weekdays, 0900–1200 Saturdays, closed Sunday.

Water At the marina wall. Madeiran water is exceptionally pure and sweet.

Shore power A few power points on the marina wall (220 volt, 50Hz).

Bottled gas Camping Gaz is available from the chandlers; it may be possible to get other bottles filled.

Ice From the fish dock at the western end of the harbour.

Showers In the marina complex; key from marina office.

Laundry/laundrette Next to the showers.

Banks Many, open 0830–1145 and 1300–1445, weekdays only. Most have ATMs.

General shopping Good and varied, though with a strong bias towards tourist items.

Provisioning Several well-stocked and reasonably priced supermarkets, and a minimarket in the marina. The fresh produce market in the eastern part of the town is a must – flowers, vegetables and fruit on two levels, with a busy fish market at the rear. Take your own egg boxes and plastic bags (and a camera).

Restaurants/hotels Very wide choice at all levels.

Medical services There is a health services information centre for visitors at 1 Rua das Pretas, plus several well-equipped hospitals, two of which have a 24-hour Accident and Emergency service.

Communications

Mailing address C/o the main post office or the Marina do Funchal, Funchal 9000, Madeira, Portugal.

Fax services At the marina office (fax: 225524) and the main post office.

Post office On Avenida Zarco. Open 0830–2000 weekdays, 0900–1230 Saturdays. Stamps can be bought at any shop displaying the green *correio* sign.

Telephones At the main post office, the marina office and elsewhere.

Bus service Cheap and reliable. A timetable is available from the tourist office.

Taxis/car hire Wide choice.

Ferry services Regular ferries to Porto Santo.

Air services Direct flights to London, Portugal and Porto Santo. Santa Catarina airport is 20km (12 miles) north-east from Funchal.

12 Harbours in the Canaries

Centred on *28°32'N 15°47'W UT*

Springs: 2.4m*		***Range*** 2.1m*	
Neaps: 1.8m*		***Range*** 0.8m*	
Flag: Spain		***Currency:*** Euro	

Tel/fax – Country code: 34, Area codes:
928 (Lanzarote, Fuerteventura and Gran Canaria)
922 (Tenerife, La Gomera, La Palma and El Hierro)

Charts**	Admiralty		US	
General	3133	(1:250,000)	51380	(1:263,900)
	3134	(1:250,000)	51260	(1:300,000)
Local	1869	(1:300,000)		
	1870	(1:300,000)		

General

Mention has already been made in Part II of the difficulty – if not impossibility – of finding an empty berth in many of the marinas in the Canary Islands. This is because nearly all the private marinas were built alongside holiday complexes, and in most cases a high proportion of the berths were sold together with the properties. The vast majority of the remaining berths are let annually.

For this reason, rather than covering one or two harbours in detail, it seemed more useful to describe four, scattered over as many islands. As of early 2003, all these harbours anticipated having berths available for transient yachts, even during the busy autumn season, and there are also new marinas or extensions of existing ones being built. However, it should be stressed that it is always worth telephoning ahead to check the current situation and to make a booking.

The main criteria for inclusion here is that all offer secure alongside or bow- or stern-to berthing, can be entered in all normal conditions, and can meet at least day-to-day shopping needs. Two – Puerto de la Luz at Las Palmas de Gran Canaria and Marina Atlantico at Santa Cruz de Tenerife – are close to major cities where a yacht can be provisioned for Atlantic passage. Puerto Calero, Lanzarote and San Sebastian de la Gomera are smaller and more remote, but also cleaner and more peaceful. Harbours are taken on a general north-east to south-west trend since few skippers will choose to pass through the islands in any other direction.

It should not be assumed that these are the only harbours worth visiting. If conditions are favourable, La Sociedad (Caleta Sebo) on Isla Graciosa, north of Lanzarote, makes a delightful landfall, provided almost nothing is required ashore. For those who do not mind the noise and smells of a busy fishing harbour, the anchorage inside Puerto de Naos (Lanzarote) gives total protection from the elements and convenient access to the city of Arrecife. Gran Canaria has possibly the most crowded marinas of the archipelago, though either Pasito Blanco or Puerto Rico may be able to find space for a visitor and both have well-run boatyards. Mogan has long been a favourite with British sailors, but seldom has a berth available.

On Tenerife, the small marina at Radazul can sometimes take visitors and has good workshop facilities. Further west there are anchorages at Las Galletas and Los Cristianos, though the latter is in theory closed to yachts other than those waiting for the travel lift (strictly DIY, but with the lowest prices in the Canaries). Puerto Colón no longer accepts visiting yachts, but Los Gigantes can sometimes take one or two.

On the smaller islands, Santa Cruz de la Palma offers pleasant, relaxed surroundings in which to make final preparations for the Atlantic passage, together with good shopping facilities and excellent tap water (rare in the Canaries). However, visiting yachts, though welcome, do not yet have custom-built berthing, and commercial berths are not always suitable. On El Hierro, the smallest and least visited of the Canaries, Puerto de la Restinga in the south offers a friendly if somewhat remote last stop before the Atlantic Ocean, together with some yard facilities. If planning to cruise the Canaries in any detail, the purchase of a cruising guide will be more than justified.

Shelter from stress of weather

The requirement to shelter a yacht at risk from heavy weather is generally honoured, though she may be requested to leave as soon as conditions have moderated. However, there appears to be no formal definition of 'heavy weather', presumably leaving a decision to the discretion of harbour staff.

Note:
* These figures are the mean over the island group.
** There are four further larger-scale Admiralty charts of harbours in the group and the Ilhas Selvagens.
  Spanish charts are more detailed and should be considered for use if cruising extensively among the islands.

Puerto Calero, Lanzarote
28°55'.1N 13°42'W

Charts	Admiralty	US
Approach	886 (1:75,000)	–

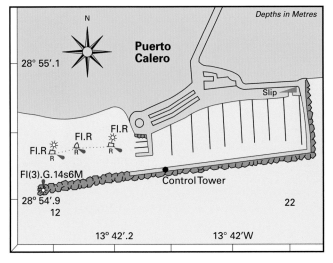

Plan 41 *Puerto Calero, Lanzarote.*

General

A spotlessly clean but expensive private marina, Puerto Calero has recently expanded from some 250 to 420 berths. The marina is surrounded by a small tourist complex, including a supermarket and restaurants, but it would be necessary to organise a hire car or taxi to Arrecife for serious shopping.

Approach and entrance

Puerto Calero is situated some 9 miles west-south-west of Arrecife. The harbour opens to the west but is somewhat protected by the curve of the coast towards Punta Gorda and Punta Papagayo and the recent extension has increased the shelter. It is best identified from off-shore by the white upper part of the octagonal marina office near the middle of the south mole.

On closing the coast, the bottom shelves suddenly and steeply and a sharp turn to starboard is needed round the end of the breakwater; a row of three red (Fl.R) buoys joined by a line of white pellets mark the north limit of a safe approach once round the breakwater end. Entrance is then straightforward and visitors should secure to the reception berth beneath the office.

Radio

VHF watch is kept on channels 09 and 16 from 0800 to 2000 daily (tel: 928 511285, fax: 514568).

Facilities

Boatyard/engineers/electronics Small but active boatyard, with contractors available if required; 75+ tonne travel lift.

Sailmaker Drizas Velas in the marina complex, or Lanzarote Sail Repairs (tel: 592351).

Chandlery Jewel Marine Services next to the boatyard (tel: 512468, fax: 512777) for electronics; Efectos Navales Duarte (tel: 811117, fax: 802108) at Puerto de Naos.

Fuel At the reception berth.

Water Throughout the marina, but unpleasant to drink.

Shore power Throughout the marina. Both 220 and 380 volts available.

Bottled gas From the DISA plant north of Puerto de Mármoles. Any cylinder can be filled, generally while you wait. Camping Gaz exchanges may be available in the Alamar supermarket.

Showers Well maintained and open 24 hours a day.

Laundrette At the supermarket.

Bank In Puerto del Carmen, about 10km (6 miles) by road. Small quantities of currency can be exchanged at Alamar supermarket.

General shopping/provisioning Small supermarket near the harbour. Otherwise, in Puerto del Carmen.

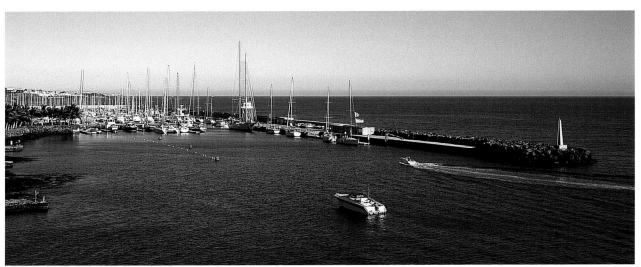

The marina entrance at Puerto Calero, Lanzarote, looking SE. Photo John Lytle.

Puerto Calero marina looking SW from the slip. Photo John Lytle.

Restaurant In the octagonal grey building near the root of the north mole, and several others.

Medical services Cruz Roja post in the marina.

Communications

Mailing address C/o Puerto Calero, PO Box 45, 35510, Puerto del Carmen, Lanzarote, Islas Canarias, España.

Fax and internet services At Alamar (fax: 514382).

Post office In Puerto del Carmen (stamps at Alamar).

Telephones At Alamar and elsewhere.

Taxis Available by phone. No buses.

Car hire In Puerto del Carmen, or arrange via Alamar.

Air services International airport west of Arrecife, some 16km (10 miles) by road.

Puerto de la Luz, Las Palmas de Gran Canaria
28°07'.7N 15°25'.4W

Charts	Admiralty	US
Approach	1856 (1:75,000)	51344 (1:30,000)
Harbour	1856 (1:12,500)	51244 (1:10,000)

General

A large yacht marina with all the usual facilities, but sharing its approach with that of Gran Canaria's largest commercial harbour. Puerto de la Luz is very crowded in late November before the start of the ARC rally, when non-participating yachts have to wait at anchor outside, but can normally accommodate visitors at other times. However, much has been done recently to extend this marina both to increase the berths available and the protection afforded. Some of these improvements have suffered in the winter gales, but there are now positive improvements that look as if they may last.

Approach and entrance

The solid buildings of Las Palmas are unmistakable for many miles offshore. Head for a point some 0.5 miles south-west of the head of the Dique Reina Sofia (the main outer breakwater), keeping a good watch for commercial traffic, then turn north-west for the outer head of the marina breakwater.

Arrivals generally secure to the Texaco fuel berth on the breakwater.

Radio

Call port control on VHF channel 16 or 12 (24 hours). The marina guards channels 16 and 09 (0800–1400, Monday to Saturday). Contact the Harbourmaster tel/fax: 928 243 606.

Berthing

Large yachts are usually berthed stern-to against the outer wall just south of the fuel berth. Visitors' berths are provided with buoys and lazy lines to the pontoon, with the finger pontoons in the southern part of the basin being reserved for local boats.

Anchorage

Anchoring, for which a small charge is made, is permitted north of the marina. Holding is said to be good, but a trip line might be advisable. The marina extensions have improved the shelter in the anchorage.

Formalities

The marina office (tel: 928 244 101; e-mail: palmasport @palmasport.es), where customs and other formalities

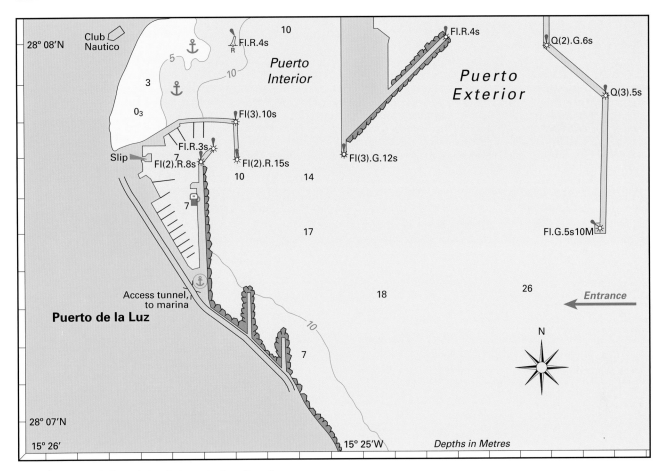

Plan 42 *Puerto de la Luz`, Las Palmas de Gran Canaria.*

are also handled, is at the south end of the basin beside the road that leads (via a tunnel) out of the harbour. Ship's papers and crew passports are held until final departure.

Facilities

Boatyard Serious boatyard in the north-west part of the harbour, where major wood and GRP repairs can be carried out. Equipment includes a 60-tonne travel lift.

Engineers Ask at the marina office. There are local agents for Perkins, Volvo, Evinrude, Johnson, Mercury, Suzuki and Yamaha.

Sailmakers Charles Linton of Velas Linton (tel/fax: 291934), Olivier Youf of O'Sails (tel/fax: 261553) and Velas Benoit Claveau (tel: 280939).

Chandlery Alcorde, at Calle Luis Antunex 51 (tel: 242484, fax: 249526) and others.

Liferafts Can be serviced by Ocean Products Española (tel: 270962/272716) on Muelle de Rivera near the root of the Dique del Léon y Castillo.

Fuel All varieties, plus oils etc, at the Texaco fuel dock.

Water At all berths, but unpleasant to drink.

Shore power 220 volts at all berths, with 380 volts south of the fuel dock.

Bottled gas Exchange or refills available via the fuel dock. The latter (refilled at the DISA plant south of Las Palmas) may take several days.

Showers Built into the wall near the harbour office and

opposite pontoon 10, with a card entry system.

Laundry At the corner of Calle de Sagasta and Isla Hierro.

Banks Many, with credit card facilities.

General shopping/provisioning Three large supermarkets: El Cortes Ingles, Supersol and Hiperdino, plus a produce and fish market near the commercial harbour. The small store at the fuel dock stocks bread, milk, wine, etc.

Restaurants, bars and hotels A very wide choice, some handy to the marina.

Medical services Hospital near the marina.

Communications

Mailing address C/o Oficina del Puerto, Muelle Deportivo, E-35004 Las Palmas de Gran Canaria, Islas Canarias, España.

Fax and internet services At the marina office (fax: 300466).

Post office In the town.

Telephones On the fuel dock and near the port office, as well as in town.

Bus services To the airport, etc.

Taxis/car hire Readily available.

Ferry services Jetfoil to Fuerteventura and Tenerife plus inter-island car ferry.

Air services International airport 16km (10 miles) south of Las Palmas.

Marina Atlantico, Santa Cruz de Tenerife
28°27'.3N 16°14'.8W

Charts	Admiralty		US	
Approach	1858	(1:75,000)	51341	(1:50,000)
Harbour	1857	(1:12,000)	51341	(1:10,000)

General

Several years ago plans were produced for a large, full-service marina in the Dársena de los Llanos, the southernmost of Santa Cruz's four commercial basins. A barrier was installed near the head of the basin – the outer part is still used by container and Ro-Ro traffic – and work has accelerated in the last two years, with several more pontoons and better facilities installed. This progress is expected to continue slowly.

Marina Atlantico is very convenient to the city. The older Marina Tenerife, situated in the Dársena Pesquera to the north, seldom has space for visiting yachts.

Approach and entrance

The Dársena de los Llanos lies at the southern end of the harbour complex, less than 1 mile north of the chimneys and fuelling berths of Puerto Caballo. Its entrance opens almost due south, with leading lights on 353°. The basin is used by commercial shipping and, providing lights and buoys are observed, should present no problems to a yacht. However, it should be noted that only the eastern of the two entrances to the marina is passable – the western is narrow with what appears to be a wave baffle, presumably to limit wash from the commercial harbour.

Formalities

The port office is north of the marina, overlooking the Dársena Sur (tel: 605472, fax: 605481). Visit with the usual ship's papers and passports.

Facilities

Boatyard No yacht yards in Santa Cruz (though several shipyards). Hauling is best done at Los Cristianos, where there is a 60-tonne travel lift operated by the fishermen's co-operative (tel: 790014/793912, fax: 751785). Engineers at Puerto Radazul, about 6 miles south-west of Santa Cruz.

Sailmaker Spinnaker (tel: 243975, fax: 293830), which also handles stainless steel rigging.

Chandlery Good selection – Spinnaker (see above), La Marina (tel: 271246, fax: 247246), Sucesores Tomás Fernandez Blanco (tel: 275014/275058, fax: 279769) and H Oscar Martín Fariña (tel: 281550/281554, fax: 285174).

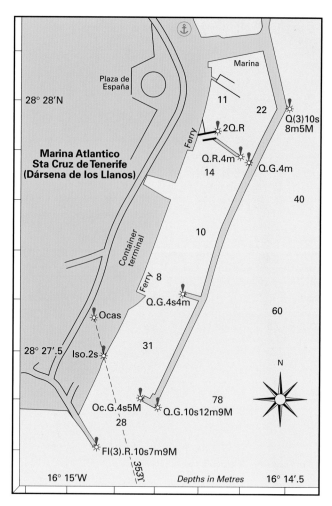

Plan 43 *Santa Cruz de Tenerife.*

Fuel None at the Marina Atlantico, but available in the Dársena Pesquera from the rear of the filling station about halfway up the harbour on the inner side.

Water On the pontoons, but unpleasant to drink.

Shore power On the pontoons.

Bottled gas Camping Gaz exchanges at Tomás Fernandez Blanco and elsewhere. Other cylinders can be filled at DISA (tel: 224966) next to the Palacio de Ferias.

Showers On the jetty at the Marina Atlantico.

Laundrettes Several in the city, including Lavandería la Rosa (tel: 283382).

Banks Many, with ATMs.

General shopping/provisioning Excellent supermarkets and other shops in Santa Cruz. Also, several freezer warehouses near the Dársena Pesquera which sell a wide range of frozen fish and meat at good prices with no minimum quantity restrictions.

Restaurants/hotels Many in the town.

Medical services Several hospitals plus a first aid station.

Communications

Mailing address C/o the main post office: *Poste Restante*, Correos de Santa Cruz, Plaza de España, Santa Cruz de Tenerife, Islas Canarias, España.

Fax and internet services At the port office (fax: 605481), and various internet cafés.

Marina Atlantico, Santa Cruz de Tenerife, looking NNW from the entrance. Photo Anne Hammick.

Post office Across the road from the marina.

Telephones At the port office and elsewhere.

*Bus service*s Regular bus service, including to both air-ports.

Taxis/car hire Readily available.

Ferry services Jetfoil to Gran Canaria and Fuerteventura. Car ferries to Gomera and La Palma.

Air services International flights mainly from Reina Sophia in the south, inter-island services from Los Rodeos in the north.

San Sebastián de la Gomera
28°05′N 17°06′.5W

Charts	Admiralty	US
Harbour	1858 (1:10,000)	—

General

San Sebastián is a small harbour mainly handling car ferries to Tenerife and El Hierro, and tucked inside is a 275-berth marina which welcomes visiting yachts but is becoming very crowded. The building of a spur to the entrance to the marina now provides complete shelter in all conditions. Anchoring in the harbour is no longer permitted; this poses problems if the marina has no further room. Prior booking of a berth at the marina is advised.

The town has strong links with Columbus, whose house is now an art gallery. The Church of Our Lady of the Assumption, where Columbus and his crew said Mass before their departure, is on the main street (though rebuilt a number of times), and San Sebastián would still be an excellent place from which to leave for the Atlantic crossing.

La Gomera, like the other western islands, is extremely beautiful in parts and every effort should be made to explore inland, whether by bus, hire car or on foot.

Radio

Port authority and marina monitor VHF channel 09 (0830–2030 daily).

Approach and entrance

From north-east, the radio mast makes a fine landmark. The lighthouse is less conspicuous and the breakwater and town are concealed by the headland. From south or east the town on the north side of the valley can be seen and the breakwater will be raised on close approach.

Plan 44 *San Sebastián de la Gomera.*

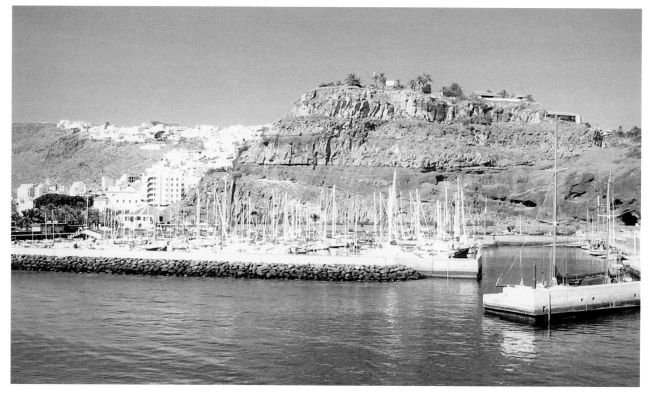

San Sebastián de la Gomera looking north, showing the new breakwater at the marina entrance on the right. Photo Anne Hammick.

There are no outlying dangers, and course can be set to clear the breakwater end. Keep a lookout for the hydrofoil and car ferry and keep well clear if either is entering or leaving. The marina entrance is close west of the breakwater root and well marked by day or night. There is normally someone on duty until 2100, otherwise arrivals should berth either on the head of the pontoon nearest the entrance or alongside the eastern quay.

Formalities

The port office is at the head of the marina ramp and is manned by English-speaking staff (tel: 141769, fax: 871362) during office hours.

Facilities

Boatyard/engineers Enquire at the port office. Several small workshops, but not a place for major work. There is no travel lift here – the nearest is a 64-tonne one at Puerto de Santiago.

Chandlery Nothing – best to order from Tenerife (see Marina Atlantico, above).

Fuel In cans from CEPSA filling station on main road.

Water Good drinking water on the pontoons, with hoses provided.

Shore power On the pontoons.

Bottled gas Bottles can be refilled at a plant in the southwest part of the town. Allow plenty of time.

Showers Good showers in the marina.

Laundry Lavandería Hecu on Calle del Medio.

Banks Several, with credit card facilities.

General shopping/provisioning Two or three supermarkets plus a produce/fish market where purchases can be frozen to order.

Restaurants/hotels All grades, including the four star Parador.

Medical services Hospital in the town.

Communications

Mailing address C/o Puerto Deportivo, CP 38800/ Autoridad Porturia, San Sebastián de la Gomera, Islas Canarias, España.

Fax services At the port office (fax: 141310).

Post office Near the church.

Telephones In the square opposite the marina and elsewhere.

Bus services Throughout the island. Details from the tourist office.

Taxis/car hire In the ferry booking office on the breakwater.

Ferry service To Tenerife and El Hierro.

Air services Airport for inter-island flights only.

Porto Grande (Mindelo), São Vicente, Cape Verdes
16°53'N 25°00'W UT–1

Springs: 1.2m	Range 0.9m	
Neaps: 1.0m	**Range** 0.4m	

Flag: Republic of Cape Verde

Currency: Cape Verdean escudo

Tel/fax – Country code: 238, **Area code:** none

Charts	Admiralty	US
General	366 (1:500,000)	51500 (1:250,000)
Approach	367 (1:150,000)	–
Harbour	367 (Various)	51500 (1:20,000)
	369 (Various)	

General

After years of receiving a bad press – if mentioned at all – the Cape Verde Islands are at last being recognised as an interesting port of call for Atlantic voyagers. The distance to the Caribbean is reduced by 700 miles if you leave from the Cape Verdes rather than from the Canaries. Porto Grande (also known as Mindelo) is an excellent natural harbour, a port of entry (see below), and facilities for yachts have improved.

Many of the local people are very poor, and theft from yachts is endemic. Dinghies are a tempting target, and padlocks should be employed on the outboard and oars, as well as to secure the dinghy to the yacht or landing. However, major crime, assault and armed theft are minimal. The employment of a 'boat boy' is a good insurance and provides a water taxi.

Approach

Most yachts will approach from the north through the Canal de São Vicente. The small and rocky Ilhèu do Pássaros [Fl (3) 13s 86m 14M] can be passed on either side.

Caution: Refer to the warnings in Chapters 12 and 13 regarding frequent poor visibility and the unreliability of lights and other navigational aids.

Radio

The port authorities operate on VHF channel 15, with the pilot service using channels 13 and 16.

Entrance

This is very straightforward both by day and night, with good depths throughout the northern part of the bay. The grey stone breakwaters are deep close-to, and well lit. A new jetty, with steps and a slipway, has been built near the yacht anchorage. Various ships' mooring buoys, mostly unlit, are scattered in the southern part of the bay while a number of wrecks line the beach.

Anchorage and moorings

The yacht anchorage is in the north-east corner of Porto Grande Bay, with good holding in sand. Depths of 5–6m (17–20ft) in the outer part of the anchorage shoal

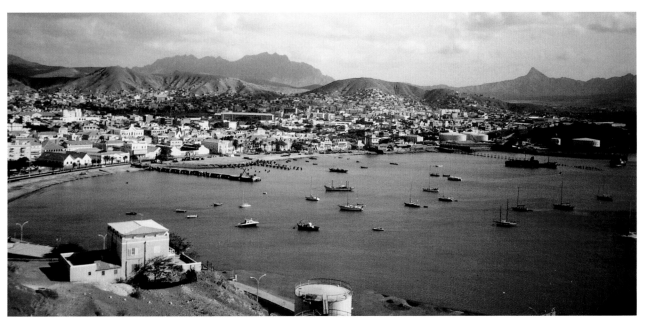

Port Grande (Mindelo), Cape Verdes, looking SE over yacht anchorage. There is the wreck of a steamer below the oil tanks. Photo Anne Hammick.

Plan 45 *Porto Grande, São Vicente, Cape Verde Islands.*

gradually towards the beach. There are no yacht moorings and the steel mooring buoys in the outer part of the bay should be avoided.

Berthing

It may be possible to lie alongside in the inner harbour, though the east side of the inner breakwater is used by ferries. No yacht lying alongside should ever be left unattended – even employing a watchman does not give complete security.

A German, Kai Brosnan, runs a yacht charter business and may be able to provide facilities. He has an office in the YC.

Formalities

In 2002 the Cape Verdes introduced legislation restricting the number of ports where yachts may clear in, and transgression of the rules can lead to hefty fines. Check with any Cape Verdean embassy or the RYA on the current situation before departure. Fly the Q flag on arrival. Officials from the port captain's office and immigration may board the yacht, or it may be necessary to seek them out ashore – try and ascertain current procedure from earlier arrivals. If a courtesy flag is not already hoisted they will be delighted to sell you one. Ship's papers and passports are no longer retained and visiting sailors do not require visas. Crew leaving the yacht must ensure that their passports are correctly stamped on entry. Make sure that you take evidence of departure from the islands with you if leaving for another country.

Facilities

Boatyards/engineering/electronics The Cabnave shipyard (tel: 314122/314233/314389, fax: 312874) in the bay north of Porto Grande has good facilities, including well-equipped engineering and electronics workshops; can haul anything from a yacht to a 3,000-tonne ship; and will carry out repairs in wood, glassfibre, steel and aluminium. It is one of the few places in the archipelago where a yacht may safely be laid up ashore. Several of the senior management there speak English. Onave (tel: 312270, fax: 312522), about 0.5 miles south of the anchorage, is a smaller concern, but does have diesel engineers.

Agents It may well be worth employing an agent if you need to import spares as this will probably speed things up and avoid heavy import duties.

Sailmaker None as such, though repairs can be handled locally – however, any new cloth needed must be provided.

Chandlery None as such, but several hardware stores sell both chandlery and tools.

Yacht club The Clube Náutico occupies the low white building with two gables immediately opposite the anchorage and beach.

Diesel Available alongside, by prearrangement with the Shell office, or from filling stations in the town.

Petrol From filling stations in the town.

Water Either by can from a tap on the new jetty beside the anchorage, or by hose, arranged via an office on the fuelling jetty. Quality is variable, and it would be wise to conserve Madeiran or Canaries water for the Atlantic crossing, and not to mix it.

Bottled gas Camping Gaz cylinders can be exchanged at the Shell garage, and other bottles taken to ENACOL, just south of town, for refilling.

Ice From the fish-freezing plant in the dock area (icebox rather than drinks quality).

Showers Try one of the larger hotels.

Laundry/laundrette Laundrette at 56 Avenida Unidade Africana or via Kai Brosnan.

Banks Two, where foreign currency or traveller's cheques can be exchanged and cash drawn against a credit card (no machines). Identification will be required.

General shopping Most needs can be met, but prices tend to be high.

Provisioning There are three supermarkets near the harbour offering a good range; however, fresh meat (except chicken) is scarce. There is a good produce market and the fish market is worth visiting. Fish is also hawked to yachts at anchor.

Restaurants/hotels Several, at reasonable prices.

Medical services Hospital east of the town, reported to be more than satisfactory. Some English is spoken.

Communications

Mailing address C/o the main post office.

Post office At the south end of the Praça Amilcar Cabral. Open weekdays only, 0800–1200 and 1430–1700.

Telephones At the post office, but open 0800–2200 weekdays, 0800–1130 and 1500–1700 Saturday, and 0800–1130 Sunday. Some card-operated phone booths.

Bus services Services link different parts of the island, but may not return the same day.

Ferry services The regular inter-island service employs two purpose-built vessels. There is also a daily service to Santo Antão.

Taxis/car hire Readily available, but rates should always be negotiated in advance and to include hidden extras such as tax, mileage and fuel.

Air services Daily flights from the small airfield at San Pedro to Ilha do Sal, from which there are international services, and to other Cape Verde Islands. Credit cards cannot yet be used to pay for flights.

Springs: 1.1m	Range 0.6m		
Neaps: 1.0m	Range 0.7m		
Flag: Trinidad	Currency: Trinidad & Tobago dollar		
Tel/fax – Country code: 1-868, Area code: none			
Charts	Admiralty	US	Imray/Iolaire
General	493 (1:300,000)	25400 (1:250,000) 24404 (1:175,000)	B (1:745,000)
Approach	484 (1:50,000)	24405 (1:75,000)	D11 (1:240,700)
Harbour	479 (1:25,000)	24406 (1:17,500)	—

General

Trinidad has developed into one of the south-east Caribbean's leading yachting centres. Its position south of the normal hurricane belt increases its appeal as a safe venue to leave a boat during the summer – and makes it acceptable to most insurers. Yachting services are largely concentrated in the north-west of the island, many of them in the Chaguaramas Bay area where marinas and boatyards offer extensive facilities for haul-out, lay-up and servicing. Foreign yachts are frequently stored ashore while their owners return home on one of the regular flights to the United Kingdom, United States and Canada. It has indeed become so popular that it is often difficult to get work done, and advance booking of a berth afloat or ashore is essential.

Carnival – in theory held over the three days preceding Lent, but with a build-up starting around New Year – is also a major attraction. Described with only slight exaggeration as 'the greatest show on earth', many local people spend the entire year planning costumes. Equally, visiting sailors are more than welcome to take part, and costumes can often be hired.

Approach and entrance

Chacachacare Light [Fl 10s 26M] on the island of that name is the principal navigation light for the approach to Trinidad. From the north, the light should be kept well to starboard until close to land in order to counter east-flowing currents and prevailing westerly winds.

Yachts approaching from the north usually pass through the Boca de Monos, the most easterly of the three *bocas* (literally 'mouths'). Le Chapeau rock [Fl (3) 10s] lies on the starboard hand in the entrance, after which a course of 170° clears Têteron Rock [Fl G 4s 7m 4M] at the southern end of the *boca*. There is good water between the islands of Caspar Grande and Gasparillo, leading directly into Chaguaramas Bay.

Yachts arriving from Venezuela generally enter the Gulf of Paria via either the Boca de Navios, east of Chacachacare Island, or south of Chacachacare Island and its two companions. Again there are no particular hazards.

Radio

The National SAR Agency is the Trinidad and Tobago Coast Guard and all emergency contact is through North Port Radio on 2182 kHz or VHF channel 16

Chaguaramas, looking NE with the anchorage in the foreground and boatyards and marinas behind. Carenage Bay can be seen top right.

Plan 46 *Chaguaramas Bay, Trinidad.*

(emergency tel: 634 2131). North Post Radio operates on 2735, 3165, on channels 24, 25, 26 and 27. Customs and immigration also monitor VHF channel 16. Of the commercial concerns, CrewsInn Marina uses channel 77, Power Boats channel 72, and Peake Yacht Services channel 68. The smaller yards also use channel 68 with both yacht clubs in Carenage Bay, as well as businesses ranging from chandleries to taxis.

Anchorage and moorings

There is a designated yacht anchorage in the eastern part of Chaguaramas Bay marked by large white buoys, and a hefty fine will be imposed for ignoring them. Holding is patchy in sand and mud, and a chain scope of at least 5:1 is advised locally.

The Trinidad & Tobago Yachting Association (tel: 634 3276/4210, 4519, fax: 634 4376) in Carenage Bay, to the east of Point Gourde, has 16 visitors' moorings – another possibility is to anchor off the Trinidad Yacht Club (tel: 633 7420, fax: 633 6388) further east on Cumana Bay.

Berthing and marinas

At least seven companies of varying size offer berthing on the shores of Chaguaramas Bay. Taken anticlockwise these include:

1   CrewsInn Marina and Boatyard (tel: 634 4384/4385, fax: 634 4828), the biggest and newest concern in the area, which caters purely for visiting yachts. The marina has 60 berths capable of taking vessels up to 40m (130ft).
2   Tropical Marine (tel: 634 4502, fax: 634 4453), Tardieu Marine (tel: 634 4534) and Calypso Marine

Services (tel: 634 4551), all relatively small boat-yards each with some berthing available. They share the eastern corner of the bay, the latter two in a narrow and well-sheltered creek.

3 Humming Bird Marine (tel/fax: 634 4046), some-times referred to as Stella Maris, also situated in the corner creek and owned by Harold La Borde, well-known in Caribbean sailing circles for having circumnavigated twice during the last 25 years, both times in home-built yachts. Humming Bird Marine has expanded over the years and now provides 17 stern-to berths on its new jetty as well as nine or ten slots alongside.

4 The much larger Power Boat Mutual Facilities (tel: 634 4303, fax: 634 4327), generally known as simply 'Power Boats', immediately west of the creek with 20 stern-to berths for yachts up to 21m (70 ft).

5 Peake Yacht Services (tel: 634 4420/4423/ 4427, fax: 634 4387), further west again, offering 16 stern-to berths for yachts up to 30m (100 ft).

In addition, the Trinidad Yacht Club (tel: 633 7420, fax: 633 6388), situated 4 miles to the east on Cumana Bay, reserve 40 of their 80 berths for visiting yachts up to 17m (56ft).

Formalities

Entry formalities are completed at Chaguaramas customs and immigration office in the CrewsInn Marina complex, where there is a dedicated customs jetty which arriving yachts must use. The office is manned around the clock, and the entire crew is expected to present themselves without delay. However, sizeable overtime fees are charged for arrival outside normal office hours (0800–1200 and 1300–1600, weekdays only), appar-ently also levied for *entering territorial waters 12 miles offshore* outside these hours. More modest dues are payable for each 30-day period spent in the country. The officials are friendly and efficient, but in peak periods the offices can be under-staffed.

Facilities

Although based at Power Boats, the Yacht Service Association of Trinidad and Tobago (tel/fax: 634 4938) represents most yacht-related businesses in the country. They can recommend who to go to for what (if not covered below), as well as supplying current haulage and lay-up charges, etc to those considering sailing to Trinidad for this purpose.

Boatyards CrewsInn Marina and Boatyard (tel: 634 4384/4385, boatyard fax: 634 4828) has a 200-tonne travel lift plus a 60-tonne crane with 43m (140ft) boom, backed by comprehensive yard facilities and a large lay-up area, some of it under cover. All work is done by boatyard staff, and DIY work is not normally permitted.

Power Boats (tel: 634 4303, fax: 634 4327) has a 50-tonne travel lift and dry storage space for 160 boats. Other than actual hauling, work is normally subcontracted out to carefully vetted specialists, some of them based in the yard. Semi-skilled labour is avail-able and DIY work permitted. Peake Yacht Services (tel: 634 4420/4427/4423, fax: 634 4387) use a 150-tonne travel lift. They can take around 300 yachts ashore and also have large covered workshops. Again, DIY work is permitted. Industrial Marine Services (IMS) (tel: 634 4328, fax: 634 4437) have a 70-tonne travel lift and room for some 130 boats ashore. Most work is carried out by Atlantic Yacht Services (tel: 634 4337, fax: 634 4437), which is based in the yard.

Finally, all the smaller yards previously listed under 'Berthing and marinas' (above) offer space for mainte-nance ashore, generally with a DIY option.

Engineers/electronics Bowen Marine at the CrewsInn Marina Boatyard, plus several engineering concerns on and around the Power Boats site and at Peake Yacht Services.

Sailmaker Ocean Sails International (tel/fax: 634 4560) at IMS can make or repair sails of all sizes. Also, Barrow Sail Loft (tel/fax: 634 4137) at Power Boats, and Soca Sails (tel: 634 4384, ext 117) at the CrewsInn Boatyard. Rigging services are available at Ocean Sails, Peake Yacht Services and CrewsInn Boatyard.

Chandlery Very good stocks at Peake Yacht Services Chandlery, at Budget Marine (tel/fax: 8634 4382) in the Formula III Building on Western Main Road, and at the Boat Shop II (tel: 634 2628, tel/fax: 634 4148) at Power Boats. All are willing to order items not in stock.

Yacht clubs The Trinidad & Tobago Yachting Assoc-iation (tel: 634 3276/4210, fax: 634 4376) and the Trinidad Yacht Club (tel: 633 7420, fax: 633 6388) are both situated east of Point Gourde, facing Carenage Bay and Cumana Bay respectively. Both make bona fide visiting sailors very welcome.

Diesel Fuel jetties at Power Boats and the CrewsInn Marina; Peake Yacht Services is supplied by a fuel truck.

Water At all marinas, boatyards and clubs.

Electricity At all marinas, boatyards and clubs. Normally 110 volts, though 220 volts is sometimes available.

Bottled gas Propane is readily available, but pure butane is not obtainable – a propane/butane mix is normally used to fill yachtsmen's cylinders.

Ice Plentiful everywhere.

Showers At all marinas, boatyards and clubs.

Laundrettes At Power Boats, Peake Yacht Services and IMS. Also Chin's Laundry and Dry Cleaning (tel: 622 3733), which offers free pick-up and delivery.

Banks At Peake Yacht Services and CrewsInn Marina, with credit card facilities, plus many others elsewhere.

General shopping Excellent, with several American-style shopping malls in and around Port of Spain.

Provisioning Grocery stores at or near Peake Yacht Services, Power Boats and CrewsInn Marina (which also has a range of other shops). There is an even better choice further afield, with a wide range of domestic and imported produce available.

Restaurants/hotels Something for every pocket, including a café, and/or restaurant at each of the larger marinas and boatyards. Peake Marine Services and CrewsInn boast hotels, with rental apartments at Power Boats.

Medical services Several hospitals and medical centres in and around Port of Spain.

Communications

Mailing addresses C/o CrewsInn Marina and Boatyard, PO Bag 518, Carenage; Power Boat Mutual Facilities, PO Box 3163, Carenage; Peake Yacht Services, PO Box 3168, Carenage; the Trinidad & Tobago Yachting Association, PO Box 3140, Carenage; or the Trinidad Yacht Club, Bayshore, and others (in all cases followed by 'Trinidad, West Indies') by prior arrangement.

Fax services At Power Boats (fax: 634 4327), Peake Yacht Services (fax: 634 4387), CrewsInn Marina and Boat-yard (marina fax: 634 4542, boatyard fax: 634 4828), Humming Bird Marine (tel/fax: 634 4046), both the yacht clubs and elsewhere.

Post office On Carenage Bay east of Pointe Gourde. Power Boats sells stamps and will take visitors' mail to the post office.

Telephones Card-operated telephones at all marinas, boatyards and clubs, where cards are also on sale.

Bus services Local people favour 'maxi-taxis' – minibuses that operate much as regular buses would elsewhere. They normally stop only at marked bus stops, and must be waved down. Like private taxis, they have H number plates – confirm that you are boarding the type you want.

Taxis Readily available, but private taxis are much more expensive than the shared variety.

Car hire Mark's Rentals (tel: 632 8984) at Power Boats and Convenient Rental (tel/fax: 634 4017) at Peake Yacht Services (where bicycles can also be hired). Driving is on the left.

Air services The island is served by regular flights to the United States, Canada and London, as well as to other Caribbean countries.

15

Prickly Bay, Grenada
12°00'N 61°45'.8W UT–4

Charts	Admiralty	US	Imray/Iolaire
Springs: 0.7m	**Range** 0.4m		
Neaps: 0.4m	**Range** 0.3m		
Flag: Grenada	**Currency:** EC dollar		
Tel/fax – Country code: 1-473, **Area code:** none			

Charts	Admiralty	US	Imray/Iolaire
General	597 (1:175,000)	25400 (1:250,000)	B5 (1:510,700)
Approach	797 (1:60,000)	25481 (1:60,000)	B3 (1:162,000)
			B32 (1:86,000)
Harbour	797 (1:25,000)	—	B32 (Inset)

General

Prickly Bay, also known as L'anse aux Epines, is one of the few recommended harbours that is not in a town, although it is only a short bus or taxi ride from the capital, St George's, which does provide an alternative entry port. However, the incidence of theft in St George's makes Prickly Bay a preferable port of call for yachts. It is particularly attractive even by the high standards of the Caribbean, and is an official port of entry. Fuel, alcohol and many goods are duty free.

Approach

The majority of yachts approach from the north, down the western (lee) side of Grenada. If a course is shaped directly for Point Saline at the western extremity of the island all outlying rocks will be cleared, but if coming from the direction of St George's, Long Point Shoal to the north-west of Long Point (itself at the western end of the spectacular Grande Anse beach) carries less than

1m (3ft). The old, striped lighthouse at Point Saline fell victim to the airport development and the replacement [Q (9) 15s 7M] is a poor substitute. After rounding Point Saline, Prickly Point to the east of Prickly Bay should be seen about 2.5 miles distant, extending further south than the intermediate headlands. Glover Island can be left on either side.

If approaching from eastwards, or from the south, the chief hazard is The Porpoises, a group of rocks with 0.9m (3ft) on which the swell breaks, about 0.7 miles south of Prickly Point. They are unmarked and unlit, and have claimed more than one yacht. In fact, lights along this entire coast are poor, and if approaching in darkness there is much to be said for taking the traditional line and heaving-to until daylight, but beware of being set past the island by the strong current.

Radio

Spice Island Marine Services monitors 4125 kHz (Voice) and VHF channels 16 and 68. The water taxi service and other services are also on channel 68.

Entrance

There are reefs close to both sides of the entrance, but these generally present no problem. More dangerous is the isolated coral patch in the centre of the bay, west of Spice Island Marine Services, which is *sometimes* marked by an inconspicuous buoy. The water in Prickly Bay, though clean, is often cloudy, and if in doubt keep well east, towards the Spice Island Marine pontoon. There is a second shoal close inshore on the eastern part of the bay just north of the boatyard.

Anchorage and moorings

Most yachts anchor either in the north-east corner of the bay or off Spice Island Marine, the best place for landing by dinghy. Otherwise, choose almost any part of the bay in 10m (30ft) or so over mud and sand, though anchoring within 100m (330ft) of the beach at the Calabash Hotel at the head of the bay is forbidden. Some swell may find its way in from the south, but Prickly Bay is often both flat and breezy – the best possible Caribbean combination. As with all Caribbean anchorages, keep a careful watch for swimmers if going ashore by outboard-powered dinghy.

Berthing and marinas

Spice Island Marine offers stern-to berthing for 30 yachts, as well as providing dinghy dockage and other

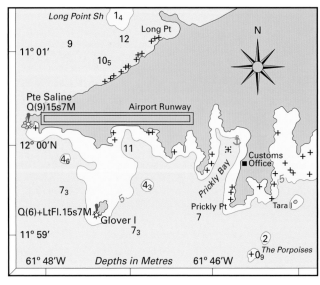

Plan 47 *The south-west coast of Granada.*

services to those anchored off. It must be one of very few top Caribbean destinations to have remained operational but unspoilt by the yachting explosion of the last two decades; with its lawns, flowers and trees, long may it remain so.

Formalities

Customs and immigration inhabit the upper floor of the building just to the north of the disused slipway. All the usual documents are required, but the attitude is pleasant and relaxed. Office hours are 0800–1145 and 1300–1545 weekdays only, and as overtime fees are likely to be accompanied by separate taxi fares for several officials, the charge can mount up dramatically. Endeavour to arrive in office hours.

Facilities

Boatyards Spice Island Marine Services (tel: 444 4257/ 4342, fax: 444 2816) has a 35-tonne travel lift and allows DIY work.

Engineers/electronics At Spice Island Marine, or McIntyre Bros (tel: 440 3944, fax: 444 2899) on the road to the airport; Enza Marine also undertake electrical, mechanical and refrigeration engineering.

Sailmaker Michael at Spice Island Marine. Jeff Fisher (tel/fax: 440 2556) is agent for Neil Pryde Sails of Hong Kong, which claims a six-week delivery. Also, Johnny Sails & Canvas (tel: 444 1108/9619, fax: 444 1108) on the St George's road, which also deals with rigging etc.

Chandlery Well-stocked chandlery at Spice Island Marine.

Yacht club The Grenada Yacht Club (tel: 440 3050, fax: 440 4128) is a good reason for going to St George's. There is a 30-berth dock, and it might be preferable to Prickly Bay if major provisioning is necessary.

Diesel On the pontoon at Spice Island Marine.

Water On the pontoon at Spice Island Marine, plus taps elsewhere in the boatyard. Grenada has some of the sweetest water in the Lesser Antilles.

Electricity Available (220 volt, 50 Hz) if berthed stern-to.

Bottled gas Propane refills available at Spice Island Marine or at Huggins on the Carenage in St George's.

Ice At Spice Island Marine.

Showers At Spice Island Marine. A small charge is made if not berthed in the marina.

Laundry/laundrette At Spice Island Marine.

Banks Several in St George's, with ATMs.

General shopping Not too much locally, but a good range in St George's.

Provisioning An essentials mini-market at Spice Island Marine, with a wider choice at several supermarkets on the road into St George's. Local women sometimes bring baskets of fresh produce out to the boatyard, but nothing rivals the excellent and colourful market in the centre of St George's – go early, and take a camera and several bags.

Restaurants Pleasant bar/restaurant at Spice Island Marine (with really good local steel band on Friday nights).

Plan 48 *Prickly Bay, Grenada.*

Just down the road are the long-established Red Crab Restaurant (tel: 444 4424), the Choo Light (tel: 444 2196) which also does take-aways, and the Bolero (tel: 444 1250). In town, the Nutmeg, overlooking the Carenage, deserves a visit – try their calaloo soup and rotis.

Hotels Many at all levels, including several overlooking Prickly Bay.

Medical services Hospital outside St George's.

Communications

Mailing addresses C/o General Delivery at the main post office, or c/o Spice Island Marine Services, Prickly Bay, L'Anse aux Epines, St George's, Grenada, West Indies.

Fax services At Spice Island Marine Services' office (fax: 444 2816).

Post office On the waterfront in St George's.

Telephones At Spice Island Marine and elsewhere.

Bus services Irregular buses from the boatyard, or walk up the road to the T junction for more frequent services.

Taxis Plenty, both cars and mini-buses. Many of the drivers are delighted to double as tour guides.

Car hire McIntyre Brothers (tel: 440 3944) and others. Driving is on the left.

Air services The airport at Point Saline has direct flights to the United Kingdom, the United States and Canada, as well as offering inter-island services.

16

Bridgetown/Port St Charles, Barbados
13°16'N 59°39'W UT–4

Springs:	0.8m	Range	0.6m
Neaps:	0.7m	Range	0.3m
Flag: Barbados		Currency: Barbados dollar	
Tel/fax – Country code: 1-246, Area code: none			

Charts	Admiralty	US	Imray/Iolaire
General	956 (1:644,000)	—	B5 (1:510,700)
Approach	2485 (1:100,000)	25485 (1:100,000)	B2 (1:56,900)
Harbour	502 (1:12,500)	25485 (1:25,000)	B2 (Inset)
		25487 (1:10,000)	

General

Barbados is a popular island for an Atlantic landfall – it is well lit, offers some of the best general shopping of any ex-British island in the West Indies, and has direct flights to the United Kingdom, the United States and Canada among other countries. There was a time, though, when its popularity waned as there was no marina and clearance

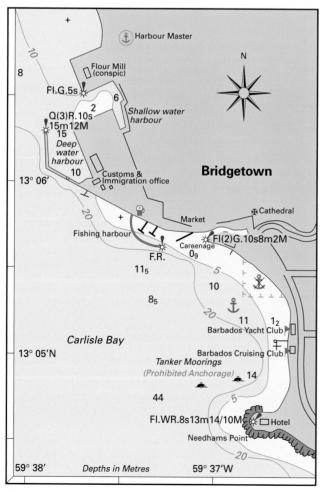

Plan 49 Bridgetown, Barbados.

procedures were difficult. However, the advent of Port St Charles Marina on the north-west coast, offering easier clearance, has restored the popularity of Barbados, even if, due to the marina's limited capacity, most visitors have to go on to Carlisle Bay at Bridgetown after clearance.

With Barbados lying nearly 100 miles to the east of the main chain of islands, it is logical to visit it first, though boats do occasionally beat out from Martinique or St Lucia. And, of course, a call at Barbados cuts at least a day off the Atlantic passage.

Approach

Barbados differs from most West Indian islands in that it is low-lying with only one high point, Mount Misery, at 329m (1,086ft). It is logical to approach round the north end of the island to clear in at Port St Charles. From North Point, it is 6 miles to Port St Charles and 17 miles to Bridgetown in the lee of the land.

You should keep at least 1 mile clear of the land around the north and north-east coasts until the end of Port St Charles breakwater bears 150° or less; keeping outside the 100m line will achieve the same, but the bottom drops away very sharply from 20m (66ft) to 200m (660ft).

Approaching from round the south end, a large bank known as The Shallows, with a least depth of 60m (200ft), and which lies about 4 miles south-east of South Point, should be avoided. This area can be very rough when a westerly swell meets an east-going current. From South Point, it is 8 miles to Bridgetown.

Radio

Barbados port authority monitors VHF channel 16 and uses channel 12 as its working channel (24 hours). Port control should be called on channel 16 on the approach, as should Port St Charles (on channel 77) if calling there first. Barbados Coast Guard is the national search and rescue agency and watches 2182 kHz and channel 16 continuously.

Entrance

Port St Charles The marina lies just over 1 mile south of the conspicuous Arawak jetty and cement works, and 0.5 miles north of Speightstown. The entrance is around a rubble breakwater with a square white tower halfway along it. The fuelling/customs jetty (18m (60ft) in length), immediately inside the end of the break-water, is in a channel no more than 50m (165ft) wide with a least depth of 4.3m (14ft). The shoal close to the east is marked by a row of red (FlR) buoys.

Bridgetown/Carlisle Bay After calling port control, secure alongside in the deep water harbour in the south-east corner where the offices are situated. A swell often enters here and good fendering will be needed. Arrivals are then directed to anchor in Carlisle Bay 1.5 miles to the east-south-east.

Anchorage and moorings

Port St Charles Anchor well clear of the entrance in 3–10m (10–30ft), in sand, avoiding the occasional coral outcrop.

Carlisle Bay The yacht anchorage is to the south of the careenage and Fort Willoughby [Fl(2)G10s] in 10m (30ft) or less over sand. There are wrecks and dive sites south of this area. The mooring buoys off the yacht clubs at the south end of the bay are available for residents only.

The Boatyard Restaurant has ten moorings in the north end of the bay that may be available. Although in some ways a classic Caribbean anchorage, with clear blue water backed by a long sandy beach, Carlisle Bay frequently suffers from swell, causing monohulls to roll, and making landing by dinghy a distinctly wet affair; however, a jetty has been built opposite the Boatyard Restaurant, and this helps. If surf is breaking heavily on the beach it may be best to take the dinghy into the careenage. Otherwise, until you've got the measure of it, avoid carrying cameras (except the waterproof kind) or other valuables, and transport money, shoes etc in sealed polythene bags.

Berthing and marinas

Port St Charles There are alongside berths for six transients behind the breakwater, but they are configured more for those larger yachts up to 35m (116ft). Booking is necessary. There are berths and room for residents only in the lagoon.

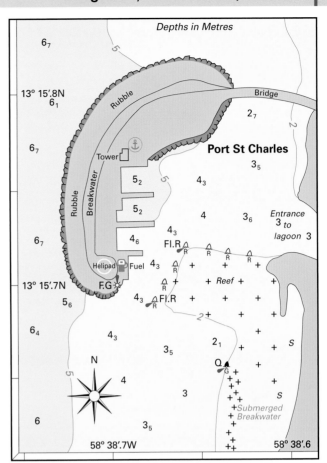

Plan 50 *Port St Charles, Barbados.*

Carlisle Bay Visitors are not allowed to lie in the shallow water harbour (mostly dredged to 6m (20ft)) to the north of the town unless using the travel lift at Willie's. A possibility is to berth in the careenage, for which permission will be needed from the Barbados port authority (tel: 430 4700), but there are only suitable berths for a couple of 10m (30ft) yachts and the frequent surge will put severe strain on warps and fenders. However, most crews will want to celebrate their arrival in the Caribbean by swimming from the boat – impossible in either of the above.

Port St Charles breakwater, Barbados, looking NE with arrival/fuel berth behind the hut on the right. Photo Port St Charles Development Co Ltd.

The anchorage at Carlisle Bay, Barbados. Photo John Melling.

Formalities

Fly the Q flag on approaching Barbados. As already mentioned, yachts must go to Port St Charles or into the deep water harbour to clear customs and immigration. Note that clearance out may be expected to be the same place as clearance in; this should be checked on arrival.

First call Port St Charles on VHF channel 16 or 77, or Bridgetown Harbour Signal Station on channel 12 for clearance to enter the harbour. At Bridgetown out of hours, you may be directed to Carlisle Bay until the morning.

Customs and immigration are housed adjacent to the arrivals berth at Port St Charles, and in a large building just to the south of the deep water harbour, and function 0600–2200 seven days a week. The usual papers, including outward clearance from the previous port, will be required, and a charge of around US$25 made, covering boat and crew. Anchorage and light dues are payable on departure.

It is normally necessary to return to Port St Charles or the deep water harbour *with the yacht* to obtain outward clearance, which remains valid for 24 hours. However, it seems as if this rule may sometimes be relaxed and outward clearance granted to skippers who have walked over from Carlisle Bay – check the current position when clearing in. Once cleared out, the yacht must leave directly to sea towards her next port of call and cannot return to the anchorage.

Coastal cruising

Customs clearance is required to cruise along the coast including from Port St Charles to Bridgetown. If intending to do this, check the procedure either on arrival or through the Coast Guard on VHF channel 16, and which anchorages can be used.

Facilities

Boatyard Willie's Diving and Marine Services is at the south end of the shallow water harbour with a 45-tonne travel lift and draught limit of 2.2m (7ft). Most repair and engineering work can be arranged.

Engineers/Electronics Enquire at Willie's.

Sailmaker Doyle Sailmakers Caribbean (tel: 423 4600, fax: 423 4499) at 6 Crossroads, St Philip, on the east side of the island are major sailmakers, exporting throughout the Caribbean and worldwide. They will collect and deliver.

Chandlery Port Hole Marine Supplies (at Willie's and very limited) and Carter's Fishermans Corner (in Bridgetown, with limited yacht stocks but will order from the United States).

Yacht club Both the Barbados Yacht Club (tel: 427 1125) and the Barbados Cruising Club (tel: 426 4434) have premises facing the southern part of Carlisle Bay. Both offer one week's free membership to visiting sailors and make them welcome. The Barbados Yacht Club is open all the time and expects a reasonable standard of dress; the Barbados Cruising Club is only open at weekends. Both are friendly and helpful to visitors.

Diesel In the shallow water harbour or the fishing harbour. There is 4m (13ft) in the fishing harbour, but little room inside to turn. Also, at Port St Charles.

Petrol From the service station near the Barbados Yacht Club, and also from the fuel berth at Port St Charles.

Water In the careenage, the deep water harbour (while clearing in) or the fishing harbour (where water is free if also taking on diesel). Unless large quantities are required, it may be easier to carry it by can from the Boatyard; also, water is available from the fuel berth at Port St Charles.

Bottled gas Texaco tank farm north of the deep water harbour. Propane and butane are both available.

Ice The Boatyard Restaurant and most filling stations.

Showers Barbados Yacht Club or the Barbados Cruising Club.

Laundry/laundrette This can be arranged by the Boatyard Restaurant.

Banks Several, with ATMs. Both Barbados and US dollars are used, but the former are not accepted elsewhere in the Caribbean except by banks. It may be convenient to pay the anchorage and light dues (usually US$5–10) in Bajan dollars on departure.

General shopping Relatively good, though inevitably slanted towards the thousands of cruise ship and hotel tourists.

Provisioning Several large supermarkets, mostly stocking American brands but also British, plus good produce and fish markets. A supermarket on the beach on the south side of the jetty at Speightstown is very convenient for yachts; there is also one by the

east side of the inner basin in the careenage that is convenient for dinghies.

Restaurants/hotels A vast choice. The bar/restaurant at the Boatyard is a favourite evening venue with cruisers, and there are dozens more in Bridgetown. There is a great range of price between the tourist bars and the 'rum-shops', but both are equally welcoming to visitors.

Medical services The small private Bayview Hospital is situated within walking distance of the Barbados Yacht Club. The Queen Elizabeth Hospital is publicly run, and is about ten minutes from the careenage. There is a large modern hospital just outside Bridgetown.

Communications

Mailing addresses C/o General Delivery at the main post office in Bridgetown (identification will be required on collection), either of the yacht clubs, or the Boatyard Restaurant, Bay Street, Bridgetown, Barbados, all by prior arrangement.

Post office A large building, with General Delivery occupying its own floor.

Telephones At the yacht clubs, the Boatyard Restaurant, the post office and elsewhere.

Bus services Buses all over the island – a cheap, fun way to travel. An island tour can be had for about BD$4.50.

Taxis Plentiful.

Car hire Several agencies. Driving is on the left.

Air services International air services to Europe and the Americas, and local air services to eastern Caribbean islands. Grantley Adams airport is 21km (13 miles) from Bridgetown.

Rodney Bay, St Lucia
14°04'.5N 60°57'.5W UT–4

Springs: 0.6m	Range 0.2m	
Neaps: 0.5m	Range 0.2m	
Flag: St Lucia	Currency: EC dollar	
Tel/fax – Country code: 1-758, Area code: none		
Charts	Admiralty	US	Imray/Iolaire
General	596 (1:175,000)	—	B5/A4 (1:510,700)
Approach	1273 (1:60,000)	25521 (1:75,000)	B1 (1:72,000)
Harbour	197 (1:25,000)	—	B1 (Inset)
	197 (1:5,000)		

General

Rodney Bay Marina, St Lucia, inside the lagoon at Rodney Bay (also known as Gros Islet Bay), has become a popular Atlantic landfall over the last few years. The smaller A-Frame Marina is just to the south of it and the Boatyard to the north in the lagoon. Certainly the range of on-the-spot facilities is the widest in the Windward Islands, and several large charter fleets are based here. It is the arrival port for the annual ARC rally from the Canaries and, for those not taking part, it may be time to avoid the island for up to a month after race arrival. The incidence of minor crime also tends to increase during this time.

The lagoon's most obvious disadvantages are in being some way from Castries – though this is partly offset by excellent shopping etc nearby – and even further from the international airport. The protection offered by the narrow entrance also means that the water inside is stagnant and unsuitable for swimming, though admittedly it is only a short walk or dinghy ride to the beach. It all comes down to priorities.

Approach

Rodney Bay lies within a couple of miles of the northern end of St Lucia, one of the more mountainous of the Lesser Antilles. Although Pointe du Cap at the extreme north of the island has no outlying hazards, neither is it lit, and the light at Cape Marquis [Fl(2) 20s 60m] 3 miles further south on the windward coast only has a 5-mile visibility.

Having rounded Pointe du Cap, Pigeon Island will be seen rising to over 100m (330ft) at the end of a low artificial causeway. Beyond is Rodney Bay, where fish traps with their associated floats and lines can be a hazard.

Rodney Bay Marina, St Lucia, looking north. Photo John Gibb.

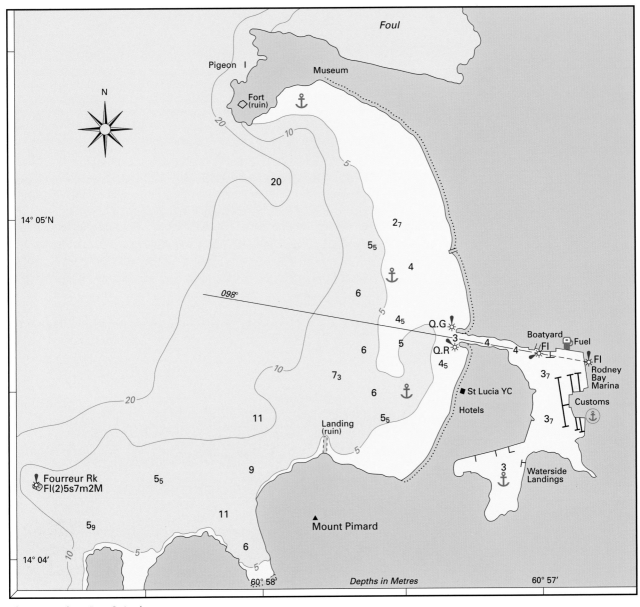

Plan 51 *Rodney Bay, St Lucia.*

Radio

The Royal St Lucia Police Force is the search and rescue agency and keeps watch on 2182 kHz and VHF channel 16. They operate in conjunction with the Maritime Rescue Co-ordination Centre in Martinique (tel: 596 596 719292).

Rodney Bay Marina operates on channel 16, with Rodney Bay Marina Boatyard on channel 68, and A-Frame Marina on channels 16 and 17. As is usual in the Caribbean, a number of other concerns – ranging from charter companies to restaurants – monitor VHF, generally channel 16.

Entrance

The entrance to the lagoon lies near the middle of the bay, between Gros Islet village to the north and Reduit Beach to the south. It is not hard to identify by daylight

and is lit at night, but the channel is narrow and marked by two unlit red and green buoys. If approaching after dark, the first-time visitor might do better to anchor outside and enter in daylight. There is 3m (10ft) or more in the entrance channel and 4m (13ft) in much of the lagoon itself.

Anchorage and moorings

It may be possible to anchor to the south of the marina in the main lagoon in 3m (10ft), or in the slightly shallower inner lagoon to the south-west, but moorings are increasingly encroaching in these areas. Both offer reasonable holding in thick mud and a guaranteed escape from rolling, but the insects can reach you if the wind is down. The alternative is to return to the outer bay after completing formalities and anchor either off Reduit Beach or to the south-east of Pigeon Island, but both may be subject to swell.

Berthing and marinas

If intending to berth at Rodney Bay Marina (tel: 452 0324, fax: 452 0185) it is best to telephone or call up on VHF channel 16 before arrival to be allocated a berth, as there is no reception pontoon. Failing this, secure in any space available until a berth can be arranged. Security is good.

The smaller A-Frame Marina (tel: 452 9800) is situated to the south of the larger marina, with most of its 20 berths stern-to.

Formalities

Rodney Bay is one of four ports of entry in St Lucia. There is a clearance berth opposite the customs and immigration office, but only if planning to anchor off is it necessary to secure here first. If staying in the marina the skipper can take the usual papers and go on foot. Office hours are 0800–1800, but overtime is charged after 1600.

Facilities

Boatyard/engineers/electronics Rodney Bay Marina Boatyard (now called Destination Saint Lucia Ltd) (tel: 452 8531, fax: 452 0183) has the best boatyard facilities in the southern Antilles, including a 50-tonne travel lift and large lay-up area. DIY, or hire local labour. Also Rodney Bay Ship Services (tel: 452 9973, fax: 452 9974) at the A-Frame Marina.

Electronics Regis Electronics (tel: 452 0205, fax: 452 0206) in the Rodney Bay Marina.

Sailmaker The Sail Loft (tel: 452 8648, fax: 452 0839), who will also deal with rigging and winches.

Chandlery Johnsons Marine Centre (tel: 452 0299, fax: 452 0311), opposite the Rodney Bay Marina, has extensive stocks.

Diesel On the fuel dock to the north of the marina (available duty free following outward clearance).

Water On pontoon berths and at the fuel dock, also at the A-Frame Marina.

Electricity On pontoon berths (220 volt, 50Hz).

Bottled gas Most types of propane and butane cylinders from Rodney Bay Marina.

Ice Block ice from Rodney Bay Marina, cube ice from stores and the mini-market.

Showers In the Rodney Bay Marina complex and at the A-Frame Marina.

Laundry/laundrette In the Rodney Bay Marina complex.

Banks In the Rodney Bay Marina complex, with ATMs.

General shopping Plenty of tourist shops, boutiques etc locally, but for wider variety go to Castries.

Provisioning Several supermarkets and bakeries etc in the Rodney Bay Marina complex, and a large shopping centre and more supermarkets on the Castries road, but for the best fresh produce visit the market in Castries.

Restaurants Dozens within walking or dinghy distance.

Hotels Many, scattered throughout the island.

Medical services Various clinics, plus a hospital south of Castries.

Communications

Mailing address C/o Rodney Bay Marina, PO Box 1538, Castries, St Lucia, West Indies.

Fax services At the Rodney Bay Marina office (fax: 452 8363).

Post office In Castries.

Telephones In the Rodney Bay Marina complex and elsewhere.

Bus services Buses to Castries.

Taxis/car hire In the Rodney Bay Marina complex. Driving is on the left.

Air services Inter-island flights from Tapion airport at Vigie Cove near Castries, but long-haul carriers use Hewannora airport, adjacent to Vieux Fort at the south end of the island.

18 Fort de France, Martinique

14°36'N 61°05'W UT–4

Springs:	0.7m	Range	0.1m	
Neaps:	0.6m	Range	0.2m	
Flag: France		Currency: Euro		
Tel/fax – Country code: 596, Area code: none				

Charts	Admiralty	US		Imray/Iolaire
General	594 (1:175,000)	—		A4 (1:388,000)
Approach	371 (1:75,000)	25524 (1:75,000)		A30 (1:92,000)
Harbour	371 (1:25,000)	25527 (1:15,000)		A30 (Inset)

General

Fort de France is one of the very few cities in the Caribbean islands that truly merits the title in terms of both size and atmosphere. It became the capital of Martinique in 1902 following the eruption of Mt Pelée and the destruction of the previous capital, St Pierre, and has more than made up for lost time. Facilities are generally excellent, and not surprisingly landfalls in Martinique, and to a lesser extent Guadeloupe, are very popular among French-speaking yachtsmen.

An alternative port of entry is Marin at the east end of the south coast of the island where there is a big marina, moorings and anchorage in a large, sheltered bay with good facilities ashore.

All the French islands of the Caribbean chain are technically part of France and receive large subsidies from their parent country, some of which appear to go into the comprehensive and generally well-maintained system of buoys and lights. Much of the infrastructure comes from France, along with the legal and education systems plus, somehow, that indefinable chic in dress and bearing that so many French West Indian women share with their Parisienne counterparts. Not for nothing did Napoleon's Empress Josephine come from Martinique.

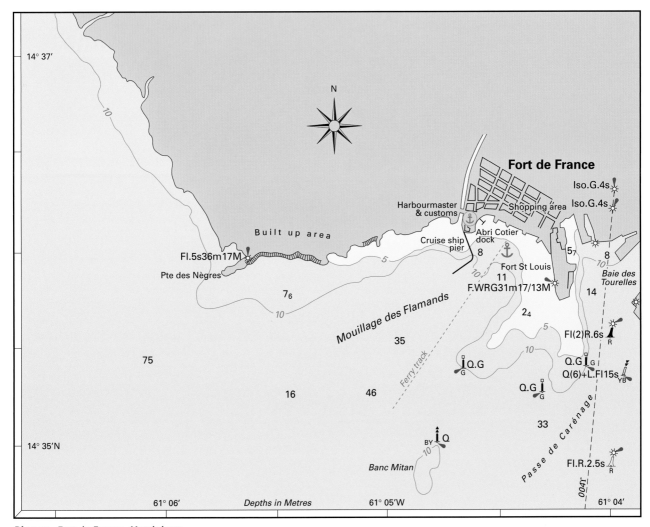

Plan 52 *Fort de France, Martinique.*

Fort de France, Martinique, looking north from the anchorage.

Approach

Martinique is one of the more mountainous islands of the Caribbean, and Fort de France lies on the northern shores of a large bay somewhat south of the island's centre. If making landfall there after a transatlantic passage it makes sense to approach around the southern end of the island, if only to avoid the long and often windless stretch from Pte du Macouba in the extreme north. Reefs and offlying islets fringe much of the windward coast, which should be given a wide berth.

Approaching around the south, Ilet Cabrits [FlR 5s 43m 16M] can be cleared at a mile or so and Rocher du Diamant (Diamond Rock) at the same distance. This will avoid the 4.0m (13ft) Banc du Diamant shoal where the seas can be rough. The south-west coast has no outlying hazards.

The large bay in which Fort de France lies has many attractive anchorages and a few small marinas where it is possible to leave a yacht. Some of these may be designated 'hurricane holes', but they offer no more safety than any others of the same genre throughout the islands. Nevertheless, Baie de Fort de France is a delightful area to explore for a few days.

Radio

The search and rescue agency (COSMA) is situated in the Maritime Rescue Co-ordination Centre at Fort de France, which keeps watch on 2182 kHz and VHF channel 16 (tel: 596 719292). The port authority operates on channels 12, 13 and 16.

Entrance

The entrance to the Baie de Fort de France is over 3 miles wide, between Pointe des Nègres [Fl 5s 36m 17M] in the north and Ilet a Ramiers (unlit) in the south. An unlit red buoy, Banc du Gros Ilet, lies almost in the centre of the mouth to mark shoals carrying a least depth of 6.2m (20ft). Other buoys, mostly lit, mark other shoals to the east of the main yacht anchorage.

Anchorage and moorings

The yacht anchorage is in the Mouillage des Flamands, to the west of Fort St Louis and directly off the city and public gardens. However, with the two ferry piers to the east, and the cruise ship pier to the west, space is tight. Some moorings have also been laid in the area, contributing to the chronic overcrowding. It may be possible for a smaller yacht to find space close inshore, but crews of larger yachts (or those needing scope for a nylon anchor rode) may be faced with a long dinghy ride. Dinghies can be left free of charge at the floating pontoon near the Abri Cotier dock. Holding is reasonably good in mud.

Winds from south of east make the Mouillage des Flamands uncomfortable, and an alternative is to cross to Anse Mitan, sheltered by Pte du Bout on the southern shore, from which a regular ferry service runs to Fort de France.

Berthing and marinas

It may be possible to lie stern-to at the Abri Cotier dock, but this is usually fully occupied by charter boats. There are some alongside berths if having work done in Baie des Tourelles.

Formalities

The customs and immigration office is situated near the new cruise ship pier. Office hours are 0700–1100 and 1430–1700 daily.

Facilities

Boatyards Carenantilles in Baie des Tourelles (tel: 637674, fax: 716683) has a 35-tonne travel lift and there are several others in the same area and around Baie de Fort de France. There are specialists in GRP, wooden boats and stainless steel work.

Engineers Madia Boat (tel: 631061, fax: 634870), Multicap Caraibes (tel: 714181, fax: 714183) Martinique Diesel (tel: 511613/513433) and several others.

Electronics Carib Electronic Engineering (tel: 600700, fax: 636014) for electronics, and Cadet Petit (tel: 637918) for electrical work.

Sailmaker R Helenon (tel: 602205, fax: 631763) has premises overlooking the canal to the north, or the cruise ship pier, and sails can be delivered and retrieved by dinghy; also, North Sails Martinique (tel: 680334, fax: 685069).

Chandlery Sea Services (tel/fax: 702669) is the largest and it also has a rigging workshop; Plus Nautique has secondhand goods, plus a good range of new items, and is a Plastimo agent (tel: 605848).

Yacht club The Yacht Club de la Martinique is situated in the military and commercial port on the eastern side of the Fort St Louis peninsula. It has its own small marina, but vacant berths are extremely rare.

Diesel/petrol From the CBS dock in Baie des Tourelles; also, at Ponton du Bakoua (tel: 660545, fax: 660950) in Anse Mitan.

Water From the CBS dock and Abri Cotier dock.

Bottled gas Camping Gaz exchanges readily available. Calor Gas and other non-standard bottles can be filled at Antilles Gas (tel: 503330) in the industrial area to the east.

Ice At the CBS dock or Glaciers Modernes.

Showers At the Abri Cotier dock and at the yacht club.

Laundry/laundrette In the city.

Banks Many, with ATMs.

General shopping Excellent – the place to treat yourself.

Provisioning Up to the best French standards, with cheese and paté abounding, and a good place to stock up on wine. Several of the larger supermarkets will deliver to the Abri Cotier dock. Don't miss the large covered produce market, and the fish market on the banks of the canal to the west of the city. There are several super-/hypermarkets in the industrial area to the east of the city, but a taxi would be needed (at least on the return trip).

Restaurants Many and excellent, at all prices.

Hotels At all levels.

Medical services Large modern hospital outside the city.

Communications

Mailing addresses C/o Carenantilles, Baie des Tourelles, 97200 Fort de France, Martinique, French West Indies, by prior arrangement, or c/o *Poste restante* at the main post office.

Post office On the main road opposite the attractive Place de la Savanne public gardens.

Telephones Many around the city, using cards bought in post offices; good mobile coverage.

Internet and e-mail services There are at least two internet cafés; the Web Café is behind the post office.

Bus services Mini-buses run all over the island from the square next to the customs office.

Ferry services Regular ferries to Anse Mitan and Trois Islets.

Taxis From the same square as the mini-buses. Communal taxis are the norm, and very economical – you specify where you want to go, but the driver can then pick up more passengers en route. Sole-use taxis are expensive.

Car hire Several agencies. Driving is on the right.

Air services International airport to the east of the Baie de Fort de France with flights to the United States, Canada and Europe.

Springs: 0.6m	Range 0.3m		
Neaps: 0.4m	Range 0.1m		
Flag: Antigua	Currency: EC dollar		
Tel/fax – Country code: 1-268, Area code: none			
Charts	Admiralty	US	Imray/Iolaire
General	584 (1:175,000)	25550 (1:250,000)	A3 (1:394,000)
Approach	2064 (1:50,000)	25570 (1:75,000)	A27 (1:57,600)
Harbour	2064 (1:20,000)	—	A271 (Inset)

General

English Harbour, Antigua, features high on the 'must visit' list for most British and American cruising sailors. Semi-derelict until the 1950s, Nelson's Dockyard and its surrounds are now one of the busiest yachting centres in the Caribbean, particularly during Antigua Race Week at the end of April. Probably less than a quarter of the yachts present actually race, but there is plenty going on ashore and, if you don't mind crowds, it provides a fun contrast to the 'deserted beaches' aspect of the Caribbean. (If you can't stand crowds and adore deserted beaches, clear in at Antigua and then sail on to Barbuda, its smaller and much less developed sister island to the north.)

English Harbour is never deserted. Until a decade or so ago, most visiting yachts used the same small protected anchorage favoured by the eighteenth-century British fleet, but since then ever-increasing numbers have turned to the adjoining Falmouth Bay, preferring the open, breezy anchorage of Falmouth to its more enclosed neighbour.

Almost all the development fringing both harbours is yacht or tourist related, and with nearly all requirements met locally it would be possible, though a pity, to spend several weeks in Antigua without ever visiting the capital, St John's, or venturing more than a mile from your boat.

Approach

At one time Antigua had a poor reputation as an Atlantic landfall, not least because its vicious windward reefs are unmarked by lights of any kind. While this is still true, the bright lights of the airport in the north of the island now effectively announce Antigua's presence from afar. They appear to burn all night, and should be quite sufficient to prevent the unwary from running up

The approach to English Harbour, Antigua, with the Pillars of Hercules on the right. Photo Anne Hammick.

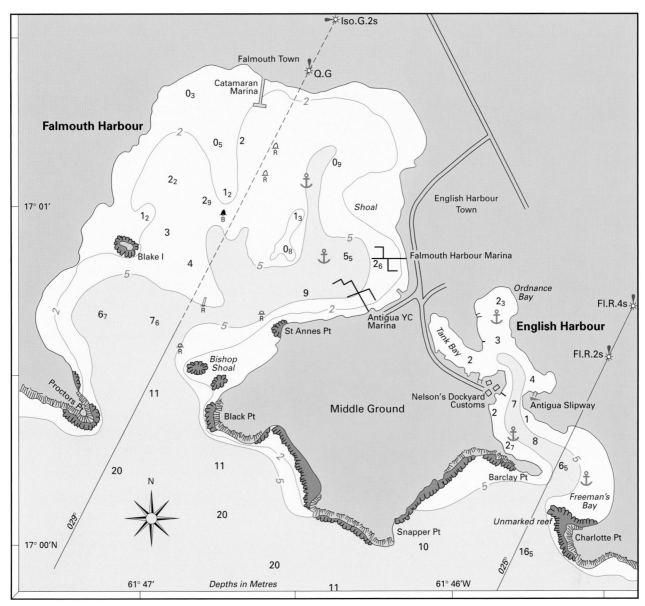

Plan 53 *English Harbour/Falmouth Bay, Antigua.*

on the island unawares even without GPS. If Antigua is sighted at dusk, consideration should be given to reducing speed or even heaving-to for the night, but this might be said of many Caribbean landfalls.

The entrances to English Harbour and Falmouth Bay lie almost in the centre of the south coast, and are somewhat easier to identify when approaching from eastwards than from the south. Coming in from the east in daylight the bluff promontory of Cape Shirley [Fl (4) 20s 150m 20M] is unmistakable. This headland is the place to close the coast, and a mile or so onwards the entrances first to English Harbour and then to Falmouth Bay will open up.

From the south the approach is straightforward, although the entrances are not always easy to pinpoint. Inland there are rolling hills, but the lower, slightly darker patch in front is Middle Ground, which separates the two entrances. On closer approach, the sandstone cliffs of Cape Shirley and Shirley Heights will be seen to terminate at their western end (Charlotte Point)

in some unusual vertical columns, aptly named the Pillars of Hercules. If coming in from the south be careful not to get set too far to the west – Middle and Cade Reefs lurk off the south-west tip of Antigua and have claimed several yachts.

Radio

English Harbour Radio in the Yacht Control Centre operates on 8294 kHz, 2582 and 2750 kHz (Voice), and VHF channels 16 and 68. Antigua Slipway (English Harbour) also watches channel 68. Catamaran Club Marina in Falmouth Bay monitors channels 16 and 68.

Entrance

English Harbour To the north-west, the low crenellations of Barclay Point are unmistakable from nearby, while to the south-east, Charlotte Point is marked by the equally distinctive Pillars of Hercules. A reef extends

English Harbour, Antigua, looking NW with Nelson's Dockyard in the centre, Falmouth Bay in the background. Photo Anne Hammick.

north-west from Charlotte Point directly towards Barclay Point, and best depths will be found by keeping between half and three-quarters of the way across the gap – ie nearer to Barclay Point.

The leading marks are a pair of orange boards positioned further to the north which transit on approximately 025°. Their lights [FlR 2 and 4s] should not be relied upon, and first-time entry after dark is best avoided.

Falmouth Bay Although much larger, wide stretches of Falmouth Bay are shallow and there are several isolated coral patches. Bishop Shoal extends nearly 0.5 miles offshore on the starboard hand soon after entering and often breaks, but the central shoal (supposedly buoyed) does not. Again there are leading lights [Iso and QG] on 029°, and again they do not always work. As a stranger, do not enter the bay in darkness if the leading lights cannot be seen.

There is a 4-knot speed limit in both harbours that applies to everything, including dinghies; the financial penalties for transgression are severe.

Anchorage and moorings

English Harbour Pick any spot that offers swinging room and does not impede the channel to Antigua Slipway and Nelson's Dockyard. Some prefer the breeze and cleaner water of Freeman's Bay, some the greater convenience of being nearer the Dockyard, perhaps in Ordnance Bay on its northern side. Dinghies can be landed on the beach in Freeman's Bay or at the purpose-built dinghy landing by the boundary wall of the old Dockyard.

Falmouth Bay Again a case of finding a convenient spot, though the majority of yachts favour the south-east corner of the bay off the Antigua Yacht Club Marina. Anchoring is prohibited close off both the Antigua Yacht Club and the Falmouth Harbour Marina. Dinghies can be left at the pontoon near the customs building.

Berthing and marinas

English Harbour A limited number of yachts can berth stern-to at Nelson's Dockyard (tel: 463 1053/1379/ 1380), but space is not always available. Call up on VHF channel 68 before arrival. The Dockyard is administered by the National Parks Authority, PO Box 1283, English Harbour. A few yachts may also be able to lie alongside at Antigua Slipway (tel: 463 1056, fax: 460 1156) on the eastern shore, but this is usually reserved for boats undergoing work.

Falmouth Bay The long-established Antigua Yacht Club has branched out into the marina business (tel: 460 1544, fax: 460 1444), with a pontoon to which about 30 yachts (some of them mega-yachts) can moor stern-to. The Catamaran Club (tel: 460 1503/1505, fax: 460 1506) runs a marina in the northern part of the bay, but it is usually full and is at a distance from many of the shoreside facilities.

Formalities

After entering with the Q flag hoisted, the skipper should go ashore with ship's papers, passports and previous port clearance to the combined customs and immigration office at the eastern end of the balconied Officers' Quarters building in Nelson's Dockyard. Hours are 0800–1630 daily, with dues payable for anchoring and for a cruising permit (whether or not you plan to cruise the island). Before departure, a receipt must be obtained from the Harbour Office before outward clearance will be granted.

Facilities

Boatyards Antigua Slipway (tel: 460 1056, fax: 460 1566) can haul yachts up to 120 tonnes and also has a travel lift.

Engineers Antigua Slipway; Marine Power Services (tel: 460 1850) at the head of Falmouth Bay; Caribbean International Yacht Services (tel: 462 9525, fax: 462 9526) on the road between the Dockyard and Falmouth Bay.

Electrical/electronics The Signal Locker (tel: 460 1528, fax: 460 1148), which has an excellent reputation and is the local agent for a wide variety of UK and US manufacturers. Cay Electronics are in Falmouth Harbour (tel: 460 1040, fax: 460 1227) and have agents all over the Caribbean and the US east coast.

Sailmaker A & F Sails (tel: 460 1522, fax: 460 1152) in Nelson's Dockyard.

Chandlery Good stock upstairs at Antigua Slipway, also chandleries at Antigua Yacht Club Marina, Catamaran Marina and Falmouth Harbour Marina in Falmouth Harbour.

Chart agent The Map Shop (tel: 460 3993, fax: 460 3995) on St Mary's Street in St John's stocks BA, US DMA and Imray-Iolaire charts, plus local cruising guides. Lord Jim's Locker (tel: 460 1093, fax: 460 1524) in Nelson's Dockyard stocks Imray-Iolaire charts and cruising guides.

Yacht club Antigua Yacht Club on Falmouth Bay organises evening racing throughout the winter season, and has a relaxed bar and good restaurant.

Weather forecast Broadcast by English Harbour Radio on VHF channel 06 at 0900 local time, following an announcement on channel 68.

Diesel/petrol Antigua Slipway, Antigua Yacht Club Marina, Falmouth Harbour Marina and at the Catamaran Club Marina.

Water At all the above, plus hoses to yachts lying stern-to in the Dockyard.

Electricity Stern-to in Nelson's Dockyard, and Antigua Slipway, Antigua Yacht Club Marina, Falmouth Harbour Marina and the Catamaran Club Marina.

Bottled gas Hinckley Yacht Services (tel: 460 2711, fax: 460 3740), propane only.

Ice Antigua Slipway, Antigua Yacht Club Marina, Falmouth Harbour Marina and the Catamaran Club Marina.

Showers At all the marinas and in Nelson's Dockyard.

Laundry/laundrette Sam & Dave Laundry (tel: 460 1266) at Falmouth, plus services offered by several local women who can be found in the Dockyard.

Banks Two in the Dockyard area and others in St John's, with ATMs.

General shopping Mostly tourist shops locally, but a wider selection in St John's.

Provisioning Malone's store opposite the head of Tank Bay, which is owned by Seventh Day Adventists (closed Saturday, open Sunday). Mini-markets at the marinas; Bailey's supermarket behind Catamaran Marina, who will deliver; and there are several others of all sizes, with the largest in St John's.

Restaurants Spoilt for choice. The Admiral's Inn (tel: 460 1027, fax: 460 1534) has the atmosphere, and the Lookout on Shirley Heights (tel: 460 1785) has the view, but neither are cheap. Many, many others at all levels.

Hotels At least three overlooking English Harbour, with many more throughout the rest of the island. Antigua's economy depends heavily on tourism.

Medical services Doctors and dentists in St John's, plus a modern hospital outside the town.

Communications

Mailing addresses C/o Nicholson's Yacht Charters, English Harbour Post Office, English Harbour, Antigua, West Indies; Caribbean International Yacht Services, Stanley's Tavern, English Harbour, Antigua, West Indies; Hinckley Yacht Services, PO Box 2242, St John's, Antigua, West Indies (although located at English Harbour), or Antigua Yacht Club Marina, Falmouth Bay, Antigua, West Indies, all by prior arrangement.

Post office In the building just outside the Dockyard gates and in St John's.

Fax and internet services At Hinckley Yacht Services (fax: 460 3740) and Caribbean International Yacht Services (fax: 462 9526).

Telephones Outside the Dockyard gates, at the marinas and elsewhere.

Bus services Mini-buses to St John's from the car park outside the Dockyard gates.

Taxis Plentiful, but not cheap.

Car hire Several agencies nearby. Driving is on the left.

Air services Direct flights to the United Kingdom, United States, Canada etc.

Road Town, Tortola   *18°25'N 64°37'W UT–4*
Virgin Gorda Yacht Harbour,
British Virgin Islands   *18°27'N 64°26'W UT–4*

Springs: 0.6m		**Range** 0.2m		
Neaps: 0.3m		**Range** 0.1m		
Flag: British Virgin Islands		**Currency:** US dollar		
Tel/fax – Country code: 1-284, **Area code:** none				

Charts	Admiralty		US		Imray/Iolaire
General	130	(1:282,000)	25600	(1:250,000)	A2 (1:416,000)
Approach	2019	(1:35,000)	25609	(1:80,000)	A231 (1:88,300)
	2005	(1:35,000)	25611	(1:30,000)	A232 (1:87,550)
Harbour	2020	(1:15,000)	25611	(1:15,000)	A231 (Insets)

General

Unlike anchorages such as English Harbour, Fort de France, etc, where many cruising sailors stay for several weeks, once cleared into the British Virgin Islands few yachts will stay in one harbour long – the whole appeal is to explore by water.

Road Town is the capital of the British Virgin Islands and a centre for bareboat charters, and has all facilities necessary to prepare for departure northwards. However, some skippers prefer to clear in and out at one of the other ports in the area, only visiting Road Town for essential shopping.

Approach

If coming from eastwards – ie St Martin or Anguilla – aim to arrive at dawn and enter through Round Rock Passage, between Ginger Island [Fl 5s 152m 14M] and the jumbled rocks known as Fallen Jerusalem off the south end of Virgin Gorda (unlit). Then either head north for Virgin Gorda Yacht Harbour or continue down the Sir Francis Drake Channel towards Road Town, about halfway along the south coast of Tortola.

Landfall from northwards – ie Bermuda or the United States – is more of a problem because of the dangers posed by the low-lying island of Anegada. Approach from the north-west and be certain to arrive in daylight, even if you have GPS. If coming from this direction it may be convenient to clear into the British Virgin Islands at Great Harbour on Jost Van Dyke.

Radio

VHF channel 16 is used throughout the islands for international distress and calling. The US Coast Guard uses channel 22A. Channels 06 and 68 are used for intership traffic and channel 03 for weather. Road Harbour and Port Purcell use channels 16 and 14, and Virgin Gorda Yacht Harbour uses channel 16.

Road Town, Tortola, looking ESE. Wickhams Cay is to the left with the yacht anchorage beyond.
Photo British Virgin Islands Tourist Boards.

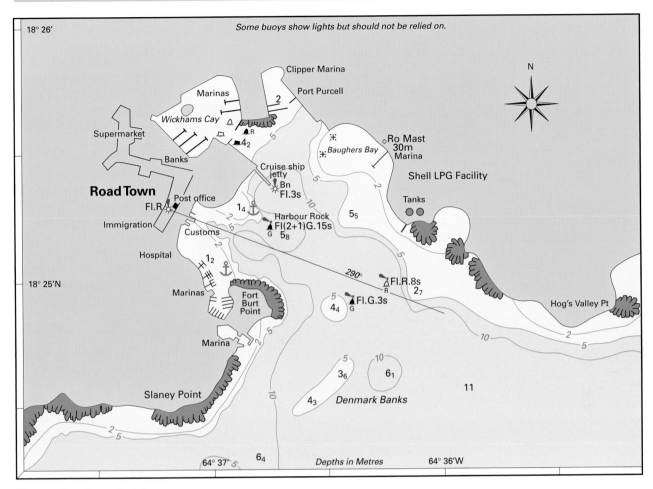

Some buoys show lights but should not be relied on.

Plan 54 *Road Town, Tortola.*

Entrance

Road Town Road Bay is unmistakable, with many buildings and large fuel tanks on the eastern side near the entrance. Although various shoal patches dot the entrance, all carry at least 3.6m (12ft), so can be ignored by the majority of yachts. However, avoid approaching Fort Burt Point too closely, and beware of Harbour Spit which runs south-east towards the middle of the harbour, supposedly marked by a lit buoy. If continuing into Wickhams Cay at the north end of the bay, having left the cruise ship dock to port, keep carefully to the channel – it is narrow with a distinct dog-leg, but well buoyed (but see 'Formalities', below).

Virgin Gorda Yacht Harbour The marina lies north of the famous Baths on the west coast of the island. The channel is buoyed, with a sharp turn first to the south and then eastwards into the marina proper.

Anchorage and moorings

Road Town Yachts anchor along the western shores of the outer harbour to the north of Fort Burt, with a dinghy landing at the ferry pier in the north-west corner. More protected, and with several marinas with visitors' berths, is Wickhams Cay. A notice forbidding yachts to anchor may be visible, but no one seems to take much notice provided access to the marinas is not impeded. Visitors are also accepted in the marinas just to the west of Fort Burt.

Virgin Gorda Yacht Harbour St Thomas Bay outside the entrance to the marina provides a pleasant temporary anchorage in 6m (20ft) or more over sand while clearing in. For both safety and comfort, keep well north of the approach to the ferry pier.

Berthing and marinas

Road Town Either Village Cay Marina (tel: 494 2771, fax: 494 2773) on the west side of Wickhams Cay or the Moorings/Mariners Inn (tel: 494 2331, fax: 494 3776) to the east may have a berth available – check before arrival. Their reception pontoons are clearly marked.

Virgin Gorda Yacht Harbour (tel: 495 5500, fax: 495 5706) This harbour can berth just over 100 yachts. The reception pontoon is nearly opposite the entrance and again is well marked. There is little room to manoeuvre once inside, so if short on crew go in with lines and fenders ready (port side-to).

Formalities

Fly the Q flag on arrival. If wishing to clear in at Road Town it is, in theory, still necessary to anchor off the customs dock while the skipper alone goes ashore to clear,

Plan 55 *Virgin Gorda Yacht Harbour, Virgin Gorda.*

taking all the usual papers plus clearance from the last port of call. In practice, it may be permissible to go on foot from a marina berth – check the current situation with the marina by radio before berthing. In Road Town the offices are at the head of the ferry and customs pier, in Virgin Gorda Yacht Harbour in the main administration block, and hours are 0830–1530. Outward clearance is valid for 24 hours, but if you admit that you intend to depart outside working hours you may well be charged overtime!

American citizens should note that a valid passport is now required to enter the British Virgin Islands. A birth certificate plus photographic identification is no longer sufficient.

Facilities

Boatyards/engineers/electronics Both Tortola Yacht Services (tel: 494 2124, fax: 474 4707) close east of the Moorings, and Virgin Gorda Yacht Harbour Boatyard (tel: 495 5318, fax: 495 5685) have 70-tonne travel lifts with full boatyard facilities on site.

Engineers Parts & Power (tel: 494 2830, fax: 494 6972) at Tortola Yacht Services.

Sailmaker Doyle Sailmakers Caribbean (tel: 494 2569, fax: 494 2034), who have a branch near the Moorings, and Tortola Yacht Services. Both in Road Town.

Chandlery At all three of the marinas listed, and at Tortola Yacht Services.

Diesel At all the marinas.

Water At all the marinas. Water is scarce in the British Virgin Islands and a charge will be made.

Electricity At all the marinas.

Bottled gas Enquire at the marina office or at Tortola Yacht Services.

Ice At all the marinas and at many shops and filling stations.

Showers At all the marinas. It may be possible for crews from yachts anchored off to use marina showers by arrangement, but expect to pay.

Laundry/laundrette At Village Cay Marina and Virgin Gorda Yacht Harbour, and in Road Town.

Banks In Road Town and at Virgin Gorda Yacht Harbour, with ATMs.

General shopping Reasonable shopping in Road Town, though with a strong tourist slant.

Provisioning Several large supermarkets in Road Town. Everything in Virgin Gorda must be brought over on the ferry, so although the store in the Village Cay Marina complex is well stocked, prices are high.

Restaurants Dozens, both tourist and local.

Hotels Everything from small guest houses to five-star developments, including one in the Village Cay Marina complex.

Medical services Doctors on Tortola and Virgin Gorda, hospital outside Road Town.

Communications

Mailing addresses C/o Road Town Post Office (not recommended); Village Cay Marina, Wickhams Cay I, Road Town, Tortola, BVI; Virgin Gorda Yacht Harbour, Spanish Town, Virgin Gorda, BVI; or possibly Tortola Yacht Services, PO Box 74, Tortola, BVI, all by prior arrangement.

Post offices Near the customs building in Road Town; south of the marina at Virgin Gorda.

Telephones At post offices, marinas and elsewhere.

Bus services Buses to Beef Island airport and other destinations.

Taxis/car hire No problem. Driving is on the left.

Ferry services Frequent ferries between Road Town and Virgin Gorda.

Air services Beef Island airport, Tortola (about 16km (10 miles) from Road Town) has links with other Caribbean islands, including Antigua and Puerto Rico, but no long-haul flights. There is a convenient anchorage in nearby Trellis Bay. Virgin Gorda has a small airstrip – but, having seen it, most sailors would probably rather go by water!

21 Fort Lauderdale, Florida, USA

26°05'N 80°07'W UT–5

Springs: 0.9m	Range 0.9m
Neaps: 0.7m	Range 0.2m
Flag: USA	Currency: US dollar

Tel/fax – Country code: 1, Area code: (1) 954

Charts	Admiralty	US
General	2866 (1:500,000)	11460 (1:466,940)
Approach	3699 (1:80,000)	11466 (1:80,000)
Harbour	3684 (1:20,000)	11470 (1:10,000)

General

Most yachts approaching Fort Lauderdale – or more correctly Port Everglades – will be doing so to enter the Intracoastal Waterway, which runs northwards for more than 1,600km (1,000 miles) to Norfolk, Virginia. There is considerable commercial activity in the port, and priority must always be given to ships when entering or leaving. Fort Lauderdale's 'Miracle Mile' may in fact hold a greater concentration of sizeable yachts than anywhere else in the United States (or the world).

Approach

The east coast of Florida shelves gently with no offlying hazards in the Fort Lauderdale area. However, nearly all the shoreline is built up, and it may be difficult to pinpoint the narrow entrance to Port Everglades from offshore, particularly in daylight. The outer fairway buoy about 1.5 miles off the entrance is lit and has a racon [Fl Mo (A)]; this may help as it is almost on the leading line [Dir WRG and FG].

Plan 56 *Fort Lauderdale, Florida.*

Radio

The harbourmaster monitors VHF channel 16 and operates on channel 14; these two channels should be monitored by all vessels in the port. Causeway Bridge operates on channel 09. Pier 66 Marina guards channel 71, Bahia Mar Marina channel 68, Hall of Fame Marina channel 08. There are many other marinas on various frequencies, but all monitor channel 16, as does the US Coast Guard.

Entrance

The red and white outer fairway buoy, marked 'PE' [Fl Mo (A)], lies about 1.5 miles due east of the harbour entrance. The first pair of channel markers – '2' to starboard and '3' to port – will be found about 1 mile offshore and from then on the channel, known as Outer Bar Cut, is clearly marked. Submerged breakwaters run from each side of the entrance out towards these buoys, and any yacht tempted to take a short cut should do so only with the aid of large-scale charts. Dir WRG and FG leading lights on 270° mark the fairway, the narrow white sector showing the centreline.

The entrance to Port Everglades is relatively narrow, and protected by the North and South Jetties. Inside is the large Turning Basin with wharves on the western side. The marked channel turns sharply northwards, hugging the eastern shore and passing under the 17th Street Causeway Bridge to join the Stranahan River. (The bridge has an air height of only 7.6m (25ft), but opens on demand – provided it has been closed for at least 15 minutes.) About 0.5 miles further on this converges with the New River and the Intracoastal Waterway proper. Currents can run strongly in this section, reaching 3 knots beneath the bridge.

Anchorage and moorings

The city authorities provide a very limited number of moorings (many of them permanently occupied) in the bight opposite the municipal marina at Birch-Las Olas

Docks about 1 mile north up the Intracoastal Waterway. (Call the dockmaster on channel 09.) It is also possible to anchor here, though stays are limited to a few nights. Holding is good, but passing traffic may make for a bumpy night. Dinghies can be left at the marina.

Berthing and marinas

There are approaching twenty marinas in and around Fort Lauderdale, and only those nearest the entrance that have visitors' berths are mentioned here. If none have space, keep going up the Intracoastal Waterway or New River until one is found. Pier 66 (tel: 728 3570, fax: 728 3588) and Marina Inn (tel: 525 3484) are situated on the east side immediately north of Causeway bascule Bridge; around the second bend of the channel of the Waterway lie Bahia Mar Yachting Center (tel: 764 2233, fax: 627 6356) and Hall of Fame Marinas (tel: 764 3975, fax: 779 3658); further north are the Birch-Las Olas Docks municipal marina (tel: 761 5423) with more visitors' berths. Bahia Mar has, at 200, the greatest number of visitors' berths, though Pier 66, the Birch-Las Olas Docks and Marriott Portside keep, respectively, 60, 38 and 33 transient berths free. There are many more marinas further north and south, as well as on the New River which branches westwards about 1 mile north of the entrance.

Formalities

Fly the Q flag from offshore if arriving from abroad. The skipper *only* should go ashore immediately after berthing and telephone 1 800 973 2867 (toll free). This national centre will supply the number for the local customs office, which can (and should) be called at any time of the day or night, though normal office hours are 0800–1700. (Alternatively, the marina may know the number or even have a direct line.) If requested, customs will notify the immigration services.

The yacht will then be visited, by launch if necessary. There is no charge for clearance within office hours and a free cruising license, valid for one year, will be issued to a foreign yacht at the first port of call. Ship's papers, passports (with visas as appropriate) and previous port clearance will be required – see 'Formalities: the United States' in Chapter 18.

Facilities

Fort Lauderdale possesses hundreds of marine-related businesses and it would not be possible to include them all here. Those listed over are merely an indication of what is available.

Fort Lauderdale, looking SW. Photo Jerry E Clark, JE Clark Photographics.

Boatyards It is necessary to go beyond the city centre for specialist services, though Everglades Marina has a 30-tonne travel lift and some repair facilities.

Engineers RPM Diesel Engine Co (tel: 587 1620) and many others.

Electronics At Everglades Marina, or Ward's Marine Electric Inc (tel: 523 2815) for electrical repairs.

Chandlery Boat/US (tel: 523 7993) on W Broward Blvd, West Marine (tel: 527 5540) on S Federal Highway and at Pier 66 and Lauderdale Marinas. Sailorman (tel: 522 6716) on E State Road also carries used equipment.

Chart agent Bluewater Books & Charts (tel: 763 6533) on 17th Street.

Diesel Pier 66, Lauderdale Marina and Bahia Mar.

Water At all the marinas.

Electricity At all the marinas, with both 110 volts and 220 volts generally available.

Bottled gas Lauderdale Marina and in the city.

Showers At all the marinas.

Holding tank pump-out Nearly all marinas have facilities.

Laundry/laundrette Pier 66, Marina Inn, Marriott Portside, Bahia Mar and Hall of Fame.

Banks Many, with ATMs.

General shopping Good, nearly all needs can be met.

Provisioning Supermarkets and shopping malls abound.

Restaurants/hotels Hundreds, at all levels.

Medical services Several large hospitals in the area, including Broward General Medical Center (tel: 355 4400), plus the usual doctors and dentists.

Communications

Mailing addresses C/o any of the marinas by prior arrangement.

Fax and internet services Most of the marinas provide these.

Post office In the city.

Telephones At the marinas and elsewhere.

Taxis/car hire No shortage.

Air services Fort Lauderdale International airport a few miles away, or Miami International for most European flights.

Beaufort/Morehead City, North Carolina, USA

34°43'N 76°42'W UT–5

Springs: 1.0m		Range 1.0m	
Neaps: 0.9m		Range 0.7m	
Flag: USA		Currency: US dollar	
Tel/fax – Country code: 1, Area code: (1) 252			
Charts	Admiralty	US	
General	2864 (1:500,000)	11520	(1:432,720)
Approach	3686 (1:100,000)	11543	(1:80,000)
Harbour	3686 (1:15,000)	11547	(1:12,500)

General

Beaufort and its twin town of Morehead City to the west are popular both as stops on the Intracoastal Waterway and as an entry point for yachts heading north and wishing to avoid Cape Hatteras. They are often referred to as the US gateway to the Caribbean, as for many yachts it is a four-day sail to the Bahamas, five to Bermuda, and between seven and ten days direct to the Virgin Islands.

The North Carolina Maritime Museum (tel: 728 7317) on Front Street, Beaufort, is particularly helpful towards visiting sailors.

Approach

For details of Cape Hatteras some 70 miles to the north-east, see Chapter 18. The later approaches to Beaufort Inlet receive good protection from Cape Lookout, just under 10 miles to the south-east, though the vicinity of the Cape and its offlying shoals extending 10 miles to the south-south-east is dangerous and should be given wide clearance. It should further be noted that the powerful light [Fl 15s 48m 25M] is displayed from a tower about 1.5 miles north of the point itself, though the outlying shoals are well buoyed.

The coast to the west of Beaufort Inlet runs on an almost east/west axis, with good water within 0.5 miles or less of the shore.

Radio

Port operations monitor VHF channel 16 and work on channels 10, 13, 14 and 16. The Coast Guard monitors channel 16 and operates on channel 22A. All the marinas monitor channel 16 during daylight hours; Town Creek Marina also uses channel 08, Beaufort Docks uses channel 09, and Morehead City Yacht Basin uses channel 71.

Beaufort: looking north over Taylor's Creek towards Beaufort Docks. Photo Tom Doe.

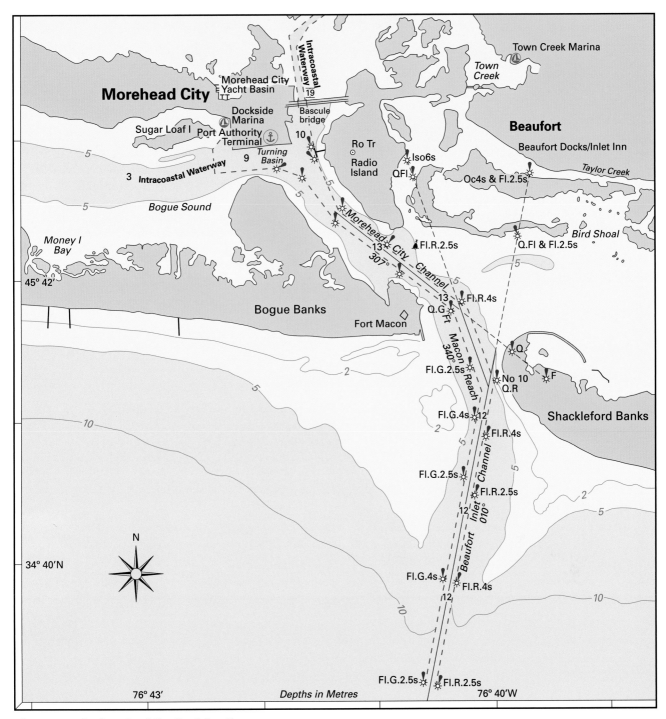

Plan 57 *Beaufort/Morehead City, North Carolina.*

Entrance

The long, buoyed Beaufort Inlet Channel is one of the safest on the coast and begins/ends at the red and white BM seabuoy [Fl Mo (A)] almost 7 miles offshore. It is entered on a bearing of 011°, with leading lights at night. Once close off Shackleford Point, this line is abandoned for one on 340°, which leads up Fort Macon Reach and into the well-buoyed Morehead City Channel. Fort Macon, on the port hand when entering, is unlit.

If making for Beaufort, once in the Morehead City Channel look for red pillar buoy R2 [Fl R 2.5s] and the nearby marker G1 [Fl G 4s 4.5m 4M], after which the channel is buoyed on the starboard hand.

Tidal streams in the Beaufort Inlet Channel may run at 2–3 knots and an opposing wind will cause steep seas. In the vicinity of the Port Authority Terminal the stream can reach more than 4 knots at springs.

Anchorage and moorings

The two best anchorages are on the south side of Taylor Creek, in a marked area opposite the Beaufort Docks, or in Town Creek to the north of Beaufort. The latter anchorage is quieter, but still convenient for the town.

A spot must be chosen clear of the main channel and a bahamian moor is essential in the strong streams. There is a public dinghy dock opposite the post office on Front Street, Beaufort.

Berthing and marinas

There are many marinas in the area, but those with most visitors' berths are the Dockside Marina (tel/fax: 247 4890) just to the west of the Port Authority Terminal, and Morehead City Yacht Basin (tel: 726 6862, fax: 726 1939), which is up a channel to port after the two bridges. On the Beaufort side, Town Creek Marina (tel: 728 6111, fax: 728 4053) is through another bridge and Beaufort Docks (tel: 728 2503), which caters for visiting yachts only, is on the north side of Taylor Creek.

Morehead City Yacht Basin is approached via a bascule bridge which carries the railway and is normally open unless a train is due, and a fixed bridge with 20m (65ft) air height. Town Creek Marina is reached via a bascule road bridge which opens on the hour and at 20-minute intervals.

Formalities

Fly the Q flag from offshore if arriving from abroad. The skipper *only* should go ashore immediately after berthing and telephone 1 800 973 2867 (toll free). This national centre will supply the number for the local customs office, which can (and should) be called at any time of the day or night, though normal office hours are 0800–1700. (Alternatively, the marina may know the number or even have a direct line.) If requested, customs will notify the immigration services.

The yacht will then be visited, by launch if necessary. There is no charge for clearance within office hours and a free cruising license, valid for one year, will be issued to a foreign yacht at the first port of call. Ship's papers, passports (with visas as appropriate) and previous port clearance will be required – see 'Formalities: the United States' in Chapter 18.

Facilities

Boatyards There is a 50-tonne travel lift with full service boatyard at Town Creek Marina, and a wide range of repair facilities are also available at Beaufort Docks. Jarrett Bay, a few miles up the Intracoastal Waterway, can lift boats up to 220 tonnes and 50m (165ft) and has all the attendant facilities.

Engineers At Beaufort Docks and Town Creek Marina.

Electronics West Marine in Morehead City and at Town Creek Marina.

Sail repairs At Beaufort Docks.

Chandlery Beaufort Marine Discount on Front Street and in Morehead City.

Charts The North Carolina Maritime Museum or Scuttlebutt, both on Front Street, Beaufort.

Weather forecast Rolling forecast with hurricane information on VHF weather channel WX 2.

Diesel At Beaufort Docks and Town Creek Marina.

Water At all the marinas.

Electricity At all the marinas; 110 volts and 220 volts available at Beaufort Docks.

Bottled gas Propane at all the marinas.

Showers At all the marinas.

Holding tank pump-out Beaufort Docks and elsewhere.

Laundry/laundrette On Front Street and Town Creek Marina in Beaufort, and at Dockside Marina in Morehead City.

Banks Several, with ATMs.

General shopping Somewhat limited in Beaufort, good in Morehead City.

Provisioning No problem in Morehead City, and several grocery stores in Beaufort. On production of a driving licence, the Maritime Museum will lend a car for two hours to visit the excellent shopping mall just out of town on Route 70. Several of the marinas offer a similar service.

Restaurants A wide selection.

Medical services Hospital in Morehead City; doctors and dentists in both Morehead City and Beaufort.

Communications

Mailing addresses C/o The North Carolina Maritime Museum, Front Street, Beaufort, NC 28516; or General Delivery, Main Post Office, Front Street. Otherwise, c/o Town Creek Marina, 232 West Beaufort Street, Beaufort, NC 28516; Beaufort Docks, 500 Front Street, Beaufort, NC 28516; or Dockside Marina, PO Box 3398, 301 Arendell Street, Morehead City, NC 28557, by prior arrangement.

Fax and internet services At Town Creek Marina (fax: 728 4053); many internet cafés in Beaufort and Morehead.

Post office On Front Street in Beaufort and in Morehead City.

Telephones At the marinas and elsewhere.

Taxis/car hire No problem.

Air services National airport at New Bern, 64km (40 miles) away.

23 Norfolk, Virginia, USA
36°51'N 76°18'W UT–5

Charts	Admiralty	US	
Springs: 0.9m	**Range** 0.9m		
Neaps: 0.7m	**Range** 0.7m		
Flag: USA	**Currency:** US dollar		
Tel/fax – Country code: 1, **Area code:** (1) 757			
Charts	**Admiralty**	**US**	
General	–	12280	(1:200,000)
Approach	2919 (1:80,000)	12221	(1:80,000)
		12222	(1:40,000)
Harbour	2814 (1:20,000)	12245	(1:20,000)
		12253	(1:20,000)

General

Norfolk lies at the mouth of the Elizabeth River and marks the emergence of the Intracoastal Waterway into the Chesapeake Bay, and most yachts passing through Norfolk will be either joining or leaving the Waterway. The seaward approach is via Hampton Roads – the lower stretches of the James River – where a bridge-tunnel combination links Norfolk with Hampton and Newport News on the northern shore. Hampton Roads is a busy area for both naval and commercial shipping, and the Norfolk Naval Base is the largest in the world (tours of the base are run daily in summer). Although yachtsmen generally refer to the area as Norfolk, several of the marinas listed below are actually in Portsmouth, on the west bank of the Elizabeth River.

Approach

Norfolk may be approached from further north up the Bay, or from the Atlantic via the Chesapeake Bay Channel between Cape Charles [Fl 5s 55m 24M] on the northern shore and Cape Henry [Mo (U) WR 20s 50m 17/15M] to the south. Some 6 miles to the east of Cape Henry lies the Chesapeake Bay Bridge Tunnel complex, with the well-buoyed Thimble Shoal Channel leading through it just over 3 miles from the southern shore. Strong currents can run in the area, sometimes exceeding 3 knots, and particular care must be taken in the vicinity of the bridge. The Thimble Shoal Channel extends a further 6 miles west-north-west towards Old Point Comfort [LFl (2) W/R 12s 16m 16/14M] and the northern end of the bridge tunnel combination linking Norfolk and Hampton. Fort Wool [Fl 4s 8m 8M] marks the southern side of the navigable area.

Radio

Both Coast Guard and harbourmaster monitor VHF channel 16. All the marinas listen on channel 16, with the Waterside Marina, Tidewater Yacht Agency, Scott's Creek Marina, Portsmouth Boating Center and the Ocean Marine water taxi also using channel 68.

Entrance

A direct course can be shaped from the Hampton tunnel area past the narrow but well-marked channel for

Plan 58 *Norfolk, Virginia.*

Plan 59 *Norfolk Harbor and the Elizabeth River, Virginia.*

Willoughby Bay and thence south-west down Entrance Reach. Norfolk Harbor Reach then leads south past the Naval Base into the Elizabeth River. The wide-mouthed Lafayette River flows in from the east, before the channel narrows into the Southern Branch and the Waterway proper. The entire area is extremely well buoyed.

Anchorage and moorings

There are several possible anchorages convenient to Norfolk and Portsmouth. The northernmost – and deepest – is on the west side of the channel opposite Lamberts Point in about 8.0m (26ft), with others just south of Lamberts Point and south of Hospital Point on Town Point Reach in 4.0m (13ft) or so. The latter offers convenient dinghy access to both Norfolk and Portsmouth city centres. Dinghies can be left at the Waterside Marina for a nominal charge, and a dinghy dock is also being installed at the Nauticus centre just north of Waterside Marina. The Ocean Marine water taxi covers the inner harbour from 0700 daily.

Berthing and marinas

There are numerous marinas around Norfolk and Portsmouth, with more at Hampton on the north bank.

Willoughby Harbor Marina (tel: 583 4150, fax: 583 1846) is located on the north side of Willoughby Bay about 4 miles from Norfolk city centre, near the southern end of the Hampton Roads Bridge Tunnel. It is some distance out of town, but there are good facilities locally and a courtesy car may be available. A current of up to 2 knots can flow in the marina basin. Much closer to the city centre on the Norfolk shore is the Waterside Marina (tel: 625 2000, fax: 623 8477), an all-transient facility with 50 berths and able to take mega-yachts up to 120m (400ft).

On the Portsmouth side are the Nautical Boats Marina (tel: 483 6148), Scott's Creek Marina (tel: 393 2628), which has 135 berths for yachts up to 20m (66ft), and Tidewater Yacht Agency (tel: 393 2525, fax: 393 7845). Of these, Tidewater Yacht Agency is the largest, with 325 berths for vessels up to 30m (100ft), a hundred of them reserved for visiting yachts, and is situated right opposite Waterside Marina and the Norfolk city centre.

Formalities

Fly the Q flag from offshore if arriving from abroad. The skipper *only* should go ashore immediately after berthing and telephone 1 800 973 2867 (toll free). This national centre will supply the number for the local customs office, which can (and should) be called at any time of the day or night, though normal office hours are 0800–1700. (Alternatively, the marina may know the number or even have a direct line.) If requested, customs will notify the immigration services.

The yacht will then be visited, by launch if necessary. There is no charge for clearance within office hours and a free cruising license, valid for one year, will be issued to a foreign yacht at the first port of call. Ship's papers, passports (with visas as appropriate) and previous port clearance will be required – see 'Formalities: the United States', in Chapter 18.

Facilities

Boatyards Ocean Marine (tel: 391 3000, fax: 399 3088) at Tidewater Yacht Agency has a 60-tonne travel lift and 25m (80 ft) enclosed wet slip, and can handle all normal work. There is also a boatyard next to Willoughby Harbor Marina.

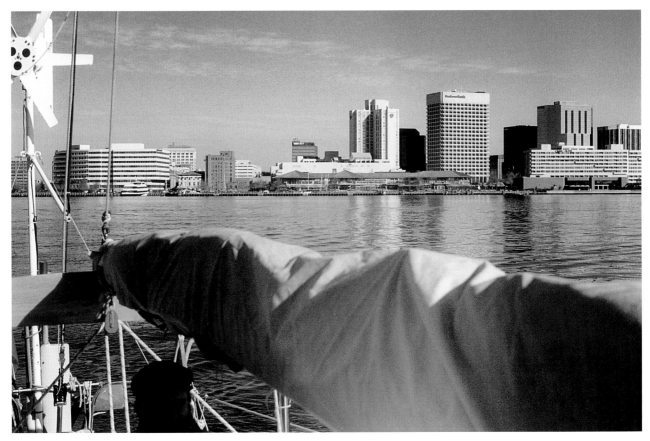

Downtown Norfolk with Waterside Marina in the foreground looking NW across Town Point Reach. Photo Gavin McLaren.

Engineers At Ocean Marine, plus a mobile mechanical service at Waterside Marina.

Electronics Ocean Marine.

Chandlery West Marine (E&B Marine), a short bus ride from Waterside Marina, and at most of the marinas.

Diesel At all the marinas.

Water At all the marinas.

Electricity At all the marinas, with both 110 volts and 220 volts generally available.

Showers At all the marinas.

Holding tank pump-out At Willoughby Harbor Marina, Waterside Marina, Scott's Creek Marina and Tidewater Yacht Agency.

Laundry/laundrette At Willoughby Harbor Marina, Waterside Marina, Scott's Creek Marina, Tidewater Yacht Agency, and in the city.

Banks Many, with credit card facilities and ATMs.

General shopping Good on both sides of the river.

Provisioning All requirements can be met. Gene Walters' Marketplace store will collect customers from Waterside Marina.

Restaurants/hotels A choice in Norfolk and Portsmouth.

Medical services Several hospitals, and the usual doctors and dentists.

Communications

Mailing addresses C/o General Delivery, US Post Office/ Customs House Station, Norfolk, VA 23514 (mark 'Hold for Arrival'), or c/o one of the marinas by prior agreement: Willoughby Harbor Marina, 1525 Bayville Street, Norfolk, VA 23503; Waterside Marina, 333 Waterside Drive, Norfolk, VA 23510– 3202; H&H Marina, 3515 Shipwright Street, Portsmouth, VA; Scott's Creek Marina, 6 Harper Avenue, Portsmouth, VA 23707; or Tidewater Yacht Agency, 10 Crawford Parkway, Portsmouth, VA 23704–2606.

Fax and internet services At Willoughby Harbor Marina (fax: 583 1846), Waterside Marina (fax: 623 8477), and Tidewater Yacht Agency (fax: 393 7845), plus many internet cafés.

Post offices On both sides of the Elizabeth River.

Telephones At the marinas and elsewhere.

Bus services Local and airport buses.

Taxis/car hire Readily available.

Ferry services Two ferries link Portsmouth and Norfolk from 0700 daily.

Air services Norfolk International airport is a few minutes away.

24 Annapolis, Maryland, USA
38°58'.5N 76°29'W UT–5

Springs: 0.3m		Range 0.2m		
Neaps: 0.3m		Range 0.2m		
Flag: USA		Currency: US dollar		
Tel/fax – Country code: 1, Area code: (1) 410				
Charts	Admiralty		US	
General	—		12280	(1:200,000)
Approach	2921	(1:80,000)	12270	(1:40,000)
			12282	(1:25,000)
Harbour	—		12283	(1:10,000)

General

Annapolis, Maryland, briefly the capital of the United States and the state capital since 1695, is located on the western shore of the Chesapeake Bay some 140 miles north of the open sea. It is the yachting and sailing centre for middle Chesapeake Bay and offers all maritime services for sail, power and commercial vessels. Within the city limits are 11 marinas, which between them provide facilities ranging from transient-only to full-service and DIY, and three main creeks which offer many berths for transient vessels. From south to north these are Back Creek, Spa Creek, and Weems Creek. College Creek, although within the city limits, is unsuitable as an anchorage. Access to all three is straightforward, and Back Creek and Spa Creek provide access to all the city's marinas.

Much of the land between Spa Creek and College Creek is occupied by the United States Naval Academy. Annapolis is also the venue of the United States Sailboat Show and the United States Powerboat Show, which run consecutively for two weeks during October. The city enjoys a thriving tourist business, with many of the homes of the early settlers restored and open for viewing.

Caution
There is little tidal range even at springs, and heights are affected by wind as much as by lunar forces – a strong north-westerly breeze will reduce the water level in the Bay by as much as 1.0m (3ft).

Approach and entrance

Annapolis lies on the south-west shore of the Severn River about 0.7 miles from its mouth. Approach is simple from both north and south, with good depths available. From the south follow the buoyed channel up the Severn River until marker HP [Fl 6s 6M] is identified, and leave this to port on a north-westerly course for Spa Creek. For Back Creek, leave HP well to the

north on a south-westerly course for the Fl G 4s marker (leave to port) at the entrance to Back Creek. Back Creek is deepest along its northern shore.

In July 1997 the Coast Guard renumbered and replaced several of the channel markers in the area – ensure that the large-scale chart in use is an edition not later than 6 September 1997.

Radio

The harbourmaster monitors VHF channels 16 and 09 and uses others, principally channel 17, for communication. The marinas generally use one or more of channels 16, 17, 71, 72 and 74. The water taxi that serves Back Creek and Spa Creek monitors channel 68.

Anchorage and moorings

Anchorage may be found in Back Creek, Weems Creek and the upper reaches of Spa Creek, but holding is not good – especially in Back Creek. There is a deep anchorage to the north-west of Eastport Yacht Club known as South Anchorage, and in the outer part of Spa Creek, but again the holding is suspect. In strong winds a berth at one of the many marinas is much to be preferred.

To enter *Back Creek*, which has a minimum depth at the entrance of 3.0m (10ft), proceed as above. Special attention should be paid not to stray to the south of the buoyed channel until the marinas are reached. As well as providing anchoring space for transient vessels in indifferent holding, Back Creek is home to several large marinas.

For *Spa Creek*, continue in the main channel to buoy No 9 [Q G] before turning west on the conspic spire of St Mary's Church, bearing about 260°. There is an anchorage in 3.5–4.5m (12–15ft) near its mouth, but the holding is suspect. There is ample room further upstream beyond the bascule bridge in 3.5m (12ft). There are several marinas in the creek that have visitors' berths.

The harbour authorities maintain 59 moorings in the creek, 40 downstream of the bridge, for yachts of no more than 13m (43ft) or so, and 19 beyond it in St Mary's Cove, this time limited to 11m (36ft) overall. The city moorings are white with a blue stripe and a number, and are allocated on a 'first come, first served' basis. The harbourmaster patrols the moorings during daylight hours. Dinghies can be left at the north-west end of the City Dock inlet (labelled 'Market Slip' on DMA chart 12283) for which no charge is made.

Weems Creek, the most northerly of the three, lies between the two highway bridges crossing the Severn River. Vertical clearance is 22.8m (75ft) at the south-

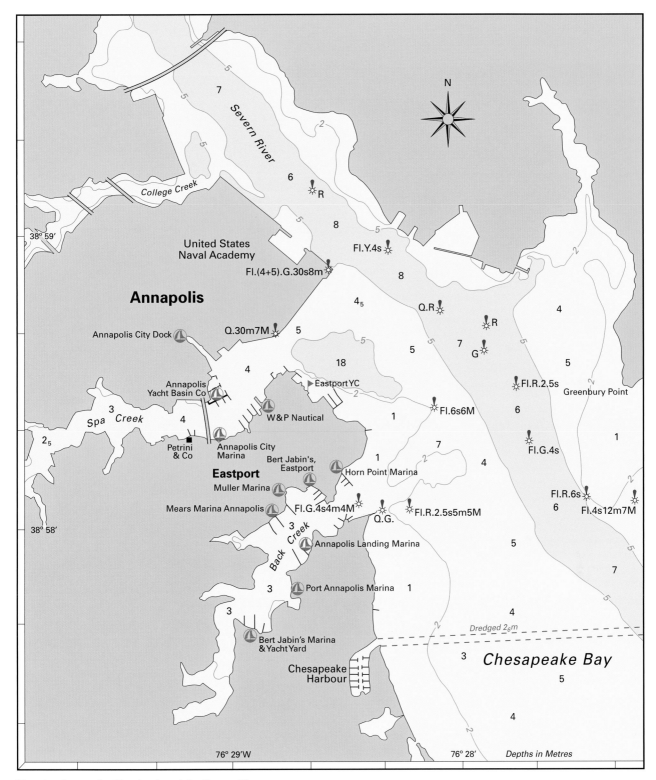

Plan 60 *Annapolis, Maryland, and the Severn River.*

east bridge and 24.3m (80ft) at the north-west one. The creek entrance is indicated by a red and green marker labelled 'WC'. A bascule bridge crosses Weems Creek about 0.5 miles from its mouth, severely limiting navigation, but depths of around 4.5m (15ft) will be carried to the bridge. It is a quiet anchorage with very limited access to the shore, though it is possible to land at a street end on the south-eastern shore, from which it is a 1-mile walk to a small shopping centre.

Berthing and marinas

As already mentioned, there are at least 11 marinas in Annapolis. All provide the usual services and some have boatyards on site.

Back Creek on the northern shore from north-east to south-west are: Horn Point Harbor Marina (tel: 263 0550), Bert Jabin's Eastport (tel: 268 6812), Muller Marina (tel: 626 1238) and Mears Marina (tel: 268 8282).

Looking ESE over Annapolis. College Creek is in the foreground, Spa Creek centre right and Back Creek just visible. To the left can be seen Greenbury Point with radio masts. Photo David Wallace.

On the south shore from north-east to south-west marinas are: Annapolis Landing Marina (tel: 263 0090), Port Annapolis Marina (tel: 269 1990), and Bert Jabin's Yacht Yard (tel: 268 9667).

Spa Creek on the northern shore has Annapolis City Dock (tel: 263 7973) and Annapolis Yacht Basin (tel: 263 3544), and on the southern shore, W & P Nautical (tel: 268 7700) and Annapolis City Marina (tel: 268 0660).

Formalities

Unlike all the other harbours in this section, Annapolis is NOT an official port of entry. Visiting sailors should clear customs and complete appropriate formalities in Baltimore, Hampton, Newport News, Norfolk or elsewhere.

Facilities

The harbourmaster (tel: 263 7973), who has his office close east of the City Dock, welcomes visiting yachts enthusiastically and will assist in any way he can. The Tourist and Visitors' Information Booth in the same building is open from 1 April to 1 November and will provide all tourist information during normal business hours.

The Port Book, which is produced annually and covers Annapolis and the eastern shore of Maryland, lists marine, tourist and travel services, bridge opening times, etc. It is available free of charge from the harbourmaster's office.

Boatyards/engineers Bert Jabin's Yacht Yard, Port Annapolis Marina, and Annapolis Yacht Yard all have travel lifts, while Mears Marina has a 50-tonne crane. All have facilities for DIY or yard work.

Electronics Bay Country Electronics (tel: 263 3000) at the City Dock, and Electronic Marine (tel: 268 8108, fax: 268 8111) on 4th Street.

Sailmakers Several international companies, including Banks (tel: 266 3666), Hood (tel: 268 4663) and North (tel: 269 5662), have sail lofts within the city limits. See *The Port Book*.

Chandlery Fawcett's Boat Supplies (tel: 267 8681, fax: 268 7547) and Viking Boat Supplies (tel: 268 8000, fax: 268 1532) both near the City Dock. West Marine (tel: 268 0129, fax: 431 5100) and Boat/US (tel: 573 5744) on the outskirts of the city, and others.

Chart agent Good selection at Fawcett's Boat Supplies.

Yacht clubs Annapolis is the home of the Annapolis Yacht Club (tel: 263 9279), the Eastport Yacht Club (tel: 267 8986) and the United States Naval Academy Sailing Squadron (tel: 293 5603).

Diesel At most marinas.

Water At all marinas and the City Dock.

Electricity At all marinas and the City Dock.

Bottled gas Propane is available at most hardware stores, True Value, and some garages. For refills, try Rental Works (tel: 268 7173) at 1919 Lincoln Drive.

Showers At all marinas and the City Dock (the latter free if berthed in the Dock, otherwise a small charge).

Holding tank pump-out At most of the marinas. In addition, the pump-out boat, provided by the city authorities, can be called on VHF channel 09.

Laundry/laundrette At most marinas, plus several readily available to the Spa Creek and Back Creek anchorages.

Banks Many in the city, all with ATMs.

General shopping On the Eastport peninsula between Back Creek and Spa Creek, and in the downtown area adjacent to the City Dock.

Provisioning Two large supermarkets, within 1 mile of Back Creek and Weems Creek respectively. No large store handy to Spa Creek, but public transport available to the above.

Restaurants To suit all tastes and pockets. Crab and other seafood dishes are specialities. In the downtown area, excellent Japanese, Italian and French cuisine is available.

Hotels Several.

Medical services The hospital at Anne Arundel Medical Center in downtown Annapolis is about five minutes from Spa Creek.

Communications

Mailing addresses C/o The Harbormaster's Office, 1 Dock Street, Annapolis, MD 21401, or General Delivery, Annapolis Post Office, Annapolis, MD 21401. In both cases mail should be marked 'Hold for Arrival'. Alternatively, c/o the destination marina by prior agreement.

Fax and internet services Annapolis Post Box (fax: 268 6245), Eastport Copy Inc (fax: 269 6399) and Minute Man Press (fax: 263 3442), and several of the marinas.

Post office On Chesapeake Avenue.

Telephones At the marinas, the City Dock and in the town.

Bus services Local bus service plus longer-distance routes.

Taxis/car hire Not a problem.

Water taxi The Jiffy Water Taxi (tel: 263 0033) operates from the City Dock and serves Spa Creek, Back Creek and the Severn River. It listens on VHF channel 68.

Air services Baltimore–Washington International airport, which provides national and international services, is about 45 minutes away and can be reached by shuttle service or public transport.

25 Newport, Rhode Island, USA
41°29'N 71°19'.5W UT–5

Springs:	1.2m	Range	1.2m	
Neaps:	0.8m	Range	0.8m	
Flag:	USA	Currency:	US dollar	

Tel/fax – Country code: 1, Area code: (1) 401

Charts	Admiralty		US	
General	2492	(1:677,000)	12300	(1:400,000)
Approach	2890	(1:100,000)	13218	(1:80,000)
			13221	(1:40,000)
Harbour	2730	(1:20,000)	13223	(1:20,000)

General

Newport, Rhode Island, lies to the east of the main entrance channel to Narragansett Bay. It has long been an important yachting centre and for many years was the venue for the America's Cup races. It is also the destination of the singlehanded transatlantic races run from Plymouth, England, and a favourite landfall for yachts heading north from Bermuda. Newport is an official port of entry and, together with the other harbours on Narragansett Bay, offers excellent facilities of all kinds but at a price.

Approach

The coast between Cape Cod and Newport is low lying, with shoal water and low islands to the south of Cape Cod. The area is very prone to fog and it can be difficult to identify the coast. If coming from the south-east or south it is advisable to make first landfall at Nantucket Shoals Lanby (see Chapter 18), thus keeping well south of the shoals themselves and ensuring an exact position from which to close the land. If approaching from the north-east, most yachts will use the Cape Cod Canal, which leads into a dredged channel at the north-east end of Buzzards Bay. A middle route, through Nantucket Sound and Vineyard Sound, is possible – but not recommended.

Heavy concentrations of shipping are likely to be encountered on the approach to Newport – fishing vessels around the various banks, and commercial traffic en route to New York, Narragansett Bay and Boston.

The entrance to Narragansett Bay is well bracketed by lights, including Buzzards Bay light [Fl 2.5s 19m 17M] 16 miles to the east, Point Judith light [Oc (3) 15s 20m 16M] 6 miles to the south-west, and Block Island SE light [Fl G 5s 80m 20M] 18 miles south-south-west. All have fog signals.

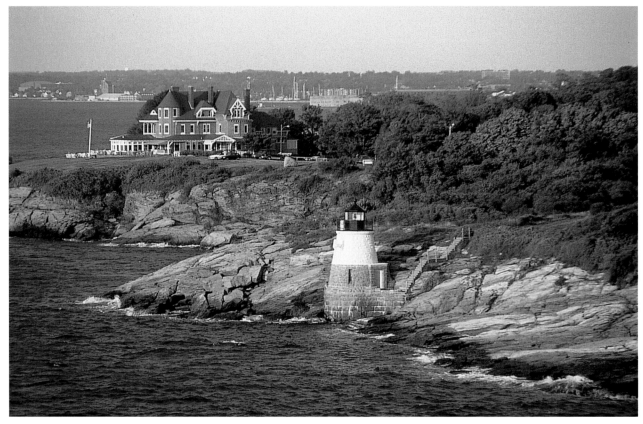

Castle Hill lighthouse on the approaches to Newport. Photo Jim Mcelholm.

Plan 61 *Newport, Rhode Island.*

If approaching from the east, head for the red and white Narragansett Bay entrance buoy [Fl 4s Mo(A) and Racon B] until a bearing on Beavertail Point [Fl 6s 20m 15M] on the west side of the entrance clears Brenton Reef whistle buoy [Fl R 4s] to starboard. This will take you well clear of Brenton Reef and the many fish nets in the area. In poor visibility, home in on Beavertail Point until abeam of the entrance buoy. If approaching from south or south-west, head directly for the entrance buoy. Do not make the mistake, as others have done when heading for Newport, by taking the West rather than the East Passage.

Radio

Castle Hill Coast Guard station maintains a 24-hour watch on VHF channel 16, but can also be called direct on channel 22A. The harbourmaster monitors channel 16, but communicates on channel 14. The marinas use channel 09 and 11, with Oldport Marine's launch listening on channel 68.

Entrance

The outer entrance lies between Beavertail Point to the west and Brenton Point to the east. From Narragansett Bay entrance buoy, steer 026° to give Castle Hill [Iso R 6s 12m 12M] good clearance to starboard. Although the rock cliff is very bold, it is essential to leave Butterball Rock bell buoy, which marks a barely awash shoal south-west of Castle Hill, to starboard. A buoyed channel then leads between Fort Adams and Goat Island into Newport Harbor.

Anchorage and moorings

Both yacht anchorages designated on BA 2730 (in Brenton Cove at the south-western corner of the harbour and between Goat Island, and the town waterfront further north) are now occupied by moorings. Most transient yachts now anchor either just north of the Ida Lewis Yacht Club or north of the causeway to Goat Island. If using the former beware the cable area – call the harbourmaster for advice.

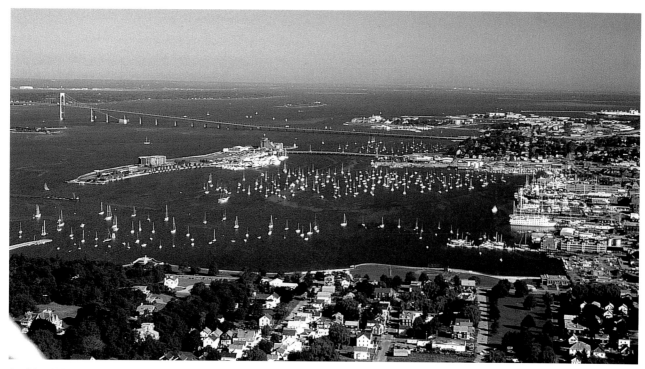

Looking NW over Newport. Goat Island with its bridge over East Passage can be seen (centre). Photo Jim Mcelholm.

The harbourmaster maintains 20 moorings available on a first come, first served basis, but there is seldom one free. Others are controlled by Oldport Marine Services (tel: 847 9109 or VHF channel 68). (They also run an excellent launch service between 0800 and midnight which will pick up and deposit anywhere in the harbour for a modest fee – call up on channel 68.) Otherwise, try Brenton Cove Moorings (tel: 849 2210). Alternatively, the Ida Lewis Yacht Club (tel: 846 1969 or channel 78A) may have a visitors' mooring available. Dinghies can be left at the Municipal Dock or the Ann Street Pier.

Berthing and marinas

There are many marinas in the Newport area. One of the largest is at Goat Island (tel: 849 5655, fax: 848 7144), situated about halfway along that island's eastern shore. It is some way from the town, but a water shuttle runs twice each hour.

Perhaps more convenient for the visiting sailor are the American Shipyard (tel: 846 6000 or channel 09), Newport Harbor Marina (tel: 847 9000 or channel 09), Oldport Marine (tel: 847 9109 or channel 68), Newport Yachting Center (tel: 847 9047), Christies Marina (tel: 848 7950) or West Wind Marina (tel: 849 4300). The Newport Yacht Club (tel: 846 9410) at the northern end of the harbour may also have berths available.

Formalities

Fly the Q flag from offshore if arriving from abroad. The skipper *only* should go ashore immediately after berthing and telephone 1 800 973 2867 (toll free). This national centre will supply the number for the local

customs office, which can (and should) be called at any time of the day or night, though normal office hours are 0800–1700. (Alternatively, the marina may know the number or even have a direct line.) If requested, customs will notify the immigration services.

The yacht will then be visited, by launch if necessary. There is no charge for clearance within office hours but a free cruising license, valid for one year, will be issued to a foreign yacht at the first port of call. Ship's papers, passports (with visas as appropriate) and previous port clearance will be required – see 'Formalities: the United States', in Chapter 18.

Facilities

The harbourmaster (tel: 848 6492) will assist with information and advice. The Visitors' Information Center at 23 America's Cup Avenue is worth a visit, as is the Fort Adams complex across the harbour.

Boatyards/engineers/electronics The American Shipyard Corporation (tel: 846 6000), Island Marine Services (tel: 848 9648), Oldport Marine Services (tel: 847 9109) and Brewer Street Boatworks (tel: 847 0321) next to Oldport. Only the first has a marine railway and can take up to 80m (260ft) LOA. Diesel engineers are available at Goat Island Marina and elsewhere.

Little Harbor Marine (tel: 683 7100) (a Ted Hood company), about 6 miles up the Bay, has a major concentration of marine industries including electronics, sailmakers, sparmakers, etc.

Sailmakers Several in the town – contact through one of the concerns listed above.

Chandlery JT's (tel: 846 7256) at 364 Thames Street has a good range, plus many others.

Chart agent The Armchair Sailor Bookstore (tel: 847 4252, fax: 847 1219) has comprehensive stocks and extremely helpful staff.

Yacht club The Ida Lewis Yacht Club (tel: 846 1969), host to many America's Cup races, has premises on the southern shores of the harbour, while the Newport Yacht Club (tel: 846 9410) is at its head. Both welcome visiting sailors. The imposing New York Yacht Club is behind the Ida Lewis Yacht Club, but casual visitors are not usually welcomed.

Diesel At Goat Island Marina, Bannister's Wharf, Newport Yachting Center, and West Wind Marina.

Electricity Alongside at all the marinas; 110 volts and/ or 220 volts may be available.

Bottled gas Island Marine Services (tel: 848 9648). Propane only is available.

Showers At all the marinas.

Holding tank pump-out At the larger marinas and the Ida Lewis Yacht Club.

Laundry/laundrette At the larger marinas and Island Yacht Services.

Banks Many in the town, with ATMs.

General shopping Good, if slightly tourist oriented.

Provisioning Several large supermarkets and many delicatessens, etc.

Restaurants/hotels Wide choice at all levels.

Medical services Newport Hospital (tel: 846 6400), and many doctors and dentists.

Communications

Mailing address C/o General Delivery at the main post office, or any of the marinas by prior arrangement.

Post office In the town.

Telephones At the marinas and elsewhere.

Fax and internet services At most marinas, and several internet cafés in the town.

Bus/rail services Buses to Providence, Rhode Island, with rail connections to Boston, New York, etc.

Taxis/car hire No problem.

Air services From Providence or Boston to international destinations.

26 Rockland, Maine, USA
44°06'N 69°06'W UT–5

Springs: 3.3m	Range 3.3m	
Neaps: 2.4m	Range 2.4m	
Flag: USA	Currency: US dollar	
Tel/fax – Country code: 1, Area code: (1) 207		
Charts	Admiralty	US
General	2492 (1:677,000)	13260 (1:378,838)
Approach	–	13302 (1:80,000)
		13305 (1:40,000)
Harbour	–	13307 (1:20,000)

General

Rockland is a large harbour that has traditionally concerned itself with fishing and commercial activities. However, these have declined sharply and considerable efforts are now made to attract yachts. There are several marinas and boatyards and all facilities are available.

Though perhaps not an obvious choice for an Atlantic landfall, Rockland would be an excellent departure point if leaving for the eastward Atlantic passage by one of the northern routes.

Approach

Rockland lies on the western shore of Penobscot Bay, about 150 miles from the Cape Cod Canal and about

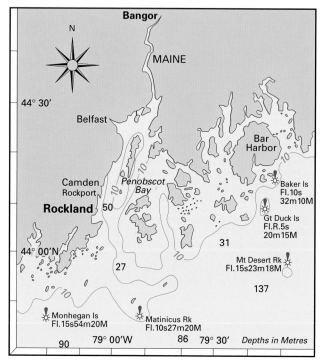

Plan 62 *Penobscot Bay, Maine.*

160 miles west-north-west of Cape Sable at the south-west tip of Nova Scotia.

If approaching from southward, landfall is probably best made at Monhegan Island [L Fl 15s 54m 20M]. From south-east, Matinicus Rock – with its powerful light [Fl 10s 27m 20M] – should be easy to identify, while from the east, Mount Desert Rock [Fl 15s 23m 18M] is the most likely landfall. Penobscot Bay is well buoyed and lit, but vast numbers of lobster pots laid within the 50m line make a night approach hazardous.

Radio

The harbourmaster monitors VHF channel 09 and works on channel 11. Both the Coast Guard and Hurricane Island Outward Bound School (which also maintains a search and rescue capability) monitor channel 16.

Of the marinas, Journey's End uses channels 09 and 18, Rockland Harbor Boatyard uses channel 09, Knight Marine Service works on channels 09 and 10, and Rockland Landings uses channels 09 and 10.

Entrance

The entrance lies between the breakwater (lit) and an unlit green can buoy 0.5 miles to the south. The buoy marks Spears Rock (1.5m (5ft)), and Lowell Ledge (drying) further inshore. Within the harbour, buoyed channels indicate the deepest water but, armed with the large-scale chart, yachts of normal draught can take their own route.

Anchorage and moorings

Free anchorage may be found anywhere within the harbour. Shelter from the prevailing winds is good, and in the occasional easterly blow protection can be found behind the breakwater.

The harbourmaster maintains moorings east of the public landing – those reserved for visitors have a white buoy with blue stripe and red number, the pick-up marked with a white flag. Both Samoset Resort Inn (tel: 594 2511) and the Hurricane Island Outward Bound School (tel: 594 5548) occasionally have moorings vacant, and several of the boatyards and marinas may also have moorings available.

Berthing and marinas

Journey's End Marina (tel: 594 4444, fax: 594 0407), situated astride the root of the granite Coast Guard Pier, has excellent facilities and is able to accommodate larger yachts – over 15m (50ft) – in their 'schooner berths'.

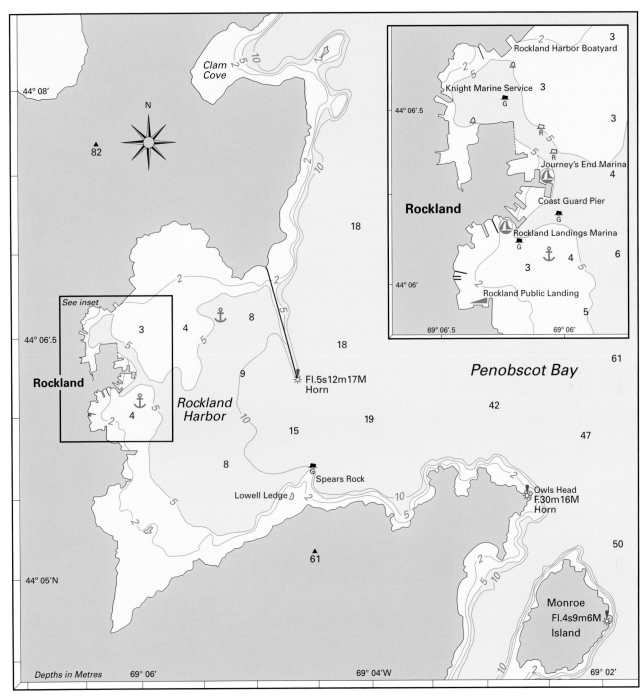

Plan 63 *Rockland, Maine.*

Rockland Landings Marina (tel: 596 6573), close south of the Coast Guard Pier, Knight Marine Service (tel: 594 4068), in the cove north of the Coast Guard Pier, and Rockland Harbor Boatyard (tel: 594 4337) all have the usual marina facilities including visitors' berths. Rockland Public Landing, just to the south of Rockland Landings Marina, and administered by the harbourmaster (tel: 594 0312), has some pontoon berths for visitors with water and electricity available.

Formalities

Fly the Q flag from offshore if arriving from abroad. The skipper *only* should go ashore immediately after berthing and telephone 1 800 973 2867 (toll free). This national centre will supply the number for the local customs office, which can (and should) be called at any time of the day or night, though normal office hours are 0800–1700. (Alternatively, the marina may know the number or even have a direct line.) If requested, customs will notify the immigration services.

The yacht will then be visited, by launch if necessary. There is no charge for clearance within office hours but a free cruising license, valid for one year, will be issued to a foreign yacht at the first port of call. Ship's papers, passports (with visas as appropriate) and previous port clearance will be required – see 'Formalities: the United States', in Chapter 18.

Rockland Harbor looking west.

Facilities

The harbourmaster (tel: 594 0312) has an office in the Chamber of Commerce building near the public landing. He and his staff welcome visiting yachts and will assist in any way they can. The Chamber of Commerce (tel: 596 0376, fax: 596 6549) provides general tourist information.

Boatyards Journey's End Marina (tel: 594 4444, fax: 594 0407) has a 50-tonne travel lift and 750- and 1,200-tonne marine railways, and can carry out all repairs. Knight Marine Service (tel: 594 4068) has a 35-tonne travel lift, backed by full boatyard facilities handling wood, steel and GRP. Rockland Harbor Boatyard (tel: 594 1766) has a 20-tonne crane and can deal with all repairs.

Engineering All boatyards, plus Shaw's Yacht Service (tel: 594 5035), which has a mobile workshop. Rockland Harbor Marine (tel: 596 0706) at Journey's End Marina handles outboards.

Electronics Omni Electronics (tel: 594 7073), Lew Grant (tel: 594 7073) at Journey's End Marina, and others.

Sail repairs Haarstick-Pope Sailmakers (tel: 596 7293) on Tilson Avenue and E S Bohndell & Co (tel: 236 3549) in nearby Rockport also provide rigging services, as do Shaw's Yacht Service (tel: 594 5035). Gemini Canvas and Sails (tel: 596 7705) at Journey's End Marina specialises in canvas and upholstery.

Chandlery Rockland Boat (tel: 594 8181) holds a mixture of fishing boat and yacht chandlery and will order items not in stock. Also, good chandleries at Journey's End Marina and Knight Marine Service.

Chart agent The Better Boating Association (tel: 617 982 4060) on Commerce Road is an agent for US DMA charts. Stocks are also held at Rockland Boat and Huston Tuttle Bookshop in Main Street.

Yacht club The Rockland Yacht Club has, as yet, no premises or facilities.

Diesel Journey's End Marina (north section), Rockland Landings Marina and Knight Marine Service.

Water All marinas and the public landing.

Electricity All marinas and the public landing.

Bottled gas Propane refills at local garages.

Showers All marinas and the harbour office building (for the public landing).

Holding tank pump-out At Journey's End Marina, Rockland Landings Marina, and the public landing.

Laundry/laundrette At the harbour authority building, plus several in town.

Banks Several, with ATMs.

General shopping Usual town shops.

Provisioning Medium-sized supermarket in town. Several larger supermarkets about 2km (1½ miles) north on the main road.

Restaurants/hotels To suit all tastes and pockets. Lobster and seafood are specialities.

Medical services The Penobscot Bay Medical Center (tel: 596 8000) in nearby Rockport.

Communications

Mailing addresses C/o The Harbourmaster's Office, PO Box 546, Rockland, ME 04841, or General Delivery, Rockland Post Office, ME 04841, in both cases marked 'Hold for Arrival'. Alternatively, c/o Journey's End Marina, 120 Tillson Avenue, Rockland, ME 04841, by prior arrangement.

Fax and internet services Chamber of Commerce (fax: 596 6549) will hold faxes provided they are clearly marked 'For visiting yacht (NAME)', also e-mail; various internet cafés in town.

Post office Off Main Street.

Telephones At the marinas, the public landing and in the town.

Bus services In summer, a 'dollar' bus runs a shuttle service around the town and to the supermarkets (see 'Provisioning', above).

Taxis/car hire Readily available.

Air services Knox County airport at nearby Owls Head has connecting flights to Boston. Bangor Intercontinental airport is 86km (54 miles) away (about 1½ hours).

27 Halifax, Nova Scotia, Canada
44°38'N 63°34'W UT–4

Charts	Admiralty	US	Canadian

Springs: 1.8m *Range* 1.5m

Neaps: 1.0m *Range* 1.0m

Flag: Canada *Currency:* Canadian dollar

Tel/fax – Country code: 1, *Area code:* 902

Charts	Admiralty	US	Canadian
General	1651 (1:725,000)	14005 (1:300,000)	4012 (1:300,000)
		14014 (1:350,000)	4013 (1:350,000)
Approach	729 (1:256,000)	14083 (1:145,000)	4320 (1:145,000)
	2027 (1:40,000)	14087 (1:38,866)	4237 (1:40,000)
Harbour	2028 (1:10,000)	14091 (1:10,000)	4203 (1:10,000)
	2029 (1:10,000)	14089 (1:10,000)	4202 (1:10,000)

General

Halifax is the capital of the Canadian province of Nova Scotia. It is a large commercial port and a naval base, and an official port of entry. Yachting activity is largely centred in the North West Arm, a long narrow bay branching off just inside the main entrance before the city and waterfront is reached, and in Bedford Basin north of the city.

Approach

The coastline of Nova Scotia is somewhat rugged and hilly with many inlets, and offlying rocks and small islands extend up to 5 miles from the coast in places. It is well buoyed, but subject to fog during the summer months, particularly with onshore winds. In clear weather the land will be visible well before any dangers are approached, but in poor visibility it is essential to exercise great caution when closing the coast.

If approaching from west of 63°30′W, care must be taken when off Pennant Point and Sambro Island. This is an area of shoal water and isolated rocks, many of which dry or are awash, and in bad weather the sea breaks fiercely. Although it is well buoyed, these may be missed in thick weather.

The final approach to Halifax is made between Chebucto Head on the western side, a 30m (100ft) headland of whitish granite with a light [Fl 20s 49m 14M] shown from a white tower close to the north, and Devils Island [Fl 10s 16m 13M] off Hartlen Point to the north-east. Between them lie Portuguese Shoal and Rock Head Shoal, both of which are buoyed. There are numerous other buoys and leading lights in the final approach.

Radio

'Halifax Traffic' operates a Vessel Traffic Management System for all vessels over 20m (65ft) and will advise smaller craft on the proximity of shipping. It monitors VHF channel 16 and works on channels 12 and 14 (channel 14 for traffic to seaward of Chebucto Head, channel 12 in the harbour itself). The harbourmaster uses channel 65A, with the Royal Nova Scotia Yacht Squadron on channel 68. The Canadian Coast Guard monitors channel 16, and works on 26 and 27. In addition, a continuous weather forecast is broadcast on channel 21B.

Halifax: the North West Arm with the Royal Nova Scotia Yacht Squadron moorings on the left. Photo John Gibb.

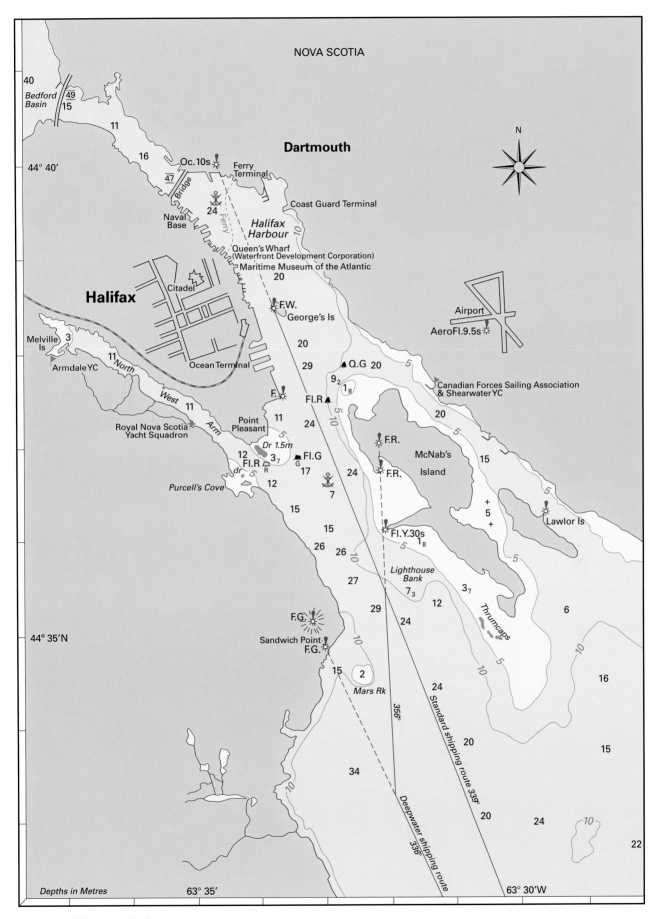

NOVA SCOTIA

40
Bedford
Basin
49
15
11
16
44° 40'
Oc.10s
Bridge
47
24
Naval
Base
Ferry
Terminal

Dartmouth

Coast Guard Terminal

*Halifax
Harbour*

Queen's Wharf
(Waterfront Development Corporation)
Maritime Museum of the Atlantic
20

N

F.W.
George's Is
20

Halifax

Citadel

Ocean Terminal
20
29

Q.G 20
9_2
1_8

Airport
AeroFl.9.5s

5

Melville
Is
3
11
North
Armdale YC

West
11
Point
Pleasant
Dr 1.5m

F.
Fl.R
24
11

Fl.R
G
17
3_7
Fl.G
12
dr
5

Royal Nova Scotia
Yacht Squadron

Arm

12

Purcell's Cove
7
24

F.R.
F.R.

Canadian Forces Sailing Association
& Shearwater YC
20

20

McNab's
Island
15

5

15

26
27

15

Fl.Y.30s
1_8

Lawlor Is

+
5
+

*Lighthouse
Bank*
7_3
3_7

Thrumcaps

6

44° 35'N

F.G.
Sandwich Point
F.G.
10
15
2
Mars Rk

29
24
12

24

356°
*Deepwater shipping route
336°*

Standard shipping route 339°
24
20
20

10
5
10

16

15

34

10
20

24

10

22

Depths in Metres
63° 35'
63° 30'W

Plan 64 *Halifax, Nova Scotia.*

Entrance

Halifax is entered between Sandwich Point and McNab's Island. Shipping generally uses one or other of the tracks indicated on the plan, and as there is good water outside the channel, yachts may do better to keep further west. The only possible hazard is a 2.0m (7ft) patch about 0.5 miles south-east of Sandwich Point.

The entire area is well buoyed, and if entering at night the leading lights at George's Island and Dartmouth will be useful (but keep a careful watch for shipping).

Anchorage and moorings

All three of the yacht club marinas listed below may also have moorings available.

If entering the North West Arm there are many yacht moorings, and care must be taken at night or in thick weather. Anchorage is prohibited inside a 'no wake corridor' which runs the entire length of the inlet, occupying approximately its centre third – speed must also be decreased if applicable. Anchoring is allowed outside this centre corridor clear of any moorings. The clubhouse of the Royal Nova Scotia Yacht Squadron (tel: 477 5653, fax: 477 6298) lies on the south-west side, about 0.5 miles up the North West Arm, with moorings off it. Visitors can anchor off, or may go alongside the floating pontoons or the 50m (165ft) wharf if space permits. The Armdale Yacht Club (tel: 477 4617) is situated on Melville Island near the head of the North West Arm, with moorings off it, and pontoon berths and jetties round the island's shore. Beware a rocky shoal patch 60m (200ft) off the western end of Melville Island.

Anchoring is not permitted in the main harbour between McNab's Island and Point Pleasant and in an area below the first bridge.

Berthing and marinas

The Canadian Forces Sailing Association (tel: 427 0550 for the military base general switchboard) has berths behind the north end of McNab's Island. They offer all the usual marina facilities other than fuel.

There are two yacht club marinas in Bedford Basin north of the city – at the Dartmouth Yacht Club (tel: 468 6050) on the east side of the Basin about 1.5 miles past the Narrows, and the Bedford Basin Yacht Club (tel: 835 3729) at the head of the Basin about 3 miles past the Narrows. Both have all the usual marina facilities, though fuel is available only at the former.

The Dartmouth Yacht Club is close to the largest industrial park in Atlantic Canada, where a wide selection of services and equipment useful to visiting yachts is available.

There are two possibilities in the city itself. The Maritime Museum of the Atlantic (tel: 424 7490, fax: 424 0612) offers free berthing for up to three days (longer if there's no competition for space), on a pontoon just south of SMCS *Sackville* and CSS *Arcadia*. However, there are no facilities other than water, and

visiting yachts inevitably become a part of the tourist attraction. There can also be a problem with wash from passing vessels. About 200m (660ft) further north is the Queen's Wharf, owned and operated by the Waterfront Development Corporation (tel: 422 6591, fax: 422 7582). This is more suited to larger yachts and shore power is available, but again wash can be a problem.

Yachts can also secure at the Dartmouth Ferry terminal on the east side of the harbour, but beware a shoal area alongside the wharf about halfway along.

Formalities

Fly the Q flag from offshore if arriving from abroad. On arrival the skipper should go ashore alone to call Canadian Customs Control on 1 888 226 7277 (toll free), with all yacht and personal details to hand – registration number, last port, names and dates of birth of all crew, etc. This number is in operation 24 hours a day. They will want to know the yacht's exact location and will then issue a Report Number. Finally, they will alert local customs who will visit the yacht to stamp the passports of non-US or Canadian nationals, for which a fee ($25) will be charged if outside normal working hours. Note that all weapons, firearms and alcohol must be declared and that there is a total ban on retaining hand guns on board; there are limitations on the amount of alcohol that can be imported.

Facilities

Boatyards/engineers The Royal Nova Scotia Yacht Squadron has a 5-tonne crane and, like the Armdale Yacht Club, has limited facilities for slipping and repair work. All the clubs will advise visitors about alternative yards if they cannot offer the necessary service.

Electronics Cross Marine Electronics (tel: 468 3993) in the Burnside Industrial Park at Dartmouth.

Chandlery The Binnacle Yachting Equipment and Accessories (tel: 423 6464, fax: 479 1518) on Purcell's Cove Road, plus others in the city.

Chart agents The Binnacle, Gabriel Aero-Marine Instruments (tel: 425 5030) and Cross Marine Electronics stock US and Canadian charts.

Yacht clubs All five yachts clubs mentioned above have good facilities and welcome visiting yachtsmen.

Weather forecast Contact the Port Meteorological Office (tel: 426 6703, fax: 426 9158) whose publication *Using the Marine Forecast* includes a map of forecast areas. (See also 'Radio', above.)

Diesel Available at the Royal Nova Scotia Yacht Squadron, the Armdale Yacht Club and the Dartmouth Yacht Club.

Water Available at all five yacht clubs and the Maritime Museum.

Electricity At the marinas and the Queen's Wharf.

Bottled gas Propane refills are normally available – enquire at one of the yacht clubs.

Showers At any of the yacht clubs with permission.

Laundry/laundrette At the Royal Nova Scotia Yacht Squadron, near the head of the North West Arm, and in the city.

Banks Several in the city, with ATMs.

General shopping All one would expect in a large, modern city.

Provisioning Supermarkets in the city and in the suburbs near the head of the North West Arm.

Restaurants Many, including those at the yacht clubs.

Hotels A wide choice.

Medical services Hospitals in the city.

Communications

Mailing addresses C/o The Royal Nova Scotia Yacht Squadron, 376 Purcell's Cove Road, Halifax, Nova Scotia B3P 1C7, Canada; the Armdale Yacht Club, PO Box 40, Armdale, Halifax, Nova Scotia B3L 4J7, Canada; The Maritime Museum of the Atlantic, 1675 Lower Water Street, Halifax, Nova Scotia B3J 1S3, Canada; The Waterfront Development Corporation, 1751 Lower Water Street, Halifax, Nova Scotia B3J 1S5, Canada; or one of the other yacht clubs. All by prior arrangement.

Post office In the city, plus a sub-post office in the suburbs near the head of the North West Arm.

Telephones At the yacht clubs and elsewhere.

Bus services A local bus route serves the area, including the North West Arm.

Rail services Halifax is served by the Canadian National Railway system. The main station is near the southern end of the docks.

Taxis/car hire Plentiful.

Air services The airport is some 40km (25 miles) north of the city and offers flights to destinations within Canada, the United States and Europe. The airport shown on the plan is a Services one.

Charts	Admiralty	US	Canadian
Springs: 1.3m	Range 1.0m		
Neaps: 1.0m	Range 0.5m		
Flag: Canada	Currency: Canadian dollar		
Tel/fax – Country code: 1, Area code: 709			
General	232A (1:565,700)	14360 (1:284,330)	4017 (1:350,000)
Approach	298 (1:60,000)	14373 (1:75,106)	4846 (1:60,000)
		14364 (1:37,506)	
Harbour	298 (1:5,000)	14365 (1:3,609)	4846 (1:5,000)

General

St John's is the capital and principal port of Newfoundland, situated on the Atlantic coast of the Avalon Peninsula near the south-east corner of the island. The harbour is landlocked and well sheltered; it is mainly commercial, but with some facilities for yachts. Its principal importance to the transatlantic sailor is in being the nearest port to Europe. It is an official port of entry.

Approach

The approaches to Newfoundland lie in one of the foggiest areas in the world. However, it is often clear within a few miles of the shore – even when there is thick fog further out. Icebergs carried south by the Labrador Current may pose a further hazard (see Chapters 10 and 18).

The coastline is generally very steep, rising directly to 60m (200ft) in many places, with a somewhat barren appearance and few signs of habitation. Hills of 150m to 250m (500ft to 800ft) lie close inland and identification of the exact landfall can be difficult. The bluff coastline can also result in squally winds or wind shadows when close inshore. The shore is generally steep-to and clear of underwater rocks, and in thick weather can be approached using the depth sounder. The 40m line lies between 0.2 and 0.5 miles offshore.

Sugarloaf Head 4 miles north of St John's is conspicuous – 168m (550ft) high with a sheer cliff face. It appears wedge-shaped when seen from north of north-east, but as a truncated cone from east-north-east round to the

St John's, Newfoundland: looking west through the inner entrance. The fishing harbour is on the left; the yacht pontoon is in line with the right-hand edge of the fishing harbour, to the left of the red building. Photo Department of Fisheries and Oceans.

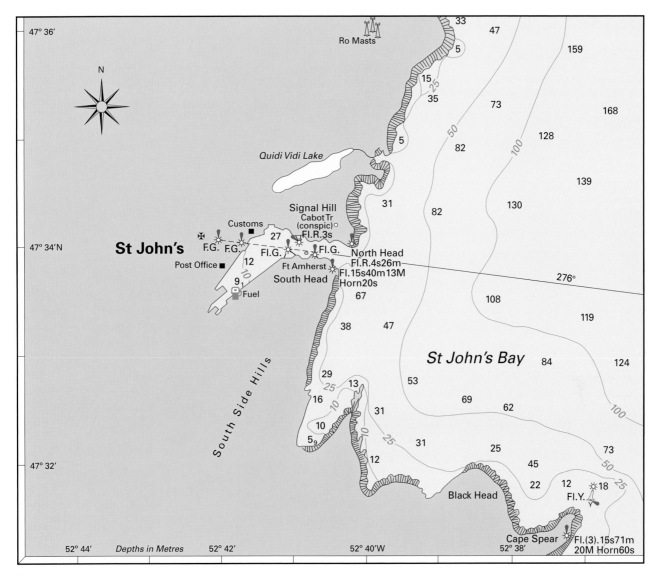

Plan 65 *St John's, Newfoundland.*

south-east. There are a number of radio masts close south of it. Cape Spear, 3.5 miles south-east of St John's, is a promontory some 80m (260ft) high, projecting north-eastward from the coast. A light is shown [Fl (3) 15s 71m 20M] from a 10.7m (35ft) white tower, with an old light structure about 200m (660ft) to the south-west.

Radio

St John's Radio broadcasts weather forecasts and ice reports as well as providing radio communications, and monitors VHF channel 16. A Vessel Traffic Management System is administered from Signal Hill and may be contacted on VHF channel 11 or 14 as 'St John's Traffic'. The Canadian Coast Guard monitors VHF channels 16 and 26. In addition, a continuous weather forecast is broadcast on channel 21B.

Entrance

St John's harbour is entered between North and South Head. Though not easily identified from a distance, it

becomes clearer as the land is closed. North Head is a steep headland of 72m (240ft) rising to 150m (500ft) immediately to its north-west as Signal Hill, topped by the conspicuous Cabot Tower. A light [Fl R 4s 26m] is shown from a mast at the entrance. South Head is marked by Fort Amherst Light [Fl 15s 40m 13M], on a square white tower. There is also a fog horn. The final approach is straightforward, with no offlying dangers other than Vestal Rock with a depth of 3.7m (12ft) some 65m (215ft) south-east of the headland.

In thick weather care must be taken not to mistake the entrance to Quidi Vidi harbour 1 mile further north for that of St John's. Quidi Vidi has no lighthouses or fog signals.

Enter between the two headlands on a course of 276°. There are daymarks and leading lights [F G 29m and F G 59m] on this bearing, but they are difficult to identify. The twin towers of the Roman Catholic Cathedral break the skyline on the outskirts of the city – the rear light (itself mounted on a church tower) is just to the north of these towers and almost level with their bases. If the leading line cannot be identified, continue on 276° until through the narrows, observing the buoys that mark shoals on both sides of the channel. Once inside, the harbour opens up to the south-west.

Anchorage and moorings

The harbour is busy and anchoring is only allowed under the direction of the harbourmaster. There is good holding in mud.

Berthing and marinas

There is pontoon berthing for yachts just south of the leading line opposite the entrance and just to the south of a large red building adjacent to the pilot boat berth. Alternatively, a berth may be found in the small boat harbour in the south-west of the port. The harbour is quite polluted, and care must be taken when handling lines that have been in the water.

Formalities

Fly the Q flag from offshore if arriving from abroad. On arrival, the skipper should go ashore alone to call Canadian Customs Control on 1 888 226 7277 (toll free), with all yacht and personal details to hand – registration number, last port, names and dates of birth of all crew, etc. This number is in operation 24 hours a day. They will want to know the yacht's exact location and will then issue a Report Number. Finally, they will alert local customs who will visit the yacht to stamp the passports of non-US or Canadian nationals, for which a fee ($25) will be charged if outside normal working hours. Note that all weapons, firearms and alcohol must be declared and that there is a total ban on retaining hand guns on board; there are limitations on the amount of alcohol that can be imported.

Facilities

Boatyards There are no yacht yards at St John's, though Down East Boat Works (tel: 576 6672) handles general boat maintenance, and Dawson Newman (tel: 782 3964) repairs in GRP. The Royal Newfoundland Yacht Club has a 50-tonne travel lift in Conception Bay, some 40 miles by sea from St John's.

Engineers Machine shops at D F Barnes (tel: 579 5041), in the south-west corner, and East Coast Marine (tel: 722 8600). Engine repairs by Detroit Diesel-Allison (tel: 579 7341) for Volvo and Perkins, and Liftow (tel: 754 3010) for Volvo and Yanmar. Fuel systems by Diesel Injection Sales (tel: 726 6774).

Electrical Terra Nova Marine (tel: 747 1565).

Electronics Canadian Marconi (tel: 726 2422) for Raytheon and Atlantic Electronics (tel: 368 8853) for Furuno.

Sail repairs United Sail Works (tel: 754 2131) and Creative Canvas (tel: 747 1988). IMP (tel: 722 4221) handle rigging and rope work.

Chandlery IMP, Coastal Outdoors (tel: 747 0159) and Mercer's Marine (tel: 466 7430).

Chart agent Campbell's Ship Supplies (tel: 726 6932).

Yacht club The Royal Newfoundland Yacht Club (tel: 834 5151), which welcomes visiting sailors, is based at Long Pond on the western shores of the Avalon Peninsula.

Weather forecast Contact the Port Meteorological Office (tel: 772 4798, fax: 772 2593) whose publication *Using the Marine Forecast* includes a map of forecast areas. (See also 'Radio', above.)

Diesel Contact Irving Fuel (tel: 758 3000), who are willing to deliver small quantities.

Water Water outlets in the area used by yachts. Hoses need a threaded connector.

Bottled gas Propane refills available. Superior Propane (tel: 726 1780) will assist with problems.

Showers The YMCA (tel: 754 2960), situated a couple of miles from the harbour, is helpful to visitors and has excellent facilities including showers, for which a small charge is made.

Laundry/laundrette In the city.

Banks In the city, with ATMs.

General shopping Good.

Provisioning Several large supermarkets in the south-western and eastern outskirts of the town.

Restaurants/hotels A reasonable choice.

Medical services Three large hospitals in the city, plus many doctors and dentists.

Communications

Mailing address C/o General Delivery, Main Postal Station C, 354 Water Street, St John's, Newfoundland, Canada A1C 5Y1.

Post office In the city.

Telephones Adjacent to the docks.

Bus services Daily bus service to Port-aux-Bisques (14 hours) for the ferry to Sydney, Nova Scotia.

Taxis/car hire Plentiful.

Air services St John's airport has direct flights to the United Kingdom as well as links within Canada and the United States.

29 St George's, Bermuda

32°22'.5N 64°40'.5W UT–4

Springs: 1.1m	**Range** 0.9m		
Neaps: 0.9m	**Range** 0.5m		
Flag: British (Red Ensign)			
Currency: Bermudian dollar (US$ accepted)			
Tel/fax – Country code: 1-441, **Area code:** none			
Charts	**Admiralty**		**US**
General	360 (1:300,000)		26340 (1:200,000)
	334 (1:75,000)		26341 (1:50,000)
Approach	868 (1:17,500)		26342 (1:17,500)
Harbour	1315 (1:7,500)		26343 (1:5,000)

General

St George's is Bermuda's second town, considerably smaller than the capital, Hamilton. Distances are such that travel is easy between the two, and certainly storing before departure is best done in Hamilton. There is some interesting cruising to be had around Bermuda, with many isolated and attractive anchorages.

Buoyage follows the IALA B system as used in the United States.

Approach

Brief details of the approaches to Bermuda will be found in Chapter 19.

St George's harbour is situated at the extreme eastern end of the island and is approached via a well-buoyed channel, one branch of which leads north-west around the island towards Hamilton, and the other through the Town Cut Channel into the harbour. A red and white pillar buoy [Mo(A) 6s] 2.3 miles east of the island marks the entrance to the channel. The powerful St David's Island light [F RG 63m 20M and Fl (2) 20s 65m 15M] lies about 1 mile to the south.

Radio

Bermuda Harbour Radio is part of the Rescue Co-ordination Centre. Watch is kept on 2182 and 2582 kHz RT, 4125 kHz SSB RT, VHF channels 16, 27 and 68; the Rescue Co-ordination Centre is also part of the DSC system and also keeps watch on 2187.5 kHz and channel 70. All vessels must contact Bermuda Harbour Radio on VHF channel 16 from 30 miles inwards and before entering the buoyed channel, with an ETA, when instructions about immigration and berthing will be given.

Entrance

Although the Town Cut is narrow, entry with a reliable engine is not difficult. If faced with beating in under sail, it might be wise to consider the alternative of a tow, which Bermuda Harbour Radio can arrange. In poor visibility, including heavy rain squalls, the Harbour Radio can monitor progress on radar. The Town Cut and its approaches are well lit, and in otherwise fair conditions entry after dark should not present problems. A one-way system is operated if a large vessel such as one of the many cruise liners is passing through the channel.

Once through the Cut the harbour opens out, with good water to starboard. If entering after dark, keep watch for anchored yachts, which may be unlit, and take care not to stray south out of the dredged channel.

Anchorage and moorings

The main yacht anchorage is north of the dredged channel and east of Ordnance Island in depths of 2–5m (7–17ft). Holding is good, but there are various old chains etc littering the bottom and a trip line may be advisable. Larger yachts will find greater depths in the southern part of the harbour, but it is a long dinghy ride

The narrow entrance channel to St George's, Bermuda. Photo Anne Hammick.

Plan 66 *St George's, Bermuda.*

ashore. Dinghies can be left at the steps inside Ordnance Island.

Berthing and marinas

The only marina in St George's is Captain Smokes' at Godet & Young (tel: 297 1940, fax: 297 1813) on McCallans' Wharf. This occupies the western end of the 350m (1,150ft) wharf which runs from close west of Ordnance Island. Otherwise, berthing alongside is on a strictly 'first come, first served' basis, with yachts rafting on the northern side of Ordnance Island and at Somers Wharf and the eastern part of Hunters Wharf further west. Other wharves are reserved for shipping. None of the yacht berths are very deep, and as there is

neither any charge nor any restriction on length of stay, space is seldom available. Berthing a yacht on any of the commercial quays is prohibited.

There are also marinas and yacht facilities at Ireland Island at the west end of Bermuda, Hamilton, Paget and Pembroke.

Formalities

Fly the Q flag from offshore until clearance has been obtained. All yachts must call first at St George's, even if proceeding to Hamilton or elsewhere, securing at the customs berth at the eastern end of Ordnance Island immediately upon arrival. The office is manned 24 hours a day, monitoring VHF channel 16 to be fore-

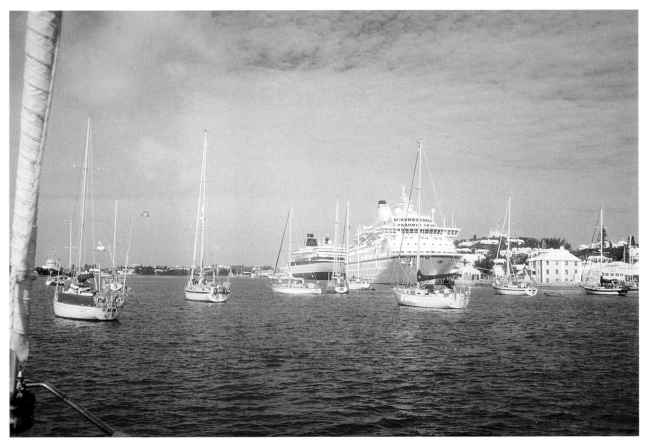

Cruise liners dwarf the yachts in the anchorage in St George's, Bermuda, looking west.

warned of arrivals. Only after the formalities have been completed may a yacht move out to anchor or continue to Hamilton. Two copies each of crew list and stores list will be required, plus ship's papers, passports and previous port clearance. A charge is made for clearance, currently of $15 per person.

In theory, it is necessary to revisit the dock to obtain outward clearance, but in practice the skipper may be allowed to deal with the paperwork while the yacht remains at anchor – enquire on arrival.

Facilities

Boatyards/engineers Meyer Industries Ltd (tel: 297 8078), north-east of the yacht anchorage, can haul yachts up to 60m (200ft), also St George's Boatyard (tel: 297 0877, fax: 297 0878) in the western part of the harbour.

Electronics Electronic Communications Ltd (tel: 295 2446) and Marine Communications (tel: 295 0558), both in Hamilton.

Sailmaker Ocean Sails/Doyle (tel: 297 1008/1009) have a full service sail loft, also Dockyard Canvas Co (tel: 234 2678); Triangle Rigging (tel: 297 2155) for rigging repairs.

Chandleries St George's Boatyard, Captain Smokes' Marina and Dowling's Shell Marine Station (tel: 297 1914).

Yacht and sailing clubs The St George's Dinghy Club (tel: 297 1612) has waterside premises on the road leading to the Town Cut and is friendly towards visitors. The Royal Bermuda Yacht Club has impressive premises on Front Street in Hamilton.

Weather forecast The Bermuda Yacht Reporting Service, located on Ordnance Island, displays a synoptic chart and forecast daily and, given some notice, will provide a departure weather briefing pack on request. Dedicated phone lines to the Bermuda Weather Service and a recorded marine forecast are also available. Continuous weather information is available on VHF Weather Channel 2 (WX02). Bermuda NAVTEX is on 518 kHz, identification B.

Diesel At St George's Boatyard, St David's Esso Marine (tel: 297 1996) or Dowling's Shell Marine Station (tel: 297 1914). Very large yachts may bunker at the Esso Station on the North Shore (tel: 297 1477), but it is unsuitable for the majority of yachts.

Water At Captain Smokes' Marina and St George's Boatyard.

Electricity At Captain Smokes' Marina and the marinas in Hamilton.

Bottled gas At Captain Smokes' Marina or from Bermuda Gas & Utility (tel: 295 3111). Propane is in general use in Bermuda – butane is not obtainable.

Showers At Captain Smokes' Marina and the St George's Dinghy Club. Water is a precious commodity in Bermuda and there may be a charge.

Laundry/laundrette Several in St George's and elsewhere.

Banks Many, with ATMs.

General shopping Good selection, especially Hamilton.

Provisioning Wide choice of frozen foods, but more difficult for a yacht without refrigeration – see Chapter 19. Nearly all food must be imported, and is therefore expensive.

Restaurants/hotels Many and various. Tourism plays a major part in Bermuda's economy.

Medical services The King Edward VII Memorial Hospital at Paget East, near Hamilton, plus many doctors and dentists.

Communications

Mailing addresses C/o St George's Post Office, St George's, Bermuda, or Captain Smokes' Marina, Godet & Young, PO Box GE 148, St George's, GE BX, Bermuda, by prior arrangement.

Fax and internet services At Captain Smokes' Marina (fax: 297 1813); internet cafés in St George's and Hamilton.

Post office In St George's.

Telephones At Captain Smokes' Marina and in the town.

Bus services Regular buses to Hamilton, Ireland Island at the west end of Bermuda, and elsewhere.

Taxis Easily available.

Car hire No car hire – mopeds are available instead. Island speed limit is 20mph; drive on the left.

Air services Daily air services to the United States, Canada and Europe.

30 Horta, Faial, Azores
38°32'N 28°37'.5W UT–1

Springs: 1.6m	Range 1.2m	
Neaps: 1.2m	Range 0.5m	
Flag: Portugal	Currency: Portuguese escudo	
Tel/fax – Country code: 351, Area code: 292		
Charts	Admiralty	US
General	1950 (1:1,000,000)	51002 (1:750,000)
Approach	1956 (1:175,000)	51061 (1:250,000)
Harbour	1957 (1:37,500)	51062 (1:25,000)
	1957 (1:12,000)	

General

Horta is the only town of any size on Faial, with a history reaching back to the mid-fifteenth century. The harbour is probably the best in the islands and has been a favourite with sailors since Joshua Slocum visited in 1895 – he commented then on the friendliness and hospitality of the local people, and things have changed little.

No visit to Horta would be complete without a beer (or a coffee) in the Café Sport, run by the Azevedo family for three generations. Neither would it be wise to tempt the fates by neglecting to add a painting, or at least the yacht's name, to the thousands that cover the harbour and marina walls. Many famous yachts feature here.

Approach

Approach and landfall on the Azores archipelago is covered in Chapter 20. However, it should be repeated that the stated range of the light at Vale Formoso [LFl (2) 10s 113m 11M] near the western tip of the island is optimistic and may be nearer to 5 miles. The only other major light is at Pta da Ribeirinha [Fl (3) 20.5s 131m 12M] on the east coast north of Horta.

Faial has few offlying dangers and the coast may safely be closed to within half a mile or so. If approaching from the south-east, the Baixa do Sul (also known as Chapman's Rocks), with 7.0m (23ft) depths, should be avoided if any sea is running. Horta lies near the south-east corner of the island, facing Pico across the Canal do Faial.

Lights and buoyage follow the European IALA A system.

Radio

The port authorities operate on VHF channels 16 and 11. The marina staff (who speak English, French and Spanish as well as Portuguese) monitor VHF channels 16, 11, 10 and 06, 0800–1230 and 1400–2000 daily (Marina da Horta, tel: 292 208300).

Entrance

If approaching from westwards, Horta harbour will not be seen until the last headland is rounded, when a course can be steered directly for the breakwater head which has good depths close in. However, avoid rounding it too tightly – the Pico ferry leaves at speed and tends to cut it fine. At night the breakwater light will probably be seen first, as the light of Boa Viagem tends to be overshadowed by town lights. The marina entrance is not lit, but in any case visiting yachts should secure to the reception/fuel berth on the western side of the entrance until assigned a berth.

There is at least one unlit steel ship's mooring buoy in the harbour, and if approaching the reception quay in darkness care must also be taken to avoid the yacht moorings laid opposite.

Anchorage and moorings

Anchoring in the harbour allowed when the marina is full. Though yacht moorings exist, they are all privately owned.

Berthing and marinas

The Marina da Horta (tel: 292 208300, mobile 0936 6491292) opened in 1986 and is an object lesson in how such a facility should be maintained and run. The majority of yachts are allotted finger pontoons, with the larger ones rafting up inside the mole. Only the very largest yachts (over 30m (100ft) and with draught exceeding 4.0m (13ft)) berth in the outer harbour alongside the breakwater. However, with over 1,000 yachts passing through Horta annually the marina is frequently very crowded, but an extension southwards which is now operational has eased the situation.

Formalities

The Azores are an autonomous region of Portugal and therefore part of the EU. In theory, this should mean fewer formalities for EU-registered yachts arriving from another EU country, but in practice this represents such a small percentage of total arrivals that it is likely all yachts will be expected to follow the same clearance procedures for some time to come.

Fly the Q flag on arrival unless this is from another Azorean island. It is necessary to visit the *Policia Maritima* and *Alfandega* (customs), whose offices flank that of the berthing master on the reception quay. On departure, both offices must again be visited, taking the receipted marina bill. Office hours are 0800–1230 and 1400–2000 and outward clearance remains valid for 24 hours.

Boa Viagem
Iso.G.1.5s12m9M

Horta

16

5

10

20

196°

Fl.R.3s20m11M

Unlit buoy

38° 32'N

3

3

32

2

3

4

Castle

Marina
Reception & Fuel

11

Marina extension

1₅

Travel hoist

Tr (Conspic)

Ferry Berth

Slipway

34

Iso.G.2s

Fishing
boats

Boatyard

Iso.G.2s

5

10

20

Monte
Queimado

Porto Pim

5

10

20₅

20

N

Monte da Guia

5

Caldeira
do Inferno

Pta da Greta

Pta das Garças

5

38° 31'

10

38

76

20

77

28° 38'W

Depths in Metres

28° 37'

Plan 67 *Horta, Faial, Azores.*

The marina at Horta, Faial, looking north. The extension to it has been built in the left foreground. Photo Anne Hammick.

Facilities

The establishment of Mid-Atlantic Yacht Services (MAYS) (tel: 292 391616, fax: 292 391656, e-mail: mays@mail.telepac.pt) has vastly eased the situation for visiting sailors needing to get work done. In addition to English, owners Duncan and Ruth Sweet speak French, German and Portuguese and have good contacts in mainland Portugal. MAYS, which is to be found opposite the root of the marina mole, is the Azorean agent for over a dozen international manufacturers and can organise importation and fitting of most items. The company specialises in engineering, electronics, rigging and deck hardware, but among its other services it will send and receive faxes and e-mail and handle cruisers' mail. As a bonus, MAYS even run a free book swop.

Boatyard With a 25-tonne travel lift, it is capable of rough but serviceable repairs to steel, aluminium and wood, but not so good for major GRP repairs.

Engineers/electronics Consult Mid-Atlantic Yacht Services.

Sail repairs Ralf Holzerland (tel: 23194) will collect, repair and return sails.

Chandlery Teófilo Garcia & Filhos Sa on the corner of Rua Vasco da Gama near the Café Sport; otherwise, Mid-Atlantic Yacht Services.

Yacht club The Clube Naval occupies the glass-fronted building on the water front south of the marina.

Weather forecast A three-day synoptic forecast is posted daily outside the marina office, plus a written forecast (Portuguese and English) outside the *Capitania do Porto* (near the Pico ferry berth). On channel 11 at 0900, 1000, 1900 and 2100 in Portuguese for local waters.

Diesel From a pump at the marina reception quay, 0800–1200 and 1300–2000, cash (US$ or euros) only.

Petrol By can from the diesel pump attendant or from filling stations in town.

Water On the marina pontoons.

Electricity On the pontoons (220 volt, 50 Hz). Yachts must provide their own cable and plug, plus adaptor if necessary.

Bottled gas Camping Gaz readily available. Calor Gas and other non-standard cylinders may be refilled via the Shell shop south of the Café Sport. Arrange through MAYS.

Showers In the semi-circular building in the north-west corner of the marina area. A small charge is made.

Laundry/laundrette In the shower block (attendant service by machine, or DIY at large sinks), plus at least two others.

Banks Several, with ATMs.

General shopping Surprisingly good.

Provisioning Several supermarkets, plus a small fruit and vegetable market at the northern end of the town, with a fish market beyond.

Restaurants A wide variety at very reasonable prices. Many accept eurocheques or credit cards.

Hotels Four star downwards.
Medical services Hospital outside the town.

Communications

Mailing addresses C/o Café Sport, Rua Vasco da Gama, 9900 Horta, Faial, Azores, Portugal; Mid-Atlantic Yacht Services, PT-9900 Horta, Faial, Azores, Portugal; or the Marina da Horta, Av Gago Coutinho e Sacadura Cabral 7, 9900 Horta, Faial, Azores, Portugal.

Fax services At the Café Sport (fax: 31287), the marina office (fax: 22523), Mid-Atlantic Yacht Services (fax: 31656) and the post office; e-mail services are also available.

Post office At the northern end of the town, open 0830–1830. Stamps can be bought at any shop displaying the green *correio* sign.

Telephones At the main post office, Café Sport, marina bar and others.

Bus services Circular route around the island. The tourist office will supply a timetable on request.

Taxis Taxi rank outside the Estalagem de Santa Cruz.

Car hire Choice of several (this is another thing that Mid-Atlantic Yacht Services will arrange).

Ferry services Several times daily to Pico, and also to the other islands of the 'central' group – details from the tourist office.

Air services Daily flights to Lisbon and the other islands. All United Kingdom flights are routed via Lisbon.

31 Ponta Delgada, São Miguel, Azores

37°42'N 25°40'W UT–1

Springs: 1.7m		Range 1.4m	
Neaps: 0.6m		Range 0.6m	
Flag: Portugal		Currency: Euro	
Tel/fax – Country code: 351, Area code: 296			
Charts	Admiralty		US
General	1950	(1:1,000,000)	51002 (1:75,000)
Approach	1958	(1:150,000)	51081 (1:250,000)
Harbour	1958	(1:10,000)	51082 (1:7,500)

General

Ponta Delgada is the largest town in the Azores, with a busy naval and commercial harbour. Other than Horta and Praia da Vitória (Terceira), it is the only place that can be considered safe for yachts in almost all conditions, though strong winds from between east and south can send a heavy swell into the harbour. Ponta Delgada also offers the best shopping and provisioning in the Azores. The island of São Miguel is outstandingly beautiful, with spectacular lakes and hot springs, and is well worth exploring.

Completion of a marina in 1993 has increased the appeal of Ponta Delgada as a cruising stopover, in particular making it the obvious jumping-off point for yachts bound for the Iberian peninsula.

Approach

Much of São Miguel is high and often visible from many miles away. The coastline is largely steep-to, with few offlying dangers, but many of the headlands are fringed by rocks and all should be given at least 500m (0.25 miles) clearance. If approaching from the west, Baixa da Negra lies about 0.5 miles south of the Airport Control Tower [Aero AlFlWG 10s 83m W28M/G23M] and should be given a wide berth. The island is relatively well lit, with powerful lights at Pta da Ferraria [Fl

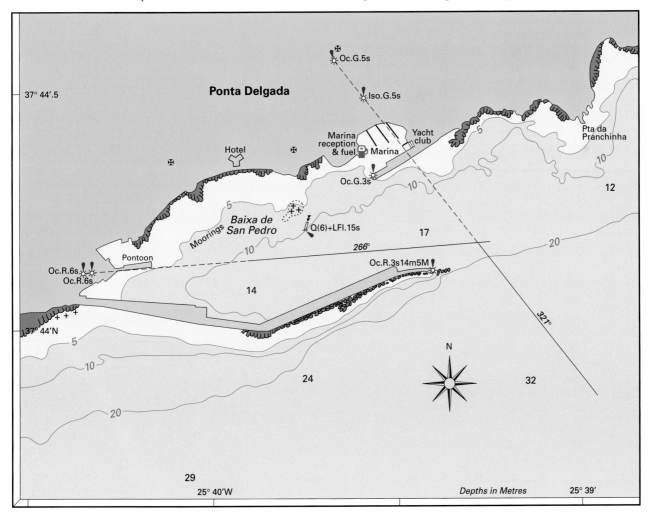

Plan 68 *Ponta Delgada, São Miguel, Azores.*

Ponta Delgado, Azores: looking south across the marina to the main breakwater (note rubble extension to breakwater end). Photo Nigel Wollen.

(3) 20s 106m 27M] at its western end and Pta do Arnel [Fl 5s 66m 25M] to the east. Santa Clara [LFl 5s 26m 15M] marks the headland to the west of Ponta Delgada.

Radio

There is a Maritime Rescue Co-ordination Centre at Ponta Delgada which is part of the DSC MF and VHF system and this also keeps watch on VHF channel 16. The port authority also operates on channel 16. The marina monitors channels 16 (24 hours) and 62, 0900–1800 daily.

Entrance

Final approach and entrance is straightforward, though the grey stone breakwater may blend with the concrete esplanade if approaching on a bearing of less than 325°. A submerged rubble extension runs out from the end of the breakwater, which should therefore be given a minimum offing of at least 100m (350ft). There are two sets of leading lights, both of them easily visible against the many shore lights behind, though if heading for the marina reception quay, the second pair will not be used.

Anchorage and moorings

There are a few mooring buoys, but most are privately owned – enquire at the Clube Naval. Otherwise, it is possible to anchor at the west of the harbour in 8–10m (26–33ft) over sand, though this is not encouraged.

Berthing and marinas

The marina – correctly the Marinaçores (tel: 296 281510) – has already gained an excellent reputation. On arrival, yachts should berth at the reception quay to visit the offices of the various officials and be assigned a berth. The depths are between 8m (26ft) and 3.5m (12ft) in the marina, the deepest being alongside the outer wall. The marina office is open 0900–1800 daily. As in Horta, most visitors are directed to pontoon berths, with larger yachts rafting up inside the marina mole, and the very largest being accommodated alongside the outer harbour wall.

Formalities

The Azores are an autonomous region of Portugal and therefore part of the EU. In theory this should mean fewer formalities for EU-registered yachts arriving from another EU country, but in practice it is likely that all yachts will be expected to follow the same clearance procedures for some time to come.

Fly the Q flag on arrival unless this is from another Azorean island. All officials have offices in the marina area. The skipper should visit the *Policia Maritima* bearing ship's papers, passports and insurance documents, and will be advised of the other officials to be seen. On departure the office must again be visited, taking the receipted marina bill.

Facilities

Boatyards Several yards where wooden fishing boats are built and steel repaired – enquire in the marina office. It is possible for yachts to be craned out on the hardstanding inside the marina mole. There is a 25-tonne travel lift in the marina.

Engineers/electronics Enquire of the marina staff, who can also arrange refrigeration repairs. It may be worth contacting Mid-Atlantic Yacht Services (MAYS) in Horta (tel: 292 391616, fax: 391656) if parts have to be imported.

Yacht club The Clube Naval de Ponta Delgada (tel: 296 283005), which occupies most of the large building at the root of the marina mole, is particularly welcoming towards visiting sailors. It has a pleasant bar and good restaurant.

Weather forecast A forecast and synoptic chart is posted daily on the notice board in the marina. This normally covers the coming 48 hours, but a one-week forecast can be prepared on request. On channel 11 at 0830 and 2000 in Portuguese for local waters. Navtex: Horta (F).

Diesel and petrol At the marina reception quay.

Water On marina pontoons. Hoses need special connectors (available in town if not already carried).

Electricity On the pontoons (220 volt, 50 Hz). Again, a locally available connector is needed, and yachts must provide their own cable and plug, plus adaptor if necessary.

Bottled gas Camping Gaz readily available. Calor Gas and other non-standard cylinders can be refilled at the Shell depot on the main road to the airport.

Ice In the marina complex, or from garages.

Showers In the marina complex.

Laundry/laundrette In the town.

Banks Several, with ATMs.

General shopping Able to meet most needs.

Restaurants/hotels Wide choice at all levels.

Medical services A hospital near the harbour, plus several medical centres.

Communications

Mailing addresses C/o Marinaçores, Av Infante D Henrique, 9500 Ponta Delgada, Azores, Portugal, or the Clube Naval de Ponta Delgada, Av Infante D Henrique, Apartado 4, 9500 Ponta Delgada, Azores, Portugal.

Fax and internet services At the marina office (fax: 296 281311).

Post office Open 0830–1830, but usually busy, with long delays. Stamps can be bought at any shop displaying the green *correio* sign.

Telephones At the marina office, the post office and elsewhere.

Bus services Good network, with a reputation for running early. Timetable from the tourist office.

Taxis/car hire No problem. Mopeds and cycles can also be hired.

Air services Daily flights to Lisbon and the other islands. All United Kingdom flights are routed via Lisbon.

Appendix A
Suggestions for Further Reading

The following suggestions for further reading are indexed by chapter for easy reference. This is by no means a complete list, nor is it implied that every book under each heading need be consulted – all books (and authors) have their strengths and weaknesses, and in many cases parts of the subject matter overlap between one title and the next. Which books will be carried on board, and which read before departure and then left at home, must depend on the size of the yacht and the priorities of her skipper.

All should be available in bookshops, chandleries or through mail order catalogues, and the ISBN (International Standard Book Number) should be quoted if you know it. Where a book is available from both UK and US publishers, be aware that the ISBN may differ.

Appropriate manufacturers' handbooks should also be carried, but for obvious reasons cannot be listed here.

The abbreviations for publishers are shown in Appendix C.

Preparations
(relevant to several chapters in Part I)

World Cruising Survey, Jimmy Cornell (ACN; IM)
Blue Water Countdown, Geoff Pack (YM)
Cruising Under Sail, incorporating *Voyaging Under Sail*, Eric Hiscock (ACN)
Handbook of Offshore Cruising, Jim Howard (ACN; SH)
Long Distance Cruising, Bobby Schenk (D&C)
Ocean Cruising on a Budget, Anne Hammick (ACN; IM)
Sell Up and Sail, Bill and Laurel Cooper (ACN; SH)
The Voyager's Handbook, Beth A Leonard (ACN; IM)
Your First Atlantic Crossing, Les Weatheritt (ACN)
Yachting Monthly's Sailing an Atlantic Circuit, Alastair Buchan (ACN)

The philosophy of ocean cruising
Sensible Cruising: The Thoreau Approach, Don Casey & Lew Hackler (IM)
The Self-Sufficient Sailor, Lin & Larry Pardey (ACN; PB)
There Be No Dragons, Reese Palley (SH; ACN)
Voyaging on a Small Income, Annie Hill (ACN)

The boat and her permanent fittings
Boat Data Book, Ian Nicolson (ACN; SH)
Elements of Yacht Strength, Dave Gerr (ACN; IM)
Seaworthiness: The Forgotten Factor, C A Marchaj (ACN)
Desirable and Undesirable Characteristics of Offshore Yachts, Technical Committee of the Cruising Club of America (WWN)
The Capable Cruiser, Lin & Larry Pardey (PB)
Fibreglass Boats, Hugo du Plessis (ACN; IM)
Surveying Small Craft, Ian Nicolson (ACN; SH)
The Cruising Multihull, Chris White (IM)

Multihull Seamanship, Dr Gavin LeSuer (FB)
Multihull Voyaging, Thomas Firth Jones (AC; SH)
Multihulls for Cruising and Racing, Derek Harvey (ACN)
Spurr's Boatbook: Upgrading the Cruising Sailboat, Daniel Spurr (IM)
The Rigging Handbook, Brian Toss (ACN; IM)
Refrigeration for Pleasureboats, Nigel Calder (IM)
Boat Engines, Dick Hewitt (FB)
The Care and Repair of Small Marine Diesels, Chris Thompson (ACN; SH)
Marine Diesel Engines, Nigel Calder (ACN; IM)
RYA Book of Diesel Engines, Tim Bartlett (ACN)
Electrics Afloat, Alastair Garrod (ACN)
Boatowner's Mechanical and Electrical Manual, Nigel Calder (ACN; IM)
Boatowner's Practical and Technical Manual, Nigel Calder (ACN; IM)
Boatowner's Wiring Manual, Charles Wing (ACN)
Marine Electrical and Electronics Bible, John C Payne (ACN; SH)
Boat Electrical Systems, Dag Pike (ACN)
The 12-Volt Bible for Boats, Miner Brotherton (ACN; IM)

Equipment for ocean and warm climate cruising
Canvas Work, Jeremy Howard-Williams (SH)
Canvaswork and Sail Repair, Don Casey (IM; ACN)
Practical Sail Care and Repair, Lisa Carr (ACN)
Nicolson on Sails, Ian Nicolson (ACN; SH)
Sails: The Way They Work, Derek Harvey (ACN; SH)
Independent Energy Guide, Kevin Jeffrey (CLGP)
Cruising in Tropical Waters and Coral, Alan Lucas (ACN)

Ocean navigation
Astro Navigation Made Easy, F Meyrier (ACN)
Celestial Navigation for Yachtsmen, Mary Blewitt (ACN)
Ocean Navigator, Kenneth Wilkes, Revised by Pat Langley-Price & Philip Ouvry (ACN)
The Sextant Handbook, Bruce Bauer (IM)
Emergency Navigation, David Burch (IM)
Simple GPS Navigation, Mik Chinery (FB)
Simple Electronic Navigation, Mik Chinery (FB)
Using GPS, Conrad Dixon (ACN; SH)
Reed's Sextant Simplified, Dag Pike (ACN; SH)
Using GPS, Conrad Dixon, revised by Geoff Hales (ACN; SH)
Using Radar, Robert Avis (ACN; SH)

Electronics and communications
Communications at Sea, Mike Harris (ACN; SH)
World Radio and TV Handbook, Sennitt Andrew (WGP)
Mariners Guide to Single Sideband, Frederick Graves (SI)
The Cruiser's Radio Guide, Roger Krautkremer (FSP)

GMDSS for Small Craft, Alan Clemmetset (FB)
GMDSS; A User's Guide, Denise Bréhaut (ACN)
Using PCs on Board, Rob Buttress and Tim Thornton (ACN; IM)

The crew
All in the Same Boat, Tom Neale (IM)
The Cruising Woman's Advisor, Diana B Jessie (IM)
Cruising with Children, Gwenda Cornell (ACN; SH)
The Hitch-Hiker's Guide to the Oceans, Alison Muir Bennett (ACN)
Born to Sail – on Other People's Boats, Jennifer P Stuart (SH)

Provisioning
Reluctant Cook, Jane Gibb (ACN)
The Care and Feeding of Sailing Crew, Lin & Larry Pardey (PB)
The Great Cruising Cookbook, John C Payne (SH; ACN)
The Cruising Chef Cookbook, Michael Greenwald (PCP)
Sailing the Farm, Ken Neumeyer (TSP)

The mechanics of ocean cruising
Living Afloat, Clare Allcard (ACN) (American title: *The Intricate Art of Living Afloat* (WWN))

Collins Gems: Guide to Flags (HCP)
Yachtsman's Ten Language Dictionary, Barbara Webb & Michael Manton with the Cruising Association (ACN; SH)

Safety
Oceanography and Seamanship, William G Van Dorn (CMTP)
The Weather Handbook, Alan Watts (WLB)
Weather at Sea, David Houghton (FB)
A Sailor's Guide to Wind, Waves and Tides, Captain Alex Simpson (ACN)
Heavy Weather Sailing, K Adlard Coles, Revised by Peter Bruce (ACN; IM)
How to Cope with Storms, D V Haeften (ACN; SH)
Storm Tactics Handbook, Lin & Larry Pardey (WLB)
Heavy Weather Cruising, Tom Cunliffe (FB)
Aground, James E Minnoch (IM)
First Aid at Sea, Douglas Justins & Colin Berry (ACN)
Your Offshore Doctor, Dr Michael H Beilan (SH; ACN)
Advanced First Aid Afloat, Peter F Eastman (CMTP)
The Ship's Captain's Medical Guide (SOP)
Where There Is No Doctor, Werner David (HF)
The Grab Bag Book, Frances and Michael Howorth (ACN)

Appendix B

Cruising Guides, Almanancs and Regional Weather

Books known to, and recommended by, the editor, and previous editors – and their wide circle of cruising contacts – are marked here by a double asterisk. However, the omission of this symbol does not imply any criticism of a particular book – more probably, the editors are simply unfamiliar with it; nor is this a complete list.

All publications should be available in bookshops, chandleries or through mail order catalogues, and the ISBN (International Standard Book Number) should be quoted if you know it. Where a book is available from both UK and US publishers, be aware that the ISBN may differ.

The abbreviations for publishers are shown in Appendix C

Atlantic Ocean and worldwide
Ocean Passages for the World, British Admiralty (NP 136) (HO) **
World Cruising Routes, Jimmy Cornell (ACN; IM) **
World Cruising Handbook, Jimmy Cornell (ACN; IM)
Atlas of Pilot Charts, North Atlantic Ocean and Caribbean, US Defense Mapping Agency (NIMA Pub 106)
Atlantic Pilot Atlas, James Clarke (ACN; IM) **
Street's Transatlantic Crossing Guide, Donald M Street Jr (WWN)
Yachting Monthly's Sailing an Atlantic Circuit, Alastair Buchan (ACN)

Atlantic coast of Europe and Africa
The Cruising Association Almanac (CA) **
The Macmillan Reeds Nautical Almanac **
The Macmillan Reeds Western Almanac (ND)
The Yachtsman's Pilot to the Western Isles, Martin Lawrence (ILNW)
The Yachtsman's Pilot to Skye and North West Scotland, Martin Lawrence (ILNW)
The Yachtsman's Pilot to the West Coast of Scotland: Crinan to Canna, Martin Lawrence (ILNW)
The Yachtsman's Pilot to the West Coast of Scotland: Clyde to Colonsay, Martin Lawrence (ILNW)
West Highland Shores, Maldwin Drummond (ACN)
CCC Sailing Directions: Outer Hebrides, Clyde Cruising Club (CCC) **
CCC Sailing Directions: Ardnamurchan to Cape Wrath, Clyde Cruising Club (CCC) **
CCC Sailing Directions: Kintyre to Ardnamurchan, Clyde Cruising Club (CCC) **
CCC Sailing Directions: Firth of Clyde, including the Solway Firth and Isle of Man, Clyde Cruising Club (CCC) **
East and North Coasts of Ireland Sailing Directions, Irish Cruising Club (ICC) **
South and West Coasts of Ireland Sailing Directions, Irish Cruising Club (ICC) **
Cruising Guide to Northwest England and Wales, George Griffiths (ILNW)
Lundy and Irish Sea Pilot, David Taylor (ILNW)
Bristol Channel and Severn Pilot, Peter Cumberlidge (ACN)
Isles of Scilly Pilot, John & Fay Garey (ILNW) **
West Country Cruising, Mark Fishwick (YM) **
The Macmillan Reeds Eastern Almanac (ND)
The Macmillan Reeds Channel Almanac (ND)
The Shell Channel Pilot, Tom Cunliffe (ILNW)
North Brittany and Channel Islands Cruising, Peter Cumberlidge (YM)
Brittany and Channel Islands Cruising Guide, David Jefferson (ACN)
North Brittany and Channel Islands, John Lawson (ILNW) **
Secret Anchorages of Brittany, Peter Cumberlidge (WLB)
North Biscay, Gavin McLaren (ILNW) **
South Biscay Pilot, John Lawson (ILNW) **
Atlantic Spain and Portugal, Anne Hammick (ILNW) **
Cruising Guide to West Africa, Steve Jones (RCCPF)

Islands in the Atlantic Ocean
Atlantic Islands, Anne Hammick (ILNW) **
Madeira and Porto Santo Cruising Guide, Gwenda Cornell (WCP)
Canary Islands Cruising Guide, Jimmy Cornell (WCP)
Yachting Guide to Bermuda, Edward Harris (BMMP)
Azores Cruising Guide, Gwenda Cornell (WCP)
Faeroe, Iceland & Greenland, RCC Pilotage Foundation (ILNW)

The Caribbean Island chain (Windward and Leeward Islands)
Concise Guide to Caribbean Weather, David Jones (NP) **
Reed's Nautical Almanac: Caribbean Edition (TRP)
Passages South: A Gentleman's Guide, Bruce Van Sant (CGP) **
RYA Book of Caribbean Cruising, Jane Gibb (ACN; SH) **
A Cruising Guide to the Caribbean, William T Stone & Anne M Hays (SH)
Cruising Guide to Trinidad and Tobago plus Barbados, Chris Doyle (CGP) **
Venezuela, Donald M Street Jr (WWN)
Cruising Guide to Venezuela and Bonaire, Chris Doyle (CGP) **
Martinique to Trinidad, Donald M Street Jr (WWN)
A Cruising Guide to the Leeward Islands, Chris Doyle (CGP) **
A Sailor's Guide to the Windward Islands, Chris Doyle (CGP) **

Yachtsman's Guide to the Windward Islands, Julius M Wilensky (WC)
Anguilla to Dominica, Donald M Street Jr (WWN)
VIP Cruising Guide – St Maarten to Antigua, William J Eiman (VIP)
Puerto Rico, the Passage Islands, the US and British Virgin Islands, Donald M Street Jr (WWN)
Virgin Anchorages, Nancy & Simon Scott (CGP)
Cruising Guide to the Virgin Islands, Nancy & Simon Scott (CGP) **
Yachtsman's Guide to the Virgin Islands, Meredith Fields (TIP)

The Bahamas
The Exuma Guide, Stephen Pavlidis (SWP) **
Exumas: Explorer Charts, Monty Lewis (LO) **
The Bahamas Cruising Guide, Mathew Wilson (IM)
Yachtsman's Guide to the Bahamas, Meredith Fields (TIP)
The Central and Southern Bahamas Guide, Stephen Pavlidis (SWP)
The Cruising Guide to Abaco, Steve Dodge (WSP) **

US East Coast and Canada
Reed's Nautical Almanac: North American East Coast (TRP)
Eldridge Tide and Pilot Book, Marion Jewett White (ETP)
Atlantic Coast, Embassy Marine (EMP)
Light List & Waypoint Guide: Maine to Texas, John & Leslie Kettlewell (IM)
Cruising Guide to the Florida Keys, Frank Papy (CGP)
Waterway Guide, Southern Edition (IPC) **
Intracoastal Waterway Facilities Guide, Bob & Barbara Smith (self-published)
The Intracoastal Waterway Chartbook, John & Leslie Kettlewell (IM)
The Intracoastal Waterway, Norfolk to Miami, Jan & Bill Moeller (IM) **
Florida's East Coast, Embassy Marine (EMP)
Cruising Guide to Eastern Florida, Claiborne S Young (CGP)
Cruising Guide to Coastal South Carolina and Georgia, Claiborne S Young (CGP)
Cruising Guide to Coastal North Carolina, Claiborne S Young (CGP)
Waterway Guide, Mid-Atlantic Edition (IPC) **
Guide to Cruising the Chesapeake Bay, Chesapeake Bay Magazine (CBM)
Cruising the Chesapeake: A Gunkholer's Guide, William Shellenberger (IM)
Chesapeake Bay Cruising Guide: Vol 1, Upper Bay, Tom Neale (WC)
A Cruising Guide to New Jersey Waters, Donald M Launer (RUP)

Waterway Guide, Northern Edition (IPC)
Long Island Sound, Embassy Marine (EMP) **
Cruising Guide to Narragansett Bay & the South Coast of Massachusetts, Linda & Patrick Childress & Tink Martin (IM)
Rhode Island, Maine and New Hampshire, Embassy Marine (EMP) **
Cruising Guide to Maine, Vol 1: Kittery to Rockland, Don Johnson (WC)
Cruising Guide to Maine, Vol 2: Rockport to Eastport, Don Johnson (WC)
Cruising Guide to the Maine Coast, Hank & Jan Taft & Curtis Rindlaub (DPP) **
Cruising Guide to the New England Coast, Roger F Duncan, John P Ware & Wallace Fenn (WWN) **
Coastal Guide to New England, Stan Patey (IM)
Where the Wind Blows: Marine Weather Canada, Peter J Bowyer (BB) **
Cruising Guide to the Bay of Fundy and the St John River, Nicholas Tracy (IM) **
Yachting Guide to the South Shore of Nova Scotia, Arthur M Dechman (SSSP)
Cruising Guide to the Nova Scotia Coast, John McKelvy (PTP) **
A Cruising Guide to Nova Scotia, Peter Loveridge (IM)**
The Cruising Guide to Newfoundland, Sandy Weld (PFP)
Cruising Guide to the Labrador, Sandy Weld (PFP)

Chart packs
CYC Caribbean charts:
    No 1, The Virgin Islands (St Thomas to Sombrero)
    No 2, The Northern Leewards (Anguilla to Guadeloupe)
    No 3, The Southern Leewards (Guadeloupe to Martinique)
    No 4, The Windwards (St Lucia to Grenada)

Maptech chart kits:
    No 2, Canada to Block Island
    No 3, New York to Nantucket
    No 4, Chesapeake & Delaware
    No 6, Norfolk to Jacksonville
    No 7, Florida East Coast
    No 9, The Bahamas
    No 10, The Virgin Islands

Maptech compact chart kits:
    Cape Sable to Clearwater
    Jacksonville to Miami
    Florida Keys

Appendix C   Publishers

ACN	–	Adlard Coles Nautical (UK)
BB	–	Breakwater Books (US)
BBA	–	Better Boating Association (US)
BMMP	–	Bermuda Maritime Museum Press
CA	–	Cruising Association (UK)
CB	–	Cadogan Books (UK)
CBM	–	Chesapeake Bay Magazine (US)
CCC	–	Clyde Cruising Club (UK)
CGP	–	Cruising Guide Publications (US)
CLGP	–	Chelsea Green Publishing (US)
CMP	–	Clyde Marine Press (UK)
CMTP	–	Cornell Maritime Press (US)
D&C	–	David & Charles (UK)
DPP	–	Diamond Pass Publishing (US)
EMP	–	Embassy Marine Publishing (US)
ETP	–	Eldridge Tide & Pilot Book (US)
FB	–	Fernhurst Books (UK)
FSP	–	Fantaseas Publications (US)
HCP	–	HarperCollins Publishers (UK)
HF	–	Hesperian Foundation (US)
HO	–	UK Hydrographic Office
ICC	–	Irish Cruising Club (UK)
ILNW	–	Imray Laurie Norie &Wilson (UK)
IM	–	International Marine (US)
IPC	–	Intertec Publishing Corp (US)
LO	–	Lewis Offshore (US)
ND	_	Nautical Data
NP	–	Nautorama Publishing (US)
PB	–	Pardey Books (US)
PCP	–	Paradise Cay Publications (US)
PFP	–	Puffin Press (US)
PPC	–	Paria Publishing Co (Trinidad)
PTP	–	Pilot Press (US)
RCCPF	–	RCC Pilotage Foundation (UK)
RUP	–	Rutgers University Press (US)
SH	–	Sheridan House (US)
SI	–	Sea Inc (US)
SOP	–	Stationery Office Publications (UK)
SSSP	–	South Shore Sailing Publishing (Can)
SWP	–	Seaworthy Publications (US)
TIP	–	Tropic Isle Publications (US)
TSP	–	Ten Speed Publications (US)
VIP	–	Virgin Islands Plus Yacht Charters (US)
WCP	–	World Cruising Publications (UK)
WGP	–	Watson-Guptill Publications (US)
WLB	–	Waterline Books (UK)
WSP	–	White Sound Press (US)
WTC	–	Wescott Cove Publishing (US)
WWN	–	WW Norton (US)
YM	–	Yachting Monthly (UK)

Appendix D

Suppliers of Books and Charts

The following is a selection of chart and book suppliers on both sides of the Atlantic, but is by no means a comprehensive list.

United Kingdom
Imray Laurie Norie and Wilson Ltd,
Wych House,
The Broadway, St Ives,
Huntingdon, Cambs PE17 4BT
(BA and Imray charts)
(tel: 01480 62114; fax: 01480 496109)
e-mail: ilnw@imray.com
website: www.imray.com.

Kelvin Hughes Ltd,
Kilgraston House,
Southampton Street,
Southampton SO15 2ED
(BA, US, Canadian charts and Imray charts)
(tel: 023 8063 4911; fax: 023 8033 0014)
e-mail: southampton@kelvinhughes.co.uk
website: www.kelvinhughes.co.uk

Sea Chest Nautical Bookshop,
Queen Anne's Battery Marina,
Coxside,
Plymouth, Devon PL4 OLP
(BA and Imray charts; new and secondhand books)
(tel: 01752 222012; fax: 01752 2526790)
e-mail: sales@seachest.co.uk
website: www.seachest.co.uk

Warsash Nautical Bookshop,
6 Dibles Road, Warsash,
Southampton, Hants SO31 9HZ
(new and secondhand books)
(tel: 01489 572348; fax: 01489 885756)
e-mail: orders@nauticalbooks.co.uk
website: www.nauticalbooks.co.uk

USA/Canada
Armchair Sailor Seabooks,
543 Thames Street,
Newport, RI 02840
(BA, US and Canadian charts)
(tel: 401 847 4252; fax: 401 847 1219)
e-mail: armchair@seabooks.com
website: www.bluewaterweb.com

Bluewater Books and Charts,
1481 SE 17th Street, Fort Lauderdale, FL 33316
(tel: 954 522 2278)
website: www.bluewaterweb.com

International Marine Publishing Company,
21 Elm Street,
Camden, Maine
(tel: 207 2366 314)
website: www.mcgrawhill.com

Maryland Nautical Sales Inc,
PO Box 6309, 1400 E Clement Street,
Baltimore, MD 21230
(BA, US and Canadian charts)
(tel: 410 752 4268; fax: 410 658 5068)
e-mail: sales@mdnautical.com
website: www.mdnautical.com

McGill Maritime Services Inc,
369 Place d'Youville,
Montreal PQ H2Y 2B7, Canada
(BA, US and Canadian charts)
(tel: 514 849 1125; fax: 514 849 5804)
e-mail: mcgill_maritime.ca@pubnix.net
website: www.mcgill_maritime.ca

The Nautical Mind,
249 Queen's Quay West,
Toronto, Ontario M5J 2N5, Canada
(tel: 416 203 1163; fax: 416 203 0729)
e-mail: books@nauticalmind.com
website: www.nauticalmind.ca

New York Nautical Instrument and Service Corp,
140 West Broadway, New York, NY 10013
(BA, US and Canadian charts)
(tel: 212 962 4522/3; fax: 212 406 8420)
e-mail: sales@newyorknautical.com
website: www.newyorknautical.com

Sheridan House Inc,
145 Palisade Street, Dobbs Ferry, NY 10522
(tel: 914 693 2410; fax: 914 693 0776)
e-mail: sheribks@aol.com
website: www.sheridanhouse.com

Tides End Ltd,
Bellingham Chart Printers Division,
PO Box 1728, Friday Harbor, WA 98250
(US charts and reproductions)
(tel: 360 468 3900; fax: 360 468 3939)
e-mail: sales@tidesend.com
website: www.tidesend.com

Appendix E

Glossary of British and American Terms, Weights and Measures, and Conversion Chart

In the same way that an American car has a hood, trunk and fenders while her English equivalent has a bonnet, boot and bumpers, many different sailing and related terms are used on either side of the Atlantic Ocean. In some cases a word may be common to both sides of the Atlantic, but with an alternative use limited to one side only. Others may be regional. Some of the following terms have nothing to do with sailing, but are included as they may be of help with the catering or other shopping.

British	American
alien	extraterrestrial
anchor cable (chain and/or rope)	anchor rode
aubergine	egg plant
barbecue	grill (noun or verb)
beacon	marker
bill (restaurant)	tab or check
biscuit	cookie
boomed staysail	club staysail
bottle screw	turnbuckle
burgee	pennant
can	jug
chips	fries, french fries
circular saw	skill saw
clinker (construction)	lapstrake
conical buoy	nun buoy
courgette	zucchini
cove line	railstripe
crisps	chips, potato chips
crosstrees	spreaders
deckhead	overhead
dodgers	weather cloths
dowel	plug
draught	draft
dustbin	trashcan
echo sounder	fathometer or depth sounder
enter (at customs etc)	clear in
excess (insurance)	deductible
eyelet	grommet
fairlead	chock
fender	fendoff or bumper
finger berth	slip
first floor	second floor
fizzy drink	soda
foreigner	alien
fretsaw	coping saw

British	American
gas bottle (or cylinder)	tank or propane tank
gas	LPG or propane
grease nipple	zerk fitting
grill	broil
ground floor	first floor
guard rails	life lines
hatch boards	drop boards
inflammable	flammable
jam	jelly or preserve
jerry can	jerry jug
jig saw	saber saw
jubilee clip	hose clip
junk rig	Chinese lug rig
kicking strap	boom vang
Kilner jar	Mason jar
lead (electrical)	cord
leecloth	bunkboard
lifejacket	PFD (personal flotation device)
masonry wall (eg pier)	bulkhead
methylated spirits	denatured alcohol, stove alcohol
mince, minced beef	ground beef
mole wrench or mole grip	vise grip
nappies	diapers
off licence	liquor store
oilskins	foul weather gear
Panadol, paracetamol	Tylenol
paraffin	kerosene
petrol	gasoline (gas)
pick-up buoy	toggle
pipe wrench	alligator pliers
plug (electrical)	connector
polyester	Dacron
polystyrene	styrofoam
polythene	polyethylene
pontoon berth (individual)	slip
pontoon	dock
pontoons	floats
post	mail
pot (for lobster etc)	trap
public telephone	pay phone
pump handle screwdriver	yankee screwdriver
pumpkin (vegetable)	squash
pushpit	stern pulpit
range	distance
registration papers (yacht's)	documentation

British	American	American	British
return (ticket)	round trip	bumper	fender
reverse charge call	collect call	bungey cord	shock cord
rigging screw	turnbuckle	bunkboard	leecloth
rowlock	oar lock	candy	sweets
rubbing strake	rubrail	check (restaurant)	bill
rubbish (biodegradable)	garbage	Chinese lug rig	junk rig
rubbish (non-biodegradable)	trash	chips, potato chips	crisps
rucksack	backpack	chock	fairlead
safety line (harness)	life line	club staysail	boomed staysail
scone	biscuit	collect call	reverse charge call
shifting spanner	crescent wrench	connector (electrical)	plug
shock cord	bungey cord	cookie	biscuit
skin fitting	thru hull	coping saw	fretsaw
skip (for rubbish)	dumpster	cord (electrical)	lead
slip	slipway	cordial	squash (orange etc)
slipped (of a yacht)	hauled	corn	sweetcorn, maize
slippery (surface)	slick	cotter key/pin/ring	split pin/ring
socket (electrical)	outlet	cracker or saltine	water biscuit
soya granules	TVP (texturised vegetable protein)	crescent wrench	shifting spanner
		Dacron	Terylene, polyester
spanner	wrench	deductible (insurance)	excess
split pin/ring	cotter/pin/ring	denatured alcohol	methylated spirits
sprayhood	dodger	depth sounder	echo sounder
squash (orange etc)	cordial	diapers	nappies
standpipe	public water supply	distance	range
stilson wrench	pipe wrench	dock	pontoon
stopping	surfacing putty or trowel cement	documentation	registration papers (yacht's)
swage	swedge	dodger	sprayhood
sweetcorn, maize	corn	draft	draught
sweets	candy	drop boards	hatch boats
Talurite	Nicopress	dumpster	skip (for rubbish)
tap	faucet	egg plant	aubergine
Terylene	Dacron	enter (at customs etc)	clear in
torch	flashlight	fathometer	echo sounder
transit	range	faucet	tap
treacle	molasses	fendoff	fender
Very pistol	flare gun	first floor	ground floor
video (player)	VCR	flammable	inflammable
visitor's berth	transient berth	flare gun	Very pistol
water biscuit	cracker or saltine	flashlight	torch
water tower	standpipe	floats	pontoons
white spirit, turps substitute	mineral spirits	foul weather gear	oilskins
yacht	sailboat	fries, french fries	chips
		garbage	biodegradable rubbish
		gasoline (gas)	petrol
American	**British**	grill (noun or verb)	barbecue
alien	foreigner	grommet	eyelet
alligator pliers	pipe wrench	ground beef	mince, minced beef
anchor rode	anchor cable (chain and/or rope)	hauled (of a yacht)	slipped
backpack	rucksack	hose clip	jubilee clip
biscuit	scone	jelly or preserve	jam
boom vang	kicking strap	jerry jug	jerry can
broil	grill	jug	can
bulkhead	masonry wall (eg pier)	kerosene	paraffin
		lapstrake (construction)	clinker
		life line (harness)	safety line
		life lines	guard rails

American	British
liquor store	off licence
LPG	gas
mail	post
marker	beacon
Mason jar	Kilner jar
mineral spirits	white spirits, turps substitute
molasses	treacle
Nicopress	Talurite
nun buoy	conical buoy
oar lock	rowlock
outlet (electrical)	socket
overhead	deckhead
pay phone	public telephone
pennant	burgee
PFD (personal flotation device)	lifejacket
pipe wrench	stilson wrench
plug	dowel
polyethylene	polythene
propane tank	gas bottle (or cylinder)
propane	gas
railstripe	cove line
range	transit
rip-rap	underwater rubble (around breakwaters etc)
round trip (ticket)	return
rubrail	rubbing strake
saber saw	jig saw
sailboat	yacht
second floor	first floor
skill saw	circular saw
slick	slippery (surface)
slip	finger or pontoon berth (individual)

American	British
slipway	slip
soda	fizzy drink
spreaders	crosstrees
squash (vegetable)	pumpkin
standpipe	water tower
stern pulpit	pushpit
stove alcohol	methylated spirits
styrofoam	polystyrene
surfacing putty	stopping
swedge	swage
tab (restaurant)	bill
tank or propane tank	gas bottle (or cylinder)
T-bone collision	port and starboard collision
thru hull	skin fitting
toggle	pick-up buoy
transient berth	visitor's berth
trap	pot (for lobster etc)
trash	non-biodegradable rubbish
trashcan	dustbin
trowel cement	stopping
turnbuckle	bottle screw or rigging screw
TVP (texturised vegetable protein)	soya granules
Tylenol	Panadol, paracetamol
VCR	video (player)
vise grip	mole wrench or mole grip
weather cloths	dodgers
wrench	spanner
yankee screwdriver	pump handle screwdriver
yawl boat	push boat (alongside)
zerk fitting	grease nipple
zucchini	courgette

Weights and measures

The following are intended as outline reminders only – full conversion tables will be found in most almanacs and some cruising guides. Liquid measures are assumed to be of water.

British	American
(Long) ton = 2240 lb Gallon = 160 fl oz Pint = 20 fl oz	(Short) ton = 2000 lb Gallon = 128 fl oz Pint = 16 fl oz Cup = 8 fl oz

Conversion chart

To convert:	Divide by:	To get:
Centimetres	2.54	Inches
Gallons (Imp)	1.20094	Gallons (US)
Grams	28.349523	Ounces
Kilograms	0.4536	Pounds
Kilometres	1.609	Miles (statute)
Litres	4.54609	Gallons (Imp)
Litres	0.56826125	Pints
Litres	3.785412	Gallons (US)
Metres	1.828804	Fathoms
Metres	0.3048	Feet
Metres	1852	Miles (nautical)
Miles (nautical)	1.1516	Miles (statute)
Millimetres	25.4	Inches
Tonnes (metric)	0.9078	Tons (short)

Note: To do the above conversions in reverse, multiply instead of divide.

Celsius to Fahrenheit: ÷ 5 x 9 + 32
Fahrenheit to Celsius: −32 ÷ 9 x 5

Appendix F

The Beaufort Wind Scale

UK shipping forecasts give wind speeds in terms of the Beaufort Scale. Note that the table below gives equivalent wind speeds in knots rather than statute miles per hour.

Beaufort number	Descriptive term	Mean wind speed		Probable mean wave height		Likely sea conditions
		Knots	m/sec			
0	Calm	0–1	0–0.2	–	_	Flat glassy calm
1	Light air	1–3	0.3–1.5	0.1m	4in	Low glassy ripples
2	Light breeze	4–6	1.6–3.3	0.2m	8in	Small waves without crests
3	Gentle breeze	7–10	3.4–5.4	0.6m	2ft	Small waves, crests beginning to break
4	Moderate breeze	11–16	5.5–7.9	1m	3ft	Longer waves, many with white crests
5	Fresh breeze	17–21	8.0–10.7	2m	6ft	Moderate cresting waves, some spray
6	Strong breeze	22–27	10.8–13.8	3m	10ft	Large waves with breaking crests
7	Near gale	28–33	13.9–17.1	4m	13ft	Large waves with some blown spume
8	Gale	34–40	17.2–20.7	5.5m	18ft	Very large waves with foam blown off crests
9	Strong gale	41–47	20.8–24.4	7m	23ft	High waves, visibility affected by spray
10	Storm	48–55	24.5–28.4	9m	30ft	Very high waves with over-hanging crests
11	Violent storm	56–63	28.5–32.6	11.5m	38ft	Very high waves, sea white with foam
12	Hurricane	64+	32.7+	14m+	46ft+	Giant waves, air full of foam and spray

Appendix G Weather Forecasts

Details of some weather forecasts are given in Chapter 10. This Appendix gives limited and selected information on some forecasts that are available on both sides of the Atlantic. There are so many available now, official and unofficial, available on the internet and ham radio as well as on published frequencies, by fax or voice, that a complete list would baffle the inquirer looking for initial information. Also, such a list would be subject to frequent changes.

Details of forecasts may be found in the current:

- *Admiralty Maritime Communications NP 289*, which covers the UK, French, Spanish and Moroccan coasts, and the Azores and Canary Islands.
- *Admiralty Maritime Communications NP 291*, which covers the United Kingdom, north-west Europe and the Baltic.
- *Admiralty Maritime Communications, Caribbean NP 290*, which covers Gibraltar, all the Atlantic islands, the north coast of Venezuela, the Caribbean and the southern US Atlantic coast.
- *Admiralty List of Radio Signals, Vol II, NP 283*, which covers the Atlantic coast of the United States and Canada, north of the area covered by *NP 290*.
- *Admiralty List of Radio Signals, Vol III, Part 2 NP 283(2)*, which gives global radio weather services including NAVTEX, weatherfax and internet services.
- *RYA Publication Weather Forecasts G5/02*, which covers UK and all European coasts.

All times given are in Universal Time (UT); frequencies, unless otherwise stated, are in kHz and are SSB.

The English forecast areas are shown in plan 69; the French mid-Atlantic areas are shown in plan 3 on page 67.

NAVTEX stations broadcast weather and navigational information continuously on 518 kHz, and some additionally on 490 kHz, but they only have a range of some 300 miles. There are 22 stations in the area covered by this book, and their details may be found in all the publications shown above.

Europe

British Met Office Shipping Forecast

Times: 0048, 0536, 1201, 1754 (but 1 hour earlier when Daylight Saving Time is in force, ie these are 'clock' times)
Frequency: 198 MW and FM.
Plan 69 shows the areas covered. This is a long-estab-

lished and accurate weather forecast that, together with NAVTEX, will meet most needs until the areas covered by Radio France Internationale (see Chapter 10) are reached.

Internet sites

There are many sites, some free. Most can be accessed from the Met Office home page (www.metoffice.com) or found in the publications above, the most convenient of which is RYA Publication *Weather Forecasts G5/02*.

Roger Brugge's links to meteorological sites worldwide also provides an excellent source (www.met.rdg.ac.uk/-brugge/main.html).

Satellite imagery

Latest visible and infra-red images from Nottingham University are available from www.ccc.nottingham.ac.uk/meteosat.

Radiofax

Northwood (UK)
Analyses times: 0300, 0400, 0500, 0900, 1100, 1200, 1500, 1800, 2100, 2300.
Frequencies: 2618.5, 4610, 8040, 11086.5, Schedule 0236, 1424.
Charts cover the north Atlantic, Europe and the Mediterranean, but there are many other Met charts on the broadcast.

Quickborn/Pinneberg (Germany)
Analysis times: 0430, 0525, 0743, 1050, 1600, 1800, 2200, plus forecasts for 24/30/72/96 hours.
Frequencies: 3855, 7880, 13882.5, Schedule 1111.

Amateur (ham) nets

Details of Transatlantic Maritime Net and Herb's Net may be found in Chapter 10.

MF and VHF forecasts

There are many of these transmitted by all European countries. See *RYA Publication Weather Forecasts G5/02* as a quick reference.

Gibraltar

Times: 0610, 0930, 1030, 1230, 1300, 1530, 1715, but less frequently at weekends.
Frequencies: 1458 and 92.3 MHz.
NAVTEX from Tarifa (G).

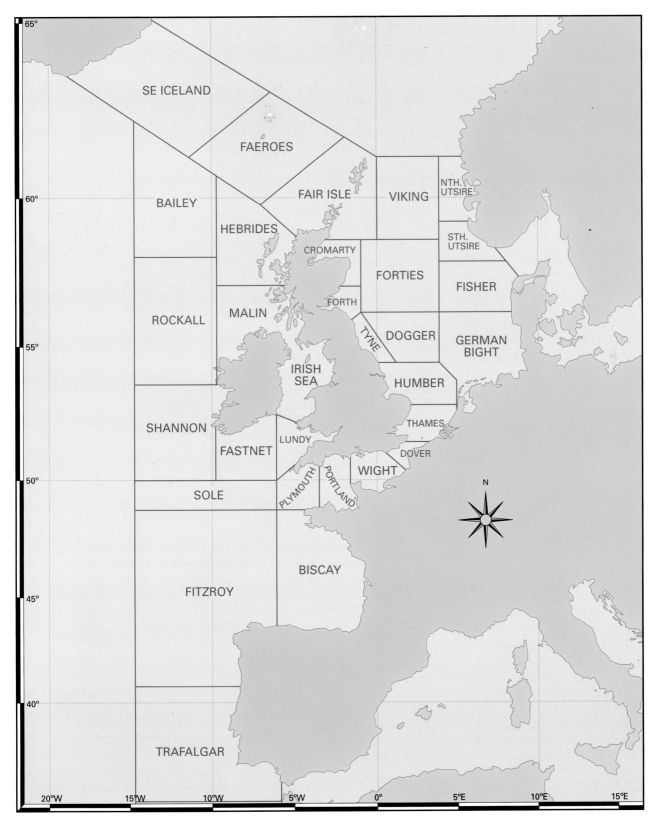

Plan 69 *BBC forecast areas.*

Azores

NAVTEX (F) from Horta and local forecasts on VHF.

Madeira

NAVTEX (P) from Porto Santo and local forecasts on VHF.

Canary Islands

NAVTEX (I) from Las Palmas and local weather forecasts on VHF.

The Caribbean

Within the Caribbean, many VHF stations give local forecasts, as do the local radio stations. These will give very frequent updates if there is a hurricane in the vicinity. Additionally, many of the popular cruising ports have a local VHF 'cruisers net'. These usually operate in the mornings, generally at some time between 0700 and 0900, and normally include a weather forecast.

Details of the Caribbean SSB Weather Net, Transatlantic Maritime Net and Antilles Emergency and Weather Net can be found in Chapter 10.

Trinidad (North Post)

Times: 1250, 1850.
Frequencies: 2735, 3165.
For Caribbean as well as local. Also, VHF broadcasts for local weather.

Radio Trinidad

Times: 1030, 1200, 1500, 1630, 2345 weekdays; 1045, 1200, 1630, 2345 Sundays.
Frequencies: 730.
Forecast for east Caribbean. NAVTEX from Curaçao (H).

San Juan (Puerto Rico)

Times: 0030, 1430.
Frequency: 2670.
Forecasts for Caribbean east of 70° and local waters. NAVTEX (R). WX1 and WC3 (see United States below for frequencies).

Nassau

Times: Every odd H+00.
Frequency: 2522.
For Bahamas and adjacent waters. Also VHF channel 27.

Bermuda Harbour Radio

Transmits on 2582 and 4125 general and weather information.

Internet site

www.caribwx.com (US)

Radiofax

New Orleans broadcasts radiofax schedules that cover the Caribbean. Details in *Admiralty Maritime Communications, Caribbean NP 290*.

United States

In addition to the High Seas Forecast mentioned in Chapter 10, American forecasts can be divided into three types:

- Inshore waters, to the limit of VHF range from the shore.
- Coastal waters, out to 1,000 fathom line, 100–150 miles offshore. This zone is divided into numbered areas starting at 1 off Maine, to 11 off Florida.
- Offshore waters, from 1,000 fathom line to about 65°W divided into two areas north and south of 32°N.

NAVTEX stations are situated at Boston (F), Portsmouth (N), Miami (A) and Savannah (E).

Inshore waters

These are covered by one of five VHF channels:

WX1 – 162.550 MHz	WX4 – 162.425 MHz
WX2 – 162.400 MHz	WX7 – 162.525 MHz
WX3 – 162.475 MHz	

Admiralty Maritime Communications, Caribbean NP 290 or *Admiralty List of Radio Signals, Vol II, NP 283* must be consulted to find out which frequency relates to each area.

Coastal waters

Again, *NP 283* or *Admiralty Maritime Communications, Caribbean 290* need to be consulted to find one of the many stations that will serve best apart from the High Seas Forecast, which is often used in the more local forecasts. HF AM weather broadcasts are made by the US Coast Guard from stations at Cape Hatteras, Cape May, Chincoteague, Charleston, Fort Macon, Mayport, Miami and Portsmouth among others.

Internet sites

National weather service – www.nws.noaa.gov
Ocean weather – www.oceanweather.com

Radiofax

Radiofax is transmitted from stations at Boston, Halifax and New Orleans. *Admiralty Maritime Communications, Caribbean NP 290* must be consulted for the frequencies and schedules.

Canada

Continuous VHF forecasts similar to those in the United States are broadcast on two frequencies: WX1 – 162.550 MHz or WX2 – 162.400 MHz.

NAVTEX

There are five NAVTEX stations in Canada. The three that provide complete cover of the south-east coast from the south-west of Nova Scotia to the north of Newfoundland are Fundy (U) and (V) (south-west of Nova Scotia), Sydney (Q) and (J) (Cape Breton Is) and St John's (O) (Newfoundland). The secondary 490 kHz transmissions are in French.

Yarmouth

Times: 0540, 1040, 1625, 1730, 2348.
Frequency: 2749.
Offshore forecasts for southern Nova Scotia and Maine waters.

Halifax

Times: 0603, 1203, 1803, 2310.
Frequency: 2749.
Offshore forecast for Nova Scotia waters.

St John's

Times: 0007, 1637.
Frequency: 2598.
Offshore forecast for Newfoundland waters.

Radiofax

Halifax transmits a radiofax weather service which covers from Greenland and Iceland to Venezuela and halfway across the Atlantic. See *Admiralty Maritime Communications, Caribbean NP 290* or *Admiralty List of Radio Signals, Vol II, NP 283* for details of frequencies and schedules.

Index

aluminium spars 5
amateur weather forecasts 68
anchor cable 16
anchorages in the Caribbean 87-8
anchors 15
Annapolis, Maryland, USA 196-9
Antigua 180-3
approach and landfall, Caribbean 84
approach to US coastline 99
approaching European coast 70
automatic steering 16
autopilots 17-18
auxiliary generators 22
awnings 22-3
Azores 107-9, 219-25
   to Bermuda 115
   to Iberia or Gibraltar 114
   to Madeira 75
   to Northern Europe 114
   to United States 116

Bahamas 92-3
Barbados 170-3
barometers 27-8
batteries 13, 32
Bayona, Spain 136-8
Beaufort Wind Scale 237
Beaufort, North Carolina, USA 190-2
below decks 7-12
Bermuda 95, 104-6, 215-18
   to Azores 113
berths 11
bilge pumps 5
biminis 22
blood transfusions 60
book list 227-8
book suppliers 232-
Brest, France 131-2
bridgedeck 4-5
Bridgetown, Barbados 170-3
British coasts 69-73
British Virgin Islands 184-6

cable, anchor 16
Calor gas 9
Camping Gaz 9
Canada 101, 208-14
   to Europe 115
Canaries to the Cape Verde Islands 76

Canary Islands 77,79-80
   Harbours 154-60
Cape Hatteras 101
Cape Verde Islands 79-80, 161-3
Caribbean Islands 85-91
chafe 7, 19
Chaguaramas Bay, Trinidad 164-7
charging batteries 13
chart datums 29
chart table 26-7
charts 28, 65
charts, electronic 34
choice of boat 2, 3-14
clothing 50-1
cockpits 4
collision 55-6
communications 35-7
   home 52
compass 27
computer systems 33, 34-5
conversion chart 236
cooking fuel 8-9
corrosion, engine 13
crew 38-40
crime 60
Crosshaven, Ireland 120-3
cruising guides 229-30
currency 90-1
currents 87, 92, 104, 107, 112
   ocean 64-5, 69

decks 4-5
   safety 53
deck-stepped masts 5
dinghies 23-4
documentation 47
dodgers 53
dorade ventilators 7
downwind sailing 19-20
drinks 44

Eastern Atlantic 74-6
echo sounder 33
electrical fires 57
electrical system 12-13
electronic charts 34
electronics 32-7
emergency steering 55
engine 4, 12-13
engine fires 56
English channel 71
English coast 70-1

English Harbour, Antigua 180-3
English ports 124-30
EPIRBs 35, 37
equipment 15-25
   failure, navigation 30-1
   lifesaving 57
Europe to the United States 116
European coasts 69-73
extinguishers, sighting 57

facilities 91,93, 105, 107
Faial 219-22
Falmouth Bay, Antigua 180-3
Falmouth 74
   to Azores 75
   to Madeira 75
Falmouth, England 124-6
fire 56-7
fire fighting equipment 57
firearms 51
first aid kit 60
fishing 43
flares 58, 59
Florida 187-9
fog 64
food storage 41-2
formalities for Europe 72-3
formalities in the Caribbean 89-9o, 93
Fort de France, Martinique 177-9
Fort Lauderdale, Florida, USA 187-9
France 131-2
French coast 71
fuel, cooking 8-9
Funchal, Madeira 151-3
further reading 227-8

gaff rig 6
galley 7-8
galley fires 56
galvanic corrosion 13
gas for cooking 8-9
gear failure 55
generators 21
   auxiliary 22
   water 21
   wind 21
genoa 19-20
Gibraltar 148-50
glossary 233-5
GMDSS 35

Gnomonic charts 30
GPS receivers 28, 30-1
Gran Canaria 156-7
Grand Banks 100
Great Circle sailing 30
Grenada 168-9
ground tackle 15
guard rails 53
guide books 66

Halifax, Nova Scotia, Canada 208-11
halyards 6
harbour awnings 22
harnesses 58-9
hatches 4-5
headsail 19
 poling out 20
 roller furling 19
heavy weather 54
Horta, Faial, Azores 219-22
hoses 4
hull 3-5
hurricanes 62-3

ice 64, 99
icebox 10
illness 59-60
inflatable dinghies 23
information, sources of 65
injury 59-60
Inmarsat C 37
Inmarsat Min-M 37
insulation 7
insurance 49-50
Ireland 120-3
Irish coast 70

keel-stepped masts 5
knockdowns 54

La Coruna, Spain 133-5
Lagos, Portugal 146-7
landfall, European 70
Lanzarote 155-6
law 50
leaks 4
leecloths 11
Leeward Islands 85-91
Leixoes, Portugal 139-41
lifebuoys 58
lifejackets 59
liferaft 57
lifesaving equipment 57-9
lightning 54-5
Lisbon, Portugal 142-5
lockers 12
log book 27

logs 33
LPG 8-9

Madeira 77-8, 151-3
 to the Canaries 76
mail 52
Maine, USA 204-7
mainsails 18-19, 20
maintenance, routine 13-14
man overboard 59
Marina Atlantico, Santa Cruz de Tenerife 158-9
Martinique 177-9
Maryland, USA 196-9
mast steps 5
masts 5
MF/HF amateur radio 36
money 48
Morehead City, North Carolina, USA 190-2
mosquito netting 23

Nantucket Shoals 100
nav-aids 33-4
navigation 26-31
NAVTEX 35
Newfoundland 100, 212-14
Newport, Rhode Island, USA 200-3
Norfolk, Virginia, USA 193-5
North American coastline 98-103
North Atlantic weather 61-4
North Carolina 190-2
Notices to Mariners 30
Nova Scotia 100, 208-11

ocean currents 64-5, 84
oil rigs 56
outboard engines 23-4

paraffin 8
passage planning charts 66
 southwards in Eastern Atlantic 74
PCs 34-5
personal safety gear 58
pests 51-2
phone calls 52
pilot books 29, 66
piracy 60
Plymouth, England 127-30
poling out headsail 20
Ponta Delgada, Sao Miguel, Azores 223-5
port information 117-225
Port St Charles, Barbados 170-3
Porto Grande (Mindelo), Sao Vicente, Cape Verdes 161-3
Portugal 139-45

position fixing systems 33
power 32
 generation 21-2
preparations for arrival 47
Prickly Bay, Grenada 168-9
propeller bar 5
propeller shaft 4
provisioning 41-4
Puerto Calero, Lanzarote 155-6
Puerto de la Luz, Las Palmas de Gran Canaria 156-7
pulpits 53

radar 33
Radio France 67
radio transmitters 35
radiofax 35
rainwater collection 22
receivers 35
recruitment of crew 38
reefing headsails
refrigeration 9-10
regional weather, European 69
repairs 24-5
replacement of crew 38
Rhode Island 200-3
RIBs 23
rigging 5-7
rigid tenders 23
Road Town, Tortola 184-6
Rockland, Maine, USA 204-7
rode, anchor 16
Rodney Bay, St Lucia 174-6
roller-furling headsails 19
routes, Atlantic 61
 Eastern Atlantic 75
running rigging 6

Sable Island 100
safety 53-60
sail repairs 24, 25
sailing directions 66
sails 18-20
San Sebastian de la Gomera 159-60
Sao Miguel 223-5
SARTs 37
satellite communications 37
Scottish coast 70
seasons for crossings 61
security 60
selecting crew 38
self-sufficiency 1
sewage disposal in US waters 102
shore power 22
sinks 8
skin fittings 3-4
skipper, role of 40
smoking 57

snuffers 19
solar panels 21
Spain 133-8
Spanish and Portuguese coast 72
spares 24
spars 5
spinnakers 19-20
St George's, Bermuda 215-18
St John's, Newfoundland, Canada 212-14
St Lucia 174-6
stainless steel rigging 6
standing rigging 5-6
steering, automatic 16
stern glands 4
storage of provisions 41
stowage 12
swaging 5

Tenerife 158-9
theft 60
thermometers 27-8
tidal streams, European 69-70
tides 69-70
time 47

timing for crossings 61
toe rails 53
tools 25
Tortola 184-6
Trade Wind crossings 82-4
Traffic Separation Schemes (TSS) 68
training crew 39
Transatlantic in the middle and northern latitudes 110
Trinidad 164-7
trysails 19

United States to Azores 114
United States to Bermuda 112-113
United States to Europe 115
US Coast Guard 102

vane gears 16-17
ventilation 7, 22-3
VHF radio 36
Virgin Gorda Yacht Harbour, British Virgin Islands 184-6
Virgin Islands 94
Virginia, USA 193-5

watchkeeping systems 45-7
water tanks 10
watermakers 110
water-powered generators 21
weather 62-4, 104, 107
weather forecast information 238-41
weather forecast transmissions 67
weather patterns in northern latitudes 111
Weatherfax 35
weights and measures 236
whales 56
wind generators 21
wind speed and direction 33
wind vane steering 16-17
windlass 16
winds 62-4
winds, Trade 82-3, 85-91
windscoops 23
Windward Islands 85-91
wooden decks 4